# ENTERTAINING

*With Style*

## PRUE LEITH & POLLY TYRER

William Morrow and Company, Inc./New York

*Produced, designed and edited by*
Shuckburgh Reynolds Limited,
289 Westbourne Grove, London WII 2QA

*Design:* David Fordham
*Design Assistant:* Carole McCleeve

*Home Economists:* Isabel Begg, Jane Harrington and Polly Tyrer
*Stylist:* Liz Hippisley

Library of Congress Catalog Card Number: 85-61142

ISBN: 0-688-04078-0

*Filmset by* SX Composing Ltd, Rayleigh, Essex, England
*Printed in* Spain by Printer Industria Grafica SA
D.L.B. 231 87 85

First U.S. Edition

1 2 3 4 5 6 7 8 9 10

PHOTOGRAPHS BY CHARLIE STEBBINGS
ILLUSTRATIONS BY SARAH JOHN

For Sam, Li-Da and Daniel

# ACKNOWLEDGEMENTS

THE AUTHORS WOULD LIKE TO THANK THE MANY people whose inspired, zany, or just plain sensible ideas they have plundered for this book. These include friends (notably Donald Douglas) whose best recipes or decor schemes have been shamelessly adapted, cookery-writers whose ideas have acted as springboards, and party caterers (especially the staff at Leith's Good Food) whose expertise has been constantly tapped.

We would also like to pay tribute to Marie Lathia's patience with the word-processor and Isabel Begg's and Jane Harrington's with the food for the photographs.

The books we have most often had recourse to in preparing this one are listed on p. 13. Special thanks are due to The General Trading Company, 144 Sloane Street, London SW1, who generously lent many items for the photographs and also to the following: The Conran Shop, 77-79 Fulham Road, London SW3; The Glass House, Long Acre, London WC1; Paul Jones, Stand Y6, Antiquarius, 135 King's Road, London SW3; Juliana's Travelling Discotheques Ltd, Unit 3a, Farm Trading Centre, Farm Lane, London SW6; David Mellor, 4 Sloane Square, London SW1; and Wilson & Gill, 137 Regent Street, London W1. Deh-ta Hsiung provided the translation and calligraphy for the Chinese menu. Martha and Grace Reynolds decorated the Easter eggs.

# CONTENTS

# INTRODUCTION

GIVING A THOROUGHLY SUCCESSFUL PARTY IS ONE OF life's most satisfactory experiences. If the whole thing has gone extraordinarily well, if the guests have left late and with reluctance, and if the washing up is made bearable by irresistible left-overs to be picked at, then the hosts will feel that wonderful but illusive frission – half proud achievement, half social triumph.

A good party is an opportunity for legitimate showing off, for flattering friends and for shuffling off the mundane and everyday in exchange for a bit of exotic fantasy. Of course giving a bad party is as positively awful, embarrassing, humiliating and as heartbreaking as giving a good one is exhilarating.

The difference between the best and the worst is not as much a question of chance as one would think. I'm often struck by the fact that hosts or hostesses, who have spent days, if not weeks, working to make a party succeed, are surprised and delighted when it does. *Of course* the thing will go with a swing if the guest list is right, the atmosphere is right, the food and the drinks are right. How could it not? It is true that torrential rain will spoil a picnic, or put paid to a tennis game, but it is unlikely to spoil the party. Friends who are gathered together for the express purpose of having a good time are not so easily cheated out of it. They'll have a good time regardless of the weather.

What makes for a bad time for the guests at a party is the feeling that they have wasted their time coming, because there has been nothing to come for, and no one has cared much if they were there or not. If the food is indifferent, the drink runs out, and there is no one interesting, or at least new, to meet, the guest cannot help feeling that he'd have been better off at home in front of the TV. However desirable it might be to be indifferent to flattery and to insult, none of us are. And if some trouble has gone into our welfare we cannot but feel pleased, just as we cannot but be slightly miffed if we arrive for dinner to find our hosts have forgotten we were coming.

Making the guests feel pleased, both with the delights on offer, and with themselves, is the secret, almost the only secret, of giving a good party. Of course that is a lot easier said that done. It takes a degree of efficiency, confidence and élan that cannot be conjured out of a hat.

But there are techniques and tricks to party-giving as there are to anything else. My co-author, Polly Tyrer, and I have been for many years professional organizers and caterers for countless London parties, from elaborate tented wedding receptions to intimate picnics for four out of a hamper. It would be vain (and a downright lie) to pretend that things in our party-catering past have never gone wrong. Once I managed to drop an entire box of knives and forks into the Thames (where it lies still, for all I know) when loading a river-cruiser for a party on the river. Time and tide wait for no caterer so the boat left without replacement silver, and the guests had to manage without. But the party was a tremendous success, because the basic structure, the fundamentals of the party, were good, and the mood was festive. What matters if the cutlery has augmented Davy Jones' Locker? And who can be glum eating salmon with a coffee spoon?

How to get it right? Well, the first thing of course is to want to give a party in the first place. If you hate parties, hate cooking, and hate your fellow man *en masse*, then this book (with the possible exception of the chapter on "Aphrodisiac Dinner for Two") is probably not for you. Good party-givers have something of the earth-mother in them – they want to feed their friends. They want to be at the dispensing end of a large table, with happy faces eagerly awaiting their slice of pecan pie. They enjoy the look of pure pleasure that a perfectly-frosted mint julep exacts from the recipient, and they are not averse to a little appreciative clapping when they bring in the *pièce de résistance*.

So, having found, or invented, a good reason for having a party, the next question is: whom to invite to it? The reason will often dictate the guest list anyway – no use asking three-year-olds (even if they come with mother) to a tennis party. They are liable to get murdered by infuriated players as they wail or shriek on the side lines. No use asking someone's twelve-year-old daughter to make up the numbers if the plan is to play risqué games after supper – her parents' concern and her embarrassment will kill the fun stone dead.

It is, I think, important to be a little ruthless over the guest list. If the plan is to have young couples for a St Valentine's dinner, then don't relent and let someone's nice old Granny come too. And do not ask anyone you do not like to a party. They will come with reluctance (the chances are they don't care for you too much either) and then they'll feel obliged to ask you back and the thing could grind on miserably for ever.

Decide on the number of guests you want, and ask that number well in advance. If they don't reply pretty quickly, do not feel embarrassed to nag them. You need time to ask second-reserve guests if anyone can't come without making late invitations so last-minute that the recipients will guess that they are stand-ins. Do not worry if you do not have the classic mix of 50 per cent male and 50 per cent female. It is better to have people who are likely to get on together than to sacrifice quality just so you can have boy-girl-boy-girl round the table. Women generally like women, and men are notorious for talking to each other even when they are offered a lady apiece. And do not worry unduly about ages either. With the possible exception of twelve-year-olds who may think ten-year-olds beneath their dignity, liking and enjoyment has little to do with age. Some of the best parties are family reunions, with adolescents discovering what delightful great-uncles they have, and elderly cousins enjoying a little permissible flirting with their youthful relations.

Of course not all parties need lengthy and elaborate preparations, special decor, music and exotic food. But all parties do need proper organization. Even a dinner for six can be the most memorable event if every aspect of it goes exactly to plan. And although it's true that the best laid plans, like the wee, sleekit beastie's, gang aft agley, if there are no plans at all anxiety and panic will follow as surely as night follows day. So how to lay the best plans? I suppose the first principle, obvious though it is, is to keep ambition within the limits of achievement. No use baying for a costume ball if time and finances dictate a knees-up with beer and sausages for the neighbors. The trick, I suspect, is to establish a budget for the party. Then do your best to stick to it. You won't be able to – I've never yet met anyone who spent no more than he set out to on a party – but at least it means that every bit of extravagance that breaks the budget will be thought about, and positively okayed or positively rejected. Do we need floodlights? A barman to stay on after midnight at time-and-a-half? Fireworks that will cost a mint and be gone in a flash, or, worse, in a fizzle? Do we want *real* caviar? Does the champagne have to be "*Grande Marque*"? And so on.

Having decided on what the party is for, who is to come to it, and how much to spend on it, what is left?

Well, there is the planning of every detail from where the guests will piddle (sorry, but *not* thinking of such things would be a mistake) to calculating how many pizzas the band will devour in the interval between "Heavy Metal" and "Soft and Soupy". Planning is pretty good fun, though I'd hate to subscribe to Robert Louis Stevenson's theory that "to travel hopefully is a better thing than to arrive, and the true success is labour". Because with any luck the successful labor will be only a prelude to a successful party. But there's no doubt that careful planning is mighty important, however prosaic it seems. I remember the louts of my class at school (and that, regrettably, included me) mocking the head-girl because she made neat lists of everything. Lists of prefects-on-duty, lists of allowable tuck, lists of "Things To Be Done". We scorned such pedantic care, but then she was head-girl and we were not. The charming, efficient and wholly likable restaurant manager of my restaurant in London is nick-named Monsieur Petit Papier, and is not too proud to write himself instructions as though to a backward child, "Ring X, Order Y, Cancel Z".

We have tried, in this book, to do much of the planning for you, with comprehensive lists of what should be done months before a party, what can be prepared weeks in advance and frozen, what must be done on the day and what at the last minute. Once the work has been methodically chopped up like this, it is surprising how easy it is to manage. I'm convinced that half the anxiety that hosts and cooks go through is caused by the fear of having forgotten something, or the unease at not knowing how long things will take. But if it is all well worked out and planned in advance, most of the terror vanishes, leaving just enough to keep the party-givers on their toes. A *little* stage-fright is no bad thing, as every actress will tell you. It sharpens the mind, speeds the hand, charmingly colors the cheek and brightens the eye.

This book is largely about "theme-parties". Some of them are extravagant, zany, even over the top. But a party is the perfect time for exaggeration and, dare I say it, for a little vulgarity. If the event is so modest and ordinary it is "just like home", then it isn't much of a party. For a real party we wear clothes we don't wear every day, we eat food and drink wines that are by no means family fare, so why shouldn't we go a bit further and alter the decor, lighting, music and, as a result, the whole mood and atmosphere of the party so that none of it is everyday or ordinary. It is a great mistake to be too conservative or too timid about these things. Do not think that because you would never have anything so vulgar as a plastic hydrangea in your house, that great tubs of them won't look spectacular for a dance or even for a garden party. What does it matter if the guests feel the petals and notice that they are phony? They will only think "How clever, I wonder where they rented them?" What would normally look like tawdry tinsel is positively romantic and exciting if its life is to be short and merry. The most obvious example is the Christmas tree. Those pretty trappings enchant us precisely *because* they are both festive and fleeting.

The party theme, especially for a grand affair, must be blindingly obvious too. No use being so gentle and subtle that no one realizes they are on a Polynesian Island or Seven Leagues Under The Sea. The more wholeheartedly the organizers throw themselves into the thing, the better it will work.

This book, which is mostly based on our own catering experiences, doesn't pretend to guarantee the host or hostess against every problem that can assail the party-giver, but we hope it is sufficiently imaginative to spark off creative enterprise in the reader and sufficiently practical to take the anxiety out of the process. Party-giving should be at least as much fun for the hosts as for the guests. I've heard it said that the proof of a good party is that the hosts were so busy they had a miserable time. That's nonsense. They should have had a great time. They are paying the piper, after all.

## HOW TO USE THIS BOOK

It is unlikely that all readers will follow the parties exactly as written. But most of the recipes, even if the party they may appear in is intended for 40 or 60 or 100, are written for 10 people. There are exceptions, and these are stated. The arithmetically-minded reader might notice that we have not always recommended doubling a recipe if it is to feed 20, or tripling if it is to feed 30. But there is good reason for this. If the dish is one of many on a buffet, many people will have a little bit of it, rather than fewer people having a goodly helping, as might happen if it was served at a sit-down lunch for 10. Also, it is a catering fact that the more people you are feeding the less food you need per head. Whether this is because the scrum at a buffet table makes some people give up unfed, or whether standing up discourages second helpings, I don't know, but you need only allow 6oz of boned raw meat or fish per head if over 40 people are to be served, whereas you need a good ½lb per head at a dinner for four or six.

This law of diminishing demands on the food is particularly true of salads. Though most people can be relied upon to serve themselves two spoonfuls of rice and two of chicken casserole from a buffet table, only about half the guests will bother with salad. Yet if six people sit down to dinner, and have a knife as well as a fork to do battle with, then an amazing amount of pretty green stuff will be consumed. We have compiled a list of catering quantities which we hope the cook will find helpful in calculating quantities not covered in the recipes given for our parties.

## METRIC CONVERSION TABLE (*Approximate equivalents*)

| | | |
|---|---|---|
| 50ml = 2 fl oz | 1¾ litres = 3 pints | ½kg = 1 lb |
| 75ml = 3 fl oz | 2 litres = 3½ pints | 600g = 1¼ lb |
| 125ml = 4 fl oz | 2½ litres = 4 pints | 700g = 1½ lb |
| 150ml = 5 fl oz | | 1kg = 2 lb |
| 175ml = 6 fl oz | 25g = 1 oz | 1¼kg = 2½ lb |
| 250ml = 8 fl oz | 40g = 1½ oz | 1½kg = 3 lb |
| 300ml = 10 fl oz | 50g = 2 oz | |
| (½ pint) | 75g = 3 oz | 5ml = 1 tsp |
| 350ml = 12 fl oz | 125g = 4 oz | 15ml = 1 tbsp |
| 450ml = 15 fl oz | 150g = 5 oz | 50ml = ¼ cup |
| 600ml = 1 pint | 175g = 6 oz | 75ml = ⅓ cup |
| 900ml = 1½ pints | 200g = 7 oz | 100ml = ½ cup |
| 1 litre = 1¾ pints | 225g = 8 oz | 150ml = ⅔ cup |
| 1¼ litres = 2 pints | 275g = 10 oz | 175ml = ¾ cup |
| 1½ litres = 2½ pints | 425g = 14 oz | 225ml = 1 cup |

# CATERING IN QUANTITY

IT IS DANGEROUS TO COOK HOT DISHES FOR MORE THAN twenty people in one batch. Large amounts of food take a long time to heat up and a long time to cool down, giving bacteria plenty of time to breed while the food is passing through those lukewarm stages. Prepare the food in several batches and cool it quickly by wedging a wooden board under the base of the pan so that the air can circulate underneath, or by standing the pan in a sinkful of cold water and constantly replenishing the sink with fresh water. Always leave the lid off the pan while you are doing this. Once the food is cool, you should transfer it immediately to the refrigerator. Chicken in particular is notorious for spoiling so always treat it with great care.

When reheating food do so in small quantities for the same reasons. Only reheat meat dishes in an oven or on a stove. Warming cabinets do not always give sufficient heat to make the food safe. Make sure, by careful stirring, that food heats thoroughly and evenly.

When preparing food for large numbers it is often best to adopt a "production line" method of working: even if you are to cook six smallish casseroles rather than one vast one (for the reasons given above), it is quicker to chop all the vegetables first, then dice all the meat, brown all the meat, soften all the vegetables, etc., then divide the ingredients into smaller pans for the cooking. Sometimes it is easier to cook ingredients separately and then combine them as described for the jambalaya on p. 189.

Similarly, sandwiches are best made by

(1) preparing all the fillings
(2) buttering all the bread
(3) laying out half the slices on a large table
(4) spreading them with the fillings
(5) seasoning them
(6) covering them with the rest of the slices
(7) stacking them in piles of 4
(8) cutting off the crusts
(9) quartering them.

## HOW MUCH TO COOK

For some reason the more people you are feeding the less food you need to allow per head – probably because people eat less if standing up. Also in a large party there may be some people who won't eat at all – something that never happens at a dinner for six. As a rough guide, if giving a party of 100 people allow full quantities for 85. If offering a selection of dishes you will need to over-cater a little to allow for people who eat both, or all, the alternatives – but expect to have some food left over. If offering a choice of main dishes allow one and a third main course portions per person and two small portions of salad. For first courses and desserts one portion per head will be sufficient. You will also need to gauge the popularity of a dish: smoked salmon is bound to be more popular than ham salad.

## CATERING QUANTITIES

**POULTRY**

| | |
|---|---|
| Chicken and Turkey | 1lb weight (plucked and drawn) per person |
| Duck | 6½lb bird for 3-4 people<br>4lb bird for 2 people |
| Goose | 8lb for 4 people<br>15lb for 7 people |

**GAME**

| | |
|---|---|
| Pheasant | Roast: 1 bird for 2 people<br>Casseroled: 1 bird for 3 people |
| Pigeon | 1 bird per person |
| Grouse | Roast: 1 young grouse per person<br>Casseroled: 2 birds for 3 people |
| Quail | 2 small birds per person, or 1 large boned stuffed bird (served on a crouton) |
| Partridge | 1 bird per person |
| Venison | Casseroled: 6oz lean meat per person<br>Braised or Roast: 4½lb cut of haunch weighed on the bone, for 8-9 people<br>Braised or Roast: 6oz per person (weighed off the bone)<br>Steaks: 6oz per person |

**MEAT**

| | |
|---|---|
| Lamb or mutton | Casseroled: 8oz per person (boneless, with fat trimmed away)<br>Roast leg: 3lb for 3-4 people<br>4½lb for 4-5 people<br>6½lb for 7-8 people<br>Roast shoulder: 4½lb shoulder for 5-6 people<br>6½lb shoulder for 7-9 people<br>Roast breast: 1lb breast for 2 people<br>Note: *These weights are for unboned joints. For boned pieces of meat allow 4-6oz per person*<br>Grilled best-end cutlets: 3-4 per person<br>Grilled loin chops: 2 per person |
| Beef | Stewed: ½lb boneless trimmed meat per person<br>Roast (off the bone): if serving men only ½lb per person; if serving men and women, 7oz per person<br>Roast (on the bone): 12oz per person<br>Roast whole fillet: 4½lb piece for 10 people<br>Grilled steaks: 8oz per person |
| Pork | Casseroled: 6oz per person<br>Roast leg or loin (off the bone): 7oz per person<br>Roast leg or loin (on the bone): 12oz per person<br>2 average tenderloin fillets will feed 3-4 people<br>Grilled: one 6oz chop or cutlet per person |
| Veal | Stews or pies: ½lb pie veal per person<br>Fried: one 6oz escalope per person |
| Minced Meat | 6oz per person for shepherd's pie, hamburgers etc.<br>¼lb per person for steak tartare<br>3oz per person for lasagne, canneloni etc.<br>4oz per person for moussaka<br>2oz per person for spaghetti |

**FISH**

| | |
|---|---|
| Large fish | Whole large fish (e.g. sea bass, salmon, whole haddock), weighed uncleaned, with head on: 12oz per person<br>Cutlets and steaks: 6oz per person<br>Fillets (e.g. from such fish as sole, lemon sole, flounder): 3 small fillets per person (total weight about 6oz)<br>Smoked fish: 3-4oz per person as a starter |
| Small fish | Whole small fish (e.g. trout, perch, small plaice, small mackerel, herring): 12oz weighed with heads for main course<br>6oz for starter<br>Fish off the bone (in fish pie, with sauce, etc): 6oz per person |
| Shellfish | Shrimp: 2-3oz per person as a fish course<br>5oz per person as a main course |

**VEGETABLES**

| | |
|---|---|
| | Weighed before preparation and cooking, and assuming three vegetables, including potatoes, served with a main course:<br>4oz per person, except |
| Green beans | 3oz per person |
| Peas | 3oz per person |
| Spinach | 12oz per person |

| | |
|---|---|
| Potatoes | Roast: 3 small per person<br>Mashed: 12oz per person<br>Parisienne: 10-15 per person<br>Château: 5 per person<br>Baked: 1 large or 2 small per person<br>New: 12oz per person |
| Rice | Plain boiled or fried:<br>2oz (¼ cup) weighed before cooking per person or ¾ cup (measured after cooking) per person<br>In risotto or pilaf:<br>1oz (1½ tbsp) per person (weighed before cooking) for first course<br>2oz (¼ cup) per person for main course |

Note: *As a general rule men eat more potatoes and less "greens" than women.*

**MISCELLANEOUS**

| | |
|---|---|
| Brown bread | 1-1½ slices (3 triangular pieces) per person |
| French bread | 1 large loaf for 15 people<br>1 small loaf for 10 people |
| Cheese | After a meal:<br>If serving one blue-veined, one hard and one cream cheese:<br>8oz piece of each for 8 people.<br>If serving one variety of cheese only:<br>3oz per person up to 8 people<br>2oz per person for up to 20 people<br>1oz per person for over 20 people<br>At a wine and cheese party:<br>4oz per person for up to 8 people<br>3oz per person for up to 20 people<br>2oz per person for over 20 people<br>Inevitably, if catering for small numbers, there will be cheese left over but this is unavoidable if the host is not to look stingy. |
| Crackers | 3 each for up to 10 people<br>2 each for up to 30 people<br>1 each for over 30 people |
| Butter | 1oz (2 tbsp) per person if bread is served with the meal<br>1½oz (2½ tbsp) per person if cheese is served as well |
| Cream | ¾ fl oz (1½ tbsp) per person for coffee<br>1½ fl oz (3 tbsp) per person for pudding or dessert |
| Milk | 1pt for 18-20 cups of tea |

**SALADS**

| | |
|---|---|
| | Obviously, the more salads served, the less guests will eat of any one salad. Allow 1½ large portions of salad, in total, per head. E.g. if only one salad is served make sure there is enough for 1½ helpings each. Conversely if 100 guests are to choose from five different salads, allow a total of 150 portions – i.e. 30 portions of each salad. |
| Tomato salad | 1lb tomatoes, sliced, serves 5 people |
| Coleslaw | 1 small cabbage, finely shredded, serves 10-12 people |
| Grated carrot salad | 1lb carrots, grated, serves 6 people |
| Potato salad | 1lb potatoes (weighed before cooking) serves 5 people |
| Green salad | Allow a loose handful of leaves for each person (i.e. a large Romaine lettuce will serve 8, a large iceberg will serve 10, a large butter or Boston lettuce will serve 4). |

COCKTAIL PARTIES

| | |
|---|---|
| | Allow 10 cocktail mouthfuls per head if served at a "cocktail party" |
| | 14 cocktail mouthfuls per head if served at lunchtime when guests are unlikely to go on to a meal |
| | 4-5 cocktail mouthfuls per head with pre-lunch or pre-dinner drinks |
| | 8 cocktail mouthfuls, plus 4 miniature sweet cakes or pastries per head, for a wedding reception |
| Sliced bread | A large loaf, thinly sliced, generally has 18-20 slices |
| Butter | 1oz (2 tbsp) soft butter will cover 8 large bread slices |
| Sausages | 1lb = 32 cocktail sausages |

## WINE
For parties of more than 50 people allow half bottle of wine per head (one bottle holds six glasses). Buy two-thirds white and one-third red if the party is at lunch time, and the reverse if in the evening. For champagne a third of a bottle per head is sufficient if a meal with wine is to follow. If it is only for a toast allow one glass each (one bottle per 6 people). For parties of between 25 and 50 people figure on two-thirds of a bottle of wine each, and for parties of under 25 people, play safe and have a bottle per head in stock.

If wine is to be served for pre-meal drinks as well as with the food, allow an extra glass per head for large parties and an extra 2 glasses for small ones.

## ICE
Allow 20lb of ice to cool two cases of wine if refrigerator space is not available.

## SPIRITS
Deciding on how much people will drink is a difficult question and the last thing the host wants at his party is to run dry. As most liquor stores will supply on a sale-or-return basis it is best to over-order. Each bottle of spirits will hold 30 tots. In our experience gin, bourbon and scotch are the most popular spirits followed by vodka and bacardi. Campari, dry and sweet vermouth and sherry should also be available if offering a 'full bar'. Supply plenty of soft drinks both for non-drinkers and for the guests who start off on the hard stuff, but try to sober up with orange juice or mineral water towards the end of the party. Children, especially if playing active games, can average six soft drinks each. For a mixed bar for a hundred people the order might be:

| | | | |
|---|---|---|---|
| Gin | 5 | Soda Water | 2 dozen "splits" |
| Bourbon or Scotch | 5 | Tonic Water | 4 dozen "splits" |
| Vodka | 2 | Ginger Ale | 3 dozen "splits" |
| Rum | 2 | Tomato Juice | 6 litres |
| Campari | 2 | Orange Juice | 24 litres |
| Dry Vermouth | 2 | Bitter Lemon | 3 dozen "splits" |
| Sweet Vermouth | 2 | Coca-Cola | 4 dozen cans |
| Dry Sherry | 2 | Lemonade | 2 dozen cans |
| Sweet Sherry | 1 | Mineral Water | 24 litres |
| Brandy | 1 | | |
| White Wine | 1 case | | |
| Red Wine | 1 case | | |

## HIRE EQUIPMENT
See the following check list for items to order. For a dinner party allow one set of salt, pepper, mustard, sauce-boats, butter dish and knife, cream pitcher, and sugar bowl and spoon per 6 guests (if for a very sophisticated dinner one set per 4 guests). For a buffet, one set per 50 is sufficient. It is a good idea to run mentally through the party from start to finish to make sure you have hired everything you need. (On what will the coats be hung? On what will the food be served? Platters? Trays? Tables? What with? How will it be heated? How will the coffee be made? Served?). Always order equipment for a few more people than you expect so that you are not caught out with breakages or extra guests.

## HIRED EQUIPMENT LIST

**CHINA**
Plates 10in
Plates 9in
Plates 6in
Soup Cups and Saucers
Pudding Bowls or Dessert Plates
Tea/Coffee Cups and Saucers
Small Coffee Cups and Saucers
Coffee Pots
Tea Pots
Sugar Bowls
Pitcher ⅔ cup
Pitcher 1 cup
Pitcher 2½ cups

**CUTLERY**
Fish Knives
Fish Forks
Soup Spoons
Table Knives
Table Forks
Dessert Knives
Dessert Forks
Dessert Spoons
Tea Spoons
Coffee Spoons
Service Spoon and Fork
Carving Knife and Fork
Cake Knife
Metal Spatula

**FURNITURE**
Trestle Tables
Card Tables
Round Tables
Chairs
Coat Rail and Hangers

**GLASSWARE**
Port/Sherry Glasses
Brandy Balloons
Tulip Champagne
Old Fashioned Tumbler
Tall Tumbler
Beer Mugs
Water Pitchers – large
                     small
Ash Trays

**TABLEWARE**
Cheeseboard and Knife
Butter Dish and Knife
Plate for Crackers
Bread Basket
Fruit Bowl
Oval Meat Dish
Vegetable Dishes
Salt and Pepper
Mustard Pot and Spoon
Sauce-boats
Ladles
Glass Dish and Spoon
Platters – large 14in
                   small 10in

**MISCELLANEOUS**
Tablecloth
Linen Napkins
Paper Napkins
Dish Cloths
Ice Bowls and Spoon
Ice Bucket
Hot Tray
Coffee Urn
Kettle

## SPACE
You need approximately 5sq ft per person for a cocktail party, 9sq ft for a buffet and 12sq ft if all the guests are to be seated. It is a good idea to make a plan of the room to scale, cut out paper shapes for the tables (also to scale) and then see how they can be fitted in. If using long trestle tables allow 1½ft per person. For round tables 3ft diameter seats six, 4½ft seats eight, and 5ft ten. Small "caterers" chairs or armless dining chairs are

economical in space but they will still take 1½ft from table edge to chairback and you will need another 1ft for people (guests and staff) to move behind. Order light chairs that can easily be moved around.

Arrange for everything to be delivered as early as is practical so that there is plenty of time to replace imperfect or forgotten items.

## TENTS
It is always important to consult a hire company for tents very early on in proceedings as they become fully booked far in advance, and their advice on how the tent should be erected may affect the way you organize the rest of the party. They will tell you what size you need and how many people will fit in. Obtain quotes from two or three companies as the quality of tents provided and the choice of linings and floorings vary considerably. It is always far less expensive to hire a tent than to have an awning exterior attached to the house as the awning has to be tailor-made especially. A covered passage can be hired comparatively inexpensively to connect house to tent.

## STAFF
For silver or "butler" service (where the waiter or waitress offers the food on a platter and the guest serves himself) one server can cope with up to 8 guests. Obviously the fewer the guests per server the better the service will be. If the staff must, as they should for a very special or formal dinner, offer vegetables, sauces and accompaniments in the same way, and pour 3 or 4 different wines, removing used glasses each time, the ratio might be as low as 4 guests to one waiter.

"Banquet service" where the staff help the guests to portion-controlled food from platters or salvers, is quicker, and one server could manage 10 guests, especially if wine, salad, bread, etc. were put on the table rather than offered individually. For a buffet meal allow one helper per 25 guests and for a cocktail party one per 35. For a full bar book one experienced bar-tender per 30 people and for a semi-bar (perhaps just wine, gin, whisky and sherry) allow one per 50 guests.

# FURTHER READING

Ager, Anne and Pamela Westland, *The Hostess Cookbook* (1983).

Bateman, Michael, Caroline Conran and Oliver Gillie, *The Sunday Times Guide to the World's Best Food* (1981).

Boxer, Arabella, *Mediterranean Cookbook* (1981), *The Sunday Times Complete Cookbook* (1983).

Brennan, Jennifer, *Thai Cooking* (1981).

Campbell, Susan, *English Cookery, New and Old* (1981).

Carrier, Robert, *Food, Wine and Friends* (1982).

Christian, Glyn, *Glyn Christian's Delicatessen Food Handbook* (1982).

Claiborne, Craig and Virginia Lee, *The Chinese Cookbook* (1973).

David, Elizabeth, *English Bread and Yeast Cookery* (1977), *French Provincial Cooking* (1960).

Dimbleby, Josceline, *Favourite Food* (1983).

Farmer, Fanny, *The Fanny Farmer Cookbook* (rev. ed. 1981), *Good Housekeeping Cookery Book* (rev. ed. 1983).

Guérard, Michel, *Cuisine Gourmande* (1978).

Hanbury-Tenison, Marika, *Book of Afternoon Tea* (1980).

Harlech, Pamela, *Pamela Harlech's Practical Guide to Cooking, Entertaining and Household Management* (1981).

Haroutunian, Arto der, *Middle Eastern Cookery* (1982).

Hazan, Marcella, *The Classic Italian Cookbook* (1980).

Hom Ken, *Chinese Cookery* (1984).

Hume, Rosemary and Constance Spry, *The Constance Spry Cookery Book*

Jaffrey, Madhur, *Indian Cookery* (1982).

Leith, Prue, *The Cook's Handbook* (1984).

Leith, Prue and Caroline Waldegrave, *Leith's Cookbook* (1985).

Lenôtre, Gaston, *Lenôtre's Desserts and Pastries* (1977).

Macdonald, Lady Macdonald of, *Season Cooking from the Isle of Skye* (1978).

Montagné, Prosper, *Larousse Gastronomique* (English ed. 1961).

Oney, Judith, *Entertainments* (1981).

Owen, Sri, *Indonesian Food and Cookery* (1980).

*Readers Digest Cookery Year* (1973).

Rose, Evelyn, *The Entertaining Cookbook* (1980).

Roux Brothers, *New Classic Cuisine* (1983).

Root, Waverley, *The Food of France* (1983).

Smith, Delia, *Delia Smith's Complete Cookery Course* (1982).

Smith, Michael, *Homes and Gardens Cookbook* (1983).

So, Yan-kit, *Classic Chinese Cookbook* (1983).

Stewart, Katie, *The Times Calendar Cookbook* (1975).

Taneja, Meera, *Indian Regional Cookery* (1982).

Time-Life Books, *Foods of the World Series* (1979-), *The Good Cook Series* (1973-81).

Tovey, John, *Table Talk with Tovey* (1981).

Troisgros, Jean and Pierre, *The Nouvelle Cuisine* (1980).

Vergé, Roger, *Cuisine of the Sun* (1979).

Wickramasinghe, Priya, *Oriental Cookbook* (1982).

Willan, Anne, *The Observer French Cookery School* (1980).

# BISTRO NIGHT

*for twenty*

*Left* The essential ingredients for a bistro night decor should be light, or rather the lack of it. Flickering candles stuck in French wine bottles provide the ideal romantic atmosphere. To get the candle wax to drip enthusiastically down the bottle, stand it in a slight draft. Twist it to get rivers of wax down the other side. Round-bowled "Paris" goblets are the classic bistro shape and can often be rented.

A S A THEME, "BISTRO NIGHT" IS PRETTY WELL FAIL-PROOF. French bistro food is generally simple, the wine not cripplingly expensive, and the setting easy enough to achieve – important factors if organizing a party for twenty or so. The essential ingredient, we think, should be lighting, or rather lack of it. Gloom should predominate, lit by candles stuck in wine bottles at four or five smallish tables, perhaps a spotlight directed at the buffet where onion strings hang, large French loaves protrude from a wicker basket and where the French cheeses are displayed on a tray covered by straw mats or leaves and at the menu chalked on a blackboard.

Lighting
*Take a tip on lighting from professional photographers. Aim a spotlight at a white wall so that the light bounces off, giving the room a subdued glow.*

### THE MENU

*Salade de Tomates*
*Pommes à l'Huile*

*Croque Monsieur*
*Choucroute Garnie*
*Salade Verte*

*Fromages*

*Tarte Maison*

Of course, you do not have to produce all that food. I've included recipes for all the dishes, but, unless you have some help, or your friends are particularly greedy, you will not need

*Below* A selection of *chèvre* (goats') blue and classic runny cheeses served on chestnut or vine leaves looks attractive. Don't be tempted to ripen cheese at home. Buy it not more than a day ahead, keep wrapped and refrigerated. Bring to room temperature half an hour before supper.

**Croque Monsieur**
*Save time by making the buttered croques monsieur in advance. Pack them in piles of four with wax paper between each sandwich to prevent them sticking together. Wrap them tightly in plastic wrap and freeze. When you need them, put them unwrapped but still frozen into the heated oven and bake until crisp, golden and hot all the way through.*

**French Cigarettes**
*Gauloises or Gitanes dotted about the room give a bistro-look and smell distinctly Parisian.*

French touches can be added with Ricard ashtrays or carafes.

the choucroute garnie *and* the croque monsieur. The choucroute costs more, but can be cooked in advance and is more of a full-scale meal. The croque monsieur is, of course, just a glorified sandwich, but is not the worse for that. It needs oven-space though. It would be unwise to attempt twenty hot sandwiches without a fan-assisted oven, a commercial sandwich maker, or a slave to fry them. From which you will gather that the sandwiches can be baked, toasted or fried. Baking will create the least last-minute hassle.

Ideally, the salads for the first course should come in rather rustic-looking earthenware or terracotta dishes, the tablecloths should be red and white check, perhaps with a plain white paper "slip cloth" on top – the kind the waiters do their sums on – and the napkins could be large, white and linen. No side plates – the French eat bread, remember, without butter, breaking it up on the tablecloth.

Of course, the food, the lighting and the separate check-clothed tables are the chief ingredients in creating bistro night. But Juliette Greco, Edith Piaf, or Charles Aznavour on the tape machine or record player, Toulouse-Lautrec posters (or Air France, Gauloise or anything else remotely French) on the walls, plus the odd small printed sign, *"Monsieur Crédit est mort"*, *"Ne crachez pas"*, *"Fermez la porte S.V.P."*, *"Toilettes"* (with a pointing hand and finger) or *"W.C."* all help.

If the host can contrive black trousers, white shirt with black bow-tie, a long white apron down to his ankles and a crumpled white napkin over his arm, all the better. You might also suggest that guests come looking like music-hall French – berets, moustaches, striped T-shirts, blue jackets *et al.* English-speaking nations protest that they hate dressing up, but once in disguise their famous social reserve vanishes with the pinstripe suit or safe little dress.

## WINE
Wine can be served direct from the bottle or, if it came in a box, from carafes or decanted into old well-washed and dried bottles. It should, we think, be red, and good enough to last the evening and not be overpowered by the cheese in the croque monsieur or the ham and sauerkraut. Perhaps a full burgundy or carbernet or a Spanish rioja.

The most authentic wine glasses are, happily, exactly the kind wine merchants will lend if the wine is bought from them, and the kind most cheaply hired or bought – the stemmed "Paris" goblet. Serve French lager, like Kronenbourg, as an alternative to wine, or one of the dry French sparkling ciders. Aperitifs, if there are to be any other than wine, could be Pernod, St Raphäel or "le Scotch".

## THE INVITATION
You could adapt the design of a typical French street sign with curved corners (see illustration on the opposite page), for the design of your invitation card and, if your French is up to it, give the wording on the card in French: *"Soyez le bienvenu (la bienvenue) chez Marie et Jean*, etc." Another idea would be to reproduce the bistro menu that you are planning on the invitation card – handwritten in pink and purple and then cyclostyled – although this does, of course, commit you to serving this particular menu that you have promised your guests a good long time in advance.

Small Perrier bottles, either with or without their labels, make good *ad hoc* vases.

**Goats' Cheese**
*There are many varieties of goats' cheese in France but all are simply described as chèvres. The flavor will vary according to the ripening period. Some chèvres are flavored with garlic or fresh herbs and others are rolled in mountain ash.*

**Invitations**
*Use postcards of France for invitations. Or better still find a friend in France to post the invitations so that they arrive complete with authentic stamp and postmark.*

SOYEZ LE
BIENVENU
CHEZ
MARIE ET JEAN

*Left* Invitations that imitate French street signs are easy to achieve. Use white lettering on a dark shiny blue background framed in green and treat corners so they look like nail holes.

## GETTING AHEAD
*Weeks or days in advance*
○ Send the invitations.
○ Collect wine bottles for the candles, and assiduously burn candles in them to get dribbles of wax down the sides.
○ Collect small Perrier bottles for the flowers.
○ Borrow a blackboard, posters, French records or tapes.
○ Do the non-perishable shopping (wine, groceries, sauerkraut).

*Below* The food, the lighting and the separate check-clothed tables are the chief ingredients for Bistro Night. From the top clockwise: croque monsieur, choucroute garnie and salade de tomates.

○ Buy a string or two of onions and garlic.
○ Organize the rental or loan of glasses, carafes, cutlery, china, tables, chairs and napkins.
○ Buy gingham paper tablecloths or make them out of the cheapest check fabric.

### Two days in advance
○ Do the rest of the shopping, other than the French bread, salad and cheese.
○ Make the apple tarts.
○ Make, but do not cook, the sandwiches. Keep covered in plastic wrap. (If the bread is a little stale it crisps up better in the oven.)
○ Make the three salad dressings.

### The day before
○ Make a few extra trays of ice cubes, storing them in a box – useful for aperitifs.
○ Skin the tomatoes and refrigerate them.
○ Set up the room, lay tables, put the wine on sideboard, put up posters, get the lighting right.
○ Peel and cook the potatoes and cool in dressing.

### On the morning of the party
○ Buy the salad, French bread, and cheeses.
○ Make the choucroute garnie. It will reheat in a low oven or in a microwave. (But do not add the parsley until the last minute.)
○ Slice the tomatoes and cover in dressing.

### On the afternoon of the party
○ Decant the wine or open a few bottles and put the corks back. (This is for convenience, not to let the wine "breathe", which is not necessary or a good idea anyway.)
○ Put bread and cheese out on the buffet. Cover the cheese with plastic wrap until the last minute.
○ Get the kitchen as clear as you can.
○ Wash and drain the lettuce.

### Before the guests arrive
○ Dish everything up.
○ If making the croque monsieur, turn the oven on high so that when you get to the last-minute sandwich-baking there is no panic. If doing choucroute, turn the oven on low and put the choucroute in to warm up.

### Half an hour before supper
○ Put the first course salads on the table, and put the sandwiches into bake. Once cooked, you can turn the oven to low and not worry about them.
○ Dress the green salad.

**Peeling Tomatoes**
*Skin the tomatoes by dipping them in boiling water for 5 seconds, then plunging them immediately into cold water. The peel should come off easily. If not, reboil briefly.*

If your French is shaky, use a dictionary to avoid the mockery of your friends.

**Buying Brie**
*Brie is best bought ripe. Look for a downy white crust and check for a creamy texture by pressing the top lightly with your fingertips. It should give a little and not feel at all firm. Leave an under-ripe Brie in a cool airy place for a few days to mature. Refrigerate over-ripe Brie until half an hour before serving, or it will run all over the table.*

# BISTRO NIGHT RECIPES

## SALADE DE TOMATES
SERVES 20
*10lbs large ripe tomatoes (preferably "beefsteak" variety)*
FOR DECORATION
*1 bunch chopped scallions, or 3/4 cup chopped onions*
DRESSING
*2/3 cup olive oil*
*2/3 cup peanut oil*
*juice of 1 lemon*
*2 tbsp red wine vinegar*
*salt and freshly ground black pepper*

1. Dip the tomatoes into boiling water for 5 seconds, then skin them.
2. Slice the tomatoes and arrange them overlapping in 4 shallow dishes. Scatter over the onions.
3. Mix the ingredients for the dressing in a screw-top jar or, better still, a blender. Pour over the tomatoes. Refrigerate until serving.
4. Serve with French bread.

## POMMES À L'HUILE
SERVES 20
*5lbs potatoes*
DRESSING
*2 cups olive oil*
*2/3 cup wine vinegar*
*juice of 1 onion (squeezed on a lemon squeezer)*
*3 cloves garlic, crushed*
FOR DECORATION
*chopped coriander (cilantro) leaves*

1. Peel the potatoes and cut into walnut-sized pieces. Place in cold salted water, bring slowly to the boil and simmer gently until the potatoes are just tender, approximately 10 minutes.
2. Meanwhile beat together the ingredients for the dressing.
3. Drain the potatoes well and immediately turn them in the dressing. Cool.
4. Turn the potatoes again just before serving and scatter over the chopped coriander (cilantro) leaves.

## CROQUE MONSIEUR
SERVES 20
*40 thin slices crustless white bread*
*butter for spreading*
*20 thin slices Swiss cheese*
*20 thin slices ham*

1. Preheat the oven, setting the temperature control to 425°.
2. Butter the bread and lay half of them, butter side down, on the work surface.
3. Place a layer of cheese and then one of ham on the unbuttered side.

4. Cover with the remaining bread, so that you have a sandwich with the butter on the outside. Press the edges together.
5. Place the sandwiches on baking sheets and bake for 10 minutes, turn them over and bake for a further 5 minutes.

## CHOUCROUTE GARNIE
SERVES 20
*4lb sauerkraut*
*8oz garlic sausage, sliced*
*8oz smoked sausage, sliced (preferably saucisse de Strasbourg)*
*2 1/2lb ham steaks, cut into strips*
*1 tbsp well-crushed juniper berries*
*2 1/2 cups white wine*
*1 1/2lb small peeled steamed potatoes*
FOR DECORATION
*chopped parsley*

1. Put the sauerkraut and its liquid in a large pan and lay the sliced sausages and ham strips on top. Sprinkle over the juniper berries. Place the pan on the heat and pour in the wine.
2. Cover and leave to simmer slowly for about 40 minutes, or until the ham is tender.
3. Tip the choucroute into a warm serving bowl with the meats mostly on top. Decorate with hot quartered potatoes, and a scattering of chopped parsley.

## SALADE VERTE
SERVES 20
*3 large Romaine lettuces or 8-10 Boston or butter lettuces*
DRESSING
*2 cups walnut oil*
*4 tbsp wine vinegar*
*squeeze of lemon juice*
*1/2 cup chopped walnuts*
*salt*
*freshly ground black pepper*
*dried mustard*

1. Wash lettuce and drain well.
2. Break the large leaves in half and leave the other leaves whole.
3. Place all the dressing ingredients together in a screw-top jar and shake well.
4. Just before serving pour the dressing over the lettuce and turn carefully.

## FROMAGES
SERVES 20
*2 chèvre (goats') cheeses weighing about 6oz each*
*2 whole Bresse Bleu*
*1/2 a full-size Brie*
*3 baguettes French bread*

## TARTE MAISON
MAKES TWO 12IN TARTS
FOR THE PASTRY
*4 cups all-purpose flour*
*pinch of salt*
*1 cup softened butter*
*1 cup sugar*
*8 egg yolks*
*2 tsp grated lemon rind*
FOR FILLING AND TOPPING
*20 medium-sized eating apples*
*3/4 cup sugar*
APRICOT GLAZE
*6 tbsp smooth apricot jam*
*2 tbsp water*
*juice of 1 lemon*

1. To make the pastry in a food processor: halve all the ingredients and process in two batches, using the chopping blade of the food processor to mix everything together.
2. If making by hand, make the pastry as follows: sift the flour and salt on to a table top and make a hollow or well in the center of the pile. Place the remaining pastry ingredients in the well and, with the fingertips of one hand only, combine the butter, sugar, yolks and rind in a smooth, soft paste. Gradually draw in the surrounding flour. Knead quickly and lightly until you have a smooth paste.
3. Wrap this up in plastic wrap and place in the refrigerator for 30 minutes.
4. Preheat the oven, setting the temperature control to 375°.
5. Roll out the pastry and line two 12in fluted flan rings placed on cookie sheets. Chill again for a further 10 minutes.
6. Line the pastry with a double sheet of wax paper and then weigh it down with something heavy – pebbles, pennies, marbles or "blind beans" are all suitable for this purpose.
7. Peel, quarter and core the apples. Using a stainless steel knife, thinly slice them into the flan ring, liberally sprinkling with sugar. When the flan is nearly full, arrange the top layer of apple slices very neatly in overlapping circles.
8. Dust well with sugar and bake in the oven for about 20 minutes, or until the apples are tender and the pastry is crisp and brown.
9. Slip the flan rings up off the pastry and return to the oven for 7-8 minutes.
10. Slowly melt the glaze ingredients together. When smooth brush all over the tart tops.
11. Return the tarts to the oven for 5 more minutes.

# CHINESE PANCAKE DINNER *for Six*

*Left* A Cantonese "chrysanthemum" pot is much the same thing as a Mongolian fire-pot. Make sure the table is protected under the cloth. Chinese wine is best served well chilled.

THERE IS SOMETHING FRIENDLY AND ATTRACTIVE ABOUT do-it-yourself cooking at the table along fondue party or Cantonese fire-pot lines. The very fact that the guests have to do something other than eat and chat, seems to unite them in party-mood. Our Chinese pancake dinner is no exception. The guests cook their own meat for the first course in the communal broth, deftly wielding chopsticks if they are able and tongs if they are not. Once all the meats have been eaten, the cooking broth is then served as a clear soup.

Next – more diner participation: this time the guests pick tiny warm pancakes from a central dish, and fill them to their own specification or whim, with pork, shrimp or roast duck, adding raw cucumber and scallions, or spicy sweet sauce as they like. Because the pancakes are tiny and because it is tempting to try at least *one* of each type of filling, and most of all because the pancakes are delicious, a surprising number of them will be eaten. So dinner should take a long time, with much leisurely chat between courses and between pancakes.

A simple and unusual fruit salad would make a refreshing dessert or plain fresh lychees could be served. Fresh lychees, especially if they can be bought in large bunches rather than separated into single fruits, are quite beautiful to look at. The skin of the lychee should be brown or, better still, browny-orange, and when cracked the brilliant white flesh inside should almost burst from its tight shell. Leave the guests to pick, peel and eat them with no help other than a plate, a fingerbowl, and a dish for debris. Do not have more than six people round the table – the first course would take too long to cook, and a table bigger than 4ft would be awkward.

Of course Chinese bowls, chopsticks and teapots would make the table look authentic and exquisite, but they are not necessary. Expensive metal fire-pots can be bought in Chinese supermarkets and small rattan steaming baskets could be used to hold the pancakes and filling ingredients – not an authentic use for them of course (they are properly used for cooking *dim-sum*) but nevertheless they would look exotic and pretty.

Steaming baskets are traditionally used for cooking "*dimsum*". They are stacked, with a lid on the top one, over a bubbling wok. But they make pretty containers for any food – perhaps the ingredients for our fire-pot.

*Below* Exquisitely pretty, reuseable chopsticks are cheap enough to buy. For the clumsy or embarrassed Westerner buy hinged plastic chopsticks.

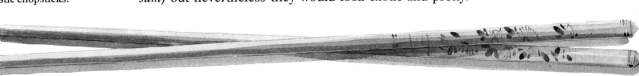

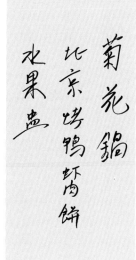

Chinese Hors d'Ouvres
*Good nibbles to serve with drinks might be tiny pieces of pork deep-fried in batter and served with sweet and sour dip; or hard-boiled quails' eggs with hot chili sauce; crabs' claws with a soy and ginger dip; or samosas (deep-fried pastry cases) filled with seafood and scallions.*

**THE MENU**

Cantonese Chrysanthemum Pot
Peking Pancakes with Duck, Pork and Shrimp Filling
Chinese Fruit Salad

## GETTING AHEAD

*A few weeks before the party*
○ Invite the guests.
○ If possible find suitable Chinese serving dishes. Bowls, plates, tiny sauce dishes and cups for tea or wine are easily available at Oriental stores. Buy wine or tea.
○ Find a Chinese fire-pot, fondue set or electric ring.
○ Collect sufficient chopsticks, tongs or small ladles.
○ Make some strong chicken stock and freeze.
○ Make a shopping list from the recipes.
○ Buy items like chili sauce, hot mustard and Hoisin sauce.
○ Buy a tape of Chinese music.

*The day before the dinner*
○ Do all the shopping.
○ Coat the duck in honey and lemon syrup and hang up to dry.
○ Make the soy and sesame dip.
○ Make the sesame caramel chips; store in an airtight container.
○ Defrost the chicken stock.

*The morning of the party*
○ Arrange the room, set the table and prepare a tray for tea.
○ Prepare all the ingredients for the chrysanthemum pot, put into serving dishes, cover and refrigerate.
○ Chop the scallions and ginger for the shrimp filling.
○ Chop the chili for the pork filling.
○ Prepare the pancakes and cover tightly with plastic wrap.
○ Make the Chinese fruit salad, but leave the orange shreds and caramel chips separately.

*Two hours before the guests arrive*
○ Cook the duck.
○ Measure all the ingredients for the shrimp and pork fillings and put out ready to finish off at the last minute.
○ Put a steamer ready to steam the pancakes.
○ Put the chicken stock into a pan ready to heat.

*Half an hour before the guests arrive*
○ Put the sauces into serving dishes and set on the table.
○ Arrange the prepared ingredients for the chrysanthemum pot on the table.
○ Make sure that the heater or pot to keep the stock hot is in place and ready to be used.
○ Strip the duck flesh and skin from the bone and keep warm, uncovered, in a low oven (to keep the skin crisp).

*After the guests arrive*
○ Boil the chicken stock and serve the chrysanthemum pot.
○ Steam the pancakes and stir-fry the pork and shrimp fillings.
○ Decorate the fruit salad.

Perhaps your local Chinese restaurant would lend you a hand in producing an authentic Chinese menu card.

Chinese Wine
*Wine is increasingly drunk by the Westernized Chinese and imported light white wines (with names like the Great Wall of China) are available in Chinese supermarkets in some areas. However it might be wiser to sacrifice the theme and buy a riesling which would be excellent throughout the meal.*

Making Stock
*The secret of good stock is long, slow simmering and careful skimming to remove the fat. Use little onion and plenty of leek as strongly flavored vegetables give an overpowering taste. To store: reduce by simmering to a syrupy consistency and keep refrigerated or freeze in cartons or in ice-cube trays.*

China Teas
*There are three broad categories of tea made in China: Black fermented teas such as Lapsang-Souchong and Keemum (the former has strong smoky taste and the latter is mild and fragrant); green teas are unfermented and include the well-known gunpowder. Oolong is part-fermented and is often flavored with jasmine, gardenia, orange or lemon.*

The prettiest traditional china is so thin that you can see the "rice-grain" pattern.

# CHINESE PANCAKE DINNER RECIPES

## CANTONESE CHRYSANTHEMUM POT
**SERVES 6 AS A STARTER**
*¾ cup boned chicken breasts*
*8oz lean lamb, skinned and boned*
*8oz firm white fish (halibut, turbot, plaice or sole)*
*6 large scallops*
*4oz bean curd (tofu)*
*2 cups fresh spinach, trimmed*
*2 cups Chinese cabbage*
*1⅓ cups small button mushrooms*
*4oz Chinese egg noodles*
*5 cups chicken stock*
*1 clove garlic, crushed*
*1 tbsp fresh coriander (cilantro) leaves*
**FOR THE DIPPING SAUCES**
*Chinese chili sauce*
*hot mustard*
*soy and sesame dip (see below)*
**SOY AND SESAME DIP**
*2 tbsp tahini or peanut butter*
*1 tbsp soy sauce*
*1 tbsp dry sherry*
*1 tbsp sugar*
*1 tbsp hot water*

1. Trim the chicken breasts, lamb, and white fish well and cut into fine slivers.
2. Wash the scallops and cut them into quarters.
3. Cut the bean curd into bite-sized chunks. Wash the spinach and cut into fine shreds. Wash and tear or cut the Chinese cabbage into small pieces. Wipe and slice the mushrooms.
4. Dish up the dipping sauces. Every person should have a tiny individual dish of each sauce. The soy and sesame dip is made by mixing all the ingredients.
5. In the absence of a proper Chinese fire-pot, use a fondue set or a large round casserole over an electric ring or chafing-dish. Give each guest a plate with an assortment of raw chicken, lamb, fish and scallop. Put the bean curd into one dish and the spinach, Chinese cabbage, button mushrooms and Chinese noodles together in another.
6. Bring the chicken stock to the boil and add the garlic and coriander leaves. Transfer this to the fondue pot and keep just below simmering point.
7. Each guest needs a pair of chopsticks or a small wire ladle or simply a fork to dip the raw meat and fish into the stock to cook it. When all this is eaten cook the bean curd and let everyone help themselves.
8. Bring the stock back to the boil and add the dish of vegetables and noodles. Cook through and then ladle into bowls.

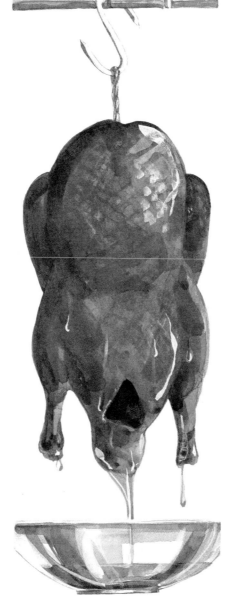

## PEKING PANCAKES WITH DUCK, PORK AND SHRIMP FILLINGS
**SERVES 6**
**FOR THE PEKING PANCAKES**
*4 cups all-purpose flour*
*1¼ cups very hot water*
*2 tbsp sesame oil*
**FOR THE PEKING DUCK**
*1 young duckling*
*1 lemon*
*5 cups water*
*3 tbsp honey*
*3 tbsp soy sauce*
*⅔ cup dry sherry*

**FOR THE SHRIMP FILLING**
*1⅓ cups shelled shrimp*
*1 tbsp scallions, finely chopped*
*2in piece of fresh ginger, finely chopped*
*1 tbsp dry sherry*
*1 tsp soy sauce*
*1 tbsp chicken stock*
**FOR THE PORK AND CASHEW FILLING**
*1½ cups (about 12oz) ground pork*
*1 tbsp oil*
*½ red chili*
*½ cup cashew nuts*
*2 tbsp soy sauce*
*1 tbsp dry sherry*
*1 tsp sugar*
*salt and black pepper*
**TO SERVE**
*2 bunches scallions, cleaned and cut into fine strips*
*½ cucumber, cut into fine sticks*
*Hoisin sauce*

1. Prepare the duck on the day before cooking. Wash and dry it well with kitchen paper. Slice the lemon thickly and put it in a pan with the remaining ingredients. Bring to the boil and simmer for about 30 minutes.
2. Ladle the honey and lemon syrup over the duck several times, until it is completely coated with the mixture. Hang the duck in a cool, well ventilated place and leave to dry overnight. Place a roasting pan to catch any drips.
3. The following day, prepare the pancakes: sift the flour into a large bowl. Gradually add enough of the hot water to form a soft but not sticky dough. Knead the dough for 10 minutes until it is soft and smooth, cover it with a damp cloth and leave for 30 minutes.
4. After the dough has rested, knead it again for 5 minutes. Shape it into 2 sausages each about 12in long and cut each roll into 1in pieces. Shape each piece into a ball.
5. Take two balls at a time and dip one side of one ball in the sesame oil, put the oiled side on top of the other ball and roll the two together into a 6in circle.
6. Heat a heavy frying-pan or griddle and cook the pancake until it has dried on one side, then cook the other side. Remove from the pan and peel the two sides apart. Continue to roll and cook the pancakes. Cover tightly in plastic wrap until you are ready to use them.
7. To finish the duck: heat the oven, setting the temperature to 500°. Place the duck breast-side up on a wire rack. Stand the rack over a roasting pan filled with ¾ cup water. Cook the duck for 15

minutes then turn the oven down to 350° and continue to cook for one hour or until the juices from the cavity are no longer pink. Allow the duck to stand for about 10 minutes, and then remove the meat from the bone and carefully cut both meat and skin into neat slices. Keep warm.

8. Prepare the shrimp filling: put the scallions, fresh ginger, sherry, soy sauce and chicken stock together in a frying-pan or wok. Bring to the boil and simmer for 2 minutes. Add the shrimp and cook for a further 2 minutes. Turn into a heated serving dish and keep warm in a low oven.

9. Prepare the pork and cashew filling: heat the oil in a frying-pan or wok, add the chili and fry until it turns dark, then remove from the pan. Stir-fry the ground pork in the oil, breaking up any lumps of meat. Remove the pork from the pan and drain off all but one table-spoon of the fat. When the fat is very hot, add the cashew nuts and stir-fry for 1 minute. Return the pork to the pan and add the soy sauce, sherry and sugar, and season with salt and black pepper. Continue to stir-fry for 5 minutes or until the meat is cooked. Turn into a serving dish and keep warm.

10. To serve the pancakes: give each guest a tiny dish of Hoisin sauce. Dry the scallions and cucumbers well and put into serving dishes. Steam the pancakes to reheat them and serve at once with the various hot fillings. The guests help themselves to duck, scallions and cucumber (dipped into Hoisin sauce if they like), or to the other fillings, wrap them in the pancakes and eat with chopsticks or fingers.

## CHINESE FRUIT SALAD
SERVES 6
*½ cup sugar*
*1¼ cups water*
*3 apples*
*3 oranges*
*½ ripe honeydew melon*
*1lb fresh or canned lychees*
FOR THE SESAME CARAMEL CHIPS
*¼ cup sugar for the caramel*
*1 tbsp sesame seeds*

1. Place the sugar and water together in a small pan, heat gently until the sugar has dissolved then boil rapidly for a few minutes until the syrup is clear.
2. Peel, quarter and core the apples and place them in the sugar syrup. Simmer them very, very gently until just tender.

Remove the apples and leave to cool.
3. Thinly pare the rind from one orange, taking care to remove only the rind and not the bitter pith. Cut the rind into very thin shreds, put into the syrup, boil for one minute, lift out and cool.
4. Peel the oranges with a sharp knife removing all the pith. Cut into neat segments, discarding seeds and membrane.
5. Cut the melon into cubes or scoop out balls with a melon baller. Peel and stone fresh lychees or if using canned lychees, drain them.

6. Mix all the fruit together, pour over the sugar syrup and chill in the refrigerator.
7. Make the sesame caramel chips: put the sugar and sesame seeds into a small heavy-based pan over a low heat until the sugar dissolves and becomes dark golden. Pour the hot caramel on to an oiled baking sheet and when it is cold break it into chips.
8. Serve the fruit salad with orange shreds and sesame caramel chips scattered over the top at the last minute.

*Below* Peking pancakes provide elegant do-it-yourself dining. The oval dish contains Peking duck slices; below it (clockwise) shrimp filling, scallions and cucumber, soy sauce, pork filling. In bottles, Hoisin sauce and Chinese mustard. Assemble pancakes by first spreading with Hoisin sauce (bottom right); then (moving round the table counter-clockwise), add vegetables, then duck or fillings. Season with soy.

# ST. VALENTINE'S DAY DINNER *for Eight*

To make a St Valentine's dinner really work you must be prepared to be laughably sentimental and, almost more important, you must ask only couples who are devoted to each other, or are likely (perhaps under the influence of this dinner) to become so.

The best St Valentine's dinner is hearts and flowers all the way. Everything – the food, the invitation, the place names – that can possibly be heart-shaped, should be heart-shaped.

The invitations – which might for example be postcards of Valentino at his most ardent or copies of a "Love is . . ." cartoon – could, if the budget will bear it, be delivered by a florist with a single rose.

Almost every food known to man has been thought aphrodisiac at some time by some nation. Caviar, oysters, rare beef, wild mushrooms, seafood, avocados, chocolate and strawberries are the West's alleged aphrodisiacs – washed down by pink champagne, "gold wasser" (an incredibly pretty German wine with flakes of gold leaf floating in it) or brandy. Our menu doesn't call for all that, but is pretty, unusual and definitely romantic.

be my VALENTINE

*Left* The best St Valentine's dinner should be hearts and flowers all the way. A silk and lace heart-shaped invitation could be delivered with a perfect red rose.

*Above* Peppermint creams, cookies and hazelnut clusters can all be heart-shaped. "Love-heart" sweets are cheap and easy to obtain.

## HEART-SHAPED FOOD

It might be fun to make heart-shaped chocolate-covered cookies for after dinner with the guests' initials, and pipe entwined hearts on them in coffee-colored icing.

Heart-shaped cake pans are easy enough to get. Heart-shaped confectioners' chocolate molds can be had and heart-shaped chocolates, or chocolates in heart-shaped boxes are sold in the run-up to 14 February. "Love-Heart" sweets have sentimental messages on them and can be bought at almost any sweet shop.

Once you start, it's hard to stop. You can cut red and pink paper napkins so that, when unfolded, they turn out to be heart-shaped.

Our menu is almost all heart-shaped – the avocados, the sole and shrimp pie (Lovers' Surprise), even the carrots and spinach molds. Vegetable purées, if stiff enough, can be shaped into large heart-shapes on flat serving dishes. A spinach one could form one side of the heart, creamed potato the other.

Some trailing ivies and geraniums have heart-shaped leaves, as does the sweetheart plant *Philodendron Scandens*. If trailed about the table with red roses (another wonderful romantic cliché), it looks extraordinarily pretty. And, of course, the guests should wear their hearts on their sleeves – give them a name-badge cut to a heart-shape with their beloved's name upon it. It will make them laugh at least.

Of course the lights should be low, the table lit by candle-light and sentimental music should just be heard. The flowers might get a romantic boost from a squirt of Chanel or Hermès – or, if they smell wonderful already, the napkins might benefit. Oh, it's all enough to make one fall in love!

## WINE

Pink wine is considered romantic though pink champagne is actually "heavier" than white. A provençale rosé would go well with the fish, preceded perhaps by pink champagne with the avocado. Kir (cassis-flavored white wine) or kir royale (cassis-flavored champagne) are pretty and delicious aperitifs. Or what about fresh strawberries crushed and added to champagne, or a dash of framboise liqueur added to any sparkling white wine?

Heart-shaped napkins
*Cut a cardboard template in the shape of half a heart, large enough to fill a paper napkin folded in half completely. Use best quality napkins and cut out the shape of the template. Open the napkin out to a full heart shape and add frilly edges with strips of paper doily. Cut out silver paper arrows to pierce the center of the heart. (Do not get too carried away – the napkins must remain functional!)*

*Right* The pink and pretty, hearts and flowers, theme can be carried right through the dinner. Here the avocado half is peeled and cut to a heart-shape and set on a strawberry vinaigrette. For the heart-shaped light in the background, cut a heart out of a large dark card, light it from behind and drop a white sheet (crumpled attractively) in front of it.

Ice Cubes
*Look for trays to make heart-shaped ice cubes. Make pink ice cubes by adding a dash of food coloring or Angostura bitters. Ice cubes flavored with crème de cassis are delicious served in a glass of white wine or champagne.*

St Valentine
*St Valentine was a third-century Roman priest. By pure chance his Saint's Day coincided with the Roman pagan festival* Lupercalia *or the choosing of sweethearts.*

THE MENU

*Avocado Hearts*
*with Strawberry Vinaigrette*

*Lovers' Surprise*
*Spinach and Leek Hearts*
*Carrot Kisses*

*Ice-Maiden with Passion Sauce*

*Frivolities and Friandises*

Menu Cards
*Cut out a large pink cardboard heart. Paint a little glue around the edge of the card and sprinkle on silver glitter. Use a contrast marker pen for instant silver writing and outlining in shocking pink or purple for writing the menu. Cut out a second heart a little larger than the first and stick on red velvet to cover the outside edge. Attach the pink heart on top and tape a cardboard wedge to the back to prop the menu up. Individual mini-menus can be made the same way for each guest.*

Really kitsch menu cards made with pink card, glitter dust, and perhaps framed in red velvet will make amusing mementos of the evening.

## GETTING AHEAD

*Weeks or days in advance*

- Make and send invitations, or arrange delivery of single roses-plus-invitation with florist.
- Make heart-shaped napkins, place names, heart-on-the-sleeve badges or bands, etc.
- Buy, or borrow, pastel-colored tablecloth.
- Buy pastel-colored candles to complement the tablecloth.

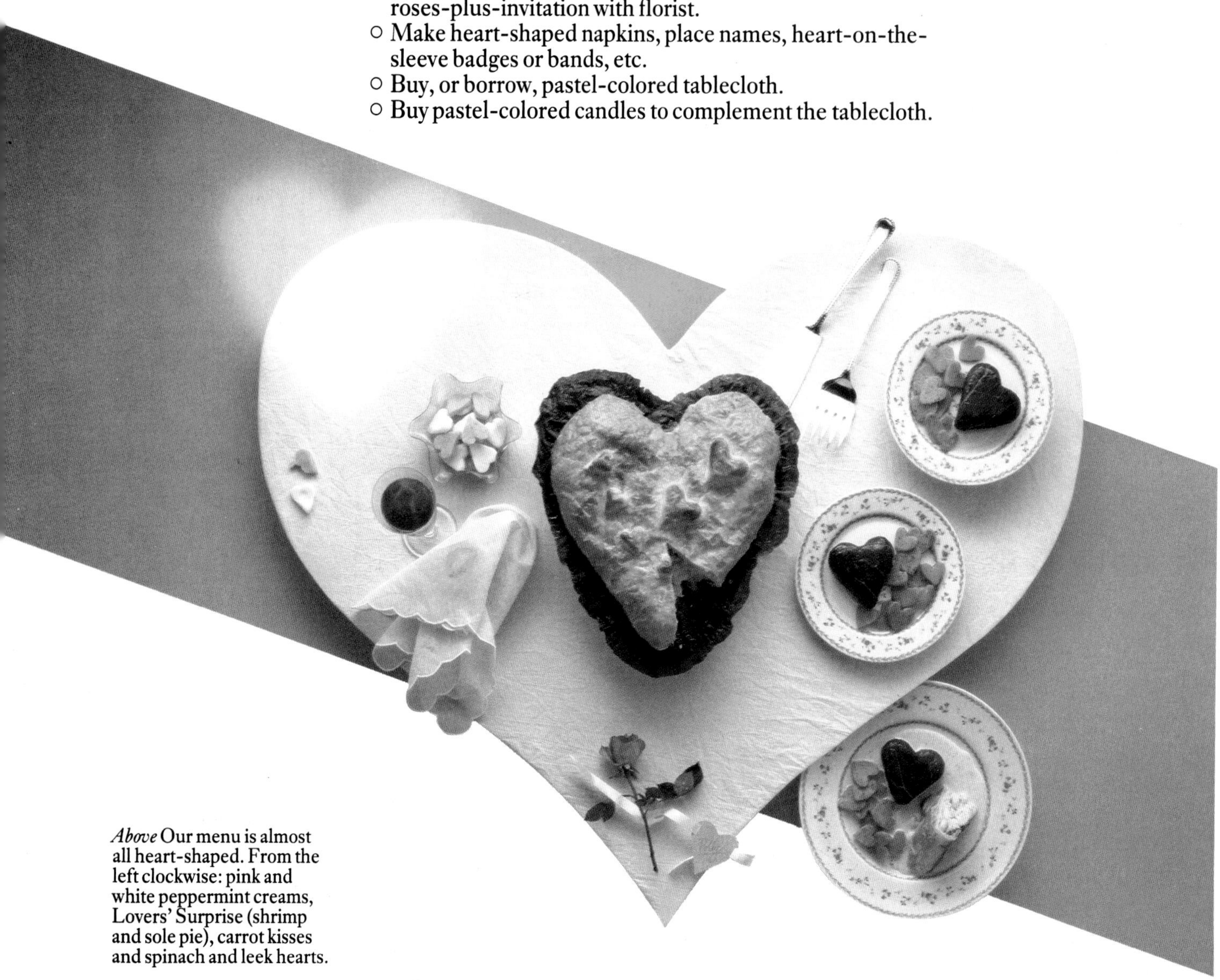

*Above* Our menu is almost all heart-shaped. From the left clockwise: pink and white peppermint creams, Lovers' Surprise (shrimp and sole pie), carrot kisses and spinach and leek hearts.

*Romantic music*
*A must to greet the guests is Roger's and Hart's "My Funny Valentine". Make a tape of this and other thirties songs by Cole Porter, George Gershwin and Noel Coward. The Beatles' music included many love themes and even Elvis Presley sang many a romantic ballad. Or you could weep to Vera Lynn's sentimental songs or swell the room with a passionate Verdi aria.*

○ Sort through the record collection and pick out some suitably romantic music.
○ Make the meringue base and top and store in an airtight container.
○ Buy small molds for the leek and spinach hearts (coeur à la crème cheese drainers would do).
○ Buy wines and drinks.
○ Make a shopping list and buy all the non-perishable items.

*Two days before the party*
○ Do all the shopping except for the fish. Order this to collect next day.
○ Make the mango ice cream and freeze.
○ Make the frivolities and friandises: put everything in separate airtight containers once ready.
○ Make the sugar syrup for the passion sauce.

*The day before the party*
○ Make the strawberry vinaigrette.
○ Collect the fish.
○ Make the fish stock from the fish bones.
○ Defrost the puff pastry if using frozen. Keep refrigerated.
○ Prepare the leek and spinach molds ready to be heated the following evening.
○ Chill the wines if pink or white.

*On the morning of the party*
○ Do the flower arrangements.
○ Set the table, prepare the coffee tray.
○ Chill champagne.
○ Set out glasses for drinks.
○ Sort out the service dishes and plates for each course.
○ Peel, shape and slice the carrots.
○ Fill the meringue heart with ice cream and return to the freezer.
○ Scoop the passion fruit flesh into the sugar syrup, pour into a pitcher ready for serving.
○ Make the sole and shrimp en croûte but leave at the end of stage 8, when the pastry is raw on top, and cover in plastic wrap. Refrigerate.
○ Make the tarragon sauce.
○ Arrange the frivolities and friandises on plates.

*Half an hour before the guests arrive*
○ Heat the oven.
○ Place meringue ice cream in the refrigerator to soften and add the mini-meringue border.
○ Prepare a hot water bath to heat the spinach and leek molds.
○ Put the tarragon sauce in a pan ready to be heated.
○ Put the carrots in a pan of salted water.
○ Set out the avocados, lemon juice, dressing, plates, a sharp knife and a board, ready to prepare the first course.
○ Warm the main course plates.

*Once the guests arrive*
○ Brush the sole and shrimp en croûte with beaten egg and bake.
○ Heat the spinach and leek molds in the oven.
○ Cook the carrots.
○ Heat the tarragon sauce.
○ Dish up the avocado with strawberry vinaigrette and place on the table.

Half strawberries can be perfectly heart-shaped. In February only imported ones will be available.

Carrot kisses: carve the carrots so that they are heart-shaped in section, then cut into slices. Cut lemon slices into pieces each containing two segments. Trim as shown.

Vegetable Purée
*Make one large heart by simply spreading the purée into shape on a flat serving dish. Or make individual ones by filling greased heart-shaped molds with purée. Heat in a moderate oven in a roasting pan filled with a little water. Turn them on to side plates for serving.*

# ST. VALENTINE'S DAY DINNER RECIPES

## AVOCADO HEARTS WITH STRAWBERRY VINAIGRETTE
SERVES 8
*4 ripe avocados*
*lemon juice*
FOR THE STRAWBERRY VINAIGRETTE
*1½ cups vegetable oil*
*juice of 1 lemon*
*8oz strawberries*
*salt and black pepper*
FOR DECORATION
*4 large strawberries with hulls left on*
*3 slices lemon*

1. First make the dressing: place all the ingredients together in a blender or food processor and blend until smooth. Season with salt and pepper.
2. Cut the avocados in half lengthways. Remove the stone and peel.
3. Cut a 'V' in the top of each half of avocado to make it look like a heart, then brush each one with lemon juice.
4. Serve on individual plates: coat the base of each plate with a thin lake of strawberry vinaigrette. Place the avocado, cut side down, on top.
5. Place half a perfect strawberry, flat side down, in the sauce, to the side.
6. Cut the lemon slices as shown on p.29 and place on top.

## LOVERS' SURPRISE
(SOLE AND SHRIMP IN PASTRY)
SERVES 8
*1½lbs puff pastry*
*3 tbsp semolina or bread flour*
FOR THE FILLING
*6 lemon sole, filleted and skinned*
*1lb cooked shrimp*
*1 tbsp finely chopped parsley*
*few sprigs fresh tarragon*
*⅓ cup butter*
*white pepper and salt*
*lemon juice*
*beaten egg*
FOR THE SAUCE
*¼ cup butter*
*2 tbsp flour*
*1¼ cups fish stock (see below)*
*¼ cup glass white wine*
*1 tbsp chopped parsley*
*1 tbsp tarragon*
*2 tbsp heavy cream*
FOR THE STOCK
*2 slices onion and 1 leek*
*small bunch parsley and 1 bay leaf*
*6 peppercorns*
*skin, bones and heads from sole*
*2½ cups water*
FOR DECORATION
*6 whole shrimp*

1. Place all the ingredients for the stock together and simmer for 20 minutes. Strain into a measuring jug.
2. Preheat the oven, setting the temperature control to 450°.
3. Roll out one-third of the pastry to a 12in square about the thickness of a penny. Flour well, fold in half gently and cut through both thicknesses to the shape of half a heart. Open the pastry up into the full heart.
4. Place on a wet baking sheet and prick all over. Leave in a cool place for 15 minutes, then bake until brown and crisp. Cool and trim if necessary.
5. Sprinkle the cooked pastry base evenly with semolina or bread flour (to prevent the fish juices from making the pastry soggy).
6. Lay half the fillets of fish on the cooked pastry, scatter over the shrimp, parsley and tarragon and dot with half the butter. Then cover with the remaining fish and dot with the rest of the butter. Season with salt, pepper and lemon juice.
7. Roll out the rest of the pastry into a large sheet and lay it over the fish. Cut around the heart shape leaving approximately a 1in border. Carefully tuck the top sheet of pastry under the cooked pastry.
8. Brush with beaten egg. Cut some pastry trimmings into heart, flower or leaf shapes and use to decorate the heart. Brush again with egg.
9. Bake for 15 minutes in the hot oven to brown and puff up the pastry. Then turn the oven down to 300° for a further 20 minutes. Cover the pastry crust with wet wax paper if it looks in danger of browning. To test if the fish is cooked push a skewer through the pastry and fish from the side. It should glide in easily.

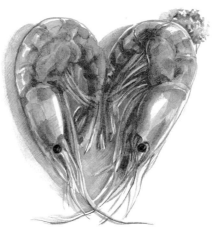

10. While the fish is cooking make the sauce: melt half the butter in a saucepan, add the flour and cook, stirring, for one minute. Gradually add the stock and wine, stirring all the time until smooth and boiling. Boil rapidly until you have a sauce the consistency of thin cream.
11. Add the chopped parsley, tarragon and cream. Beat in the remaining butter bit by bit. Pour into a warmed sauceboat.

## SPINACH AND LEEK HEARTS
SERVES 8
*8 large spinach leaves*
*melted butter*
*8 young leeks*
*¼ cup butter*
*2 tbsp heavy cream*
*lemon juice*
*salt, black pepper and nutmeg*
*carrot hearts to decorate (see pp.29 and 31)*

1. Wash the spinach well, and remove the tough stalks. Cook in boiling salted water for 1 minute, rinse under cold water, drain and pat dry.
2. Brush out eight 3in heart-shaped molds with melted butter.
3. Wash the leeks and remove the dark green leaves. Cut into 2in pieces. Then cut each piece lengthwise into fine strips.
4. Melt the butter in a sauté pan or frying-pan, add the leeks and cook gently until soft and tender but not colored.
5. Add the heavy cream. Bring to the boil. Season to taste with lemon juice, salt, black pepper and nutmeg.
6. Preheat the oven, setting the temperature control to 350°.
7. Carefully line each of the heart-shaped molds with a spinach leaf. Make sure that the leaves will be large enough to fold over the top of the mold once it is filled.
8. Fill each mold with some of the leek mixture. Wrap the rest of the spinach leaf over the top, making sure that the leek is completely sealed in.
9. Stand the molds in a roasting pan full of boiling water and bake for 20 minutes to heat the molds all the way through.
10. Tip the molds out and serve them on individual warmed side plates surrounded with carrot kisses.

NOTE:
If using china coeur à la crème molds for this, steam over water rather than standing the molds in it. The perforated bases would let in the water.

## CARROT KISSES
SERVES 8
*2lb carrots (evenly sized)*
*melted butter*
*salt*
*black pepper*
FOR DECORATION
*parsley, finely chopped*

1. Peel the carrots.
2. Using a sharp knife, remove a V-shaped strip along the length of each carrot. With a vegetable peeler, shave the sides of each carrot to bring them to a slight point opposite the V so that, in section, the carrots look heart-shaped.
3. Cut the carrots into ¼in-thick "heart-shaped" slices.
4. Place in boiling salted water and cook until tender – perhaps 8 minutes.
5. Drain. Toss in melted butter and season with salt and pepper. Sprinkle with very finely chopped parsley just before serving.

## ICE-MAIDEN WITH PASSION SAUCE
SERVES 8
FOR THE FILLING
*2 ripe or even over-ripe mangoes*
*1¼ cups heavy cream*
*2oz confectioners' sugar, sifted*
FOR THE MERINGUE
*4 egg whites*
*1 cup sugar*
*a little light brown sugar*
FOR THE SAUCE
*1¼ cups water*
*⅔ cup sugar*
*grated rind and juice of ½ lemon*
*4 passion fruit*

1. To make the filling: peel the mangoes and cut the flesh away from the stone. Purée the flesh.
2. Lightly whip the cream and fold in the purée with the confectioners' sugar.
3. Turn the mixture into a chilled tray and freeze. Whisk with a fork every 30 minutes until the mixture is frozen solid.
4. To make the meringue: preheat the oven, setting the temperature control to 200°. Lay two pieces of wax paper on two baking sheets. Draw a heart-shape approximately 10in long on one of the pieces of paper and brush both pieces lightly with oil.
5. Beat the egg whites until the mixture will stand up in stiff peaks if the whisk is lifted. Add a tablespoon of the sugar and continue to whisk until very stiff and shiny. Fold in the remaining sugar.

6. Pipe or spread two-thirds of the meringue to fill the heart. Carefully spoon, or pipe, the remaining third into even mini-meringues on the second piece of oiled paper. Sprinkle with the brown sugar.
7. Place the meringues in the oven to dry out. They are done when light and dry and the paper will peel off easily. (The small meringues will take about 2 hours, the large one 3 hours.)
8. To make the sauce: put the water, sugar and grated lemon rind together in a pan. Heat slowly until dissolved. Bring to the boil and cook until the syrup feels sticky between finger and thumb. Allow to cool. Remove the lemon rind and pour into a sauce boat.
9. Cut the passion fruit in half. Scoop the pulp into the sugar syrup. Add lemon juice to taste. (The sauce should be sharp to contrast with the sweetness of the meringue.)
10. To serve: place the ice cream filling in the refrigerator for 40 minutes to soften before serving. Spoon over the base of the meringue. Make a border on top of the heart-shape with the tiny meringues. Hand passion sauce separately.

## FRIVOLITIES AND FRIANDISES

### PINK AND WHITE PEPPERMINT CREAMS
*2 cups sifted confectioners' sugar*
*1 tsp lemon juice*
*a few drops of peppermint extract*
*½ egg white, lightly beaten*
*pink food coloring*

1. Mix together the sugar, lemon juice, peppermint flavoring and enough egg white to make a pliable "dough".
2. Dust the work surface with confectioners' sugar. Divide the mixture in half. Add 1-2 drops of pink coloring to one half. Knead the two pieces of mixture until smooth.
3. Using a little more confectioners' sugar to prevent the mixture sticking, roll it out to ¼in thick. Stamp out the peppermint creams with a small heart-shaped cutter and lay on a sheet of wax paper. Leave in a cool place for 24 hours to dry out.
4. Store in an airtight container.

### CHOCOLATE SHORTBREAD HEARTS
*¼ cup butter*
*2 tbsp sugar*
*¾ cup all-purpose flour*
*2oz bittersweet chocolate*

1. Preheat the oven, setting the temperature control to 375°.
2. Beat the butter and sugar together until soft and creamy.
3. Gently work in the flour.
4. Pat the paste into a smooth ball and then into a square about ¼in thick. Cut the dough into tiny hearts using a shaped pastry cutter. Place on a floured baking sheet.
5. Bake to a pale beige color. Cool.
6. Melt the chocolate over a pan of simmering water. Dip the cookies halfway in so that the hearts are half plain and half chocolate-coated. Place on a wire rack for the chocolate to harden.

### COFFEE KISSES
*1 egg white*
*½ cup sugar*
*pinch cinnamon*
FOR THE FILLING
*2 tbsp unsalted butter*
*½ cup confectioners' sugar, sifted*
*1 tsp instant coffee dissolved in a little boiling water*
*½ egg yolk*

1. Preheat the oven, setting the temperature control to 200°. Cover a baking tray with a sheet of oiled wax paper.
2. Beat the egg white until stiff. Add half the sugar and continue to beat until very stiff and shiny.
3. Fold in the remaining sugar and pinch of cinnamon.
4. Put the meringue into a piping bag fitted with a ⅙in plain nozzle and pipe tiny flat heart shapes on to the prepared baking tray.
5. Place the meringues in the oven until they are light and dry and will easily pull off the paper. This will take about one hour. Cool on a wire rack.
6. To make the filling: soften the butter, carefully beat in the remaining ingredients and continue to beat until light and fluffy.
7. Sandwich the meringue hearts together with the coffee filling.

### HAZELNUT DELIGHTS
*4oz bittersweet chocolate*
*2oz whole hazelnuts*

1. Brush a sheet of wax paper with oil and place it on a tray.
2. Melt the chocolate in a bowl over a pan of simmering water.
3. Stir in the hazelnuts. With a teaspoon lift the chocolate-coated nuts out and place in clusters of three on the prepared wax paper. Leave to set.

# TENNIS PARTY
## *for Six*

*Left* A classic English teatray set on the lawn is a welcome sight to tired tennis players. Fresh air, exercise and sunshine make the keenest health-enthusiast hungry, so be generous with the easy fruit cake and the almond tartlets.

Croquet
*This is a more complicated game than it looks. Use an encyclopaedia of games or the instructions leaflet in a croquet mallet box for strictly-by-the-rules croquet. But the general idea is to race your opponent round the croquet lawn, knocking your ball through the hoops in a race to the central pin. Players take turns. Dastardly tactics are allowed, like hitting your opponent's ball with yours which entitles you to snuggle your ball up close to his, put your foot on your own to hold it steady while clonking hard with the mallet to send his ball anywhere that he doesn't want it to be.*

THE VERY IDEA OF A TENNIS PARTY IS WONDERFULLY old-fashioned, perhaps belonging to the twenties or thirties with pert young women with bobbed hair and bandeaux across their foreheads being very jolly. Modern tennis tends to take place on municipal courts or at the club, the aura being more of competitive sweat and Coca Cola than of the Salad Days of pre-war summers.

Which makes a nostalgic tennis party all the better. Obviously, a tennis party requires a tennis court and people who can play tennis. If it has to be held at public courts, then it had better be a picnic, with cool drinks for between games, plenty of ice and something summery and alcoholic for when the last game is done – say Pimm's or a grapefruit and rum punch. If it has to be at a club, then tea and drinks are likely to be provided by the club caterers who are unlikely to care for any self-catering on the part of the club members.

So this party is really designed for the host with a private tennis court, or access to one. If there is no tennis court to be had, or the guests are not athletic, then a croquet party is just as much fun, even more competitive (whacking your opponent into the shrubbery and making enemies for life is traditional) and easier to achieve. All you need is a good-sized lawn and a croquet set and six people (four play at once, two a side). No experience on the part of host or guests is necessary. Croquet is one of the few games that you can enjoy the first time you try, and it gets better as you get better. You need written rules, though, because everyone gets tempted to make them up as they go.

But back to tennis: six people is a perfect number. That means two sit out and chat while four play. Eight means the same four people play together all the afternoon, and four means you are all on the court all the time and there is no chance for the host or hostess to sneak off and get tea or drinks on the go. It is important that all the players are roughly the same standard. A beginner playing with even moderately good players feels a real rabbit, and prevents anyone else getting a decent game, and a wretched time is had by all,

Afternoon tennis parties are more fun than morning ones, partly because there is more time to play, but also because there is more scope for the cook. One can hardly serve a great groaning tea party at mid-morning. People get very hungry

For summery drinks add candy-striped straws and slices of cucumber or fruit to long, tall, cool glasses.

33

playing tennis, so provide a goodly spread. Our suggestions are very British, and we've included the recipes for the cakes. But an excellent tea can be had from the supermarket – bought gingerbread spread generously with unsalted butter, buttered fruit muffins with honey, English muffins with clotted cream and jam, good quality biscuits, etc.

The tea should be good too, and it might be nice to offer China tea (say Lapsan Souchong or Keemun), as well as Darjeeling or Ceylon. Make plenty of it – everyone drinks at least three cups. A non-alcoholic iced homemade lemonade is good too and could be kept in a large thermos for hot and panting players.

The tea-tray, or more likely trays, should appear about two hours after the start of play. By then everyone should have played at least one set, and be ready for a rest and some refreshment. A silver tea-tray and a large jam-filled sponge cake sitting on the green grass must be the most romantic and most welcome of summer sights.

*Above* An excellent tea for the non-cook can be had from the supermarket – sticky gingerbread, good quality jam, fresh muffins and chocolate cookies.

Choose a good leaf tea, perhaps China or Darjeeling, and be sure to make plenty of it.

> **THE MENU**
>
> *Cucumber Sandwiches*
>
> *Almond Tartlets*
>
> *Classic Sponge*
>
> *Easy Fruit Cake*
>
> *Lemonade or Tea*

## GETTING AHEAD
*A month before the party*
○ Telephone the guests to invite them.
○ Make sure you have 2 cans of new tennis balls.
○ Make a shopping list.
○ The classic sponge cake freezes well without filling. So make this now.
○ Make the easy fruit cake. It will keep well wrapped in foil and stored in an airtight container.

Be Prepared For Rain
*Even in summer the weather cannot be relied upon so make a contingency plan in case it should rain. Borrow an indoor croquet set or buy a set of carpet bowls. Or you could produce a couple of packs of cards and turn the Tennis Party into a Bridge Tea.*

**Lining Pastry Cases**

*Cut the pastry about ⅓in above the rim of the pan. The lip can be left plain or crimped between the thumb and forefinger. Chill the pastry before baking. The result will be a deep pastry case even if it should shrink back a little during cooking.*

*Two days before the party*
○ Do all the shopping.
○ Wash and iron your tennis clothes.
○ Make the pastry for the almond tartlets and chill.
○ Assemble tea-tray, teapots and china and polish if necessary.

*The day before the party*
○ Make the almond tartlets.
○ Make the lemonade and leave overnight.

*The morning of the party*
○ Sweep or mow the tennis court.
○ Check the net.
○ Put out tennis balls.
○ Make sure clean towels and soap are handy.
○ Strain the lemonade and leave in pitchers in the refrigerator.
○ Set out the tea-tray with cups, saucers, sugar, napkins, milk jug, plates, teapot and strainer.
○ Put a rug on the grass near the court if there isn't a bench or chairs handy.
○ Take the classic sponge cake out of the freezer.

*Half an hour before the guests arrive*
○ Make the cucumber sandwiches, arrange on plates, decorate and cover with plastic wrap.
○ Fill the sponge cake and dust with confectioners' sugar.
○ Put the almond tartlets on to a plate.
○ Set out the easy fruit cake with a sharp knife for cutting.

*To serve the tea*
○ Add ice and mint to the lemonade.
○ Make the tea.

**Cake Making**

*The appearance of a finished cake depends largely on the care with which the cake pans have been prepared before baking. They should always be greased and floured or lined with paper. It is best to let most cakes settle in their pans for about 5 minutes before turning them out on to a wire rack to cool.*

*Below* Lemon barley water is a traditional part of the summer tennis scene, as are thinly cut cucumber sandwiches. Simple plastic dishes can serve as trays or plates – lighter to carry to the court.

# TENNIS PARTY RECIPES

## CUCUMBER SANDWICHES
SERVES 6

You will need to allow two slices of bread for each guest. Any thinly sliced brown or white bread will do, or make each round with one brown slice and one white. An average cucumber will cover twenty slices of bread. Slice it very thinly just before making the sandwiches. If slicing the cucumber in advance keep it in a plastic bag to prevent it from drying out.

Make the sandwiches at the last possible moment so they do not become soggy; season well with salt and black pepper. Don't skimp on the butter – it will prevent moisture from the cucumber soaking into the bread. 1 cup butter should cover twenty slices of bread. Remove the crusts and cut into neat squares or triangles. Set them upright on the platter so that the filling can be seen easily. Decorate the sandwiches with fresh watercress. Cover them with a damp dish cloth.

NOTE:
Cucumber sandwiches cannot be frozen.

## ALMOND TARTLETS
MAKES 12 TARTLETS
*1 cup flour-quantity French flan pastry*
*   (see Tarte Maison p. 19)*
FOR THE ALMOND FILLING
*¼ cup unsalted butter*
*¼ cup sugar*
*1 egg*
*lemon juice*
*½ cup ground almonds*
*1½ tbsp all-purpose flour*
*½ cup flaked almonds*
FOR DECORATION
*apricot or redcurrant glaze*

1. Preheat the oven, setting the temperature control to 375°.
2. Use the pastry to line 12 tartlet molds. Prick the pastry with a fork and chill while you make the filling.
3. Cream the butter and sugar together and beat in the egg. Add a squeeze of lemon juice.
4. Fold in the almonds and flour. Carefully spoon or pipe this filling into the pastry cases, filling each one to just below the top.
5. Scatter the tartlets with the flaked almonds and bake for 15-20 minutes.
6. As soon as the tartlets are well browned, remove them from the molds and brush the tops with the hot apricot or redcurrant glaze.

## CLASSIC SPONGE
MAKES ONE 8-INCH CAKE
*1¼ cups all-purpose flour*
*pinch of salt*
*4 eggs*
*1 cup sugar*
*grated rind of 1 lemon*
FOR THE FILLING
*jam or lemon curd*
*a little confectioners' sugar*

1. Preheat the oven, setting the temperature to 350°. Grease a 8in round springform cake pan and line the bottom with greased wax paper.
2. Sift flour and salt. Separate the eggs.
3. Place the yolks with half the sugar and the lemon rind and beat them until pale yellow and mousse-like.
4. Beat the egg whites until stiff. If using a machine gradually beat in the remaining sugar a spoonful at a time, continue to beat until the mixture forms stiff peaks. If beating by hand, add the sugar at the end and fold lightly.
5. Using a metal spoon, carefully fold the egg whites and flour into the yolks.
6. Pour the mixture into the prepared pan and bake for about 45 minutes until the cake is well risen, golden brown and firm when pressed with the fingertips.

7. When the cake is cool split in half with a large sharp knife. Spread with jam or lemon curd and sandwich back together again.
8. Dust the top of the cake with a little confectioners' sugar and store in an airtight container.

## EASY FRUIT CAKE
MAKES ONE 8-INCH CAKE
*1 cup soft "tub" margarine*
*1 cup sugar*
*2½ cups all-purpose flour*
*4 large eggs*
*¾ cup ground almonds*
*1 tsp salt*
*¼ cup mixed peel*
*¼ cup chopped glacé cherries*
*2 cups currants*
*2 cups golden raisins*
*1 tsp ground allspice*
*1¼ cups beer*

1. Preheat the oven, setting the temperature control to 350°. Carefully line a 8in cake pan with a double layer of greased wax paper.
2. Put all ingredients together in a large mixing bowl and beat well. Turn into the prepared cake pan, and bake for one hour.
3. Turn the oven to 300°. Cover the top of the cake with wax paper to prevent it from browning too much.
4. Continue to cook for a further 2½-3 hours. The cake is cooked when a skewer will emerge clean when stuck into the center.

NOTE:
For a boozier cake prick with a skewer and brush with brandy or rum.

## LEMONADE
MAKES ONE DRINK EACH FOR 6 PEOPLE
*6 lemons*
*6oz sugar cubes*
*7½ cups boiling water*
TO SERVE
*ice cubes*
*mint leaves*

1. Rub the sugar cubes all over the lemons to extract the oils (and the flavor) in the rind. If this is too tedious, finely grate the rind while taking great care not to grate the bitter white pith.
2. Slice the lemons and put them with the sugar (and rind) in a bowl.
3. Add the boiling water and leave in a cool place for about 12 hours. Strain and refrigerate until needed.
4. Serve in large glass jugs with plenty of ice and mint leaves.

# ITALIAN LUNCH
*for Eight*

### Parmesan
*Parmesan is the most famous and expensive of Italian grana (hard, grainy cheeses). The texture is the result of a slow ageing process and low moisture content. Grana Padano is cheaper than true Parmesan and often used in cooking.*

THIS IS A LUNCH PARTY FOR A LONG LAZY SUNDAY afternoon with hours for indulgence. It should be a family and best-friends affair, casual, relaxed, with very good food and plenty of easy-drinking Italian wine. The lunch itself, except for the childishly simple and undeniably fattening chocolate pudding, is pretty and light, and perfect for a summer day.

Our menu amounts to a 3-hour party. Salad is served Italian-style as a separate course, and the meal consists of five courses without the traditional Italian dessert of fresh fruit, and without any cheese. A less lengthy lunch could be had by omitting either the spaghetti and sauce or (if a vegetarian lunch was called for) the chicken breasts, and replacing the pudding with fresh Pecorino or Parmesan cheese with a few perfect pears or grapes.

The first course of crudités and hot dip might best be served as an accompaniment to a glass of frascati before sitting down to the serious business of lunch. Children find lengthy sojourns at the table very tedious so perhaps they could take around the crudités to standing grown-ups, then sit down demurely with them for spaghetti and chicken, and be allowed to escape during the salad course. They could always return, restored by a chase around garden or house, for the chocolate pudding.

### Pecorino
*This is another hard grainy cheese made with ewes' milk. It has a strong salty flavor. Use older grana cheeses for grating and cooking and the young moist ones for eating in chunks.*

*Below* Hot anchovy and garlic dip contrasts wonderfully with crisp fresh crudités. One small bowl of dip is enough for three or four replenishments of vegetables.

Make sure bread sticks are very fresh. Unsalted butter may not be classic or Italian but it is delicious served with them. Or dip the bread sticks in the hot anchovy and garlic dip.

If the party is to be an Italian Evening rather than an Italian Lunch, the same menu, perhaps with the additions of such Italian classics as gambaretti (boiled shrimp), seafood salad, tomato and Mozzarella salad and Neapolitan ice cream would make an excellent spread on the buffet table.

## WINE

Any type of Italian wine would be suitable – fresh white frascati or soave at lunch time perhaps, or the heavier red bardolinos, barolos or chianti classicos for dinner. Be careful when buying Italian wine. Many Italians like a sunny, rather "cooked" taste which people used to young California wines find too hard and oxidized. Check that the color is purpley-red or pure red, rather than brownish, if the wines are young. Older wines can legitimately be browner but they need to be very good to last (and improve) in bottle, so take the advice of an expert if at all unsure.

---

### THE MENU

*Crudités with Hot Anchovy and Garlic Dip
(to serve with drinks)*

*Spaghetti with Fresh Tomato Sauce*

*Breast of Chicken Stuffed with Mushrooms
served with Sweetbreads in Cream*

*Spinach Gnocchi*

*Saladini*

*Italian Chocolate Pudding*

---

## GETTING AHEAD

*A couple of weeks before the lunch*
○ Telephone the guests to invite them.

*Two days before the lunch*
○ Make a list from the recipes and buy all the ingredients needed and also wine and soft drinks.
○ Think about suitable flowers, plates, napkins, tablecloth, etc. It is possible to buy colored Italian-style paper tablecloths.
○ Borrow an expresso coffee machine, if possible.

*The day before the lunch*
○ Prepare the crudités. Secure vegetables cut into sticks in bunches with a rubber band at each end to prevent them curling. Store in cold water overnight.
○ Prepare the tomato sauce, cover tightly and chill overnight.
○ Soak the sweetbreads.
○ Fill the chicken breasts with mushroom stuffing, cover with plastic wrap and chill.
○ Line the ramekins with spinach leaves and prepare the spinach filling. Fill the molds, cover tightly and chill overnight.
○ Make the chocolate pudding.
○ Chill the wine.

Seafood Salad
*Use 4oz of assorted cooked seafood for each portion. Add finely shredded raw leek and carrot and slices of raw button mushroom. Toss the salad in garlic-flavored vinaigrette dressing and sprinkle with chopped parsley.*

Zabaglione
*This is the lightest of desserts and can be served alone or as a sauce to accompany ice cream or fruit. For each person mix 1 egg yolk, 1 tbsp sugar and 1 tbsp marsala in a bowl and set it over a pan of simmering water. Beat until it is thick and mousse-like. Serve warm.*

*Right* A table laden with courses for a long, lazy Sunday afternoon. On the left: plates of chicken, mushroom and sweetbreads in cream served with spinach gnocchi and saladini. In the center: Amaretti cookies (tiny macaroons in paper), fresh grated Parmesan and (right foreground) spaghetti with fresh tomato sauce. Chilled soave or frascati would be perfect on a sunny day; a gutsy red on a chilly one.

**Italian Coffee**
*Expresso is a strong, rich cup of coffee made by forcing steam and water through finely ground coffee beans. Italian coffee beans are roast exceptionally dark. If they are not available, use high roast coffee at double strength. A true expresso coffee-maker is an expensive machine but a moka express is an inexpensive substitute. Cappucino is made by adding frothy milk to expresso coffee with a pinch of cinnamon or cocoa. The milk is made to froth by steam under pressure but the same effect can be achieved by whizzing hot milk in a blender.*

○ Prepare the saladini dressing in a screw-top jar.
○ Set the table.
○ Prepare equipment and a tray for coffee.
○ Organize glasses and ice for pre-lunch drinks.
○ Prepare the saladini but do not dress, cover with plastic wrap and chill.
○ Stand the gnocchi in a roasting pan.
○ Arrange the crudités and bread sticks.
○ Simmer and slice the sweetbreads and reduce the liquid and set them aside.
○ Measure the ingredients for the cream sauce.
○ Set out ingredients for the anchovy and garlic dip.
○ Dust the chicken breasts with flour and brown in hot butter with the onion and mushrooms. Lay them in a roasting pan with cold chicken stock. Cover with foil.
○ Turn out the chocolate pudding and cover with whipped cream.
○ Decorate with grated chocolate.

*Just before the guests arrive*
○ Make the anchovy and garlic dip.

*After the guests arrive*
○ Serve the crudités with anchovy dip.
○ Put the chicken breasts into the preheated oven.
○ Pour boiling water around the spinach molds and put in the oven.
○ Boil a pan of water to cook the spaghetti.

*30 minutes after the guests arrive*
○ Cook the spaghetti.
○ While the spaghetti is cooking, turn out the spinach gnocchi and keep warm.
○ Put the chicken breasts on to a serving dish. Finish off the sweetbread cream sauce. Pour over the chicken breasts. Cover and keep warm.
○ Dress the saladini.
○ Drain the spaghetti and keep it warm by tossing it lightly with olive oil or a little of the sauce to prevent the strands sticking together.
○ Serve the spaghetti with a spoonful of tomato sauce on the top.

**Dips**
*Other possible dips are plain or horseradish-flavored cream cheese beaten together with tomato ketchup, Worcestershire sauce and crushed garlic. Or a very ripe avocado finely chopped with a peeled and seeded tomato, 1 tsp grated onion and seasoned with Tabasco and lemon juice. Or try blue Brie mashed and mixed with cream.*

**Italian Wines**
*In most years Italy is the most prolific wine producer in the world. Italian white wines are clean and refreshing but the hot climate means that the best Italian wines are full-bodied reds, especially those from Piedmont in the north-west and Tuscany in the Central Apenines.*

**Chicken Breasts**
*These are also delicious stuffed with spinach, cheese and prosciutto or crabmeat and served with a light cream sauce.*

*Right Freshly grated Parmigiano (Parmesan) or Pecorino is infinitely better than dried, pre-grated cheese.*

**Wholewheat Spaghetti**
*This has a nutty, full flavor. Fresh pasta shops sometimes sell it colored pink (with tomato purée) or green (with spinach). Chopped basil is the classic pasta herb but marjoram, chives and tarragon are all good.*

# ITALIAN LUNCH RECIPES

## CRUDITÉS WITH HOT ANCHOVY AND GARLIC DIP
SERVES 8
*½ cucumber, seeded and cut into sticks*
*2 carrots, peeled and cut into sticks*
*1 red pepper, seeded and cut into sticks*
*1 green pepper, seeded and cut into sticks*
*1 bunch of scallions, cleaned and neatly*
*    trimmed*
*12 cherry tomatoes*
*¼ cup fresh white button mushrooms*
*Italian bread sticks*
FOR THE DIP
*2 cups heavy cream*
*¼ cup butter*
*8 anchovy fillets, finely chopped*
*1 large clove of garlic, crushed*

1. Prepare the vegetables and leave to soak in a bowl of iced water for an hour to become crisp. Drain.
2. Arrange on a round plate and chill. Put the bread sticks in a tall glass.
3. Put the cream into a heavy-based pan, bring to the boil and simmer gently for 15 to 20 minutes until thickened and reduced to 1¼ cups.
4. Melt the butter over a low heat. Add the anchovy fillets and garlic and cook gently for one minute. Slowly add the reduced cream, stirring constantly.
5. Serve immediately in a fondue pot or a flameproof dish that will fit over a candle or burner and stand. Serve the bread sticks and vegetables separately.

NOTE:
The sauce is good cold or tepid, so do not worry if there is no means of keeping it hot. See the margin note on p. 40 for other dips to serve with crudités.

## SPAGHETTI WITH FRESH TOMATO SAUCE
SERVES 8 AS A STARTER
*1lb spaghetti*
*salt*
*1 tbsp olive oil*
*⅓ cup grated Parmesan cheese*
*salt*
*freshly ground black pepper*
FOR THE TOMATO SAUCE
*1½lb sweet ripe tomatoes*
*4-6 shallots, finely chopped*
*2 tbsp fresh basil, chopped*
*3 whole cloves garlic*
*⅔ cup olive oil*
*salt*
*black pepper*

1. Skin and seed the tomatoes. Chop the flesh finely. Place in a bowl with the shallot and basil.

2. Flatten the cloves of garlic with the flat blade of a knife so that they are a little crushed but still in one piece. Peel them and add to the tomato mixture. Season with salt and freshly ground black pepper.
3. Pour the olive oil over the garlic and tomato mixture and then leave to stand for 3 to 4 hours. Remove the garlic cloves.
4. Bring a large pan of water to the boil, add the salt and olive oil. Cook the spaghetti in the water for about 10 minutes. Drain and rinse in boiling water. Season with salt and black pepper.
5. Place a helping of spaghetti on each plate with a large spoonful of tomato sauce on top.
6. Serve the freshly grated Parmesan cheese separately.

## BREAST OF CHICKEN STUFFED WITH MUSHROOMS WITH SWEETBREADS IN CREAM
SERVES 8
FOR THE SWEETBREADS IN CREAM
*8oz lambs' or calves' sweetbreads*
*2 tbsp butter*
*3½ tbsp flour*
*⅔ cup light white wine*
*2 tbsp heavy or whipping cream*
*squeeze of lemon juice*
*salt*
*ground white pepper*

FOR THE CHICKEN BREASTS
*8 chicken breasts, skinned and boned*
*⅓ cup butter*
*1 onion, finely chopped*
*1 cup mushrooms, finely chopped*
*salt and ground black pepper*
*⅔ cup chicken stock*

1. Start with the sweetbreads: soak them in successive changes of cold water until the water is no longer tinged pink. Drain, then cover with boiling water and drain again. Place in a pan of fresh boiling water and simmer for 6 minutes. Remove the sweetbreads from the liquid and boil it down to approximately ⅔ cup. When the sweetbreads are cool remove any sinew or membrane and cut into slices. Set the sweetbreads and stock to one side.
2. Preheat the oven, setting the temperature control to 375°.
3. Now prepare the chicken breasts: melt half the butter in a frying-pan over low heat and in it soften the onion, add the mushrooms and fry gently until very soft. Season with salt and pepper. Cool.
4. Split each chicken breast horizontally in its thicker part, but without cutting completely through. Open it out like a book and gently beat it with a rolling-pin or mallet to flatten it slightly.
5. Sprinkle each breast with salt and pepper and spread a little of the mushroom mixture on each one, making sure that none is overlapping the edge.
6. Fold the chicken breasts carefully so that the filling is tightly enclosed. Dust with flour and fry gently in the remaining butter until golden brown. Place in a roasting pan and pour over the chicken stock. Cover and cook in the heated oven for 30 minutes or until the chicken breasts are tender.
7. Lift the breasts on to a serving dish and keep warm in a low oven. Reserve the chicken stock.
8. To finish the sweetbreads in cream: melt the butter in a frying-pan, and fry the sweetbreads on all sides until lightly golden. Remove from the pan and put to one side. Add the flour and cook for one minute. Gradually pour in the reserved chicken and sweetbread stocks and the white wine, stirring constantly. Bring to the boil and simmer until the sauce has reduced by approximately one-third.
9. Return the sweetbreads to the pan and simmer for 1 minute. Stir in the cream and lemon juice and season. Pour the sauce over the chicken breasts and serve immediately.

*Above* A good party leaves a merry mess! Here too much wine has led to third helpings of chocolate pudding and the children have ended up playing model-car games on the table.

## SPINACH GNOCCHI
SERVES 8

*3 lb fresh spinach*
*¼ cup butter*
*1 cup Ricotta cheese*
*2 tbsp flour*
*3 eggs, lightly beaten*
*3 tbsp heavy or whipping cream*
*¼ cup grated Parmesan cheese*
*salt*
*freshly ground black pepper*
*pinch of nutmeg*

1. Trim the stalks and wash two-thirds of the spinach. Cook it briefly in boiling water (2 minutes), drain well, press dry, then chop finely.
2. Melt the butter in a heavy-based pan, add the chopped spinach and heat, stirring constantly until any liquid has boiled away and the spinach begins to stick slightly to the pan.
3. Stir in the Ricotta cheese and continue to cook the mixture for a further 3 to 4 minutes until the cheese has melted and completely mixed with the spinach.

4. Turn the mixture into a bowl and beat in the flour, eggs, cream and grated Parmesan cheese. Season with salt, black pepper and nutmeg. Chill for 30 minutes.
5. Remove the tough stalks from the remaining spinach leaves and wash well. Cook in boiling salted water for one minute. Drain and plunge immediately into cold water. Lay out flat and pat dry.
6. Preheat the oven, setting the temperature control to 375°. Butter 8 ramekin dishes. Line them with the spinach leaves.
7. Spoon the gnocchi mixture into the ramekins. Stand the ramekins in a roasting pan, and pour a little boiling water into the base of the pan. Cover the whole roasting pan with foil and bake for 30 minutes or until the gnocchi feel firm to the touch.
8. Turn the spinach gnocchi out of the ramekin dishes. Serve to accompany a main course or as a starter with tomato sauce.

## SALADINI

Buy a mixture of young salad leaves including any lettuces (Romaine, Boston, butter, iceberg) or endives (curly endive, Belgian endive, radicchio) and watercress, lamb's lettuce, arugula, fennel tops, celery leaves, etc.

Dress with olive oil flavored with lemon juice, crushed garlic, salt and freshly ground coarse black pepper.

## ITALIAN CHOCOLATE PUDDING
SERVES 8

*oil*
*3¾ tbsp cornstarch*
*2½ cups milk*
*8 oz bittersweet chocolate*
*⅓ cup sugar*
*½ tsp vanilla extract*
FOR DECORATION
*1½ cups heavy cream, whipped*
*1 oz bittersweet chocolate, grated*

1. Lightly oil a 5-cup decorative mold. Turn upside down to allow the excess oil to drain.
2. Mix the cornstarch to a smooth paste with a little of the cold milk.
3. Put the remaining milk, chocolate and sugar in a pan and place over a low heat until the chocolate has melted.
4. Pour the warm liquid on to the cornstarch paste, mix well, return to the pan and stir over the heat until the mixture is smooth, thick and boiling. Add the vanilla.
5. Pour into the oiled mold, allow to cool, then cover and chill until set.
6. To turn the chocolate pudding out of the mold, loosen the edges with the fingertips. Turn upside down over a serving plate. Give a sharp shake to loosen the mold.
7. Cover with whipped cream and scatter the grated chocolate over the top just before serving.

# SUNDAY BRUNCH

*for twelve*

**Cinnamon Toast**
*For each slice of toast you will need 1 heaped tsp of sugar and a good pinch of cinnamon mixed together. Spread each slice of toast with butter and sprinkle over the cinnamon and sugar mixture. This also makes a deliciously sticky topping for hot muffins or buns.*

BRUNCH, THAT DELIGHTFUL HYBRID OF BREAKFAST AND lunch, is a relaxed way to combine a family Sunday with entertaining friends.

Make it the start of a long lazy day, with newspapers to browse through, comics for the children, and perhaps follow it with a Sunday walk (or a nap for the truly sybaritic), after which a proper knees-under afternoon tea with cinnamon toast and cake will wind up the proceedings nicely and send the guests home before the demands of children, homework and the coming week make themselves felt.

The best brunches combine something of the conservative breakfast, say cereal and scrambled eggs for the guests who have just tumbled out of bed, and something more exciting, more like party fare, for later in the morning. The famous brunch on the Orient-Express train has everything on the groaning buffet from cornflakes and porridge to Beluga caviar and foie gras. But ordinary mortals can hardly go to such extremes.

The essential should be that whatever last-minute cooking is necessary should be easy to accomplish with friends getting in the way – scrambled eggs are suitable; eggs and bacon, sausages and ham are not. The more glamorous dishes should be pre-preparable, and the addition of exotic fruit in a basket, and interesting and unusual breads and preserves will enhance the meal without adding labor.

**News For Children**
*To keep the children amused, a hired video film or video game might be a good idea, or they could be set the task of making a giant collage of last week's news in pictures – with several pairs of scissors, some flour-and-water paste and last week's newspapers and magazines.*

*Below* A simple selection of different breads and rolls will look homely but attractive. Few bakers work on Sundays but bread freezes well. Warm small breads and rolls from frozen but thaw large loaves first.

One of the features of a good brunch is that it lasts all morning. Such is food conservatism that, given half a chance, early arrivals will eat eggs, muffins and marmalade at eleven o'clock, and then come back at one o'clock for seafood crepes or kebabs. Coffee will give way to orange juice, which will then get upgraded to Mimosas with the addition of sparkling wine or champagne, and finally everyone will be drinking unadulterated fizz. Or the orange juice could gradually get spiked with vodka as the morning progresses, or tomato juice might turn into Bloody Mary. Fresh brews of coffee will need to be made throughout the morning, to cater for late arrivals, and also because coffee loses its flavor if kept warm on the hotplate for more than half an hour.

Buffet service is obviously the simplest and best for this sort of coming and going. Plates should be good and hot for the breakfast-style dishes which tend to cool fast.

*Right* A formal arrangement of the food would be inappropriate for such a casual, relaxed occasion. From the top clockwise: seafood crepes, a decorative basket of brambles, toasted muffins, marmalade, blackcurrant jam, honey, strong black coffee, a selection of rolls, scrambled egg with chives and fried bread. In the center mushroom, bacon and tomato kebabs.

---

### THE MENU

*Peach Granola*
*Pineapple Fruit Salad*

*Scrambled Eggs with Chives and Fried Bread Croûtes*
*Seafood Crepes*
*Hash Browns with Onions*
*Mushroom, Bacon and Tomato Kebabs*

*Rolls and Hot Muffins*
*Butter*
*Marmalade and Preserves*

*Coffee*

---

## GETTING AHEAD

*Far in advance*
○ Telephone your friends and invite them to come.
○ Buy or borrow extra hotplates or chafing dishes.
○ Buy kebab sticks or skewers.
○ Buy or borrow several thermos jugs for hot milk and coffee.
○ Make the crepes and freeze them.
○ Check that you have enough cutlery, china and glasses.
○ Make a food shopping list from the recipes.
○ Buy champagne, wine or vodka, orange and tomato juice.
○ Order extra Sunday newspapers.
○ Buy paper napkins or wash and press linen ones.

*Two days before*
○ Order the fresh seafood and do all the other shopping.
○ Put breads, rolls or muffins in the freezer.

*The day or evening before*
○ Pick or buy a vase or two of flowers and greenery.
○ Arrange the buffet table. Put the cloth on and lay hot plates and chafing dishes. Set with cutlery, china, coffee cups and napkins. Put plates on hotplates ready to warm.
○ Chill champagne or wine.
○ Collect the seafood.
○ Defrost the crepes. Make the filling for the crepes, taking care not to overcook. Fill the crepes and keep them refrigerated, covered in plastic wrap.

Wooden handles on kebab skewers prevent burnt fingers. Or cool metal handles with a cold, wet cloth before serving.

Muesli or Granola
*This is even more delicious if homemade. For each portion mix 2 tbsps of rolled oats with 1 heaped tbsp of assorted dried fruits and chopped nuts. Add 2 heaped tsps each of wheatgerm, brown sugar and powdered milk. To make granola add enough melted honey or corn syrup to coat the mixture. Spread it on to an oiled baking sheet and bake in a hot oven until golden brown and crunchy. Cool and crumble into small pieces.*

*Left* You will need a good supply of trays to carry all the food quickly to the table. From left to right: fresh orange juice, peach granola, pineapple fruit salad, hash browns, bacon, mushroom and tomato kebabs, and hot buttered toast.

**Fresh Milk**
*Milk can become tainted with the flavor of aromatic fruits such as pineapple, melon or strawberries if they are stored together in the refrigerator. Make sure that both milk and the fruits are tightly wrapped or covered to avoid this.*

**Removing the Skin**
*To remove skin from milk without using a strainer: beat briskly or pour into a jug from a height. Keep in a thermos to prevent skin forming and to keep hot.*

**Barbecue Brunch**
*Combine Sunday Brunch with a barbecue to ease the last-minute rush of breakfast cooking. Sausages, jumbo shrimp or scallop and bacon kebabs would be good additions to the menu. Barbecued bananas or peach halves could be served instead of the peach granola.*

○ Make the croûtes to decorate the eggs.
○ Skewer the tomato, mushroom and bacon kebabs. Place on a baking tray, cover with plastic wrap and refrigerate overnight.
○ Grate the fruit rind and squeeze the juice for the peach granola.
○ Prepare the pineapple, melon and berries for the fruit salad and chill, well-wrapped to prevent the milk in the refrigerator becoming tainted.
○ Clean the pineapple leaves, removing any discolored ones.
○ Peel the potatoes, boil them and cut up roughly.
○ Fry the onions and keep in a bowl, covered tightly.

*On the morning of the party*
○ Add breads (which will thaw fast), butter, jams, marmalades, cream, sugar, fruit juices, drinks, glasses and ice to the buffet.
○ If the muffins are to be warmed, put them in the warmer or directly on the hotplate.
○ Mix the scrambled eggs and season. Place the butter ready in a pan.
○ Put croûtes on a flat tray on the hot plate, ready to warm.
○ Arrange the chilled fruit in the pineapple shell and set on the buffet table.

*Half an hour before the guests arrive*
○ Switch on the hotplate.
○ Make the peach granola and put on the buffet.
○ Put the ice cream (if served) in the refrigerator to soften.
○ Finish frying the hash browns and keep warm.
○ Heat the crepes, broil the top and place in a low oven.
○ Heat milk for the coffee and keep warm in a vacuum jug.
○ Turn up the oven and cook the kebabs. Put in a low oven.

*Once the guests arrive*
○ Scramble the eggs.
○ Make the coffee.
○ Put hash browns, crepes, kebabs, scrambled eggs, warm muffins, ice cream and coffee on the buffet.

**Scrambled Eggs**
*To make scrambled eggs in quantity use the following method: heat 1¼ cups milk in a large pan with ¼ cup butter. Season well with salt and ground black pepper. Break 20 eggs into a mixing bowl and beat together. Just before serving, stir the eggs into the hot milk; they will scramble evenly and almost instantly. Remove from the heat just before the eggs are set, and by the time they are served they will be just the right consistency.*

# SUNDAY BRUNCH RECIPES

## PEACH GRANOLA
SERVES 6

*6 fresh peaches (or canned peach halves)*
*grated rind and juice of ½ orange and ½*
  *lemon*
*¼ cup brandy*
*¼ cup butter*
*¼ cup soft brown sugar*
*1⅓ cups muesli or granola-type cereal*
TO SERVE
*ice cream or*
*whipped cream*

1. Dip the peaches in boiling water for 6 seconds.
2. Peel the peaches. Cut them in half and remove the stone. Place them in a shallow flameproof dish.
3. Sprinkle over the orange and lemon rinds and juices.
4. Pour the brandy into a ladle. Warm and then set light to it. Pour it over the peaches.
5. Preheat the broiler to high.
6. Melt the butter in a frying-pan. Add the sugar and allow to dissolve and caramelize a little.
7. Stir in the cereal and mix thoroughly with the sugar.
8. Spoon the cereal mixture over the peaches. Place under the broiler until hot and bubbling.
9. Allow to cool a little before serving, preferably with ice cream or whipped cream offered separately.

## PINEAPPLE FRUIT SALAD
SERVES 12 SMALL PORTIONS

*1 large sized pineapple*
*1 small ripe melon*
*1lb mixed strawberries, raspberries,*
  *blackberries or redcurrants*

1. Cut the pineapple in half lengthwise. With a grapefruit knife carefully remove the flesh, leaving both the half-shells intact.
2. Cut the flesh into cubes, removing any woody core.
3. Using a melon baller, scoop the melon flesh into balls, or cut them carefully into cubes.
4. Hull the strawberries. Wash all the berries if dusty.
5. Clean the green leaves of the pineapple and give them a shine with a piece of absorbent paper towel dipped in a little cooking oil.
6. Arrange the pineapple and melon in the pineapple shell.
7. Scatter the berries over the top.
8. Chill in the refrigerator for at least one hour before serving.

## SCRAMBLED EGGS WITH CHIVES AND FRIED BREAD CROÛTES
SERVES 9-12 PORTIONS

*12 large eggs*
*1¼ cups milk*
*salt and black pepper*
*½ cup butter*
*2 tbsp chopped chives*
FOR THE CROÛTES
*3 slices white bread*
*oil for frying*

1. Make the croûtes: remove crusts and cut each slice diagonally into four.
2. Heat the oil in a heavy-based frying-pan. Fry the triangles of bread on each side until brown and crisp. Drain and sprinkle with salt. Keep warm.
3. Beat eggs and milk. Season.
4. In the same frying-pan melt the butter. Add eggs and stir over a low heat until thick and creamy. Stir in the chopped chives and serve immediately in a heated dish with the croûtes.

## SEAFOOD CREPES
SERVES 12
FOR THE CREPES
*1 cup all-purpose flour*
*2 eggs*
*pinch of salt*
*1¼ cups milk or milk and water mixed*
*1 tbsp oil (for frying)*
FOR THE FILLING
*12oz raw scallops*
*12oz raw, shelled shrimp*
*⅓ cup butter*
*2 shallots, finely chopped*
*juice of 1 lemon*
*1 tbsp finely chopped parsley*
*salt*
*pepper*
TO SERVE
*2 tbsp melted butter*
*2 tbsp grated Parmesan cheese*

1. Mix the flour, eggs, salt, milk and water to a smooth batter in a blender.
2. Lightly grease a frying-pan with oil. Heat it, and pour in a little batter. Tip the pan so it coats the surface very thinly.
3. Fry gently until set. With the help of a spatula or egg turner flip the pancake over and brown the other side. Repeat until you have 12 crepes.
4. Remove the tough muscles (opposite the coral) from the scallops. Cut each scallop and each shrimp into four.
5. Melt the butter gently in a frying-pan and soften the finely chopped shallots in it for one minute until they are translucent.
6. Add the scallops and shrimp and fry briskly for one minute or until the seafood is pale brown but still tender.
7. Add the lemon juice, parsley and seasoning and toss for 10-15 seconds over the flame.
8. Place a spoonful of the mixture in the corner of each crepe and fold into four to make small triangles.
9. Arrange the crepes in a flameproof dish. Brush melted butter over the top and sprinkle with Parmesan cheese.
10. Reheat gently in a low oven 15 minutes before serving, then broil briefly to brown the top.

## HASH BROWNS WITH FRIED ONIONS
SERVES 12

*4lb boiled potatoes*
*1lb onions, sliced*
*¾ cup butter, bacon dripping, chicken fat*
  *or oil*
*salt*

1. Cut the potatoes into uneven smallish cubes.
2. Fry the onions slowly in ¼ cup of the fat until translucent and pale brown.
3. Tip the onions out of the pan, put in the rest of the fat and fry the potatoes slowly, turning them as they brown. When they are a good color and before they are too mashed, add the onions, toss over the heat until sizzling and dish up. Sprinkle with salt.

## BACON, MUSHROOM AND TOMATO KEBABS
SERVES 12

*36 button mushrooms*
*butter for frying*
*18 rashers streaky bacon*
*12 small tomatoes*
*salt and black pepper*
*12 wooden kebab sticks or skewers*
TO SERVE
*watercress*

1. Preheat the oven, setting the temperature control to 350°.
2. Fry the mushrooms briskly in butter.
3. Stretch each rasher of bacon with the back of a knife. Cut them in half, roll up and grill until golden brown.
4. Cut the tomatoes in half.
5. Thread the mushrooms, bacon rolls and tomatoes alternately on to the kebab sticks.
6. Place the kebabs in a buttered oven-proof dish and cook for 10 minutes or until the tomatoes are hot.
7. Serve decorated with watercress.

# ELEGANT VEGETARIAN DINNER for Six

*Left* Texture is particularly important in meatless meals. The crisp crunch of the tartlets contrasts seductively with the soft eggs and velvety smooth tarragon hollandaise. In the middle of the table a formal salad, carefully arranged, and a neat hot spinach roulade filled with mushroom and eggplant. Back right: an unusual vegetable "floral" arrangement.

VEGETARIANS ARE COMING INTO THEIR OWN. A VEGET-arian dinner, to a meat-eater, would once have seemed cranky and clumsy, or at best commendably worthy. Today many best-selling cookbooks are vegetarian and recipes range from the farmhouse "bean-stew" variety to the most elegant reaches of the *Nouvelle Cuisine*.

Our dinner is decidedly elegant, designed to dispel any lingering idea that vegetarian food is hefty and dull. But it does take a deal of time, careful shopping and detailed planning. We have assumed six guests, all keen gourmets who will appreciate the culinary effort that has gone towards their delight.

More than six guests would be difficult to handle without help and extra plates – the meal consists of six tiny courses.

As the food is to be exquisite, the setting should match up. So pull out the best dishes and glasses, spend time on the seemingly unimportant details, like pressing the napkins, arranging the flowers and cutting fine slices of lemon or lime for the drinks. Perhaps dinner jackets is going too far but tell your friends that you will be wearing your party finery. It is a curious fact that if people have put some effort into a party – like getting dressed up in their gladdest rags, they will arrive pre-disposed to make the effort worthwhile – set, in fact, to have a good time.

The first courses would be good with a flowery not-very-alcoholic wine, such as a dry moselle, and the main course of spinach and mushroom pie is robust enough to take a good full red wine.

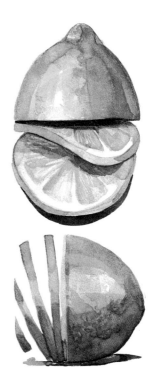

Limes have a fruitier, milder taste than lemons and are a treat for most of us. Delicious and tart while green, they become milder as they yellow. Use a sharp serrated knife to get paper-thin slices.

### THE MENU

*Zucchini with Stuffed Flowers*

*Egg Tartlets with Tarragon Hollandaise*

*Spinach Roulade with Mushroom and Egg Plant*

*Formal Salad*

*Dried Fruit Compote*

*Coeurs à la Crème*

For an Informal Dinner
*To make the dinner party less formal, omit one of the first two courses or serve the salad with the main course and the coeurs à la crème as a topping for the fruit compote.*

**Dried Fruit**
*This is sweeter and richer than fresh. The expensive dried fruits are plump and moist although the flavor of the less expensive and drier kind is often just as good and may contain less preservative. However, they will need to be soaked for much longer. Soak dried fruits in weak tea to enhance their flavor.*

Tiny charming bouquets will emphasize the careful, elegant theme. Individual ones could be arranged in an egg cup or, as here, the stems wrapped in wet cotton and foil as a gift for each guest.

**Spinach Roulade**
*This can be made in advance, filled, cooked, and covered with plastic wrap and then reheated to perfection in a microwave oven set at "reheat".*

## GETTING AHEAD

*A month before the dinner party*
○ Telephone your friends and ask them to come.
○ Make a list of ingredients from the recipes. Buy all the dry goods and the wine.
○ Make the cheese and walnut pastry and freeze it.

*A few days before the dinner party*
○ Make the dried fruit compote. Store in an airtight container.
○ If you do not grow zucchini, arrange to pick some (with flowers attached) from a friend's garden. Or try to order them from a specialty greengrocer.
○ Check over the best table linen, china, cutlery and glassware.

*The day before the dinner party*
○ Do all the shopping.
○ Pick the zucchini with flowers.
○ Take the walnut pastry out of the freezer. When defrosted make the tartlet cases.
○ Make the coeurs à la crème.
○ Make the herb filling for the zucchini.
○ Make the mushrooms and eggplant filling for the roulade.

*The morning of the dinner party*
○ Polish the glasses and silver.
○ Set the table.
○ Make a small bouquet of fresh or wild flowers to decorate the table.
○ Set up the drinks tray and coffee tray.
○ Put out all the serving dishes and plates.
○ Stuff the zucchini flowers, put on a wire rack or steamer and cover with foil ready to be steamed.
○ Skin, seed and slice the tomatoes.
○ Make the sauce for the zucchini.
○ Measure all the ingredients for the hollandaise sauce.
○ Line the pan for the roulade. Measure out the ingredients. Wash, cook and purée the spinach.
○ Reduce the stock for the zucchini sauce. Thicken it with egg and cream.

*An hour before the guests arrive*
○ Dish up the fruit compote and the coeurs à la crème.
○ Set out the tartlet cases.
○ Prepare a pan to poach the eggs.

*Half an hour before the guests arrive*
○ Make the hollandaise sauce and stand it in a pan of hot water.
○ Prepare the spinach roulade to stage 4. Preheat the oven.
○ Heat up the mushroom and eggplant filling and keep warm.
○ Prepare all the salad ingredients and arrange the salad, make dressing, cover and chill.

*After the guests arrive*
○ 15 minutes before dinner whip the egg whites, fold into the spinach mixture and bake.
○ Cook the zucchini and quickly reheat the sauce without boiling. Add the tomato.
○ Poach the eggs, put them in the tartlet cases, spoon over the sauce and broil.
○ Fill the roulade and roll up.

If zucchini with flowers are not available, buy baby zucchini, cook them in boiling water for 1 minute, drain them and split them in half. Scoop out the seeds with a teaspoon or melon-baller and fill the hollows with the Ricotta and herb mousse; then steam as the stuffed flowers or bake in a low oven until tender.

*Right* More of the first-course moselle would be light and fresh with the rich coeurs à la crème and sticky fruit compote. For lingerers at the table fresh nuts (here walnuts and hazelnuts) provide an excuse for lethargy.

# ELEGANT VEGETARIAN DINNER RECIPES

## ZUCCHINI WITH STUFFED FLOWERS

SERVES 6

*6 baby zucchini with flowers still attached*

FOR THE MOUSSE

*½ cup Ricotta cheese or sieved cottage cheese*

*2 tsp tomato paste*

*1 egg yolk*

*1 tsp fresh breadcrumbs*

*1 tbsp fresh finely chopped basil*

*1 tbsp heavy cream*

FOR THE SAUCE

*1¼ cups strong vegetable stock*

*⅔ cup heavy cream*

*1 egg yolk*

*2 tomatoes, blanched, skinned, seeded and cut into fine shreds*

1. Carefully wash the zucchini, open up the flower petals gently and pinch the stamens out of the flowers.

2. Place the Ricotta cheese in a small pan over a low heat. Beat with a wooden spoon until the cheese is warm and sticky. Add the tomato paste.

3. Remove from the heat and gradually beat in the egg yolk and crumbs. Add the fresh basil and heavy cream, cover and chill for about two hours.

4. Spoon the mousse into the zucchini flowers and carefully lay the zucchini on a greased wire rack and cover with foil. Steam over simmering water for 10 to 15 minutes until the zucchini are tender

Zucchini flowers will stay fresh if left attached to the zucchini for a day or two. Treat them gently when stuffing them lest the petals tear. Pumpkin, marrow or squash flowers are all suitable. Even the male flowers which grow high up on the plant (not attached to the fruits) can be used.

and the mousse cooked. Or better still, cook, covered in plastic wrap, in a microwave on "high" until the zucchini are tender.

5. Meanwhile make the sauce: put the stock in a pan, bring to the boil and reduce by half. Mix the egg yolk with the heavy cream; slowly pour on the hot liquid, stirring all the time; return the sauce to the heat and stir without boiling until it is thick enough to coat the back of a spoon.

6. Add the tomatoes to the sauce and check the seasoning.

7. Make a lake of sauce on six warmed plates. Lay a zucchini on top of each plate.

8. Serve immediately.

## EGG TARTLETS WITH TARRAGON HOLLANDAISE

SERVES 6

*6 large fresh eggs*

FOR THE PASTRY

*1 cup all-purpose flour*

*⅓ cup ground walnuts*

*3 tbsp finely grated Cheddar or Parmesan cheese*

*1 egg, beaten*

*4 tbsp butter*

*salt and ground black pepper*

FOR THE SAUCE

*1 shallot, finely chopped or 2 tbsp onion, finely chopped*

*2 tbsp fresh chopped tarragon or 1 tsp dried*

*4 tbsp tarragon vinegar*

*6 peppercorns*

*1 bay leaf*

*2 egg yolks*

*1 cup softened unsalted butter*

*salt and ground black pepper*

*squeeze of lemon juice*

*2 tsp tomato paste*

FOR DECORATION

*cayenne pepper*

*6 whole tarragon leaves or chopped parsley*

1. Preheat the oven, setting the temperature control to 400°. Make the pastry in a food processor or by hand: sift the flour on to the work-top, make a well in the center. Sprinkle over the walnuts and cheese. Place the egg and

butter in the well and mix them together using the fingertips. Draw in the flour and knead lightly until the pastry is smooth. Chill for 30 minutes.

2. Roll the pastry out thinly and use to line six 3-4in tartlet molds. If the pastry is too crumbly to roll, press it into the molds with the fingertips. Chill again for 15 minutes before cooking. Line the molds with wax paper and fill with baking beans or rice. Bake for 20 minutes, removing the paper and beans halfway through cooking to allow the pastry to become crisp and brown.

3. To make the sauce: put the shallot, half the tarragon, vinegar, peppercorns and bay leaf into a pan. Boil until the liquid is reduced to about a tablespoon. Cool slightly.

4. Mix the egg yolks with 1 tbsp of butter and a pinch of salt, strain in the hot vinegar and stir well. Place the basin over a pan of simmering water. Gradually beat in the butter a little at a time, allowing the sauce to thicken before adding more. When all the butter has been added, season with salt, black pepper and lemon juice and add the remaining tarragon. Color pink with the tomato purée. Keep warm by standing in a bowl of hot water.

5. Heat the broiler.

6. Poach the eggs for 3 minutes. Drain them well. Place one in each tartlet case. Cover each egg with a spoonful of the warm sauce, then place the tartlets under the broiler for about one minute to slightly brown the top of the hollandaise sauce. Sprinkle with cayenne pepper, lay a tarragon leaf on the top of each one or sprinkle with parsley. Serve straightaway.

## SPINACH ROULADE WITH MUSHROOM AND EGGPLANT
SERVES 6
FOR THE ROULADE
*2lb fresh spinach or 12oz frozen*
*2 tbsp butter*
*6 eggs, separated*
*salt*
*ground black pepper*
*grated nutmeg*
FOR THE FILLING
*1lb flat mushrooms*
*1 medium-sized eggplant*
*1 tbsp cooking oil*
*¼ cup butter*
*1 small onion, finely chopped*
*1 clove garlic, crushed*
*salt and black pepper*
*1 tsp dried marjoram*

1. Make the filling: chop the mushrooms; peel and chop the eggplant. Heat the oil and butter in a heavy-based pan, add the onion and garlic and fry gently until softened. Add the mushroom, eggplant flesh, and salt and pepper. Turn the heat down very low and put a lid on the saucepan. Cook the filling very slowly for half an hour or until all the vegetables are soft and pulpy. Add the marjoram and check the seasoning.

2. Wash and cook the spinach. Drain thoroughly and purée in a blender or food processor.

3. Preheat the oven, setting the temperature control to 375°. Line a large roasting pan with wax paper and brush with melted butter or oil.

4. Melt the butter in a saucepan, add the spinach and stir over high heat until the excess moisture has evaporated leaving a thick purée. Cool a little, then beat in the egg yolks.

5. Stiffly beat the egg whites and fold them into the spinach mixture. Season with salt, pepper and nutmeg.

6. Pour into the prepared pan, spread evenly and bake for 10 to 12 minutes until dry to the touch.

7. Lay a sheet of wax paper on the work-top and turn the roulade out on to it. Spread the hot filling over the roulade and roll it up like a jelly roll.

8. Lift the roulade on to a warmed dish and serve immediately.

## FORMAL SALAD
SERVES 6
*¼ large iceberg lettuce*
*4oz fresh alfalfa sprouts*
*1 ripe avocado*
*2 large tomatoes*
*4oz tofu (bean curd)*
*12 black olives*
FOR THE DRESSING
*4 tbsp olive oil*
*2 tsp tahini (sesame paste)*
*1½ tbsp lemon juice*
*1 tsp clear honey*
*1 tbsp assorted fresh herbs, chopped*
*salt and black pepper*

1. Wash and shake dry the lettuce. Tear into small pieces and lay over the base of a wide shallow dish.

2. Scatter the alfalfa sprouts over the top of the lettuce.

3. Cut the avocado in half, remove the stone and skin, cut into slices and brush with lemon juice. Arrange overlapping in a circle near the edge of the dish.

4. Skin and slice the tomatoes. Arrange in a circle inside the avocado.

5. Cut the tofu into cubes. Cut the olives in half and remove the stones. Pile them together in the center of the dish.

6. Put the dressing ingredients together in a bowl and mix well with a whisk. Just before serving, spoon over the salad.

## DRIED FRUIT COMPOTE
SERVES 6
*1½lb assorted dried fruit (say prunes, apricots, peaches, figs, apples and raisins)*
*1¼ cups water*
*pared rind and juice of one orange*
*pared rind and juice of one lemon*
*small piece of cinnamon stick, cloves, 1 bay leaf and 1 crushed cardamom, all tied together in a muslin bag*
*2 tbsp honey*
TO SERVE
*ice cubes*
*coeurs à la creme (see below) or whipped cream or yogurt*

1. Place all the ingredients together in a pan. Slowly bring to the boil.

2. Cover and remove from the heat. Allow to cool to room temperature. Remove the fruit rinds and the muslin bag.

3. Chill in the refrigerator. Add cubes of ice before serving in a glass bowl. The whipped cream, yogurt or *coeurs à la crème* can be handed separately.

NOTE:
If the compote is not sweet enough for your taste add more honey or dark brown sugar.

## COEURS À LA CRÈME
SERVES 6
*1 cup cottage cheese*
*1¼ cups heavy cream*
*2 egg whites*
*½ cup confectioners' sugar, sifted*
*1¼ cups light cream, to serve*

1. Sieve the cottage cheese. Slightly whip the heavy cream and mix with the cheese. Beat the egg whites until stiff and fold into the cheese mixture. Sweeten to taste with the sugar.

2. Spoon into coeurs à la crème molds, or line a sieve with a clean piece of muslin and place over a bowl. Turn the cheese mixture into the muslin and leave to set (at least 4 hours).

3. Turn the heart-shaped molds out on to serving plates. If you have not used molds, turn the cheese in the sieve out on to a plate. Coat the cheese with the light cream and serve at once.

# SURREALIST DINNER

*for Eight*

*Above* If candles are gently warmed in the oven, they can be twisted into exotic shapes and stood upright as here, or curled like snakes on the table with only the wick end rearing up.

*Below right* A pastiche of Dali's famous hanging clocks. Several twigs could form a table arrangement.

THIS IS AN EXTRAORDINARY, SOPHISTICATED CONCEPT and will only work if the guests are modern art lovers, or at least able to recognize the visual jokes. It is no good having the central table decoration a bare branch over sandy rocks with wrist-watches draped about if the guests are not going to recognize it as a send-up of Dali's "The Persistence of Memory". The pictures of Miró, Magritte and Picasso all provide inspiration for cooks with a sense of humor. The whole point is to amuse and astonish. Long thin candles can be softened by gentle warming in the oven until pliable and then bent into sinuous snakes with heads rearing and tongues aflame. An eerie gelatin hand could form an edible sculpture (well, almost edible) for the table. Or a kinetic mobile or "musical sculpture" can be constructed out of wire and bits of plastic.

Food can be carefully arranged on plates to form abstract and curious designs, such as our Picasso-like ham dish or the electric-colored green pear with two sauces in our menu. But the essential thing, which is easy to lose sight of, is that the food, however amazing it looks, must taste wonderful. No sophisticated decor or clever effects will compensate for mediocre food.

Our dinner consists of a delicious, light and pretty seafood salad starter, arranged like a picture on a plate. The main course is a sugar-coated boned ham, sliced and served hot on pre-decorated plates, with eyes slipped into place by the host when carving. The vegetables are thick purées and could be arranged in a flat dish in an abstract design.

Flower Arrangement
*Turn a bowler hat upside down. If the top is rounded and the hat wobbles, secure it to the table with scotch tape. Find a small bowl to sit inside the hat and fill it with simple bold flowers, such as marguerites. Arrange the flowers so that they will appear to be growing out of the hat.*

The possibilities are endless. A morning in a public library with a few books on modern painting will produce all sorts of curious ideas. They do not, of course, have to be direct cribs from surrealist painters. The gelatin hand described below is suitably strange and sinister.

## INSTRUCTIONS FOR MAKING GELATIN HAND

The hands need to be set very firmly in order to unmold them, and therefore are best used for decoration rather than eating. If you want to be able to eat them use a large packet of flavored Jello jelly, and add an extra tablespoon of unflavored gelatin.

Use fine surgical gloves (the small size looks best) which can be bought from a good pharmacist. Rinse the gloves out well with cold water. Put 1 cup of water into a small pan and sprinkle over 2 tbsp unflavored gelatin. Leave to soak for 10 minutes, then warm over a low heat until liquid and clear. Put 1 cup hot tap water into a bowl. Add food coloring. Stir in the melted gelatin, then pour the mixture into the glove, filling it to just above the wrist.

Make sure no air is left in the glove and tie it tightly with string round the wrist near the hand. Lay the hand palm-side down on a metal tray. Tie another piece of string about 2in further back from the first one and nearer the opening. When you have done this, untie the first piece of string so that the gelatin flows back towards the wrist. This is to ensure that all the air is removed and that the glove is not too full which would make the hand an odd fat shape and difficult to unmold.

Put the hand in the refrigerator to set until very solid. To unmold the hand, use a pair of sharp scissors and cut the glove from the wrist to the end of the palm. Gently ease it away from the fingertips.

## THE INVITATION

The invitation, of course, could be on a simple postcard from the Museum of Modern Art, or it could be a home-made collage, Picasso-style.

A SURREAL INVITATION

Any color Jello can be used for the sinister hand. Surgical gloves work best as molds. If using domestic rubber gloves turn them inside out so that the smooth side is the one in contact with the setting gelatin.

*Right* Imagination can be let rip to produce stylish food designs in the surrealist tradition. Here ham faces are given mustard noses, hard-boiled egg eyes and beards or quiffs of bean purée. The giant "artist's palette" table is cut from plywood, sprayed black and supported with scaffolding clamps. The paint splodge placemats are cut from paper. In the center, beet and lima bean purée.

*Left* A marzipan and icing model of a fried egg enclosed with the invitation would alert the guests to the surreal aspects of your party.

**Surrealist Bottles**
*If the labels on the wine bottles are not too impressive to be hidden, cover the whole bottle with fur or fur fabric to imitate the telephone and cup and saucer portrayed by surrealist artists.*

## THE WINE
A chablis would be delicious with the seafood salad and a good robust burgundy or rhône would not be overpowered by the ham. If curiously shaped decanters or bottles (or chemists' flasks) can be found, so much the better.

**Picasso Purées**
*Arrange the purées to look like a Picasso face. Shape the bean purée into a bold nose and chin. Pipe in the beet purée to fill the rest of the dish.*

**THE MENU**

*Sunset Salad*

*Ham Face with Hollandaise Sauce*
*Beet and Lima Bean Purée*

*Picasso Pear Sablés*

## GETTING AHEAD

*Far in advance*
○ Choose or make the invitations.
○ Make the table decorations and "snake" candles.
○ Make a shopping list, buy the dry ingredients and drinks.

*Two days before the party*
○ Order the seafood and do the rest of the shopping.
○ Make the sablé pastry and chill.
○ Make the melba sauce.
○ Poach the green pears and store in the syrup.

*The day before the party*
○ Roll out the sablé pastry, cut and bake, store in an airtight container.
○ Cook the French beans for the sunset salad.
○ Purée the beets and make the lima bean purée.

*The morning of the party*
○ Collect the seafood.
○ Make the seafood sauce.
○ Cook the seafood and leave to cool.
○ Make the custard.
○ Set the table, arrange the bar and coffee tray.
○ Make plenty of ice cubes.
○ Set out the serving dishes.
○ Boil the quails' eggs and blanch the cucumber skin.
○ Slice the oranges for the sunset salad.

*Two hours before the guests arrive*
○ Cook the ham and make the filling for the pear sablés.
○ Get the ingredients for the hollandaise sauce ready.
○ Slice the quails' eggs and make cucumber-skin lashes.

*45 minutes before the guests arrive*
○ Heat both purées, dish up, cover in foil and keep warm.
○ Dish up the first course and set on the table.
○ Prepare a hot water bath for the hollandaise sauce.

*15 minutes before the guests arrive*
○ Sandwich together the sablés with the pear filling.
○ Make a custard lake on eight plates. Carefully add the melba sauce and green pears, but not the sablés.
○ Bake the ham to reheat it and brown the sugar glaze.
○ Warm main-course plates.
○ Make the hollandaise sauce. Leave standing in hot water to prevent separating.
○ Pipe the mustard noses on the serving plates, put the lump-fish roe on the slices of egg.

*After the guests arrive*
○ Carve the ham and decorate the faces.
○ Place pear sablés on the custard lakes just before serving.

Use angles or curves as the dividing line between the purées. Brightly contrasting colors make the vegetables look appetizing, though strange!

**Menu Card**
*Paint a square of cardboard with blue sky and clouds. Cut out the shape of a fish in white and on it draw an eye and neatly write the menu. Paste the fish over the clouds so that it looks as if it is suspended in the sky.*

**Decorations**
*Make rocks in the shape of human bodies out of oasis, paint them grey and pierce them with forks. Buy plastic ants and leave them crawling over the table! Paint blown egg shells in bold colors and suspend them from twigs with thread.*

**Hollandaise Sauce**
*This is an emulsion of egg yolk and butter. If the butter is added too quickly it may curdle. Re-emulsify it by adding it drop by drop to a spoonful of warm vinegar in a clean bowl. If it becomes too hot the yolks may scramble, so keep the sauce warm just by standing it in a pan of hot water.*

# SURREALIST DINNER RECIPES

## SUNSET SALAD
SERVES 8
*4oz squid, cleaned*
*1pt fresh mussels or 4oz frozen mussels*
*4oz scallops, shelled*
*4oz button mushrooms*
*4oz cooked, shelled shrimp*
FOR THE DRESSING
*2 tbsp olive oil*
*2 shallots, finely chopped*
*2 tbsp dry white wine*
*2 cups water*
*2 tbsp tomato paste*
*1 clove garlic, crushed*
*6 coriander seeds*
*½ tsp dried or 1 tsp fresh fennel leaves*
*6 black peppercorns*
*pinch of salt*
*lemon juice*
FOR DECORATION
*1 orange*
*4oz fine French (green) beans*
*8 large cooked shrimp with shells on*

1. Cut the cleaned squid into fine strips. If using fresh mussels, scrub them well and wash thoroughly in cold water, pulling off the stringy beard. Be sure to discard any that will not close when tapped or which float to the top. Wash the scallops and remove the tough muscle opposite the pink coral. Cut the mushrooms into quarters.
2. Heat the oil in a saucepan. Fry the shallots for 1 minute.
3. Add the white wine and a third of the water. Bring to the boil and simmer for 5 minutes.
4. Add the mussels, put on the lid and steam over a low heat, shaking the pan occasionally, for about 5 minutes. Lift out the mussels with a draining spoon. By now the shells should have all opened. Discard any that have not. Remove the mussels from their shells and leave to cool.
5. Add all the remaining dressing ingredients to the pan, bring to the boil and simmer for 20 minutes.
6. Put the squid, shrimp, scallops and mushrooms into the pan with the dressing and cook gently for 4-5 minutes or until the seafood is just tender. Remove the seafood and mushrooms.
7. Boil the sauce rapidly until it has reduced to ¾ cup. Strain and leave to cool.
8. Meanwhile prepare the decoration: peel the orange with a knife, removing all the pith and peel at the same time. Slice the orange into rounds and cut each slice in half. Top and tail the beans

and cut them into 1in sticks. Boil them for 5 minutes, then rinse under cold water.
9. Arrange the salad on individual plates: cut the scallops into quarters and mix with the squid, mussels, shrimp and mushrooms. Add enough dressing just to coat the salad. Divide the seafood between the eight plates, spreading to cover the base of half of each plate completely.
10. To decorate: place a half slice of orange above the seafood, in the center of the plate so that it looks like the setting sun. Arrange the beans around each orange slice like sunrays.
11. Place a whole shrimp on each plate so that it looks as if it is "leaping" out of the sea.

## HAM FACE WITH HOLLANDAISE SAUCE
SERVES 8
*4lb ready-to-eat ham in one piece, boned and rolled if necessary (ask for this to be done when you order or buy the ham)*
*¾ cup brown sugar*
*⅔ cup dry cider*
FOR THE SAUCE
*4 tbsp cider vinegar*
*6 peppercorns*
*bay leaf*
*3 egg yolks*
*pinch of salt*
*¾ cup unsalted butter, softened*
*2 tsp lemon juice*

FOR DECORATION
*8 fresh quails' eggs, or bottled ones, drained*
*strips of cucumber skin*
*½ cup prepared English mustard*
*lumpfish roe*

1. Preheat the oven, setting the temperature control to 400°.
2. Put the ham, fat-side up, into a roasting pan and pour in the cider. Bake the ham for 18 to 22 minutes per pound. Before the last 20 minutes, remove the ham from the oven and turn up the temperature control to 425°.
3. Take off any rind and with a sharp knife cut diagonal gashes in the fat, press on the brown sugar, then return the ham to the oven.
4. Boil the quails' eggs for 3 minutes. Cool and cut in half and then into 16 thin slices.
5. Drop the cucumber skin into boiling water for 30 seconds. Plunge it into cold water.
6. Using a very sharp knife, carefully cut 8 sets of "eyelashes".
7. Make the sauce: place the vinegar, peppercorns and bay leaf into a pan and reduce by boiling to 1 tbsp.
8. In a small bowl, mix the egg yolks with 1 tbsp butter and a pinch of salt. Set this in a double boiler over a gentle heat or in a heatproof bowl set in the quiet end of a roasting pan of simmering water, only half of which is over the burner. Stir the mixture until slightly thickened, then pour in the reduced vinegar.
9. Gradually beat in the rest of the butter, allowing the sauce to thicken each time before adding more. When all the butter has been added, remove the sauce from the heat, add the lemon juice and beat well.
10. Keep the sauce warm by standing it in a bowl of hot water.
11. To serve: spoon the mustard into a piping bag fitted with a plain nozzle. Prepare 8 plates with a mustard nose and mouth piped slightly off center. Carve the cooked ham into ¼in slices and lay a slice on the wider side of each nose. Put two quails'-egg eyes on the face, one on the slice of ham and one on the plate. Arrange one eye-lash over the eye on the ham. Put a small pile of lumpfish roe in the center of the egg yolk to look like a pupil. Then decorate the faces with the hollandaise sauce or bean purée to make strands of hair or beards.
12. Serve extra sauce separately.

*Above* A bracelet around the gelatin hand is a macabre touch. The electric-colored green pear tastes wonderful despite its lurid looks and is served with a buttery sablé pastry and creamy sauce in our Picasso pear sablés.

## BEET AND LIMA BEAN PURÉE
SERVES 8
FOR THE BEET PURÉE
*1 ½lb cooked (but not pickled) beets*
*½ cup butter*
*3 tbsp heavy cream*
*½ tsp cumin*
*salt and black pepper*
FOR THE LIMA BEAN PURÉE
*2lb frozen lima beans or hulled fresh beans*
*½ cup butter*
*1 small onion*
*⅔ cup chicken stock*
*1 cup cooked, mashed potatoes*
*salt and black pepper*
*pinch of thyme*

1. To make the beet purée: first purée all the beets in a blender or food processor.
2. Melt a little of the butter in a heavy-based pan. Add the cumin and fry for 1 minute.
3. Pour in the cream and bring the mixture to the boil.
4. Gradually beat in the purée and remaining butter until the mixture is thick and smooth.
5. Season with salt and pepper and keep warm.
6. To make the lima bean purée: put the beans, butter, onion and stock together in a pan and simmer for 10 minutes.
7. Remove the beans from their grey skins.
8. Purée the beans with the onion and any remaining stock.
9. Beat the potato into the beans, season with salt, black pepper and thyme.
10. Serve the purées on any unusually shaped plate that you can find. You might arrange the beet purée in a triangular shape, and then arrange the lima bean purée to fill the rest of the plate. Or you could arrange them with the join in the shape of an "S", or as the spirit moves you. (See margin note Picasso Purées on p.56.)

## PICASSO PEAR SABLÉS
SERVES 8
FOR THE SABLÉ PASTRY
*2 cups all-purpose flour*
*2 egg yolks*
*¾ cup butter*
*1 cup confectioners' sugar*
FOR THE SABLÉ FILLING
*2 tbsp marsala or Pear William liqueur*
*2 poached pears, peeled and cut into thin slices*
*1 ¼ cups heavy cream, whipped*
FOR THE CUSTARD
*1 ¼ cups milk*
*2 tbsp heavy or whipping cream*
*3 egg yolks*
*2 tbsp sugar*
*1 tsp cornstarch*
*few drops of vanilla extract*
FOR THE GREEN PEARS
*8 small ripe pears (each approximately 2in long)*
*1 cup sugar*
*2 cups water*
*strip of pared lemon rind*
*a few drops of green coloring*
FOR THE MELBA SAUCE
*8oz fresh or frozen raspberries*
*confectioners' sugar*

1. To make the pastry: sift the flour on to the work-top and make a hollow in the middle. Place the egg yolks, butter and confectioners' sugar in the hollow and using the fingertips of one hand only, combine until it is a smooth, soft paste. Gradually draw in the flour and using fingertips and a metal spatula, work the mixture to a smooth dough. Wrap up in plastic wrap and chill for 30 minutes.
2. Roll out the pastry to the thickness of a coin. With the help of a ruler cut out 24 rectangles 2in × 3in. Lay them on a baking sheet and chill again for 15 minutes before baking until pale golden brown (about 10 minutes). Cool.
3. Next, make the filling: fold the liqueur and pear slices into the whipped cream.
4. To prepare the custard: heat the milk and cream until steaming but not boiling. Beat the yolks, sugar and cornstarch together in a bowl. Pour the milk and cream on to the yolks, stirring well. Return to the pan and continue to stir over a very gentle heat until the mixture thickens enough to coat the back of a wooden spoon. Add the vanilla. Immediately remove from the heat and allow the mixture to cool and then chill.
5. Now make the green pears: place the sugar, water, lemon rind and green coloring in a saucepan over a low heat. When the sugar has dissolved boil rapidly to a syrupy consistency.
6. Meanwhile peel the whole pears without removing the stalks. Place them in the syrup and cover the pan with a lid. Simmer gently for at least 20 minutes. The pears should be bright green and very tender. Drain the pears very well.
7. To prepare the melba sauce: liquidize and sieve the raspberries. Sweeten to taste with confectioners' sugar. The sauce should be a sharp contrast to the sweet pears.
8. To assemble the pear sablés use eight individual plates. Make eight three-decker sablé "sandwiches" by layering the pastry rectangles together with the cream and pear filling.
9. Pour a thin lake of custard on to each plate. Carefully lay a pear sablé to the top left-hand corner of the lake. Swirl a spoonful of melba sauce in the custard or "marble" the sauce as shown in the picture. Lay a green pear to the right of the sablé.
TIP:
Keep the green syrup for a later green fruit salad of kiwi fruit, melon, grapes and plums.

# HOGBAKE
## for Forty

**Ordering the Pig**
*An easier option would be to cook several small pigs as one large pig is more difficult to cook evenly. The butcher will normally stock pigs weighing about 80lb but given enough warning he will be able to supply a pig of any size required. Pork should be eaten shortly after purchase and kept well refrigerated meanwhile. Fresh pork should have little smell and be rose pink in color.*

**B**URYING A PIG IN AN ASHY PIT, AND DIGGING IT UP LATER does not sound the best basis for a good party. But in fact the whole procedure is enormous fun. It amounts to a great two-day party, perfect for a summer festival. The ambitious might even bake two or three small pigs side by side in one great pit to feed the whole community.

First there is the digging, fire-making, and initial roasting, which requires half a dozen people and is much merrier with a dozen or more. Great, blazing at first, then glowing, fires have a hypnotic attraction, and sitting round the pit, glass in hand and toasting fork at the ready, as the sun goes down and the moon comes up, is a simple pleasure sharpened both by its rarity and the feeling that you are on a fantasy film set.

Cooking food in glowing embers is of course the most ancient of barbecue methods, but today a foil-wrapped potato in the backyard bonfire is about as far as most of us are likely to go. So to go the whole hog – or small pig – is quite an adventure. Pit barbecues are, or used to be, common all over the world. The Papuans in New Guinea will wrap a young pig in many layers of banana leaves and proceed exactly as we have done, but our party is based on a South Carolina pit barbecue where less glamorous but rather more efficient kitchen foil is used instead of banana leaves.

It is not essential to *bury* the pig for the final roasting. It can be cooked on top of the pit fire but this requires about 10 hours of dutiful watching, turning, fire-tending and staying awake. On the other hand, it means you can stick a meat thermometer into the pig and see how it is getting on, which you certainly cannot do when it is two feet under. So for the nervous cook it has some attraction.

The advantages of the burying method are that once the pig is in, there is nothing more to be done until dig-up time. And the digging up is primitively exciting. If you have got it right – and you will if you follow the instructions to the letter – you can actually hear the pork sizzling as you get closer to it. It seems quite magical that while you have been fast asleep and perhaps even while the rain has been bucketing down, the intended pig has been quietly cooking to perfection down under the ground. The earth as you remove it is steaming hot, the coals are still aglow and the perfectly cooked pig, smelling delicious, is far too hot to handle.

**Cooking Pork**
*If using a meat thermometer, the internal temperature will need to be 80° for rare, 150° for medium pink and 170° for well done. We recommend that pork should always be well done. The meat will still be moist and tender at this temperature.*

Failing a proper American flag, a red and white striped towel or cloth with a blue rectangular tray in a corner set with blue plastic cups and star-shaped paper napkins gives a witty approximation.

**Marinade**
*For extra flavor you could marinate the pig before the hogbake. Pound 10 cloves of garlic and 4oz fresh ginger and mix with the juice of 6 lemons, 1¼ cups soy sauce and season with salt and pepper. Rub the pig all over with this and leave overnight.*

Firelighting
*Use seasoned and dry tinder wood to start the fire. Fire-lighters, though not very professional, ensure a good start. Remember that the fire will need to burn for around four hours to heat the pit, so have plenty of fuel ready.*

## TIMING

We have assumed that the pig is to be eaten at lunch time, which means the fire must be made the day before and the pig put to roast in the evening. But if the pig is to be eaten at night, it will mean a pre-dawn start for the workers, even if the pit has been dug and the fire laid the day before.

Start your calculations with the weight of the pig. If you give the butcher plenty of time to contact his suppliers, he will be able to get you a pig of almost any size. Figure on a pound weight feeding one person – our 45 pounder would provide about 45 people with a slice each. Tell the butcher you are talking of "dressed" weight (i.e. gutted), not live weight, and ask him to have it paunched only, not split open through the breast bone, which is usual. This helps to keep the pig in shape, looking better for the final unveiling.

Working backwards from when you want to start unearthing the feast – say half an hour before eating it, figure on 18 minutes per pound for well-done pork that is almost falling from the bone, with good brown crisp crackling. This is "buried time", but you must remember to add to that one hour's open roasting before the cover-up, and before that about five hours of "oven-heating" when a fire must be burnt steadily in the pit to heat it.

We have assumed a 45lb pig buried towards midnight, to be eaten at lunch time next day.

## LOCATION

This party is strictly for the country. It would make an unholy mess of the front lawn and it is surprising just how much space it takes both for the pit fire, the pile of earth removed from the pit, the supplementary bonfire and the stocks of wood and charcoal. The fires get extremely hot, so space to move back from them is essential. A field is the ideal location, sufficiently far from ripe crops, stubble or hayfields for safety. In any event it is important to lift the turf, not just from the immediate sites for pit and bonfire, but for a good two feet round the areas – the heat would kill it even if it did not catch fire. Also, of course, a windless night is essential if sparks are not to blow about dangerously. In any event a fire extinguisher, hose or a few buckets of water are an essential precaution.

Safety Note
*If organizing a community party, contact the local fire department in advance and arrange for them to give advice on safety precautions.*

## FUEL

Wood, if there is enough of it and especially if it is hard wood, will do for fuel, but there is no doubt that a really deep and glowing bed of fire is easier to achieve with coals than wood embers. But charcoal is expensive. The best solution is to make the initial pit fire of wood, using the opportunity to get rid of any unwanted combustible material – old planks, mattresses, etc., and keep it going with wood throughout the warm-up period. The essential thing is a really hot, deep fire, as hot as you can get it, for as long as possible *before* the pig goes in. The retained heat in pit and lining stones does as much to cook the pig as the actual burning fire. Then a good deep layer of charcoal can be added 45 minutes before cooking starts.

## FOOD FOR THE WORKERS

Our menu is concerned with the main lunchtime party – roast pig and all. But the evening-before helpers will need good supplies of wine, cider or beer and something to eat. As both

*Left* Burying a pig is primitively exciting at the same time as engendering warmth, *bonhomie* and relaxed good fellowship. But don't relax to the point of inattention – keep playing children away from the pit edge.

Sage is the classic herb for pork – pungent, aromatic and if used as decoration, very pretty.

For soft-skinned baked potatoes, prick the skins, rub all over with oil and wrap in foil. Bury deep in dying ashes of the fire. For crisp-skinned, charcoal-tasting potatoes, bury them without foil and shake off the ash before eating.

Hummers
*One sip and you hum! For each person take one tablespoon of any liqueur, one of crème de cacao and one of vanilla ice cream. Allow the ice cream to soften and mix the ingredients in a blender.*

pit fire and bonfire will be there, it seems a pity not to use them to bake a few potatoes wrapped in foil. Or pieces of chicken, spare ribs or burgers could be barbecued on shovel head or garden fork, or a fish could be quickly baked in foil while the pig is getting its open-roasting. The adventurous might even cook a chicken in primitive man's forerunner to the chicken brick: plaster a gutted but still feathered chicken in wet clay, giving it at least an inch of clay-coat. Put into the glowing embers for 90 minutes after which the clay will be rock hard. Crack off the clay. It will take the feathers with it leaving the bird brown, clean and roasted with a satisfyingly earthy flavor. Or if all this seems too much trouble with the worry of a big party on the morrow, just provide plenty of buns or rolls for toasting, and something to eat on them – perhaps lettuce leaves, salami slices and mayonnaise.

## LIGHTING

If the party is at night, lighting will be essential. If it is to take place at lunch time the previous night's fire-party will need at least some good flashlights or lanterns. Groping about in the dark can be infuriating and the pit fire is too deep to shed much light.

Candle holders that prevent the candles from blowing out can be made from old bottles. Use a glass cutter to take off the necks below the shoulder. There is another more primitive but equally effective method of denecking bottles: take a length of strong nylon string or baling twine, run it 1½ times round the bottle at the point you wish to cut it. Fix the bottle firmly or get someone to hold it. Pull first one end of the string and then the other so that the string moves backwards and forwards round the middle of the bottle, heating it by friction along the same narrow line. Then drop the bottle immediately into iced water. The glass will crack along the heated line and the top can be tapped off.

Chinese lanterns strung through the trees or on posts may not be exactly appropriate to an American hogbake but they look wonderfully pretty. Or a handy electrician could rig up a string of light bulbs. Catering outfits will often rent these lights too, worked off batteries or the mains. They may also be able to provide radiant electric outdoor heaters if the night is likely to be chilly.

If the main party is at night an extra bonfire (for toasting buns, for warming the guests, for keeping away insects and to add to the general excitement) is a good idea if the weather is still. Avoid this if there is any wind. Smoke blowing everywhere tends to spoil things, and flying sparks are dangerous to crops and buildings.

Ideally, seating should consist of straw-bales, logs and the odd ox cart. But beer boxes and wine crates will do. Something to sit on and something to put drinks and food on is essential.

## MUSIC

Music might be Country and Western from the stereo, interspersed, perhaps, with live turns from a friend's accordion, mouth organ or guitar.

## DRINKS

Beer, wine and cider would be the obvious drinks but it might be fun to have root beer and home-made ginger-pop too.

Fireside Dessert
*Carefully strip the skin back from a banana but leave it attached at the base. Cut the banana into four and insert a cube of chocolate between each slice. Replace the banana skin and wrap the whole thing in foil. Bake over the fire until the banana is soft and the chocolate just melted.*

Music
*For those who are not Country and Western buffs, there will be a headed section in your local record library for you to choose from. Dollie Parton, Loretta Lynn and Ernest Tubb all sing lively songs to start the party. A very appropriate theme song would be "All My Rowdy Friends Are Coming Over Tonight" by Hank Williams Jr. Don Williams' more mellow ballads will be just right for later.*

THE MENU

*Whole Roast Pig*
*Sesame Bread*

*Apple and Cranberry Sauce*

*Rice and Peppers*

*Everything Salad*

*Pecan Ice Cream with Hot Blueberry Sauce*

*Ginger Pop*

Prairie Oysters
*This is a well-tried hangover remedy. Put an unbroken egg yolk into a glass with a dash of Worcestershire sauce, tomato ketchup, vinegar, lemon juice and Tabasco. Take it straight from the glass as though it were an oyster.*

## GETTING AHEAD
*Weeks before the party*
○ Order the pig from the butcher.
○ Borrow or buy the items on our check list on p. 65.
○ Make a shopping list.
○ Buy the drinks.
○ Invite the guests (some of whom must be strong-armed and willing helpers to dig the pit the day before the party, start the pig off late at night and dig it up next day).
○ Buy disposable plates, cups, napkins, etc.
○ Buy or borrow lanterns, contrive outdoor candles or arrange for electric lights.
○ Make and store the ginger pop.
○ Make and freeze the ice cream.
○ Make and freeze the sesame bread.

*Above* Chinese lanterns may not be American but they are enchantingly pretty, providing a little light and much festive feeling.

*Below* If the pork is to be eaten without plates, an undressed salad – perhaps lettuce and avocado or apple, is easier to manage with fingers. Our Everything Salad could contain oranges, kidney beans, croutons, or what you will. Draft beer or draft cider are good outdoor drinks.

*Above* Use polished apples and fresh blue and yellow sage to decorate the cooked pig. Make sure the pig does spend all its allotted time in the firepit. It should be cooked to the point of melting tenderness with dark, sizzling crackling. It's better to err on the side of overcooking.

*One week before the party*
○ Make a detailed time plan to ensure the pig ritual goes without a hitch.
○ Organize tables for serving the food.
○ Buy all the dry goods.
○ Buy insect repellent or mosquito-coils if necessary.

*The day before the party*
○ Get all equipment (see p. 65) to the pit site.
○ Dig the pit and light the fire in it.
○ Keep the pit fire going for at least four hours.
○ Build the supplementary bonfire nearby but do not light yet.
○ Prepare the pig and follow instructions.
○ Make the apple and cranberry sauce.
○ Make the blueberry sauce.
○ Make the salad dressing.
○ Pick wild flowers or grasses to fill a big pot for the table.

*On the day of the party*
○ Remove the sesame bread from the freezer.
○ Prepare the table with plates, knives, forks, cups and serving spoons.
○ Arrange candles and any electric lighting or heating being used.
○ Dish up the apple and cranberry sauce.
○ Have the blueberry sauce in a pan ready to be heated.
○ Chop all the ingredients for the rice.
○ Set out the drinks. Chill the cold drinks.
○ Make the croutons for the salad.
○ Prepare all the salad ingredients except the avocados.

*Half an hour before the guests arrive*
○ Slice the sesame bread and put it into baskets.
○ Put ice cubes, chilled drinks, lemon slices, etc. out if needed.
○ Make the rice and peppers.
○ Put the ice cream into the refrigerator to soften.
○ Chop up the avocados and toss the salad.
○ Light the bonfire.
○ Set up the insect repellent.

*After the guests arrive*
○ Dig up the pig and carve it.
○ Put the rice pots into the warm pit to keep hot.
○ Dish up the ice cream and heat the blueberry sauce.

Serving the Pig
*Carefully remove the foil and, using a sharp knife, scrape away any that has burned on to the skin. Set the pig on a clean wooden board, remove the crackling and cut it into slices. Carve the meat starting with the hind legs and working towards the head.*

Ice Cream Sauces
*Use any soft fruit instead of the blueberries given in our recipe. Or make a chocolate sauce by melting Mars Bars with a little milk. For butterscotch sauce, mix equal quantities of unsalted butter and corn syrup, boil for two or three minutes stirring constantly and cool a little before serving.*

Croutons
*These are pretty in salads, scattered on top of soups and for decorating rich meat dishes. Usually they are just crisply fried pieces of bread but tiny, deep-fried spoonfuls of choux paste can also be used. Or you can flavor the croutons with garlic or toss them in Parmesan cheese.*

# HOGBAKE RECIPES

## WHOLE ROAST PIG
HOW TO DO IT
You will need, for a 45lb pig:
- At least 60lb charcoal and 2 cubic yards of wood.
- Five "turkey-size" rolls of aluminum foil.
- Firelighters.
- Big flashlights or lanterns if working at night.
- Long spills and matches.
- A piece of chicken-wire fencing measuring about 4ft square.
- A large wire or metal open-work mud-scraper mat or a piece of strong metal fencing 3×1ft.
- Wire cutters.
- Stones or bricks to line the baking pit.
- Two lengths of thin metal chain, or very strong wire 8ft long.
- Shovels for the workers.
- A trestle table for putting the cooked pig on.
- Carving knives and sharpening steel.
- Tongs.
- Serving spoons.
- Plastic sheeting or tarpaulin.

FOR THE PIG
*45lb pig, cleaned by paunching (with rib cage intact) with all bristles singed off*
*3lb eating apples*
*salt*
*handful sage leaves*

1. Dig a pit, 2ft deep and wide and long enough to take the whole pig comfortably with a good 1ft each side. Remember the pig will be stretched out so it will be longer than you expect. A 45lb pig will be at least 4.6ft long. Line the bottom with bricks or stones and carry them as far up the sides as you can – 1ft would be ideal. (If the ground is clay, the stones will not be necessary but they are vital in sand, chalk or loamy garden soil.) All this preparation can be done days or weeks in advance but the hole should be covered to prevent it filling with rain. If the pit is dug in grass, lift the turf carefully and keep the top-soil separate from the subsoil so that when the party is over, the area can be restored without too much damage.
2. Build a large bonfire of wood a little distance from the pit (if it is right at the edge it makes tending the pit fire awkward, hot and rather dangerous work). Do not light it yet. Make a fire in the pit with wood and keep it burning as strongly as possible for at least four hours to heat the "oven" thoroughly.

Use firelighters to get the fire burning evenly all over the pit, not just in the middle.
3. After four hours allow the embers to burn down until there are no flames, then add an even layer of charcoal 6in deep, and leave to burn for 45 minutes or until there are no more flames. (The coals should look ashy in daylight and glow red in the dark.)
4. Light the bonfire at the same time as adding the charcoal bed to the pit. Feed it for half an hour then allow it to die down, spread it flat and add a layer of charcoal to the top.
5. While the fires are burning prepare the pig: put the apples and sage in its belly – not too tightly packed or they will prevent the heat penetrating. Rub it all over with salt.
6. Wrap it in several layers of foil (shiny side outside) and then package it up tightly in the chicken wire.
7. Lay it on the scraper mat or strong fencing.
8. Thread the two lengths of chain or strong wire under and through the mat so that they will act as lowering and lifting handles.
9. Lower the whole thing on to the burning embers. Do not drop the chains or wires in – you will need them later for hauling the cooked pig out.
10. Leave the pig like this for half an hour, then roll it over for half an hour's roasting on the other side.
11. When the charcoal on the side fire is glowing rather than flaming (or, if in daylight, looks grey and ashy) start to shovel the coals (and embers) into the pit, around the pig and on top of it. This can be done as soon as the pig has been turned over, provided the coals are ready. New, non-burning charcoal can be added to the sides of the pit fire beside the pig where the fire beneath will soon ignite them, but only glowing coals should be piled on top.
12. When the pig has had an hour in the pit, bury it completely in hot coals and embers. Rake coals from the sides of the pit all around the pig. Then shovel back all the earth (except the topsoil). You will have a huge mound but do not be tempted to abandon the shovelling. The "oven" needs all the insulation it can get.
13. Cover the mound with a tarpaulin or waterproof sheet if there is any danger of rain (plastic sheeting will do but it will get hot and might discolor, so nothing too precious should be used).

14. Leave the pig to cook for the required time.
15. Dig it up.
16. Lift the parcel onto the trestle table.
17. Unwrap it and decorate with a bunch or two of sage and some shiny whole raw apples.
18. Do not forget to serve the cooked apples that are inside the pig when you are carving the meat.

## SESAME BREAD
MAKES ONE LOAF
*¾oz fresh yeast*
*1¼ cups lukewarm milk and water mixed*
*1 tsp sugar*
*4 cups strong white flour*
*1 tsp salt*
*2 tbsp clear honey*
*2 tbsp tahini*
*2 tbsp lemon juice*
*⅓ cup toasted sesame seeds*

1. Mix the yeast to a smooth paste with a little of the milk and water and the sugar. Warm a large mixing bowl and sift the flour and salt into it.
2. Add the remaining milk and water, honey, tahini, lemon juice and mix to a slack dough.
3. Beat the dough with your hand until it will leave the sides of the bowl. Tip it on to a floured board and knead until it is shiny and very elastic (about 15 minutes).
4. Put the dough into a clean, lightly-oiled bowl and cover it with plastic wrap. Leave in a warm place until it has doubled in size.
5. Preheat the oven, setting the temperature control to 400°. Grease an 8×4in (4 cups) loaf pan.
6. Turn the dough on to a floured surface and punch down. Continue to knead for 10 minutes, gradually adding the sesame seeds.
7. Shape the dough into an oblong and place in the greased pan, cover with oiled plastic wrap and leave to rise again to the size and shape of the loaf.
8. Bake the loaf for 10 minutes, then turn the oven down to 375° and bake for a further 25 minutes until the loaf is golden and firm.
9. Cool on a wire rack.
10. Serve the bread hot or cold with unsalted butter.

NOTE:
For a party of 40 people you should make 3 sesame bread loaves. See Catering in Quantity, p. 10.

## APPLE AND CRANBERRY SAUCE
SERVES 10
*1lb cooking apples*
*4oz fresh or frozen cranberries*
*⅓ cup brown sugar*
*2 tbsp butter*
*3 tbsp water*

1. Peel the apples and cut into small chunks.
2. Put all the ingredients together in a small heavy-based pan, place over a low heat and bring to the boil. Simmer until the apples are soft and the cranberries have burst.
3. Allow to cool, then mix well.

## RICE AND PEPPERS
SERVES 10
*1 medium onion*
*1 green pepper*
*1 red pepper*
*1 green chili pepper*
*2 tbsp oil*
*2¼ cups brown rice*
*5 cups chicken stock*
*2lb canned tomatoes*
*salt*
*black pepper*

1. Peel and chop the onion finely. Core, deseed and chop the pepper.
2. Finely chop the chili, making sure you remove all the seeds as they are fiery hot.
3. Heat the oil in a heavy-based pan, add the onion, pepper and chili, fry gently for two minutes. Add the rice and fry briskly for a further minute.
4. Pour in the stock and canned tomatoes, season with salt and black pepper. Bring to the boil and boil briskly until the water has evaporated enough to form small craters on the top of the rice.
5. Immediately cover the pan with a piece of foil and then the lid. Remove from the heat and leave to stand for 45 minutes. (The rice can happily be left for up to an hour at this stage, providing the lid is never removed.)
6. To serve the rice, stir it with a fork to loosen the grains and tip into a heated serving dish.

## EVERYTHING SALAD
SERVES 10
*½ iceberg lettuce*
*1 cucumber*
*2 large tomatoes*
*1 bunch scallions*
*7oz canned kidney beans*
*3 oranges*
*2 ripe avocados*

FOR THE CROUTONS
*4 slices white bread*
*oil for frying*
*1 tsp grated Parmesan cheese*
*salt*
FOR THE DRESSING
*½ cup olive oil*
*1 tbsp wine vinegar*
*1 tbsp orange juice*
*pinch brown sugar*
*1 tsp French mustard*
*salt and pepper*

1. To make the croutons: cut the bread into ¼in cubes. Heat the oil in a heavy-based frying-pan. Fry the croutons slowly until golden brown. Drain on absorbent paper and sprinkle with salt and Parmesan cheese.
2. Break up the iceberg lettuce with your hands, wash it and shake dry. Cut the cucumber into thin short sticks. Cut the tomatoes into wedges. Clean and chop the scallions. Drain and rinse the kidney beans. Peel the oranges with a sharp knife, as you would an apple. Cut into segments, removing seeds and pith.
3. Mix the dressing ingredients together.
4. Not more than half an hour in advance, cut the avocados in half, remove the stone and skin and cut into chunks and turn in the dressing.
5. Mix everything together and tip into a salad bowl.

## PECAN ICE CREAM WITH HOT BLUEBERRY SAUCE
SERVES 10
FOR THE ICE CREAM
*1 cup pecans*
*¾ cup sugar*
*5 cups heavy cream*
*4 egg whites*
*1 tsp vanilla*
FOR THE SAUCE
*⅓ cup sugar*
*3 tbsp water*
*8oz blueberries*
*juice of ½ lemon*

1. Put the pecan nuts with half the sugar into a very heavy-based pan. Place over a low heat until the sugar has browned and caramelized.
2. Turn the caramelized pecans on to an oiled baking sheet and leave until cold and brittle. Pound coarsely with a pestle and mortar or chop in a blender or food processor.
3. Lightly whip the cream.
4. Beat the egg whites until stiff. If using a machine add the remaining sugar and continue to beat until very stiff and shiny. If working by hand just fold the sugar in gently.
5. With a metal spoon or spatula fold the egg whites, vanilla and prepared pecans into the heavy cream. Turn into a metal tray and freeze. Stir with a fork once or twice while the ice cream is freezing.
6. To make the sauce: put the sugar and water together in a small pan and stand over low heat. When the sugar has dissolved, boil until it is reduced and syrupy, add the blueberries and simmer until they are pulpy. Add plenty of lemon juice to sharpen the taste.
7. Remove the ice cream from the freezer to the refrigerator 40 minutes before serving. Scoop the ice cream into a large glass bowl and hand the hot sauce separately.

## GINGER POP
MAKES 1 GALLON (4.5 LITRES).
*1oz fresh ginger*
*5 qts water*
*1 lemon*
*1 tsp cream of tartar*
*2 cups sugar*
*4 tsp brewer's yeast*
*1 egg white*

1. Peel and roughly slice the ginger. Put it into a large pan with the water, bring to the boil and simmer for 30 minutes. Pour into a large bowl and remove the ginger.
2. Coarsely chop the whole lemon and add it to the hot ginger liquid with the cream of tartar and the sugar. Stir until the sugar has dissolved.
3. Allow the mixture to cool until it is lukewarm then stir in the yeast. Cover the bowl with muslin or a dish cloth and leave to ferment for three days.
4. With a large perforated spoon skim any scum off the top. Beat in the egg white. Strain the beer through a fine strainer into a clean bowl.
5. Store the ginger beer in thick sterilized bottles, sealed with screw caps.

# CELEBRATION TEA

*for Twenty-five*

A CELEBRATION TEA, WITH ALL THAT THAT IMPLIES OF luxury, indulgence, frivolity and elegant excess is a pleasurable and unusual way to entertain friends and family. Children much prefer the farinaceous and sweet food that tea-time offers to the more worldly family lunch menu and, because grown-ups mostly deny themselves the pleasures of shortbread, éclairs, scones and walnut layer cake, it will delight them too.

A palm court quartet is hardly possible in the average household, but live musicians might turn a celebration anniversary or wedding tea into an occasion to remember. Of course the menu can be served buffet-style, with the guests drifting about cup-in-hand. But if it can be contrived, an old-fashioned, serious, knees-under tea, complete with tablecloths and napkins, proper plates and forks for the cake, all the better. If children are present, and they are old enough to look after themselves, a separate "nursery" table might give them the freedom to drink Coca-Cola uninhibitedly and tuck into five éclairs without parental disapproval, thus freeing the adults for gossip and second or third cups of tea without bored, fidgeting children spoiling the even tenor of tea-time.

Milkless tea is particularly refreshing. Make it weaker than normal especially if it is a fragrant Darjeeling.

Assam tea, served traditionally with milk, has great restorative powers. Make it fairly strong and provide extra hot water.

Herb Teas
*Tisanes make a refreshing change from traditional teas. They can be made with almost any fresh or dried herbs, the best-tasting being camomile, mint, lemon verbena or bergamot. The leaves should be steeped in boiling water, and the tisane should be served with a slice of lemon or sweetened with honey or sugar.*

**THE MENU**

**Sandwiches**
*Cream Cheese, Tomato and Watercress
Potted Meat
Sardine and Egg
Cucumber*

**Fancy Cakes**
*Honey and Hazelnut Cookies
Coffee Caramel Tuiles
Lemon and Nutmeg Shortbread
Mini Éclairs
Strawberry Mille Feuilles*

*Scones with Whipped Cream and Jam*

*Coffee and Walnut Layer Cake*

**Perfect Sandwiches**
*Spread the butter and filling evenly to the edge of the crusts. Trim each sandwich into a neat square when removing the crusts. Cut stacks of four rounds at a time using a sawing action, or better still an electric carving knife so as not to squash the bread.*

## QUANTITIES

It is unlikely that this menu (containing about 12 different items and feeding 25 people) will be followed word for word. It is a great deal of work. The essential thing is to allow five pieces per person – say two savory and three sweet ones. Our great choice of pastries (though it looks like tea-time in the best old-fashioned tradition) is not strictly necessary but it will allow you to select a balanced assortment (see margin note).

## GETTING AHEAD

*One month before*
○ Send invitations, either on a card with a suitable thirties Palm Court theme, or a black and white written invitation. "Mrs So and So requests the pleasure of . . .", etc.
○ Shop around for interesting teas.
○ Find or borrow damask or lace tablecloths and napkins, bone china plates and cups and saucers, tea knives and cake forks, a silver tea service and suitable serving dishes.
○ Decide whether the tea will be a buffet or a sit-down affair and how the room will be arranged.
○ Find some tapes or records of a string quartet; decide whether you want to clear a space for a small dance floor.
○ Make suitable arrangements for any children coming. Don't forget to buy soft drinks for them.
○ Make and freeze éclairs, puff pastry, scones and cake layers.
○ Make a shopping list from the recipes and buy all the dry ingredients.

*Two days before*
○ Buy all the fresh ingredients.
○ Remember to get extra milk.
○ Polish the silver tea set and cutlery.
○ Boil the eggs and make the potted meat filling for sandwiches.
○ Make the cookies and shortbread and store in an airtight container.
○ Defrost and bake the pastry for the mille feuilles.
○ Make the cake icing.

*The morning of the party*
○ Set the table with plates, knives, cake forks, napkins, milk and sugar, either in buffet-style or in set places.
○ Put all the tea cups, saucers and spoons on a tray so that the tea can be poured from a central point.
○ Put out glasses and soft drinks for the children.
○ Make and shape (but do not cut) the sandwiches.
○ Fill the hazelnut cookies and coat with chocolate.
○ Make the coffee and caramel tuiles.
○ Defrost the éclairs; whip the cream.
○ Fill the mille feuilles with layers of strawberries, jam and cream, and ice them.
○ Defrost the scones, whip the cream and put jam into a dish.
○ Fill and decorate the coffee and walnut cake.
○ Arrange a selection of cookies and fancy cakes on a plate.

*Last minute*
○ Cut and decorate the sandwiches.
○ Fill the éclairs with cream and coat with chocolate.
○ Slice the mille feuilles.
○ Arrange the scones on a plate.
○ Boil the kettle and make the tea.

**Making a Selection**
*If you are only going to make some of the items suggested, select those of different color and texture. For example, cucumber and potted meat sandwiches followed by lemon and nutmeg shortbread or scones with jam and cream and coffee and walnut layered cake.*

**Hiring Plants**
*Some Garden Centers might be willing to hire suitable potted palms just for the afternoon, or if you live in a large town you may be able to find a plant hire shop.*

**Boiled Eggs**
*After you have cooked them, plunge the boiled eggs into cold water to prevent a black rim forming around the yolk.*

**Cake Stands**
*Arrange an assortment of the cookies and pastries on a pretty cake plate or ideally on an old-fashioned tiered cake stand.*

*Right* Add interest to ordinary sandwiches by cutting them in elegant fingers, stacking various flavors together to make double-deckers, stamping into rounds with a cookie-cutter or rolling the bread and filling up like a jelly roll. In the background coffee caramel tuiles and honey and hazelnut cookies.

For irresistibly squashy cakes, provide cake forks or, failing them, ordinary dessert forks.

# RECIPES

## CREAM CHEESE, TOMATO AND WATERCRESS SANDWICHES

MAKES 12 FINGER SANDWICHES
*4 large thin slices white bread*
*2 large thin slices brown bread*
*¼ cup softened butter*
*¼ cup cream cheese*
*salt*
*black pepper*
*1 large tomato*
*½ bunch watercress, washed and dried*

1. Butter the white bread on one side and the brown bread on both sides.
2. Soften the cream cheese and season it with salt and black pepper. Thinly slice the tomato.
3. Cover two of the white slices of bread with the cress leaves. Sprinkle with salt and black pepper. Put the brown slices on top, arrange the tomato on these and season well.
4. Spread the two remaining white slices with the cream cheese and place on top with the cream cheese touching the tomato. Press down firmly.
5. Wrap in plastic wrap and chill for 30 minutes.
6. With a large, very sharp knife, cut off the crusts. Cut each layered sandwich in half lengthways and each half into three fingers.

## POTTED MEAT SANDWICHES

MAKES 15 TO 20 MINI-SANDWICHES
*2 smoked chicken pieces (i.e. half a bird)*
*½ cup melted butter*
*1 tbsp fresh chives and parsley, chopped*
*salt and ground black pepper*
*10 slices white bread*
*½ cup softened butter*

1. Remove the chicken from the bone and discard the skin. Place the meat and butter in a food processor and blend to a smooth paste, or mince the chicken and mix to a paste with the butter.
2. Season with the fresh herbs, salt and black pepper.
3. Butter the bread. Sandwich together with the potted meat.
4. Cut each sandwich into three or four rounds with a fluted pastry cutter.

## SARDINE AND EGG SANDWICHES

MAKES ABOUT 20 MINI-SANDWICHES
*10oz canned sardines*
*2 hard-boiled eggs, chopped*
*salt and ground black pepper*
*8 slices very fresh brown bread*
*⅓ cup softened butter*

If cucumber sandwiches must be made in advance, salt the cucumber slices, leave to drain, rinse and dry before use. Otherwise the juice will leak into the bread, making it soggy. On the right mini-éclairs.

1. Drain the oil from the sardines, remove any large pieces of bone and mash with the hard-boiled eggs. Season with salt and black pepper.
2. Cut the crusts off the bread. Lay two slices of bread end to end, with ¼in overlapping. Roll very lightly with a rolling pin to flatten the bread and seal the edges together.
3. Repeat with the six remaining slices of bread, rolling each pair into a long rectangle.
4. Butter the bread and spread with the sardine and egg. Roll up from the narrow end. Pack tightly together in a box or wrapped in foil or plastic to prevent unravelling. Chill for 30 minutes. Unwrap and slice each roll into five discs.

## CUCUMBER SANDWICHES
*See Tennis Party, p. 36.*

TO SERVE ALL THE SANDWICHES
*3-4 tbsp chopped parsley*
*1 bunch small radishes*

1. Arrange the various types of sandwich in alternate rows on a large oval serving dish.
2. Scatter with finely chopped parsley and small washed radishes, with the stalks left on.
3. Cover the sandwiches with a damp dish cloth or plastic wrap to prevent them drying out before serving.

## HONEY AND HAZELNUT COOKIES

MAKES 15
*½ cup butter*
*5 tbsp sugar*
*¾ cup ground hazelnuts*
*1⅓ cups all-purpose flour*
*thick honey*
*8oz bittersweet chocolate, chopped*

1. Preheat the oven, setting the temperature control to 350°.
2. Put the butter and sugar together in a bowl and beat until white and fluffy.
3. Add the hazelnuts and flour. Mixing first with a knife, and then using one hand, gently draw the mixture together to form a stiff paste.
4. Wrap in plastic wrap and chill for 30 minutes in the refrigerator.
5. Roll the dough out thinly and carefully cut it into rounds with a 2in pastry cutter. Lay the rounds well spaced out on a baking sheet and bake for 12 minutes. Cool on a wire rack.
6. Sandwich the cookies together with honey and return them to the wire rack, standing over a tray.
7. Put the chocolate in a bowl and melt over a pan of simmering water or in a microwave oven.
8. Spoon the melted chocolate over the cookies to cover them completely.
9. Allow the chocolate to set and store the cookies in an airtight container.

## COFFEE CARAMEL TUILES

MAKES 10
*1 egg white*
*¼ cup sugar*
*2 tbsp butter*
*3 tbsp all-purpose flour*
*½ tsp instant coffee*
FOR THE CARAMEL
*¼ cup sugar*

1. Preheat the oven, setting the temperature control to 375°. Oil a heavy baking sheet and the handles of three wooden spoons.
2. Beat the eggs whites until frothy. Gently fold in the sugar, melted butter, flour and coffee powder. Mix to a smooth paste.
3. Spread three or four small spoonfuls of the mixture in 2in rounds on the oiled baking sheet.
4. Bake in the oven for about 6 minutes, until golden brown on the edges. Cool for a few seconds.
5. Using a metal spatula quickly and carefully lift off the cookies and wind them tightly round the handle of an oiled wooden spoon. Speed is essential as the tuiles soon cool and harden and cannot then be rolled. Ease the tuiles off the handle and allow to cool. Store in an airtight container.
6. Decorate the tuiles with caramel just before serving: put the sugar in a heavy-based pan and set over a low heat. Allow it to melt slowly until it has turned to a rich toffee-brown.
7. Lay the tuiles on a wire rack with a sheet of wax paper underneath. With an oiled spoon or fork, carefully dribble the caramel in thin lines over the tuiles and leave to set.

## LEMON AND NUTMEG SHORTBREAD

MAKES 10
*¼ cup butter*
*2 tbsp sugar*
*¾ cup all-purpose flour*
*½ tbsp ground rice*
*¼ tsp ground nutmeg*
*grated rind of one lemon*
*squeeze of lemon juice*
FOR DECORATION
*sugar*
*grated nutmeg*

1. Preheat the oven, setting the temperature control to 375°.
2. Put the butter and sugar together in a bowl and beat until light and fluffy. Fold in the flour, ground rice, grated nutmeg and lemon rind and juice.

3. Turn the mixture on to a lightly floured surface and gently knead to form a smooth paste.
4. Roll the dough out to ¼in thick. Cut into small fingers 1×2in.
5. Place on a baking sheet and chill in the refrigerator for 30 minutes.
6. Bake for 25 minutes until turning the palest brown. Place the fingers on a wire rack and dust with sugar and nutmeg while still warm.

## MINI ÉCLAIRS

MAKES ABOUT 20
*¼ cup butter*
*⅔ cup water*
*⅔ cup all-purpose flour, sifted*
*pinch of salt*
*2 eggs*
FOR THE FILLING AND TOPPING
*1¼ cups heavy or whipping cream*
*a few drops vanilla*
*1 tsp confectioners' sugar*
*4oz bittersweet chocolate*

1. Preheat the oven, setting the temperature to 400°. Wet two baking sheets.
2. Put the butter and water together in a heavy pan. Bring slowly to the boil. Immediately the liquid boils tip in all the flour at once, remove the pan from the heat, and beat the mixture with a wooden spoon until it becomes thick and leaves the sides of the pan.
3. Add the salt. Allow to cool.

4. Beat the eggs lightly and then add them a little at a time to the flour mixture, beating thoroughly until the paste is shiny and smooth. If the eggs are large it may not be necessary to add all of them. The mixture should be a soft dropping consistency.
5. Put the paste into a pastry bag fitted with a ½in plain nozzle. Pipe 1½in lengths of choux pastry on to the prepared baking sheets. Be sure to set them well apart as choux pastry swells considerably during cooking and they can easily run into each other.
6. Bake for 20-25 minutes or until puffed up and golden brown.
7. Remove the éclairs from the baking sheet and make a small hole in the side of each one and return them to the oven for 5 minutes with the pierced sides uppermost to allow steam to escape from inside. Allow to cool.
8. Whip the cream and fold in the vanilla and the confectioners' sugar.
9. Put the cream into a pastry bag fitted with a medium nozzle and carefully pipe cream into the éclairs through the small hole.
10. Put the chocolate into a bowl and melt it over a pan of gently simmering water.
11. Dip each éclair upside down deeply into the melted chocolate so that the top becomes neatly coated.
12. Set the éclairs aside to dry.

A separate table at a discreet distance will allow the children to make an atrocious mess without parental frowns. Sturdy, near-unbreakable glasses are less likely to end up over-turned.

## STRAWBERRY MILLE FEUILLES

MAKES 10

*8oz puff pastry, defrosted if frozen*
*1¼ cups heavy cream, stiffly whipped*
*4oz strawberries*
*2 tbsp strawberry jam*
*2 cups confectioners' sugar*
*squeeze of lemon juice*

1. Preheat the oven, setting the temperature control to 425°. Wet a baking sheet.
2. Roll the pastry to a large thin rectangle about 16×10in. Lay it on the wet baking sheet and prick it all over with a fork. Chill for 30 minutes.
3. Bake the pastry in the hot oven until very crisp and brown. Loosen from the baking sheet, return it to the oven upside down for five minutes, then cool.
4. Trim the edges from the pastry with a serrated breadknife and cut it into six neat identical strips. Choose two pieces of pastry with the smoothest bases and put to one side. Arrange the remaining strips as two pairs.
5. Reserve five whole strawberries with their stems attached. Hull the rest, slice and mix with the cream.
6. Spread the four strips with strawberry jam and then with strawberries and cream. Place them on top of each other to give two double-deckers. Set the two remaining strips of pastry on top with the smooth side uppermost. Press down lightly.
7. Mix the sugar with the lemon juice and enough boiling water (a few drops only) to make it thick and smooth. Spread this over the top of the pastry.
8. With the breadknife dipped in hot water, cut each mille feuille into five neat pieces. While the icing is still soft, place half a strawberry on top of each slice.
9. Serve with plates and forks. They are far too creamy to manage with just the fingers.

## SCONES WITH WHIPPED CREAM AND JAM

MAKES 12

*2 cups all-purpose flour*
*3 tsp baking powder*
*½ tsp salt*
*¼ cup butter*
*¼ cup sugar*
*½ cup golden raisins*
*⅔ cup milk*
TO SERVE
*1½ cups heavy cream, whipped*
*good quality raspberry or strawberry jam*

1. Preheat the oven, setting the temperature control to 425°. Lightly grease a baking sheet.
2. Sift the flour with the baking powder and salt. Rub in the butter. Stir in the sugar and golden raisins.
3. Make a well in the center of the mixture. Pour in the milk and mix to a soft spongy dough with a knife.
4. Turn the dough on to a lightly floured surface and knead until smooth.
5. Roll out to ½in thick. Stamp into small rounds with a fluted pastry cutter. Lay the scones on a prepared baking sheet and bake until well risen and brown (about 12 minutes).
6. Leave the scones to cool on a wire rack. Serve with jam and cream handed separately. Or split them and serve spread first with cream, then with a spoonful of jam. (If the scones are to be buttered too, it is then usual to spread the jam thinly on top of the butter and add a spoonful or blob of cream.)

## COFFEE AND WALNUT LAYER CAKE

*4 small eggs*
*¾ cup sugar*
*1 tsp vanilla*
*1 cup all-purpose flour, sifted*
*⅓ cup ground walnuts*
FOR THE FILLING
*½ cup sugar*
*4 tbsp water*
*4 egg yolks*
*1 cup unsalted butter, softened*
*1 tbsp instant coffee powder, dissolved in a little boiling water*
FOR DECORATION
*½ cup chopped walnuts*

1. Preheat the oven, setting the temperature control to 400°. Line two baking sheets with greased wax paper. Mark two circles on each sheet using a 7in flan ring as a guide.
2. Mix the eggs and sugar together in a bowl set over a pan of simmering water and beat until pale, fluffy and thick enough to leave a trail when the beater is lifted.
3. Fold in the vanilla, sifted flour and ground walnuts. Spread the mixture on to the four circles marked on the prepared baking sheets. Bake for 10 to 12 minutes until just firm and very pale brown.
4. Turn over on a wire rack and peel off the paper.
5. To make the filling: dissolve the sugar in the water and boil rapidly to about 125° or until the syrup will form a thread when tested between the thumb and forefinger (first dipped in cold water). Remove from the heat.
6. Gradually pour the syrup on the egg yolks, beating constantly. Continue to beat until the mixture is pale and mousse-like.
7. Slowly beat the butter into the egg mixture. Add the coffee. Cool.
8. Sandwich the four layers of cake together with half the filling. Spread the remaining filling over the top and the sides.
9. Press the chopped walnuts around the sides of the cake, and mark the top with a fork in a lattice pattern.
10. Refrigerate.

NOTE:
As a variation the cake mixture may be baked for 20 minutes – it will give a crisp brown cookie-like texture which is pleasantly crunchy. Also melted dark chocolate can be used instead of the dissolved instant coffee powder.

# BURNS NIGHT DINNER

*for twelve*

The Ceremony
*The beginning of the ceremony of the haggis is heralded by the host knocking on the door with the handle of a* skean d'hu *(a dagger). The guests stand as the host leads the procession into the room followed by the bearer of the haggis and the bearer of the whisky who holds crossed bottles above his head.*

**B**URNS NIGHT (25 JANUARY) IS QUINTESSENTIALLY Scottish, not just because it celebrates Scotland's greatest poet, nor because a good deal of Scotch whisky and the famous Scotch haggis are consumed, but because it provides a licence for the Scots to be unbridledly sentimental. Tough clansman or hardy Highlander can weep without shame as the company sings "My Love is Like a Red Red Rose". The skirl of the bagpipes can be stirring stuff and the apparently ludicrous business of a haggis being ceremoniously "piped in" by kilted pipers, then "addressed" (preferably by an actor who will learn his lines and do it well) with Burns's famous poem "Address to a Haggis" can be both exciting and moving.

For a Burns Night to really work the whole thing must be taken seriously. The guests need not be Scots but it helps if some of them are, or at least have Scottish origins so that the rites and rituals have a chance of reviving latent patriotic sentiment.

The meal should be strictly traditional. Cock-a-leekie soup (a chicken broth with large pieces of chicken, leeks and prunes in it) could be substituted for the Finnan Haddie soup (Cullen Skink) but there must be no tampering with the haggis, bashed neeps, and champit tatties.

Serving the Haggis
*Once the* Address to a Haggis *has been read, the host slits the haggis open with the* skean d'hu. *The diners can drench their individual portions with Scotch, according to their preferences.*

*Below* Leeks, prunes and chicken broth are the strange but delicious combination of ingredients for cock-a-leekie soup which would make a good alternative to Finnan Haddie soup.

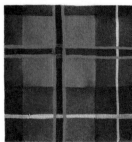

The tartans of (from the top) MacGregor, Stewart, MacDonald and Douglas. Don't be daunted by old-fashioned Scots who object to foreigners wearing their clansmen's plaids.

The traditional Burns dinner could go something like this:

**7.00 p.m.** The guests, the men in Dress Tartan (evening kilts with lacy jabots), the women in long dresses with wide tartan sashes (their own clan tartan of course) worn diagonally from shoulder to hip, arrive and are given a drink – almost certainly whisky with water but no ice.

**8.00 p.m.** Dinner is served. Whisky is served throughout. A hot punch *might* be allowable, but the haggis is always toasted in neat whisky. Its arrival is heralded by the skirl of bagpipes (or at least a recorded bagpipe march played loud on the cassette player) and it enters resting majestically on a silver platter and borne shoulder high by kilted waiter, host, cook or child. The haggis is then placed ceremoniously on the table and is solemnly addressed with the following words, spoken in the broadest Scots accent:

Fair fa' your honest, sonsie face,
Great chieftain o' the pudding race!
Aboon them a' ye tak your place,
    Painch, tripe, or thairm:
Weel are ye wordy o' a grace
    As lang's my arm.

The groaning trencher there ye fill,
Your hurdies like a distant hill,
Your pin wad help to mend a mill
    In time o' need,
While thro' your pores the dews distil
    Like amber bead.

His knife see rustic Labour dight,
An' cut you up wi' ready sleight,
Trenching your gushing entrails bright,
    Like ony ditch;
And then, O what a glorious sight,
    Warm-reekin, rich!

Then, horn for horn, they stretch an'
    strive:
Deil tak the hindmost! on they drive,
Till a' their weel-swall'd kytes belyve
    Are bent like drums;
Then auld Guidman, maist like to rive,
    "Bethanket!" hums.

Is there that owre his French **ragoût**,
Or **olio** that wad staw a sow,
Or **fricassée** wad make her spew
    Wi' perfect sconner,
Looks down wi' sneering, scornfu' view
    On sic a dinner?

Poor devil! see him owre his trash,
As feckless as a wither'd rash,
His spindle shank, a guid whip-lash,
    His nieve a nit;
Thro' bloody flood or field to dash,
    O how unfit!

But mark the Rustic, haggis-fed,
The trembling earth resounds his tread,
Clap in his walie nieve a blade,
    he'll mak it whissle;
An' legs an' arms, an' heads will sned,
    Like taps o' thrissle.

Ye Pow'rs wha mak mankind your care,
And dish them out their bill o' fare,
Auld Scotland want nae skinking ware
    That jaups in luggies;
But, if ye wish her gratefu' prayer
    Gie her a haggis!
             *Address to a Haggis*
             ROBERT BURNS

With that the haggis is pierced by its addresser, and then sliced and served. The haggis could now be followed by good roast beef if it is thought that anyone will not attempt the haggis. Or a slice of beef could be served with it. But a good bought and reheated haggis, especially if served with a traditional brown gravy, champit tatties (mashed potatoes) and buttery rutabegas ("neeps") is in fact delicious.

**10.00 p.m.** One of the men gives the Address to the Ladies. Burns was a great ladies' man, so the speech should do him justice in wit, charm and delivery. The ladies are toasted, then malt whisky and port circulate round the table while any members of the company give performances of Robbie Burns's poems or sing (solo or in unison), Scottish folk songs, such as "Ye Banks and Braes o' Bonnie Doon", "Charlie is Ma' Darling", the Skye Boat Song ("Speed, Bonny Boat"). The singers become ever more enthusiastic, sentimental and frankly drunker until they take the high road to home and bed.

Robert Burns
*The standard modern edition of Burns's works is* The Poems and Songs of Robert Burns, *edited by James Kinsley who also compiled a useful single-volume edition which is available in paperback. Both are published by Oxford University Press.*

Haggis
*Good bought haggis is now available from specialty food shops and importers. Steam the haggis over a pan of simmering water or put it (wrapped in foil) into a pan of previously boiled water, now barely simmering. Cook for 40 minutes for the first pound and then for 20 minutes per pound.*

*Right* A kilted piper to herald the haggis may not be possible but try to get friends to dress in kilt or trews, or at least very formally. Drink blended Scotch with the meal and twelve-year-old malt whisky while singing songs and reciting poetry.

Scotch Whisky
*Although many have tried to imitate it, real Scotch whisky can only be made in Scotland. The secret lies in the careful blending of malted and unmalted grains of barley.*

## DECOR

If Scottish castle decor in the form of hunting prints, stuffed birds, antlers on the wall and ancient armor can be contrived, all the better. Otherwise never mind. It's the dinner and the poetry that counts!

## THE INVITATION

January being the party season the guests should be invited well in advance. It is important that they are told (if they don't already know) what they are in for – a fiendishly Scottish (and progressively drunker) evening. It really is no good inviting abstainers to Burns Night. The Scots have two big festivals, Hogmanay (New Year) and Burns Night, and they are both unimaginable without the national drink in frequent drams. So mention the "Address to the Haggis", and add something like "Dress: Formal and Scottish" to ensure kilts and tartan. If they are not Scots they'll be in the wrong tartan, which to a true clansman is definitely the act of a cad, but for the sake of the party it is worth the risk of offending the true Stewarts, MacDonalds and Douglases.

Invitations
*Invitations could be decorated with pressed heather or snippets of tartan material. Or you might set the tone for the evening by sending a miniature bottle of Scotch whisky along with a classic white invitation card.*

*Below* Strictly traditional Burns Nicht fare. From the left: Athol Brose topped with toffee-coated oats. Center: champit taties, bashed neeps and haggis with soda bread. Right: Cullen Skink, the haddock soup.

MENU

*Finnan Haddie Soup*

*Soda Bread*

*Haggis*

*Bashed Neeps and Champit Tatties*

*Athol Brose*

*Cheese Board and Oatcakes*

**Scottish Cookies**
*Oat cookies, flapjack, parkin or shortbread could be served with the Athol Brose instead of the crunchy topping.*

**Finnan Haddock**
*This can be recognized by its pale, creamy appearance. It is named after the village of Findon in Aberdeenshire where the original method of curing the fish in the smoke of seaweed was adopted.*

# GETTING AHEAD

*One to two months before Burns Night*
- ○ Send out invitations. See margin note on p. 76.
- ○ Organize a piper or taped bagpipe music.
- ○ Decide who will be the bearer of the haggis, who will address the haggis and who will extol the ladies, and warn them of their serious duties.
- ○ Buy plenty of whisky, or other drinks if whisky is not to be the sole beverage.
- ○ Make a shopping list from the recipes and buy the dry ingredients.
- ○ Make and freeze the soda bread.
- ○ Buy, or have photocopied, song sheets and copies of Burns's "Address to a Haggis".
- ○ Obtain a copy of the complete works of Burns.

*One day before Burns Night*
- ○ Do all the shopping.
- ○ Organize the serving dishes. Old-fashioned china dishes or silver would be most suitable. A large tureen with a ladle for the soup would be festive.
- ○ Buy or make red or tartan napkins and tablecloth.
- ○ Make a table decoration – possibly of dried grasses and flowers – or a candelabra with small white candles.
- ○ If you have an open fire, make sure there are some large logs.

*The morning of Burns Night*
- ○ Defrost the soda bread.
- ○ Prepare the Finnan Haddie soup, but leave fish and soup separately.
- ○ Peel the rutabegas and potatoes and leave in cold water.
- ○ Make the Athol Brose and chill in glasses.
- ○ Make the topping for the Athol Brose and leave to cool.
- ○ Set the table.
- ○ Decorate the room.
- ○ Put out song sheets and poems.
- ○ Lay the fire.
- ○ Arrange trays of whisky and other drinks being offered.
- ○ Set a tray for coffee.

*An hour before the guests arrive*
- ○ Put the haggis on to boil or steam gently.
- ○ Cook the rutabegas and potatoes, mash them, dish them up and keep warm in a low oven.
- ○ Arrange the cheese board and put out oatcakes or crackers and butter.
- ○ Organize the music and check that everything is set for piping in the haggis.
- ○ Light the fire.

*After the guests arrive*
- ○ Heat the soup and add the smoked haddock.
- ○ Warm the soda bread.
- ○ Sprinkle the topping on the Athol Brose.

Cheaper than a miniature bottle of Scotch whisky would be an invitation rolled and inserted into a tartan-covered toilet paper tube, perhaps secured with a kilt-pin or even a safety-pin.

**Hot Punch**
*Mix one part red wine with one part soda water and one part orange juice. Add a good dash of Scotch whisky or Drambuie, slices of orange, some cloves and a cinnamon stick. Heat gently and sweeten to taste with honey.*

# BURNS NIGHT DINNER RECIPES

## FINNAN HADDIE SOUP
(Cullen Skink)
SERVES 12
*2 ½lb smoked haddock fillets*
*5 cups water*
*1 slice onion*
*1 bay leaf*
*6 peppercorns*
*1 stick celery*
*¼ cup butter*
*3 leeks, finely shredded*
*1 cup mashed potato*
*2 ½ cups milk*
*salt and pepper*
FOR DECORATION
*chopped parsley*

1. Cut the haddock fillets into large chunks.
2. Put the haddock pieces into a pan together with the water, onion, bay leaf, peppercorns and celery. Place over a low heat, bring slowly to the boil and simmer for 5 minutes.
3. Remove the fish and continue to simmer the liquid for a further 30 minutes. Strain and reserve.
4. Remove any remaining skin and bones from the haddock, keeping the pieces as large as possible.
5. Melt the butter in the pan, and gently cook the leeks over a low heat, stirring occasionally until well cooked, soft and transparent.
6. Add the mashed potato, reserved stock, and milk. Mix well and season with salt and pepper.
7. Just before serving add the cooked fish and reheat gently. Adjust the seasoning.
8. Serve the soup sprinkled with plenty of chopped parsley.
9. It should be accompanied by hot soda bread with plenty of butter.

## SODA BREAD
SERVES 12
*4⅓ cups wholewheat flour*
*1⅔ cups all-purpose flour*
*2 tsp salt*
*2 tsp baking soda*
*4 tsp cream of tartar*
*2 tsp sugar*
*¼ cup butter*
*2⅔-3⅔ cups milk*

1. Preheat the oven, setting the temperature control to 375°. Grease a baking sheet.
2. Sift the dry ingredients into a large warm bowl.
3. Rub in the butter and mix to a soft dough with the milk.

4. Shape into three small rounds about 2in thick and place them on the greased baking sheet.
5. With the handle of a wooden spoon press a deep cross on top of each loaf (at least ¾in deep).
5. Bake for 30 minutes, until the bread is brown and crusty on top and sounds hollow when tapped on the base.
6. Allow to cool a little before serving with plenty of butter.

## BASHED NEEPS AND CHAMPIT TATTIES
SERVES 12
FOR THE NEEPS
*4lb rutabagas*
*½ cup butter*
*salt and ground black pepper*
FOR THE TATTIES
*4lb floury potatoes*
*nutmeg*
*½ cup butter*
*milk*
*salt and black pepper*
TO SERVE
*extra butter*
*chopped parsley*

1. Peel and thinly slice the rutabagas.
2. Put the slices into a large, heavy-based pan. Add half the butter and season with salt and black pepper. Pour in about ½in of water. Cover tightly and simmer over the lowest heat for about 40 minutes until the rutabegas are soft all the way through.

3. Meanwhile, peel the potatoes and cook them in boiling salted water. Drain them and push them through a mincer or coarse sieve. Return to the empty pan.
4. Mash over a medium heat, allowing them to dry out as you do so. Add the butter and enough milk to moisten the potato. Continue to stir over the heat until the butter has melted.
5. Season with salt, pepper and nutmeg. Turn into a deep serving dish, filling one side only with the potatoes. Keep warm in the oven.
6. To finish the rutabegas: remove the lid from the pan and boil away any excess water, stirring and taking care not to burn on the bottom of the pan.
7. Using a potato-masher or wooden spoon, mash the rutabegas over a gentle heat, until smooth, dry and fluffy. Add the remaining butter and season with salt and ground black pepper.
8. Put the rutabegas into the dish with the potatoes. Decorate with a pat of butter and chopped parsley.

## ATHOL BROSE
SERVES 12
*3¾ cups heavy cream*
*1¼ cups Scotch whisky*
*3 tbsp runny honey*
FOR THE TOP
*1 tbsp butter*
*1 tbsp soft brown sugar*
*1 tbsp golden syrup, or light corn syrup*
*⅓ cup rolled oats*

1. Whip the cream until stiff. Fold in the whisky and honey.
2. Spoon the Athol Brose into individual glasses and chill well.
3. To make the top: melt the butter, sugar and syrup in a heavy-based pan until the sugar has dissolved. Continue to cook until the mixture has caramelized a little.
4. Stir in the oats and cook for a further minute. Allow to cool.
5. Just before serving place a spoonful of the topping on each Athol Brose.

## CHEESE BOARD
This should consist of Scottish or Scottish-type cheeses only. Cheddar and Scottish Caboc make a good contrast in richness and texture. Caboc is a double cream cheese with a 60 per cent fat content. It is made from cows' milk and coated in oatmeal. It has a mild, sweet flavour and is also good to serve with fresh fruit. Serve the cheeses with celery, scallions and radishes and hand oatcakes or crackers separately.

# CLAMBAKE
## *for Twenty*

**Sweetcorn**
*This is also known as maize. It can be dried and ground to make cornmeal or cornstarch. American sweetcorn is the most sweet and tender. When buying it, look for clean, green husks and plump, golden yellow kernels.*

ANYONE WHO HAS SEEN THAT OLD WEEPIE MUSICAL *Carousel*, will have the right idea of a clambake – a rollicking, romantic, outdoor affair with old and young alike feasting on clams, lobsters and corn, while the music plays and young love blooms.

Well, it may not be possible to contrive all that, but there is no doubt that a clambake is the best beach picnic in the world. It produces plenty of communal activity, like collecting seaweed and large smooth stones, fetching buckets of sea water, digging the pit in the sand, building and tending the fire, and finally steaming the clams.

Clams are wonderful cooked this way, but so are other shellfish, chicken and sweetcorn. Our menu consists of a mixture of all these, and the hot food could be augmented with corn bread, garlic bread, quickly heated on the stones once the clams, etc. have been removed, or even bought Greek pitta bread. Greek bread is hardly traditional for an American clambake but the flat pittas open out into convenient pockets – perfect for dropping hot food into with plenty of melted butter and a squeeze of lemon juice. A fairly substantial salad would be a good addition, or the meal might be rounded off with hearty slices of chocolate cake. If the clambake is a night-time one, it is pleasant to have a bonfire too. This can be started by the clambake embers being raked glowing from the pit, then kept going with driftwood collected by the children.

Reconnoitering the beach before a clambake is essential. Turning up on a strange beach with buckets of clams and little else could prove disastrous. The ideal setting is a deserted beach at low tide so that the sand is firm and damp and easy to dig, even far from the sea. Although a sandy beach is best, there should also be smooth round rocks about for lining the baking pit. Well-dried driftwood is piled at the high-water mark, and fresh seaweed is easily reachable from the rocks. Of course if nature does not provide, man must. Bricks (and a wheelbarrow for transporting them from road to beach) could replace the jumbo-pebbles. Seaweed might be had from the fishmarkets. Logs or charcoal are not as romantic as driftwood, but they burn as well, if not better.

Then there are other things to remember: spades for digging, the piece of chicken wire to put the clams on, buckets for the seaweed and sea water, long-handled cooking tools (or

**Clams**
*Be sure to throw away any clams that are cracked or remain open when tapped. After cooking discard the ones that remain closed. This will single out any that have died before cooking and may not be safe to eat.*

Greek pitta bread is hardly traditional clambake fare, but split open, the pitas make perfect envelopes for clams, lobster flesh, chicken pieces, etc. Add freshly-milled black pepper, butter and a squeeze of lemon.

Seaweeds
*These have long been traditional fare in Asia. A rich source of minerals, they have become popular in the Western world among health-conscious eaters. Samphire, Laver, Kelp, Dulse and Cargheen are all found in the British Isles. Wash them well in fresh water before cooking. Dried seaweeds are available from healthfood stores.*

Loire Wines
*The River Loire is the longest in France and is bordered by vineyards for almost the whole of its length. Sancerre, pouilly blanc fume, vouvray, chablis and muscadet are among the finest and best-known wines from the region.*

*Left* A clambake is the best beach picnic in the world. While the clams are cooking in the fire-pit there is plenty of time for swimming, beach games or simply lazing around.

thick gloves) for handling hot food, the square of wet canvas to hold in the steam, matches, firelighters and tinder to get the fire started, towels for sitting on, bags for rubbish, foil for wrapping food – all this and the usual paraphernalia of a picnic too. If the night is warm and balmy, insect repellent might be a good idea, and if it is dark, flashlights or lanterns will be needed. There's everyone's swimming things, warm sweaters for after a chilly dip, a transistor radio for romantic music, and wine, corkscrews and glasses to be thought of too.

But if, as the sun sets over a calm and shiny sea, you can hear the hiss of cooking clams and smell the roasting corn under the canvas, it will be worth all the slogging effort. All you will need then is a school of dolphins playing games in the surf to complete the picture.

Games are a good idea on the beach, especially if there are children to keep amused. Hopscotch, long jump and leapfrog are probably the most fun especially if played on the hard wet sand closest to the sea, where the risk of getting soaked adds an extra dimension.

## WINE
Crisp white wines are perfect with clams. Chilled beer is also traditional, and good too, but, especially at night, it might be worth bucking convention and offering red wine as well. Somehow it feels more warming after a midnight swim than a white one.

## GETTING AHEAD
*Weeks in advance*
○ Find a suitable beach and check the times of the tide.
○ Set the date and invite the guests, remembering to arrange the time about 4½ hours before you want to eat so that there are plenty of helpers to dig the pit.
○ Collect driftwood, logs or charcoal, and check that plenty of rounded stones are available.
○ Make a list of equipment you will need from our instructions, making sure that it is all available. (Remember to include games and swimming gear.)
○ Hot drinks may be welcome at the end of the evening, so collect several thermos jugs, or kettles and water containers to brew up on the fire.
○ Sort out the music and buy batteries for the portable radio or cassette player, or take an accordion or banjo for a sing-song.

*One week before the party*
○ Order the clams and lobsters.
○ Make and freeze any bread to serve with the food.
○ Buy wine and soft drinks.

*The day before the party*
○ Do all the shopping except for the shellfish.

*The day of the party*
○ Collect the clams and lobsters.
○ Collect all the equipment and other items and load up the car.
○ Get to the beach about 4½ hours before you want to eat.
○ Follow the instructions for digging the pit, preparing, and cooking the food.

Eating Lobster
*This is quite an intricate operation. First twist off the claws and legs, crack them with a hammer or nutcrackers and pick out the meat. Then, using a sharp knife, split the lobster in half from head to tail. Remove the gills from the head and the intestine running down the center of the tail. All the remaining meat is edible, including the roe and the creamy greenish liver which can also be used for sauces.*

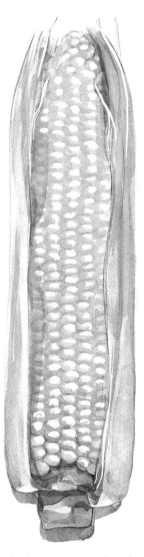

Cook young corn on the cob in their husks. They will stay hotter longer after cooking and keep moist. The husks will also prevent burning if they are against the hot stones.

Large clams, live lobsters and corn on the cob make an unbeatable combination.

## RECIPES FOR CLAMBAKE

The essentials of a good clambake, apart from convivial company that will double as a willing labour force, is split-second timing and masterly organization. For each person you will need:

*6 soft shell clams*
*1 piece of chicken*
*½ small live lobster*
*1 frankfurter*
*1 corn-on-the-cob*
*salt and pepper*
*plenty of bread and butter*

1. Start 4½ hours before the event by digging a pit in the sand about a foot deep. The width of the pit will depend on the size of the "bake". A pit three foot square would be ample for a bake for twenty people.
2. Line it with smooth stones. Build a wood fire in the pit on top of the stones. Keep feeding the fire (preferably with thick pieces of hardwood) for 2 or 3 hours, then let it die down. The idea is to get the stones white-hot.
3. While the stones are heating, wash the clams in sea water, kill the lobsters by piercing them in the back of the head with a knife, take the outside leaves from

the corn, cut the chicken into small pieces, and collect two buckets of wet rock seaweed and a bucket of sea water.
4. When the stones are white-hot, rake out the embers and put a 4-5in layer of seaweed on the stones. Work as fast as you can to prevent too much heat escaping. A piece of chicken wire laid on top of the seaweed is useful now as it prevents the food falling through and getting lost under the seaweed, but it is not vital.
5. Now put in the food – chicken pieces first, then the frankfurters, then the lobsters and the corn, and last of all the clams.
6. Add another layer of seaweed, and splash a few pints of sea water over the lot. Amply cover the pit with a piece of damp canvas, weighted down with stones to prevent the steam escaping.
7. The steaming will take about 1 hour, and the canvas should not be lifted during this time.
8. After an hour lift the cover carefully. If the clams have opened the bake is done. Lift out the food, taking care not to knock any sand in.
9. Serve with butter, pepper and salt, and crusty bread.

## PICKLED CABBAGE AND SPINACH SALAD

SERVES 10
*½ a hard white cabbage*
*8oz fresh spinach*
*6 dill pickles*

FOR THE DRESSING
*1¼ cups dairy sour cream*
*rind and juice of half a lemon*
*1 tbsp fresh dill, finely chopped or 1 tsp dill*
    *weed*
*salt*
*ground black pepper*

1. Shred the cabbage as finely as possible.
2. Remove the tough stalks from the spinach and wash thoroughly. Drain well and shred finely.
3. Cut the dill pickles into small sticks.
4. Put the dill pickles in a mixing bowl together with the shredded cabbage and shredded spinach.
5. Mix all the dressing ingredients together and season with salt and black pepper.
6. Just before serving, pour the dressing over the salad and mix well.
7. Turn the dressed salad into a clean serving dish.

# HARLEQUIN MASKED BALL

## for Two Hundred

Bought or homemade party masks can be as exotic or strange as you like.

Tᴴᴇ GREAT THING ABOUT A HARLEQUINADE IS THAT ITS origins are so muddled, its cast of characters so confusing, and its nationality so mixed, that anything goes. It is at least a costume party, and at best a masked ball. The party must have something of the uninhibited medieval revel about it, tempered perhaps by elegant mischievous intrigue. The characters should not look amiss in a medieval court – there can be kings and queens of course, and doublet-and-hose courtiers, but most of the fun seems to be had by the jesters.

The original "Arlequin" denotes a medieval French leader of a troupe of wild mountebanks who ride at night. The Italian "Arleccino" is more of a clown, and rivals Pantaloon for the affections of Colombine. The Anglo-Saxon version is sometimes the hook-nosed Punch, with poor battered Judy in tow, or a jester, buffoon or "zany", a "Jack-pudding" or a "merry-andrew". His character can be anything from evil to simple and sentimental. Mockery and fun, bawdish humor and pranks are the order of the day.

Pierrot and Pierrette can get in on the act too, with their whitened faces, loose shiny white pantaloons dotted with big black spots and deep ruffs round the neck.

Harlequin usually dresses in parti-colored bespangled tights (perhaps with one leg red and one leg yellow) and wears a visor. Indeed, everyone must be masked, but real visors might prove rather uncomfortable. But cardboard visors, helmets and exotic masks can be bought from novelty shops, and if a trick can be stolen from the *Carnevale di Venezia*, brilliantly sequinned and feathered masks can be worn by men and women alike.

Music for such an extravagant and brilliant affair should be live. The band will need a large raised platform at the end of the ballroom (or gymnasium or scout hall) so that they can be seen above the dancers. They might even agree to dress as a Pierrot troupe – Pierrots were, after all, musicians. But hiring their costumes will of course be an expense the host must bear.

The decor, as far as possible, should reflect the theme. A pretty tented effect can be had with alternate strips of crêpe paper fixed close together down the middle of the ballroom or hall ceiling, the ends fixed half-way up the walls each side, not stretched tight, but allowed to sag gently like the roof of a tent.

Make quite sure the masks are comfortable or the wearers will surely discard them.

The Band
*Remember that the band will need a break during the course of the evening so you will need to provide an additional source of music to fill the interval.*

Sparklers stuck upright in plasticine or sand and lit at midnight would look merry and festive.

Doorman
*For large parties it is a good idea to employ a security guard to check invitations and ward off gate-crashers. Make sure they will be able to deal tactfully with interlopers and make yourself available to help if necessary.*

Champagne Cocktails
*These make excellent aperitifs. Use a dash of apricot or cherry brandy, framboise or fraise de bois, top up with chilled champagne. Kir royale (a mixture of champagne and crème de cassis) is also delicious.*

The paper could be black and white to reflect the Pierrot theme, or every color under the sun for the Harlequin version.

Shiny spangles and foil stars could be suspended in profusion from the ceiling. Or great cut-outs of Pierrot or Harlequin could adorn the walls. That the hall or room must be decorated, and to within an inch of its life, goes without saying. Lighting should be dimmable so that merry revels can slowly give way to romantic intrigue, shadowy assignations and much whispering behind pillars. If the ball can be held in summer with a large tent or ballroom opening on to green lawn and fairy lights, so much the better. But if there is a garden, think about lighting it. There are few things worse than falling into a muddy ditch on the way to an illicit rendezvous.

The organization of an event like this takes months. The easiest way, and the most expensive one, is to go to a reliable caterer and hand the problem over to him. Or to enlist the services of a specialist party organizer who will engage the band, hire the tent, supervise the caterers and everything else. But big parties *can* be organized by the host or hostess. They are not much more difficult to plan than small parties. It is still a matter of decor, music, food, invitations, etc. But simply because of the numbers involved, nervousness is more likely to set in, and forward planning is all the more important. And, of course, there are some problems that don't crop up in small parties such as the need for a hired portable restroom in the garden if the ones in the house won't cope with 200 guests (you need one restroom to 40 people, very roughly). And there is the question of feeding the band, and allocating them a room to change in and to leave their instrument cases, etc. And, if there are, as there should be, professional hired waiters and waitresses, they will need feeding and changing facilities too.

Read Catering in Quantity (p. 10) carefully to make sure you have thought of every item – from flowers to coffee spoons, from ice to bottle openers, from a bankroll to pay the wage bill to matches to light the candles.

## THE INVITATION
For a masked ball to really work it must have a rigidly formal structure so that no one *dares* turn up in a business suit or T-shirt. The invitation, which should be printed and conventional (with the exception perhaps of a drawing of Harlequin or Colombine), should state time, date, that supper will be served, and that dress is strictly in costume, implying that cads and bounders who turn up ill-costumed will be barred admittance and will have to seek their entertainment at some more conventional gathering elsewhere.

## WINE
A full bar, operated by professional barmen is ideal, but very expensive. If the drinks are to be limited to wine, then choose one good red that is easy to drink all night, like a light burgundy, and a sound, not too acidic white, perhaps a chablis. If it is drier, make sure it is not too astringent – fresh acidic wines are a pleasure for a glass or two but can pall if they are to be drunk for hours on end. Stock up on orange juice, soft drinks and natural mineral water, of which a surprising amount is drunk by dancers. Get everything on "Sale or Return" from a liquor store and ask for the loan of glasses (at least 2 per head – people lose them all the time).

Lighting
*A huge variety of lighting is available for hire and can be used to enhance the decor. Faceted globes will send sparkles across the ceiling; colored plastic cut-outs revolving in front of a bulb will fill the room with rainbow patterns, or you could choose laser lights which can be used as a permanent decoration.*

Cloakroom facilities
*Don't forget to supply soap and plenty of hand towels for the restrooms, coat rails and hangers and cloakroom tickets and pins. Remember to arrange for changing facilities for the band and serving staff too.*

*Right* Color must be the central point of any Harlequin decor theme. Here the ugly scaffolding pole of a large tent is charmingly wrapped with multi-colored ribbons. On the table multi-colored pasta, a salmon encased in a Harlequin jacket of cucumber and red pepper, and bi-colored lettuce leaves.

**Menu Board**
*Have a life-size cut-out of a Harlequin made with a plain white inset on the front for the menu to be written on in bold green, red and black letters.*

**THE MENU**

*Harlequin Ham Terrine*

*Salmon Trout with Harlequin Coat*

*Red and White Pasta Salad with Green Peppers*

*Curly Endive, Radicchio and Palm Heart Salad*

*Lattice Bakewell Pie*

*Harlequin Fruit Salad*

**Harlequin Meat Platter**
*Arrange thinly-sliced roast pork and rare roast beef in rows on either side of an oval meat dish. Make a watercress and pistachio stuffing and use it to fill a boned chicken. Roast it and slice thinly. Arrange the chicken down the center of the dish and decorate with watercress.*

## GETTING AHEAD

*One year to six months in advance*

- Decide on the venue for the Harlequinade and set a date.
- If the party is to be held in a large tent consult with the contractor, and order it. Take care to specify the color of the lining, whether you need a separate service (kitchen) tent, another small tent for staff meals and the band, a stage, a dance-floor, druggits/flooring under the tables, lighting for the tent (and for covered pathways, garden and service areas), temporary heating, and electrical outlets for the disco or band equipment and for a coffee-maker for staff.
- Check on cloakroom facilities and arrange for the hire of portable coat-racks and temporary toilets if necessary.
- Design invitations and have them printed.
- Book a band and hire their costumes if necessary. Tell them to arrive one hour before the guests are due.
- Engage a florist or delegate the flower-arranging.
- Book barman and serving staff, specifying their arrival times – head waitresses to arrive early afternoon and the barman and other staff two hours before lift-off.
- Find helpers for the food and general organization: it is a good idea to delegate the making of the terrines and staff food to one person, the salads and fruit salad to another, Bakewell lattice pie to a third, leaving you with just the salmon trout to do yourself.

**Floral Decorations**
*Have garlands of flowers made to wind round the poles of the tent. Matching garlands can be looped across the front of the buffet and small bouquets placed on each table.*

*Three months in advance*

- Send the invitations.
- Make shopping lists from the recipes, one each for dry goods, the fish, meat, fruit and vegetables, dairy produce.
- Make a second list of food required by each of your helpers.
- Make a list of all equipment you need to hire (see p. 12).
- Place orders and arrange to have the food delivered.
- Order the equipment from a hire company, and specify that it is to be delivered early on the day of the party.
- Order the drinks and arrange delivery early on the party day.
- Order ice for cooling wines and for drinks to be delivered on the afternoon of the party.
- Obtain all the decorations and find helpers.
- Order, make or buy a costume for yourself.

*Weeks before the ball*

- Helper 3: make the Bakewell pies to stage 6 and freeze.
- Ring up all suppliers, staff and helpers, and confirm orders.
- Sort out boxes or deep trays for transporting food, and make sure you have plenty of plastic trash bags and ties.

Red pepper and cucumber skin, peeled thinly, can be neatly cut into diamond shapes to produce a traditional Harlequin design for the top of pâtés or poached cucumber or fish.

**Ice**
*To chill white wine or champagne, first stand the bottles in a large plastic container or bath, then pour the cubes of ice over the top. For each case of wine you will need 10lbs of ice.*

## Cooking Salmon
*A good method of cooking salmon that you are going to serve cold is to bake it in the oven. Wash the fish well and lay it on a large piece of foil. Season with salt and pepper and add dots of butter, a handful of parsley and two slices of lemon. Pour over ⅔ white wine. Wrap the fish up tightly, place it in a baking pan and bake in the oven at 400° for 5 minutes to the lb. Remove the salmon from the oven and allow to cool with the foil still sealed.*

For the Harlequin fruit salad first peel the kiwi fruit as thinly as possible; then split them neatly into quarters lengthways. Then cut across into small chunks.

### Four days before the ball
○ Buy any shopping that cannot be delivered.
○ Make mayonnaise, dressings and sauces.
○ Check with the tent contractors or local electrician that someone will be available if the lighting or power should fuse.

### One to two days before the ball
○ If you are using a tent, this should be put up now.
○ Take delivery of the food and distribute it to the helpers.
○ Poach the salmon.
○ Helper 1: make the ham terrines and keep refrigerated.
○ Helper 2: slice the palm hearts, cover and refrigerate. Cook the pasta. Chop peppers for the pasta salad.
○ Helper 3: make the royal icing.
○ Start putting up the decorations (not flowers) and take delivery of the hire equipment.
○ Check the equipment and set up tables and kitchen area.

### The morning of the ball
○ Finish the salmon.
○ Florist: arrange flowers.
○ Decor helpers: complete the decorations and clear up.
○ Helper 1: slice and dish up the ham terrines and cover tightly with plastic wrap. Make sandwiches for the staff, and collect mugs, milk, instant coffee, etc. for staff refreshment, and a coffee-maker if necessary.
○ Helper 2: pack dressings and equipment to finish off the salads there. Hull the strawberries. Cut up the kiwi fruit; mix the sugar, orange juice and kirsch. Take the bananas whole and a knife and board to cut them up before serving.
○ Helper 3: finish the Bakewell pies with jam and icing.
○ When the drinks are delivered, carefully check that it is all there. Make sure the barman checks the stocks with you and ask him to repack all the empty bottles for you to check after the party. (This way you know the wine has been consumed and has not walked off with a dishonest waiter.)

### The afternoon of the ball
○ Collect the food from your helpers or get them to deliver it.
○ Arrange for the two senior waitresses to be in charge of running the service.
○ Give them instructions to set out the tables, buffet, hire equipment, etc. and to finish off the food.
○ Remind them to feed the staff and the band.
○ Run through the bar with the barman and leave him to it.
○ Make sure a waitress will be at the door to take the coats.
○ Make time to get home for a bath and a leisurely change.

### The evening of the ball
○ Arrive early to deal with last-minute problems and to check that waitresses and barman have followed your instructions.

### After the ball
○ Before the staff leave check the drinks and count the empties.
○ See that all dirty dishes, glasses, etc. are neatly packed in the right boxes ready for collection.
○ See that the trash bags are tied and removed to litter area and the venue left clean.

### Next day
○ Remove flowers and see that all equipment is returned.

Cut the bananas diagonally into thick pieces roughly the size of the kiwi chunks.

## Salads
*Any leafy salad should be dressed just before serving as the dressing will cause the leaves to wilt if left for more than a few minutes.*

# HARLEQUIN MASKED BALL RECIPES

QUANTITY NOTE:
Adjust the quantities if catering for a large number. For a buffet for 200 make 15 of each dish (see Catering in Quantity, p. 10).

## HARLEQUIN HAM TERRINE
SERVES 10 AS A STARTER
*1½lb mild cooked ham*
*2 egg whites*
*juice of one lemon*
*⅔ cup vegetable oil*
*salt and freshly ground black pepper*
*4oz haricots verts*
*4 zucchini*
*4 carrots*
TO SERVE
*watercress*
*mustard sauce (p. 131) or*
*Cumberland sauce (p. 158)*

1. Dice and chill the ham. Place in a food processor with the egg whites, lemon juice and oil. Blend until smooth and season with salt and black pepper. Chill. (Alternatively mince and chill the ham, then gradually beat in the egg whites, lemon juice and oil with a wooden spoon.)
2. Top and tail the beans. Wash the zucchini and peel the carrots. Cut the zucchini and carrots into sticks approximately the same size as the beans. Plunge them into separate pans of boiling salted water. Cook the zucchini for 2 minutes, the carrots for 8 and the beans for 5. Rinse in cold water and pat dry.
3. Preheat the oven, setting the temperature control to 350°. Oil a 2qt loaf pan.
4. Spread a quarter of the ham mixture over the base of the loaf pan. Arrange the beans in neat rows lengthways on top leaving spaces a little wider than a bean between each row.
5. Spread a quarter of the ham mixture on top and arrange the carrots in the same way, continue with more ham and then the zucchini, finishing with a layer of ham.
6. Cover with greased wax paper and foil. Bake in the preheated oven in a roasting pan half-filled with boiling water for 2 hours.
7. Remove the foil and paper and loosen the edges of the terrine. Cool overnight.
8. The following day, turn out the terrine and cut into slices. If it will not turn out easily, stand it in hot water for a few seconds. Serve, decorated with watercress, with one of the sauces.

## SALMON TROUT WITH HARLEQUIN COAT
SERVES 10
*1×7lb salmon or salmon trout*
*(or 2×4lb ones)*
FOR THE COURT BOUILLON
*5qt water*
*⅔ cup wine vinegar*
*3 bay leaves*
*2 onions, sliced*
*large handful parsley*
*2 carrots, sliced*
*12 peppercorns*
FOR DECORATION
*finely pared skin of one cucumber*
*1lb canned red pimento*
*2 cups gelatin (packet aspic will do, or see details in 30s Cocktail Party, p. 191)*
*⅔ cup thick mayonnaise*
*1 black olive*
*1 bunch watercress*
TO SERVE
*2 cups green mayonnaise (see p. 151)*

1. To make the court bouillon: put all the ingredients together in a pan and simmer for 20 minutes. Cool.
2. Wash the salmon, making sure that any blood is removed. Remove the gills with a pair of scissors and cut the tail into a neat V. Lay the fish flat in a fish kettle and cover with the court bouillon.
3. Poach the fish very gently (so that the water is just moving but not bubbling at all) for 5 minutes to the 1lb. It is cooked when the dorsal fin will pull out easily. Cool overnight in the bouillon.
4. The following day: remove the fish from the liquid and lay it on a clean dishcloth. Carefully remove the fins, eyes and skin leaving the head and tail intact. Lay it on a serving dish.
5. To decorate the fish: drop the cucumber skin into a pan of boiling water for 30 seconds, then plunge it immediately into cold water. Cut the pimento and cucumber skin into diamonds approximately 1in long.
6. Cool the gelatin until syrupy. Pour ⅔ cup into a flat dish. Using a pin, one by one dip the diamonds of cucumber and pimento into the aspic jelly and then arrange them on the salmon, leaving space for the pale pink fish to show through so that the coat is made up of a pale pink, red and green diamond pattern. Refrigerate.
7. When the diamonds have set onto the salmon, spoon the thinnest layer of gelatin over the whole fish and allow to set. If the gelatin is already too set to spoon, heat it gently and briefly.

8. Cover the eye with half a black olive and pipe a Pierrot's collar of thick mayonnaise around the join of the head or give the fish a ruff of watercress.
9. Cut the set gelatin into ¼in cubes. Decorate the plate with cubes of jelly and watercress leaves.
10. Serve with green mayonnaise.

NOTE:
It is best to remove the bones before serving. Remove the head when cooked, carefully split the fish, remove the bones and sandwich together with mayonnaise.

## RED AND WHITE PASTA SALAD WITH GREEN PEPPERS
SERVES 10
*8oz butterfly (or "bow-tie") pasta*
*8oz red butterfly pasta*
*2 green peppers*
FOR THE DRESSING
*4 tbsp olive oil*
*2 tbsp heavy cream*
*2 tbsp wine vinegar*
*1 tbsp lemon juice*
*1 clove garlic, crushed*
*salt and ground black pepper*

1. Boil the pasta for 5 minutes if fresh (12 minutes if dried) in a large pan of salted water. Drain, rinse in hot water and drain again. Shake well to make sure that all the water has come out.
2. Remove the stalk and all the seeds from the green peppers. Cut into strips 1in wide, then cut the strips diagonally into diamonds.
3. Mix all the dressing ingredients together in a screw-top jar and shake well.
4. Just before serving toss the pasta with the pepper diamonds and dressing.

## CURLY ENDIVE, RADICCHIO AND PALM HEART SALAD
SERVES 10
*1 small curly endive*
*1 small head of radicchio*
*1lb canned palm hearts*
FOR THE DRESSING
*⅔ cup walnut oil*
*2 tbsp wine vinegar*
*2 tsp coarse-grained mustard*
*squeeze of lemon juice*
*salt and black pepper*

1. Wash the leaves of the endive and radicchio in salted water and dry.
2. Drain and slice the palm hearts.
3. Put all the dressing ingredients together in a screw-top jar and shake well.
4. Just before serving toss the salad ingredients and dressing together.

*Above* Harlequin ham terrine (at the top), to be followed by salmon trout with Harlequin coat. The pierrot's ruff round the neck of the fish is piped mayonnaise and watercress. The salad consists of radicchio, curly endive and palm hearts. The diamond design on the Bakewell pie is done with jam and white icing.

## LATTICE BAKEWELL PIE

SERVES 10

*12oz flour-quantity shortcrust pastry*

FOR THE FILLING

*4 tbsp strawberry or raspberry jam*
*⅔ cup butter*
*rind and juice of one lemon*
*2 tbsp light corn syrup*
*⅓ cup sugar*
*2 eggs*
*¾ cup self-raising flour*
*5 tbsp ground almonds*

FOR DECORATION

*pastry trimmings*
*1 egg white*
*sugar*
*3 tbsp redcurrant jelly*
*royal icing (see Victorian Wedding, p. 160)*

1. Preheat the oven, setting the temperature control to 400°.
2. Use the pastry to line one 12in diameter tart pan. Save the trimmings. Line the pastry case with wax paper and fill with baking beans or rice. Bake for 20 to 30 minutes, removing the paper and beans halfway through to allow the pastry to become crisp and brown. Cool.
3. Cream the butter with the lemon rind, corn syrup and sugar until light and fluffy. Beat in the eggs and fold in the flour and ground almonds.
4. Spread the jam over the base of the pastry and spread the filling on top of the jam.
5. Roll out the pastry trimmings thinly and cut into long strips, ½in wide. Lay the strips flat in a diagonal lattice pattern over the filling. Stick the ends down with water or with egg white, brush each strip with egg white and sprinkle with sugar.
6. Bake for 30 to 40 minutes until golden brown and a little firm when pressed on top with the fingertips. Cool.
7. Heat the redcurrant jelly with a little water until it is smooth and just runny. Place it in a pastry bag fitted with a small nozzle. Pipe the jelly into alternate spaces between the pastry lattice. Make the royal icing just runny enough to pour, put into a pastry bag and use to fill the remaining spaces between the pastry. The top should now show only golden pastry, red jelly and white royal icing.
8. Allow the icing to set before serving.

## HARLEQUIN FRUIT SALAD

SERVES 10

*1½lb small strawberries*
*4 kiwi fruit*
*4 bananas*
*2 tbsp sugar*
*⅔ cup orange juice*
*2 tbsp kirsch*

1. Hull the strawberries, rinse and pat dry.
2. Peel the kiwi fruit and cut them lengthwise into three so that you have pieces shaped like orange segments. Cut each segment into chunks about the same size as the strawberries.
3. Just before serving, peel the bananas and cut them diagonally into pieces about the same size as the other fruit. Put all the fruit into a glass bowl, sprinkle over the sugar and pour on the orange juice and kirsch. Mix gently until the sugar has dissolved.

# HARVEST SUPPER
## for Fifty

*Left* Our Harvest Supper is a nostalgic tribute to the days when tired field workers rode home on top of the last haywain or cart, looking forward to a well-earned celebration. From the top clockwise: still cider in a glass jug, a homely apple and damson pie, a whole small Stilton and a wheel of Cheddar, home-pickled pears and wheat-sheaf bread. Autumn fruits (edible or inedible) in a basket make good decorations.

Briony
*When gathering branches and berries beware the highly poisonous briony. The berries look rather like rose hips but are shiny, soft and will be found draped like garlands on bushes. They can appear from late October until early February.*

ENGLISH HARVEST SUPPERS ARE NOT WHAT THEY ONCE were, with the Lord of the Manor providing the goodly spread, the peasantry carousing at one end of the seemingly endless table with the gentry supping hardly more decorously at the other. Today they are more often communal affairs run by the village with everyone chipping in the cost of ham salad, sausage rolls and beer.

But ours is not intended as a genuine celebration for the end of long summer nights of tractor driving and mechanical baling (though it could be) but more as a nostalgic tribute to days when tired field workers riding home on top of the last haywain or cart called "Harvest Home" and looked forward to roast pork and pickles, cheese and home-baked bread, all washed down with gallons of cloudy, powerful hard cider from last year's apple crop, kept for just such a night as this.

One long table is the best arrangement for a Harvest Supper, made up perhaps of a line of trestle tables under the trees in the orchard. But failing the orchard or the weather for such romance, one head table at the top of the dining room or barn, and other tables each set for eight or ten guests would do. We have assumed about fifty guests who will help themselves from a loaded buffet, then sit down.

Harvest Supper decor should of course consist of the fruits of the earth – great sprays of hawthorn berries or shrubs with berries, sloes on the branch, rose hips, elderberries and wild plums. Late flowers like chrysanthemums and dahlias and flowering grasses will emphasize the mellow-fruitfulness theme, and a real corn-husk doll on every table would be an amusing reminder of the earth's fertility.

Preserving and Pickling
*At harvest time gardeners often find themselves with a glut of fruit and vegetables. These can be preserved in several ways: raw tender vegetables such as cucumbers or cooked tougher ones like beets can be pickled by being kept submerged in spicy vinegar. Chutneys and relishes are also easy preserves to make and almost any fruit and vegetables can be used in them. They are sweet and highly spiced and jam-like in texture, whereas the ingredients for relishes are sieved or finely chopped to give a consistency almost like a sauce. Fruits can, of course, be made into jams or jellies.*

*Below* For decorations you could use wild berries and fruits like elderberries, sloes, blackberries and rose hips.

If making corn-husk dolls is going too far and buying them prohibitively expensive, homemade breads can be made into wheat-sheaf shapes and tied with ribbon as a table centerpiece. The buffet or sideboard could be decorated with baskets of polished red apples or grapes, but beware of making the display too like the Harvest Thanksgiving altar in church – avoid large pumpkins, marrows and vegetables generally.

A Harvest Supper should be a better-dressed affair than a barn dance, but no formality is required. The invitation should say perhaps that "Mr and Mrs So and So are invited to an Old-Time Harvest Supper", and leave it at that.

It might be nice to start the party with English country music – "O Dear What Can the Matter Be", "Scarborough Fair" and "Uncle Tom Cobbley and All", even if later the music slips into rock or pop.

## DRINK

Few people would want to drink hard cider or mead right through an evening today, but a glass of either, or a good cider punch to start with, would set the mood, and jugs of wine, cider or beer set on the tables will make serving easier.

A wheat-sheaf loaf is easier to achieve than it looks.

Corn-husk dolls are ancient fertility symbols and provide an attractive reminder of the earth's fertility.

---

**THE MENU**

*Parsleyed Chicken with Green Peppercorns*

*Beef Rib Roast with Horseradish Cream*
*Roast Loin of Pork with Pickled Pears*

*Harvest Salad with Mayonnaise*

*Whole Stilton and Wheels of Cheddar*
*Pickles and Chutneys*

*Wheat-Sheaf Bread*

*Fresh Blackberries*
*Apple and Damson Pie*

---

## GETTING AHEAD
*Six months before the party*
○ Choose a date and place to hold the party.
○ You will certainly need some help with clearing the food and plates from the buffet so engage some helpful friends or paid helpers.
○ Hire trestle tables and chairs.
○ Hire any cutlery, china, glassware or table linen. You should include about 5 condiment sets and butter dishes.
○ If serving coffee, decide how it will be made and hire the necessary equipment (a large urn would do).
○ If the party area is to be decorated with bales of hay, etc. find out where they can be supplied from and how they will be transported to the venue.
○ Find a supplier for hard cider.
○ Arrange how the music will be provided.

*Two months before the party*
○ Make up and send invitations.
○ Make a shopping list and buy as many dry goods as you can.
○ Pickle the pears and store in an airtight jar.
○ Make and freeze the wheat-sheaf breads.

**Coffee**
*To make fresh coffee in quantity proceed as for making tea: pour 5 cups boiling water on to 1/3 cup freshly ground coffee; stir, then leave to stand for 3 minutes. Strain into cups.*

Hard cider in a pewter tankard. The mature cider from last year's crop, it can be deceptively alcoholic.

*Right* A plain wooden table provides a rustic setting for country fare. From the top clockwise: cider cup, roast pork with pickled pears, decorated with rosemary; rare roast beef with horseradish cream; and parsleyed chicken with green peppercorns.

Tips For Freezing
*In order to freeze food successfully it is important to wrap and pack it properly. The texture of food is best preserved by rapid freezing so use the fast-freeze compartment if you have one and pack food in small shallow parcels. Direct contact with the air inside a freezer causes dry discolored patches on the outside of food. Make sure the food is well wrapped and well labelled. The fuller a freezer is, the cheaper it is to run as the frozen food maintains its temperature more easily than circulating air.*

○ Make and freeze the pastry for the apple and damson pie.
○ Decide on the tableplan and make a plan of action for service. Break the number of guests down into tables of eight or ten, then food can be made accordingly in the right number of portions: i.e. the cold meats and cheeses can be served from a main buffet table, but the salad, bread, desserts, etc. can be made the right size for one per table. Helpers can then collect dirty dishes passed down each table, then simply put, for example, dessert plates, an apple pie, bowl of blackberries and pitcher of cream or ice cream on each table for the guests to cope with themselves.
○ Order the cheeses.
○ Order the drinks.

*Two weeks before the party*
○ Order the beef.
○ Order the pork.
○ Order the cream.
○ Make table decorations.

*Three days before the party*
○ Pick greenery and berries for decoration.
○ Buy the dry goods and collect the meat.
○ Collect the cheeses.
○ Make the plain and green mayonnaises.

*Two days before the supper*
○ Cook the chickens, cool and then clear the stock for the jelly.

To Make Mayonnaise
*Beat one egg yolk with a pinch of dry mustard and salt. Slowly add ⅔ cup oil, drip by drip, beating all the time. When about half the oil has been added and the mixture becomes very thick, add 1 tsp lemon juice and 1 tsp white wine vinegar. Continue to add the remaining oil drip by drip. Season well with salt, white pepper and more vinegar to taste.*

○ Cook the beef.
○ Cook the pork.
○ Make the parsleyed chicken.
○ Defrost the pastry.

*The day before the supper*
○ Buy the fresh vegetables, collect the cream, buy or pick the blackberries.
○ Take delivery of all equipment you have hired, check that it is all there and check for any damage.
○ Set the tables up.
○ Decorate the rooms with sheaves of wheat, wild grasses or branches full of berries, and arrange flowers or other decorations.
○ Make the apple and damson pies.
○ Hard-boil the eggs.

*The morning of the party*
○ Defrost the bread.
○ Make the horseradish cream.
○ Place the blackberries in a glass bowl.
○ Dish up the cream, cover and chill.
○ Turn out the parsleyed chicken. Keep chilled.
○ Arrange the cheeses and cover.
○ Set the tables with cutlery, glasses, etc. (so that the guests have to collect only their food from the buffet).
○ Decorate the buffet and the tables.
○ Set up the bar, put out ashtrays.
○ Chill the drinks.
○ Find the tapes or records for the music.
○ Prepare the salad vegetables.

*Three hours before the guests arrive*
○ Dish up the beef and pork. (Service is more efficient if all the meat is pre-carved but the buffet looks spectacular if some of the meat is carved and some left on the bone – the guests can then carve for themselves.)
○ Arrange the salad platters with the mayonnaise.
○ Put a loaf of bread on each table with a dish of butter.
○ Arrange the chicken and green mayonnaise, beef and horseradish, pork and pears, cheeses, pickles and salad on the buffet.
○ Stack the apple pies and berries in boxes (lightly covered with plastic wrap) under the buffet table ready to hand out later.
○ If serving coffee, prepare the cups, saucers, spoons, sugar and cream and the hot water for making it.

*Just before the guests arrive*
○ Add ice and chilled drinks to the bar.

**Clotted Cream**
*This is available in some specialty shops. Or you can easily make your own by placing heavy cream in a heavy-based pan over a low heat. Bring the cream to the boil and boil slowly until it has reduced by half. Allow to cool.*

**Staffwork**
*If the party is to run smoothly and the host-cook-organizer is to have a good time too, he or she needs to make a firm plan of how the meal will be served, cleared and washed up; to make sure all helpers understand their allotted tasks and are prepared to carry them out to the bitter end.*

**Parsleyed Chicken**
*A perfectly good, if less glamorous mold can be made with uncleared jelly. Just put the chicken pieces, parsley and peppercorns with the cool, almost set, stock into a bowl and refrigerate.*

**Washing Up**
*Enthusiasm often wanes at washing-up time when everyone is keen to join the party. Someone must be appointed chief helper and that someone needs to have the personality and powers of leadership to keep the others willingly working.*

*Below* Blackberries picked from the hedgerow are delicious (if they can be obtained). They are much smaller than the cultivated type and generally need more sugar.

# HARVEST SUPPER RECIPES

**QUANTITY NOTE:**
Adjust the quantities if catering for a large number. For 50 people you should make 2 lots of the parsleyed chicken, the pork and the beef; 4 lots of the salad; 4 or 5 loaves of bread and 5 apple and damson pies (see Catering in Quantity, p. 10).

## PARSLEYED CHICKEN WITH GREEN PEPPERCORNS
SERVES 10
*2 medium chickens*
*3 tbsp parsley, finely chopped*
*1 tbsp canned green peppercorns*
FOR THE MEAT JELLY
*5 cups water*
*1 veal hock*
*⅔ cup white wine*
*1 onion sliced*
*1 carrot sliced*
*1 tbsp tarragon vinegar*
*bunch parsley*
*½ tsp salt*
*4 tsp gelatin*
*2 egg whites and shells*
TO SERVE
*mustard or green mayonnaise (see Punk Party, p. 151)*

1. Put the chickens into a large saucepan with a well-fitting lid.
2. Cover with the water and add the veal hock, wine, onion, carrot, vinegar, parsley and salt. Put on the lid.
3. Bring to the boil, then simmer gently for 60-80 minutes or until the chicken legs will wobble loosely and the flesh has shrunk back from the hock.
4. Stand the saucepan in a washing-up bowl or larger pan and set it in the sink, so that the cold tap runs steadily into the bowl or larger pan, cooling the saucepan and its contents rapidly.
5. When the chickens are cold, lift them out, skim the fat from the liquid and strain it into a clean pan. Sprinkle the gelatin on top.
6. Strip the chicken meat from the bones and skin, and cut into neat small pieces.
7. Crush the egg shells and put together in a bowl with the egg whites. Whisk until the whites are frothy.
8. Add the whites and shells to the chicken stock and return to the heat. Continue to beat until the mixture rises and boils. As soon as it begins to rise, stop beating and remove the pan from the heat. Allow to subside.
9. Return the pan to the heat and allow to boil once more, taking care not to break the crust formed by the egg white.

After it has boiled remove the pan from the heat and leave to cool for 10 minutes.
10. Line a sieve with a double layer of muslin. Slip the egg-white crust into the lined sieve and carefully decant the liquid through both crust and sieve. If the egg white or the sediment it collects passes through the sieve, the jelly will not be clear.
11. Once all the stock has dripped through the lined sieve, chill it until nearly set to a jelly. Rinse out a large bowl or mold with water and arrange a neat layer of chicken in the bottom. Pour in enough of the nearly set jelly to hold the chicken in place when it has set. Chill.
12. Sprinkle a third of the chopped parsley and peppercorns on top of the set jelly, add another layer of chicken and just enough jelly to hold it. Chill until set.
13. Continue to layer up the chicken, parsley, peppercorns and jelly until they have all been used. Chill the finished mold in the refrigerator for at least 4 hours until it is firmly set.
14. To turn out: loosen the edge of the mold with the fingertips, dip the bowl briefly into hot water to loosen the jelly. Turn the mold upside down on to a serving plate and give a sharp shake to dislodge it.

## BEEF RIB ROAST WITH HORSERADISH CREAM
SERVES 10
*5lb beef rib roast*
*salt*
*black pepper*
*dripping or lard*
FOR THE HORSERADISH CREAM
*3 tbsp grated, fresh horseradish*
*2 tsp wine vinegar*
*1¼ cup heavy cream, lightly whipped*
*salt and ground black pepper*
FOR DECORATION
*1 bunch watercress*

1. Preheat the oven, setting the temperature control to 425°. Wipe the meat and trim off any excess fat or gristle. Season with salt and black pepper.
2. Put the meat, fat side up, with a little dripping into a roasting pan and place in the hot oven for 20 minutes. Turn the oven down to 375° and then continue to cook the meat, basting it occasionally, for a further 1½ hours. This will give medium-to-rare meat. Extend the cooking time if you prefer it better done.

3. Leave the beef on a wire rack to cool, then refrigerate.
4. To make the horseradish cream: mix all the ingredients together and season with salt and black pepper.
5. Serve the meat decorated with watercress and hand the horseradish cream separately.

## ROAST LOIN OF PORK WITH PICKLED PEARS
SERVES 10
*5lb loin of pork, boned and rolled*
*oil*
*salt*
*black pepper*
*a little flour*
*sprig of fresh rosemary*
FOR THE PICKLED PEARS
*1½lb small firm pears*
*⅔ cup cider vinegar*
*⅔ cup water*
*⅔ cup clear honey*
*6 cloves*
*rind of half a lemon*
*1 small cinnamon stick*
*1 small piece of fresh ginger*
FOR DECORATION
*fresh rosemary sprigs*
*bunch of fresh mint*

1. Preheat the oven, setting the temperature control to 400°.
2. Rub the meat with oil and then salt and flour. Sprinkle with black pepper and push the rosemary into the fold of the rolled up meat.
3. Place in a roasting pan and cook for 2½ hours. Turn the oven down to 350° for the last hour of cooking.
4. Leave the cooked pork to cool, then cover with plastic wrap and refrigerate.
5. To pickle the pears: peel, quarter and core them. Place all the remaining ingredients together in a pan and slowly bring to the boil. Add the pears and simmer gently until quite tender but still whole, about 35 minutes.
6. Lift the pears out with a draining spoon. Boil the liquid until it is reduced and syrupy. Pour over the pears and leave to cool.
7. To serve the pork: cut the meat into thin slices and arrange in an overlapping circle around the edge of a large meat dish. Drain the pears and arrange in a circle just inside the pork. Decorate the pork with sprigs of rosemary and just before serving gather the mint sprigs into a neat bunch, cut the stalks off short and "plant" in the center of the dish, like a bouquet.

## HARVEST SALAD WITH MAYONNAISE
SERVES 10
*1 large Romaine lettuce*
*1lb cherry tomatoes*
*1 bunch of scallions*
*1 cucumber*
*1 bunch of young radishes*
*5 hard-boiled eggs, shelled and quartered*
*1¼ cup mayonnaise (p. 93)*

1. Wash the lettuce and shake dry, leaving the leaves whole. Wash the tomatoes and if they are large ones cut them in half. Clean the scallions, leaving them whole with about 3in of green still attached. Cut the cucumber into shorter sticks about 2in long. Wash the radishes and trim the outer leaves leaving a little stalk at the top of each one.
2. Put the mayonnaise into a small round dish.
3. Arrange the salad on a shallow round serving platter with the bowl of mayonnaise in the center.
4. Put each sort of vegetable and the eggs in neat piles around the bowl of mayonnaise.

## WHOLE STILTON AND WHEELS OF CHEDDAR
The most attractive way of serving these whole is to have whole baby Stiltons or other blue-veined cheese and wheels of Farmhouse Cheddar. They weigh approximately 5½lb and will each be enough for about twenty people. They can usually be ordered from any good delicatessen but check well in advance.

To serve the Stilton: lay the cheese on its side, slice the top rind off, then cut ¾in slices to about halfway down the cheese. Stand the cheese the right way up putting all the slices back together again as though the cheese were whole. Now cut the slices into four or five wedges. Or you can serve the Stilton with a spoon for guests to scoop out what they want.

The Cheddar should have the dark rind removed, then be cut in the same way as the Stilton or simply arranged in a linen napkin for the guests to cut hunks off for themselves.

The cheeses can be decorated with bunches of grapes or celery, scallions and radishes.

Homemade or bought chutneys and relishes give a "country housewife" look to the table and can be eaten either with the roast meats or later with the bread and cheeses.

## WHEAT-SHEAF BREAD
SERVES 10

*½oz fresh yeast*
*1¼ cups lukewarm milk*
*1 tsp sugar*
*4 cups all-purpose flour*
*½ tsp salt*
*1 tbsp butter*
*1 egg lightly beaten*
*extra beaten egg*

1. Mix the yeast with a little of the milk and sugar.
2. Sift the flour and salt into a warmed mixing bowl, and rub in the butter.
3. Pour in the yeast mixture, beaten egg and enough of the milk to form a stiffish dough. Beat the dough until it will leave the sides of the bowl and tip it on to a floured board.
4. Knead the dough for about 15 minutes until it is elastic, smooth and shiny. Put it into a clean bowl and cover with greased plastic wrap. Leave in a warm place until it has doubled in size.
5. Turn the risen dough on to a floured surface and knead again for 10 minutes. Cut off ⅙ and reserve it. Roll the dough into a long sausage as long as your largest baking sheet. Then using a rolling pin make it about 10in wide.
6. Lay the dough on the floured baking sheet. Shape the top round and pinch the dough about a third of the way down to form a "waist".
7. Using a sharp knife, cut the lower section into long strips to look like stems. Lift them up and curl them over each other; cut some different lengths. With a pair of scissors cut large "V"s in the top section, arranging them to look like heads of wheat.
8. Shape pieces of the reserved dough to make more heads of wheat, make small snips in each head to look like seeds of corn. Add several lengths of "rope" to bind the wheatsheaf at its waist. Attach them with a little water.
9. Preheat the oven, setting the temperature control to 425°. Leave the bread to rise again for 10 minutes.
10. Brush the loaf with beaten egg and bake for 10 minutes. Turn the oven temperature down to 375° and cook the bread for a further 30 minutes, brushing with beaten egg a second time during cooking. The bread is cooked when it has turned deep golden brown and sounds hollow when tapped on the underside.
11. Cool on a wire rack and serve sliced with plenty of unsalted butter.

## FRESH BLACKBERRIES
Allow 4oz or 1 cup for each person. Remove any stalks and only if dusty rinse them gently in cold running water. Pile into a glass bowl and sprinkle with sugar. Serve with plenty of pouring cream and extra sugar.

## APPLE AND DAMSON PIE
SERVES 10
FOR THE PASTRY
*2 cups all-purpose flour*
*pinch of salt*
*⅔ cup butter*
*2 egg yolks*
*squeeze of lemon juice*
*very cold water*
*milk*
*sugar*
FOR THE FILLING
*3lb cooking apples*
*1lb damsons, stoned*
*¼ cup butter*
*½ cup sugar*
*2 strips pared lemon rind*
*4 cloves*
TO SERVE
*fresh pouring cream or ice cream*

1. Sift the flour with the salt and rub in the butter.
2. Mix the egg yolks with the lemon juice and a spoonful of water, add to the mixture and mix to a firm dough, adding a little extra water if necessary. Wrap up and chill for 30 minutes.
3. Preheat the oven, setting the temperature control to 400°.
4. Peel, quarter and core the apples. Cut into ¼in thick slices.
5. Melt the butter in a large pan. Add the sugar, lemon rind, cloves and apples. Toss over the heat for 5 minutes until the apples are just beginning to soften.
6. Mix the apples with the damsons and tip into a large pie dish.
7. Roll out the pastry to a circle about 1in larger than the size of the dish. Cut a strip to cover the rim of the pie dish.
8. Damp the rim of the dish with water and press on the pastry strip. Damp the strip with water and cover the whole pie with the remaining pastry. Cut the excess pastry away from the sides of the dish and press the two edges firmly together. Crimp the edge by pinching it between the thumb and forefinger.
9. Make a hole in the center of the pie. Brush the pastry with milk and sprinkle with sugar. Bake for 30-40 minutes until the pastry is golden brown and the apples cooked.

# EASTER EGG PARTY AND TREASURE HUNT

## *for Ten*

Store Easter eggs in a cool place but don't refrigerate them or the chocolate will lose its glossy shine.

**Simnel Cake**
*This traditional Easter cake is a rich fruit cake with a layer of marzipan baked through the center. The cake is decorated with a circle of marzipan around the edge topped with marzipan balls to represent the II faithful apostles. Brush the marzipan with beaten egg and brown briefly under the broiler before filling the center with royal or glacé icing.*

IN AMERICA EASTER MEANS EGGS. CHILDREN PAINT BOILED or hollow hens' eggs, millionaires give jewelled ones to expensive ladies, and everyone eats chocolate ones. Wonderfully pagan symbol of fertility, spring, rebirth and plenty, the egg has been happily muddled into the Christian festival of the Resurrection. The eleven faithful apostles that decorate the top of the traditional Simnel cake (Judas is banished for his sins) are represented by little marzipan eggs.

Hollow chocolate eggs, bunnies and Easter fish are not difficult to make with plastic Easter molds, which can be bought from good equipment shops, and the amateur chocolatier can produce very professional looking bonbons with the aid of toffee molds, pretty boxes and ribbons. But excellent quality chocolates and Easter eggs can be bought ready-made and as our party requires a fair amount of them as prizes in the treasure hunt, we have assumed our cook will concentrate his or her talents on the Easter lunch, all of which is egg-shaped. Nothing is very expensive but, if carefully staged, the meal will be delicious, amusing and very memorable.

We have assumed that this is a two-family party, starting with half-a-dozen children rampaging through the yard hunting for chocolate eggs (ostensibly left by the Easter bunny – a biological phenomenon that doesn't bear questioning) and ending with family lunch that grown-ups and even children, appetites blurred by too much chocolate, will enjoy.

Ideally the morning treasure hunt should last a good half hour so that the adults can have a cup of coffee and a slice of Simnel cake in peace. In practice the children either race through every clue and are back, triumphant and chocolate-fingered in two minutes flat, or they cannot understand the clues and hang around pleading for help. The best treasure hunts are not competitive – every child must have his own series of clues to follow leading to the grand prize. Tears will certainly result from any hunt that allows one child to scoop the pool.

## TO ORGANIZE A TREASURE HUNT
Each child needs about 10 clues to follow. He is handed the first, which leads him to the second, which leads him to the third and so on. He might find mini-prizes on the way, gradually leading to his Easter egg or present.

Dark chocolate, hollow eggs are generally more popular with adults but children prefer milk chocolate eggs with a surprise inside.

**Prizes**
*Candies, cream-filled eggs, chocolate chickens, fluffy rabbits, felt egg cosies make good prizes for the treasure hunt.*

**Clues**
*Write the clues on bright-colored paper so that they are not too difficult to find. Allot one color for each set of clues so that the treasure hunters can easily recognize their own papers.*

The clue-composer should do his composing the day before, if not earlier: he must decide on each hiding place for each child's trail and then write simple clues for small children and complicated riddles for big ones. It takes ages. Allow at least 15 minutes per child just to think them up.

The Easter Bunny needs time to act in secret. So the children must be packed off somewhere, or confined to quarters for at least 30 minutes while the trails are laid. It takes longer than you think, even if the clues are all carefully written out in advance. Clues should be carefully labelled too: Daniel (1) Daniel (2) Daniel (3) Jane (1) Jane (2) Jane (3), etc., to prevent the trail-layer getting in a muddle.

When laying the trail remember that the place hinted at on the slip of paper is not where the paper goes. It is surprisingly easy to get this wrong. For example, if you want the child to look in the tumble-dryer, and you write a clue something like,

*"If you turned my house on*
*I'd twist and I'd tumble*
*I'd probably melt*
*and you'd certainly grumble"*

then that clue must *lead* to the dryer, rather than be in it!

*Right* Primroses and daffodils are traditional symbols of spring. Use them to create a fantasy set-piece with Easter bunnies which the children can enjoy after the treasure hunt. The shepherdess's basket (on the log) contains veal and pork eggs in a vegetable nest.

**Hot Cross Buns**
*These can be served with morning coffee or afternoon tea. Make them from the caterpillar cake bread recipe (p. 214). Shape the mixture into 8 buns and lay shortcrust pastry crosses on the tops. Leave to rise a second time, bake and brush with milk and sugar while still hot.*

**THE MENU**

*Tea Eggs in a Tagliatelle Nest*

*Veal and Pork Eggs with Vegetable Nests*

*Ice Cream Eggs in Chestnut Nests*

## GETTING AHEAD

*Weeks in advance*
○ Fix the date with friends.
○ Start making up clues for the treasure hunt and writing them on cards.
○ Buy wine and drinks for lunch, soft drinks for the children.
○ Make the ice cream and freeze.

*Two weeks before the lunch*
○ Buy all the Easter eggs and prizes.
○ Make a shopping list and buy all the dry goods.
○ Get the children to paint eggs for decoration.

*Below* Give the children acrylic paints to decorate hard-boiled eggs. Smaller children might make splashy abstract designs and careful ten-year-olds could use Easter stencils which they could cut out themselves from thin paper.

Blown Eggs
*Soak blown eggs in bleach and water to clean the inside and to remove any grease from the surface which would prevent the paint from sticking. Seal the painted eggs with a coat of clear nail varnish.*

Easter Decoration
*Fill a large jug or vase with daffodils, pussy willow and other greenery. Hang tiny wooden chicks, rabbits and painted eggs from the branches.*

*Two days before the lunch*
○ Buy all the fresh food.
○ Pick or buy masses of daffodils and spring flowers and arrange them in vases.
○ Allow the ice cream to soften, shape into eggs and re-freeze.

*The day before the lunch*
○ Make the tea eggs, allow to cool, cover and store in the refrigerator overnight.
○ Make and shape the veal and pork eggs.
○ Melt the chocolate for the ice cream eggs, dip the eggs in and re-freeze on an oiled tray.
○ Peel and shred the root vegetables for the vegetable nests, place in a bowl of cold water and refrigerate.

*The day of the lunch*
○ First lay the treasure trail.
○ Set the tables, put out plates, serving dishes, cutlery and glasses.
○ Decorate the table with flowers and painted eggs.
○ Organize the service of drinks and soft drinks.
○ Prepare a tray for coffee.
○ Make the chestnut nests and arrange on the serving plate.
○ Cook the tagliatelle and toss in the dressing; when cool, arrange on a serving dish with the tea eggs in the center.
○ Fry the sausage eggs, make the sauce and simmer for 20 minutes. Allow to cool uncovered.
○ Drain the root vegetables and shred the spinach.

*After the guests arrive*
○ Hold the treasure hunt while the adults have a drink.
○ Reheat the sausage eggs, cook the vegetables and dish up.
○ Serve the ice cream eggs.

Quick Easter Pudding
*Make a plain sponge cake and slice into 3 layers. Fill with mango cream (p. 31) mixed with mandarin oranges and a dash of rum. Coat the whole cake with mango cream and freeze. One hour before serving transfer to the refrigerator and then decorate with mini chocolate eggs.*

*Below:* On the log, tea eggs in a tagliatelle nest.

# EASTER EGG PARTY AND TREASURE HUNT RECIPES

## TEA EGGS IN A TAGLIATELLE NEST

SERVES 10

*10 eggs*
*6 strong teabags*
*8oz green fresh tagliatelle or linguine*
*8oz white fresh tagliatelle or linguine*
*1 cup fine sliced ham, cut into strips*

FOR THE DRESSING

*4 tbsp oil*
*1 tbsp vinegar*
*salt*
*pepper*
*1 tbsp chopped basil or tarragon*
*1 clove garlic, crushed*

1. Put the eggs into boiling water for one minute, then carefully lift out and tap with a spoon to crack the shell all over.
2. Put the teabags into the egg water and return the eggs.
3. Simmer one more minute, then turn off the heat and leave to cool. The eggs, when shelled, will have the tea marbling printed on the white. They will be just soft inside.
4. For the "nests" boil the green and white thin fresh pasta and dress it, when cold, with a vinaigrette made by combining the dressing ingredients.
5. Add the thin strips of ham and toss well.
6. Arrange the pasta and ham in a shallow round bowl, making a hollow in the middle for the tea eggs.
7. Turn the tea eggs slightly in the dressing to give them a shine, and drop them carefully into the tagliatelle nest.

## VEAL AND PORK EGGS IN A VEGETABLE NEST

SERVES 10

FOR THE SAUSAGES

*2lb ground veal*
*2lb ground belly pork*
*2 tsp dried sage or 1 tbsp fresh sage, finely chopped*
*2 cloves garlic, crushed*
*1 egg, beaten*
*8 tbsp fresh white breadcrumbs*
*a little flour for shaping*
*a little shortening for frying*
*salt*
*ground black pepper*

FOR THE SAUCE

*1 small onion, finely chopped*
*1 small carrot, finely chopped*
*a few mushroom stalks*
*1 can condensed celery soup*
*1¼ cups chicken stock*
*2 tsp tomato paste*

FOR THE VEGETABLE NESTS

*8oz carrots*
*2 medium-sized parsnips*
*2 medium-sized turnips*
*8oz fresh spinach*
*¼ cup butter*
*salt and ground black pepper*

1. Put all the sausage ingredients together in a bowl and mix well.
2. With floured hands shape the meat mixture into egg shapes.
3. Heat a little shortening in a large heavy frying-pan and gently brown the sausage-eggs on all sides. Drain.
4. In the same pan fry the onion, carrot and mushroom stalks until soft.
5. Add the celery soup, stock and tomato paste to the pan, and season with salt and black pepper.
6. Return the sausage eggs to the pan, bring to the boil, cover and simmer gently for 20 minutes.

7. Meanwhile make the vegetable nests: shred the carrots, parsnips and turnips into fine ribbons with the julienne cutter of a food processor. With a sharp knife shred the spinach leaves into the thinnest ribbons.
8. Plunge the root vegetables into boiling water then drain them immediately.
9. Heat the butter in a large pan or wok. Add the root vegetables and raw spinach. Toss over the heat until hot and tender, season with salt and black pepper.
10. Arrange all the vegetables around the edge of a heated serving dish to form the nest.
11. Using a slotted spoon lift the sausage eggs into the center of the nest. Boil the sauce down briefly until syrupy, then strain over the sausages.

NOTE:
If you prefer, the "nest" could be mashed potato put through a mincer – it comes out in spaghetti-like strands.

## ICE CREAM EGGS IN A CHESTNUT NEST

SERVES 10

*1 French vanilla ice cream (recipe Creole Party, p. 190)*
*8oz bittersweet chocolate*
*2 tbsp oil*

FOR THE CHESTNUT NESTS

*2 × 1lb cans unsweetened chestnut paste*
*confectioners' sugar*

1. Place the ice cream in the refrigerator for 30 to 40 minutes, or until it is soft enough to scoop out easily with a spoon.
2. Using two large tablespoons, shape the ice cream into egg shapes. Lay them on a metal tray and freeze until they are very hard.
3. Melt the chocolate and oil together in a bowl standing over a pan of simmering water.
4. Lightly brush a metal tray with oil. When the chocolate is cool but still liquid, quickly dip in the ice cream eggs, one at a time, and place them on the oiled tray and re-freeze.
5. Put the chestnut purée through a ricer or mincer, letting it drop on to the serving plate, and dusting with confectioners' sugar as it falls.
6. With two forks, carefully arrange the strands of chestnut purée into a nest shape. Dust the finished nest with more confectioners' sugar.
7. Just before serving, carefully arrange all the ice cream eggs in the nest.

# INDIAN BUFFET *for Forty*

*Left* An ordinary sofa could be given a British Raj look with an Indian bedspread or curtain. Traditional imperial drinks – whisky with a splash of soda or "G and T" (gin and tonic) with a slice of lime – make welcome colonial sundowners. Serve them with spicy nibbles.

NEXT TO VEGETARIAN FOOD, INDIAN FOOD HAS BECOME the hottest fashion among diners-out and cooks at home. What has made modern Indian food so popular is the new availability of genuine Indian spices and fresh herbs, fresh vegetables and fruit. Lemon grass and the curry leaf, freshly ground whole spices, fresh lychees and mangoes have shifted "Indian" food in America and Europe light-years away from the flour-thickened all-purpose curry.

The setting for our Indian buffet should evoke the nostalgic atmosphere of the final years of British rule or the "Last Days of the Raj" because that is the period most easily imagined in terms of decor, with palms in pots, the punkah wallah slowly waving his fan (or more likely propeller fans lazily turning overhead), elephants' feet containing shooting sticks and Benares brass tables supporting gin slings and coolers. But the decor is easier to imagine than to achieve – elephants' feet and punkahs are not available except from specialist companies who hire them out for film sets at a pretty price. It might be possible to persuade the guests to arrive in costume – British army uniform (solar topee and cane-under-the-arm) or dhoti, and the women in that most glamorous of dresses, the sari. But artifacts are more difficult. Apart, perhaps, from some Indian shawls flung over sofas and used as tablecloths, an Edwardian lamp, epergne or glass "lustre", a potted palm or aspidistra, and some borrowed brass knick-knackery, it will be the food that must provide the authentic colonial atmosphere.

Garam Masala
*To make your own garam masala, put 1 in cinnamon stick, a small piece of nutmeg, 1 tbsp cardamom pods and 1 tsp each of coriander seeds, cumin seeds, whole cloves and peppercorns, into an electric grinder until they are all finely ground.*

*Below* An Indian mixture. Top row, from the left: okra, garlic, cumin seeds, coriander seeds, bay leaves. Bottom row, from the left: garam masala, cayenne, fresh ginger, whole cloves and cardamom pods.

**Indian Condiments**
*Indian meals are served with a variety of condiments. They stimulate the appetite with their sharp contrast of texture and flavor.*

The main thing is to have many different-patterned, different-colored and different-shaped dishes, with food simply presented – chutneys and relishes in shallow bowls or saucers, the main dishes and rice on larger flattish dishes. Brass dishes or bowls would be appropriate for serving dishes and pottery plates, if you have some, for the guests. And you must remember to organize enough trays and assistance to ensure that it all arrives on the buffet at once so that guests can pick and choose their way down the array.

Mint and coriander are both easily grown and bought herbs, heavily used in Indian cookery.

> **THE MENU**
>
> *Lamb and Mint Curry*
>
> *Almost Tandoori Chicken*
>
> *Dry Vegetable Curry with Coconut*
>
> *Basmati Rice*
>
> *Yogurt with Scallions and Walnuts*
> *Onion Relish*
> *Apple, Peach and Apricot Chutney*
> *Parathas*
>
> *Sliced Mangoes*

## GETTING AHEAD
*Weeks before the party*
- Choose some cards or postcards to send as invitations. If the party is to be a costume one, include details on the invitation.
- Decide on decorations for the room. Hire or borrow any props you may need. Find brass ornaments and candlesticks and have plenty of candlelight in the room.
- Buy incense sticks.
- Choose music (sitar, etc.).
- Make a list of requirements for the bar, including gin slings, coolers or fizzes. Buy all the ingredients, including plenty of beer.
- Make a shopping list from the recipes and buy the dry goods.

*A week or two before the party*
- Make and freeze the lamb curry, without the mint.
- Make and freeze the parathas.
- Make the apple, peach and apricot chutney. Keep cool.

*Two days before the party*
- Do all the shopping

*The day before the party*
- Marinate the tandoori chicken.
- Make the dry vegetable curry but do not add the fresh coriander.
- Take the lamb curry out of the freezer and place in the refrigerator.
- Clear the buffet room and arrange it for the next day.

*The morning of the party*
- Set the table
- Defrost the parathas.
- Make the onion relish.
- Make the yogurt with scallions and walnut relish.
- Look out serving dishes.

A joss stick or two burning in a corner will permeate the room with the exotic smell of incense.

**Raita**
*Beat together one carton of yogurt and 1 tbsp cream. Add a quarter of a cucumber, grated, 1 tbsp chopped fresh mint, a pinch of cayenne pepper, a pinch of cumin and salt and ground black pepper. Serve raita as a side dish with curries or on its own as a snack.*

Gin Sling
*Mix the juice of half a lemon, 2 tsps powdered sugar, 1 measure of gin and a dash of Angostura bitters, together in a tumbler. Add two ice cubes and top up with soda water.*

○ Prepare the bar.
○ Set a tray for serving tea or mint tea afterwards.
○ Measure the ingredients for the rice.

*Two hours before the guests arrive*
○ Put the lamb and vegetable curries in pans ready to be heated.
○ Put the relishes in serving dishes.
○ Wrap the parathas in fresh foil.
○ Prepare the mangoes, put into a serving dish and chill.
○ Place the tandoori chicken in roasting pans.

Mint Tea
*Use 1 tsp dried mint per cup of boiling water. Leave to stand for no longer than five minutes or the tea will become bitter. Serve in a glass with a sprig of fresh mint.*

Rice
*Make saffron rice by adding ½ tsp saffron strands to the rice before boiling. For spiced rice, fry a little onion, chopped green chili and 1 tsp turmeric before frying the rice; then follow our basmati rice recipe.*

*Right* Clockwise from the top right: Almost Tandoori chicken and basmati rice, tandoori marinade, apple, peach and apricot chutney, dry vegetable curry with coconut, paratha, yogurt with scallions and walnuts, lamb and mint curry. Bottom right-hand corner: onion relish.

*Half an hour before the guests arrive*
○ Preheat the oven to maximum temperature.
○ Put the lamb over a low heat to slowly heat through.
○ Warm the serving dishes.

*After the guests arrive*
○ Cook the chicken in the oven.
○ Cook the rice on the stove.
○ Heat the vegetable curry.
○ Heat the parathas.
○ Just before serving add mint and coriander to the lamb and vegetable curry.

Indian Breads
*Various breads are served with Indian meals, most of them unleavened. Some like paratha or naan bread, have pockets inside which are delicious filled with spicy vegetables or meat.*

# INDIAN BUFFET RECIPES

QUANTITY NOTE:
Adjust the quantities if catering for a large number. If part of a buffet for 40 people, you should make twice the recipe for lamb and mint curry and Almost Tandoori chicken and 3 times the vegetable curry and paratha recipes. But you will need 4 times the basmati rice and double the quantities given for the accompanying dishes (see Catering in Quantity, p. 10).

## LAMB AND MINT CURRY
SERVES 10
*4lb boneless shoulder of lamb*
*¼ cup clarified butter or ghee*
*5 whole cardamom pods*
*2 bay leaves*
*6 whole cloves*
*1 large onion, finely chopped*
*2in piece fresh ginger, finely chopped*
*3 cloves garlic, crushed*
*3 tsp turmeric*
*½ tsp cayenne pepper*
*1 tbsp ground coriander seeds*
*½ tsp garam masala*
*2½ cups strong meat or vegetable stock*
*salt*
*ground black pepper*
*1 tbsp fresh mint, finely chopped*

1. Trim some of the fat from the meat and cut into 1½in cubes.
2. Heat half the butter in a heavy-based frying-pan. Sear the meat on all sides and transfer to a large pan or casserole.
3. Heat the remaining butter, add the cardamom pods, bay leaves and cloves, shake over the heat for a minute.
4. Add the onion, ginger and garlic to the pan, fry gently until soft and lightly browned. Stir in the turmeric, cayenne pepper, coriander and garam masala and fry for one minute. Tip this mixture into the pan with the meat.
5. Pour the stock into the emptied frying-pan and bring to the boil, stirring and scraping any sediment from the bottom of the pan. Pour on to the meat. Season with salt and black pepper.
6. Simmer the meat gently over a low heat for about 1½ hours or until the meat is very tender and the liquid well reduced.
7. Add the chopped mint and simmer for a further 10 minutes.

## ALMOST TANDOORI CHICKEN
SERVES 10
*2 medium-sized roasting chickens*
*1 tsp salt*
*juice of 1 large lemon*

FOR THE MARINADE
*1¼ cups plain yogurt*
*1 clove garlic, crushed*
*1in piece fresh ginger, peeled and sliced*
*2 tbsp tomato paste*
*1 fresh, hot green chili, finely chopped*
*2 tsp garam masala*
FOR DECORATION
*wedges of lime or lemon*

1. Cut the chicken into small joints. Skin each piece and cut slits in the flesh deep enough to reach the bone. Take care that the slits do not start or finish at the edge, or the chicken may curl out of shape and possibly break up when cooking.
2. Rub the chicken pieces with salt and lemon juice and leave to stand for 20 minutes.
3. Mix all the marinade ingredients together, lay the chicken pieces in a shallow dish and pour over the marinade. Cover and chill overnight.
4. The following day: preheat the oven to its maximum temperature. Lift the chicken out of the marinade, shaking off the excess. Arrange the pieces in a shallow roasting pan, preferably on a rack. Bake for 20 to 25 minutes in the hot oven.

5. Serve hot with lime or lemon wedges.
6. Serve the marinade and the juices that run from the chicken during roasting mixed together as a sauce, handed separately.

## DRY VEGETABLE CURRY WITH COCONUT
SERVES 10
*4 tbsp vegetable oil*
*½ tsp black mustard seeds*
*2 tsp cumin seeds*
*2 cloves garlic, crushed*
*1 tsp turmeric*
*1 tsp cayenne pepper*
*1 medium-sized onion, finely chopped*
*2 green peppers, seeded and cut into slices*
*2 carrots, peeled and cut into sticks*
*2 zucchini cut into sticks*
*½ cauliflower, cut into small florets*
*4oz green beans, topped and tailed*
*4oz okra, topped and tailed*
*2 fresh hot green chilies, seeded and chopped*
*½ cup creamed coconut*
*1¼ cups boiling water*
*salt and black pepper*
*3 tbsp coriander (cilantro), finely chopped*

1. Heat the oil in a heavy pan, add the mustard seed, cumin seed and garlic, and fry until the seeds begin to pop. Stir in the turmeric and cayenne pepper and cook for one minute. Add the onion and fry gently until soft and golden brown.
2. Add the vegetables and chilies and stir gently until evenly coated with the onion mixture.
3. Dissolve the creamed coconut in the boiling water, stir into the vegetable mixture and bring to the boil. Season with salt and black pepper. Lower the heat as much as possible, cover the pan tightly and simmer for 20 minutes. The vegetables should be tender with just enough liquid remaining to coat them.
4. Stir in the coriander and allow to stand for 5 minutes before serving.

## BASMATI RICE
SERVES 10
*⅓ cup butter*
*1⅔ cups basmati rice*
*3 cups water*
*1 tsp salt*

1. Soak the rice for 15 minutes, rinse and drain.
2. Melt the butter in a large heavy-based saucepan. Stir in the rice and fry for a minute.
3. Pour in the water, add the salt and bring to the boil, cover tightly and simmer over a low heat for 25 minutes.

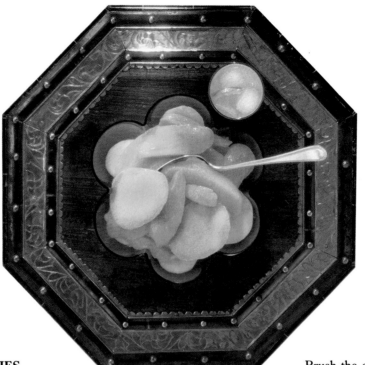

*Left* Thickly sliced, well-chilled mangoes make a refreshing dessert. The smaller mangoes are generally less fibrous and sweeter than large ones. They should feel soft to the touch and look slightly overripe.

## ACCOMPANYING DISHES

### YOGURT WITH SCALLIONS AND WALNUTS
SERVES 20
*1¼ cups plain yogurt*
*2 tbsp coriander (cilantro), finely chopped*
*⅓ cup chopped walnuts*
*5 scallions, finely chopped*
*salt*
*ground black pepper*

Mix all the ingredients together and season with salt and black pepper.

### ONION RELISH
SERVES 20
*1 large onion*
*1 tsp salt*
*juice of 1 lemon*
*½ tsp paprika*
*¼ tsp cayenne pepper*

Peel the onion, cut it in half and slice it very thinly. Lay the slices in a bowl and sprinkle all the other ingredients on top. Mix well. Leave for an hour or more.

### APPLE, PEACH AND APRICOT CHUTNEY
SERVES 20
*1lb cooking apples*
*4oz dried peaches*
*4oz dried apricots*
*⅓ cup golden raisins*
*4 cloves garlic, peeled and crushed*
*2in piece fresh ginger, peeled and
    finely grated*
*2 cups white wine vinegar*
*1¾ cups sugar*
*2 tsp salt*
*½ tsp cayenne pepper*

Put all the ingredients together in a large pan. Bring to the boil and simmer until the chutney is very thick, about 30 minutes. Stir frequently while the chutney is cooking to prevent it from sticking to the bottom of the pan.

Pour into a clean jam jar. Cover with wax paper and then a lid. Cool.

### PARATHAS
MAKES 12
*1⅓ cups wholewheat flour*
*1½ cups all-purpose flour*
*½ tsp salt*
*⅔ cup vegetable oil or clarified butter*
*7 fl oz water*
*extra oil for brushing*

1. Sift the two flours together into a mixing bowl, sprinkle the oil over the top and rub it into the flour as you would for pastry, until the mixture resembles coarse breadcrumbs.
2. Slowly add enough of the water to form a soft but not sticky dough.
3. Dust the worktop with flour and knead the dough for about 10 minutes.

Brush the outside of the dough with a thin film of oil. Wrap in plastic wrap and leave to stand for 30 minutes.
4. Heat a large cast-iron frying-pan or griddle over a low heat.
5. Knead the dough again and divide it into 12 equal balls. Keep them covered while you are working. Take one ball at a time, flatten it and dust it with plenty of flour. Roll it out to a 6in round. Brush oil over the surface of the dough and fold it in half. Brush a little more oil over the surface of the top half and then fold the dough again to form a triangle. Then roll this dough out to a larger triangle with 7in sides.
6. Brush the heated griddle with oil and lay the paratha on to it. Cook for one minute. Brush the top generously with oil. Turn the paratha over and cook the other side for another minute. Both sides should have brown spots when they are cooked.
7. Serve the parathas immediately or wrap cold parathas tightly in foil for later reheating at 400° (this will take about 15 to 20 minutes).

### SLICED MANGOES
SERVES 10
*4 ripe mangoes*
*⅔ cup fresh orange juice*

Peel all the mangoes and cut them into large thick slices. Pour on the orange juice and chill for one hour before serving.

# CABARET IN BERLIN

*for twenty*

*Left* Small tables crowded
closely together, candlelight
and black and red colors
give a nightclub
atmosphere. Old-fashioned
telephones and thirties
prints add an authentic
touch. On the plates, soused
herring with mustard sour
cream.

LIKE "BISTRO NIGHT" ON P. 15, "CABARET IN BERLIN" IS A party broadly based on the cuisine and characteristics of one country – this time Germany. It should be a rollicking, loud, rather *louche* party, with plenty of uncomplicated hefty food, free-flowing wine and good music. Do not try to be subtle or too accurate in menu or design. Never mind if some guests come in Oxford Bags (or even Tyrolean *Lederhosen*) and others arrive dressed as the Master of Ceremonies with white face, white tie and tails. Maybe some of the women will wear forties square-shouldered suits, some sequinned *décolletée*, and some fish-net stockings and leotards, complete with top hat and cane. Never mind. The idea is decadence. Excess and vulgarity are the order of the day.

Anyone who has read or seen Christopher Isherwood's Sally Bowles story as book, play or film will understand the atmosphere to aim for. Perhaps corruption in our nightclub re-creation will not go as far as live pornography acts, or even strip-tease, but the women guests should look as lustful (for sex, food, booze and money) as possible – with dyed blonde wigs and bright red mouths; the men should be elegant and decadent with an air of positively sinister evil.

Small round café tables and gilt chairs (which can be hired from a party contractor) should be packed tightly round a diminutive dance floor. At one end of the room, a stage with piano beside or on it should be contrived. Old-fashioned table-to-table telephones (or modern electronic toy ones) would allow Mr X to proposition Miss Y (for a turn on the dance floor or more exciting things elsewhere) without putting himself to the trouble of walking across the room to her.

Unless this is a big-budget party with real waiters in tails gliding through the guests with circular cocktail trays aloft, or waitresses in high heels and seamed stockings bearing sausages-and-mash on usherettes' "cigarette trays", then buffet tables are called for at one end of the room, or in the next room for guests to help themselves from.

Music should, of course, be for dancing to. It need not be authentically thirties, and indeed should probably be more 1980s disco than 1930s foxtrot. As guests arrive the dusky-voiced Dietrich could be on the record-player. Or the sound track from *Cabaret* could be belting out "Money Makes the World Go Round" or the title song "Cabaret".

Kabanos are widely available Polish pork sausages. Highly smoked, they are fairly spicy and pleasantly chewy.

German Mustards
*These are made from strong mustard flour and vinegar. They are specially blended to complement the sausages of each region but are generally mild, pungent and aromatic. In the north the mustards are hot or extra hot; in the south mild and sweet and in the Rhineland flavored with herbs and often eaten with lamb.*

Choosing Sausages
*Bierwurst is a good German sausage for slicing. When buying black pudding choose a spicy one with small pieces of fat. Bratwurst comes with a smooth or chunky filling and must be cooked.*

A cut-out bow-tie invitation would spell dressed-up frivolity.

INVITATION

## THE INVITATION
Make sure the guests realize that this is a costume affair and the more *risqué* the dress the better. The invitation card might read something like:

**"Take a break from respectability and enter the decadent world of Cabaret in Berlin. No little black dresses, business suits or persons of good reputation allowed."**

## THE WINE
Champagne or German Sekt is the obvious, if expensive, choice. But beer, especially draught beer poured from the jug into great *steins* or tankards, will quench the thirst more while making the revellers just as merry.

If wine is wanted, Moselle is a lot less alcoholic than most (about 8° of alcohol as compared to some reds such as Bordeaux at 11° or Rhônes at 12°) and so is a good choice for all-night drinking. It is also flowery and flavorsome enough not to be quelled by the rustic taste of sausages and mustard. Or red wine could be served – anything soft and easy to drink like a merlot or a gamay.

**German Beer**
*Germans brew lager-type beers which are light in color but not in potency. They are served chilled in tankards or steins.*

**A German Cheeseboard**
*A cheeseboard would be a good addition to our menu. It should consist of Tilsiter, which was originally made in Germany, Munster from the Alsace region, and rich and creamy Bavarian Blue. Serve the cheese with thick slices of rye bread and chopped raw onion.*

### MENU
*Beer Broth with Parsley Dumplings*

*Soused Herrings with Mustard Sour Cream*

*Hot Platter of Smoked Meats and Sausages*

*Boiled Potatoes with Caraway*

*Red Cabbage with Apples*

*Cherry Strudel*

**Dumplings**
*These can be seasoned to complement the dish they accompany. Mustard or grated horseradish with beef stew; caraway is delicious with goulash and herb-flavored dumplings go well with lamb. The secret of making a light dumpling is to make the mixture a little too wet to roll with the hands. Drop it in spoonfuls into the simmering casserole.*

## GETTING AHEAD

*A month or two before the party*
○ Buy cards for invitations and send them.
○ Decide on how the available space will be arranged and include a small area for dancing.
○ Order chairs and tables if you need them.
○ Buy beer, wine and other drinks.
○ Buy paper napkins.
○ Sort out suitable posters, candles and other decorations to create the right atmosphere.
○ Organize the music.

**Tables and Tablecloths**
*Remember to include tables for the buffet and linen to cover each table. The buffet should be at least 6 feet long and will need a 9 foot tablecloth.*

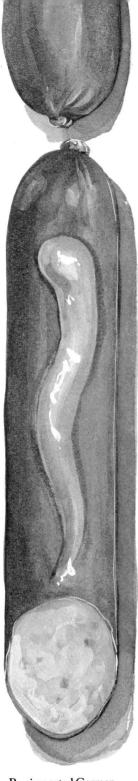

**Strudel Pastry**
*Ready-made strudel pastry can be bought in leaves from good German food shops.*

### A week before the party
○ Make a shopping list from the recipes.
○ Make plenty of ice.

### Two days before the party
○ Do the shopping.
○ Souse the herrings.
○ Cook the red cabbage.

### The day before the party
○ Take delivery of any equipment you have hired.
○ Set up tables, chairs and buffet.
○ Make a space for the bar.
○ Decorate the room.
○ Set up the music.
○ Peel potatoes or, if they are small and new, scrub them only.
○ Make the cherry strudels.

### The morning of the party
○ Set the tables.
○ Arrange candles and suitably subdued lighting.
○ Chill the wine and beer and set up the bar.
○ Make the mustard sour cream for the herrings.
○ Prepare the dumpling mixture but do not add water.
○ Slice the onions for the beer broth.
○ Slice the smoked ham and loin of pork.

### Two hours before the guests arrive
○ Brown the onions for the broth.
○ Dish up the soused herrings, cover and chill.
○ Put pans and steamers ready to reheat the sausages, ham and pork.
○ Prepare a large pan of salted water to boil the potatoes.
○ Put butter and caraway seeds for the potatoes in a small pan.
○ Put the red cabbage and strudels in suitable containers to heat in the oven.
○ Put cream into jugs to serve with the strudels.

### Just before the guests arrive
○ Decorate the herrings and put them on the buffet table with the mustard sour cream.
○ Heat the pans of water you have ready, then heat sausages in the water and ham and pork over it in a steamer.
○ Add cinnamon and ginger to the browned onions and then stock and ale or lager, bring to the boil.
○ Heat the oven to warm the red cabbage.
○ Boil the potatoes.
○ Light the candles, dim the lights and put on some music.

### After the guests arrive
○ Add water to the dumpling mixture and cook them.
○ Dish up the sausages and smoked meats and keep warm.
○ Toss the potatoes in melted butter and caraway seeds and keep warm.

### Just before serving
○ Lift the dumplings out of the broth and keep warm. Add the egg yolks to the broth and reheat without boiling. Season with lemon rind and serve with the dumplings.
○ Place the soup and the main course items on the buffet together and let the guests help themselves.
○ As you serve the main course put the cherry strudels in the oven to warm.

Buy imported German sausages and mustard rather than their imitations.

**Caraway**
*Caraway is related to the anise family and is said to be a digestive aid. In Germany it is called Kummel and is used to flavor the liqueur of that name. It is also used in baking cakes and breads and in the making of Leyden cheese.*

Bierwurst (top) is generally eaten cold but is good hot too. In the middle, black pudding. At the bottom, bratwurst.

# CABARET IN BERLIN RECIPES

QUANTITY NOTE:
Adjust the quantities for large numbers. For 20 guests make 1½ times the beer broth, herrings, hot platter and cabbage. Double the recipe for potatoes and strudel. See Catering in Quantity, p. 10.

## BEER BROTH WITH PARSLEY DUMPLINGS
SERVES 10
¼ cup butter
1lb onions, finely sliced
¼ tsp salt
¼ tsp ground cinnamon
¼ tsp ground ginger
2½ cups light ale, or lager
5 cups beef stock or bouillon
4 egg yolks
grated rind of one lemon
FOR THE DUMPLINGS
2 cups self-raising flour
pinch of salt and ground black pepper
4oz suet, very finely chopped
1 tbsp chopped parsley
⅔ cup water

1. Melt the butter in a heavy-based saucepan over very low heat and in it very gently brown the sliced onions until they are soft, transparent and evenly colored. This should take at least 40 minutes.
2. Meanwhile make the dumplings: sift the flour and salt together and add the suet and parsley. Season with pepper. Mix with water to form a soft dough.
3. With floured hands shape the dough into small walnut-sized balls.
4. When the onions have browned, stir in the salt, cinnamon and ginger, add the ale and beef stock and bring to the boil.
5. Drop the dumplings into the broth, then cover and simmer for 10 minutes. Uncover and continue to simmer for 10 more minutes.
6. Lift out the dumplings with a slotted spoon and keep warm. Mix a little broth with the egg yolks and then pour into the remaining broth and stir, taking care not to boil which would scramble the eggs.
7. Check the seasoning and add the lemon rind. Serve in a large tureen with the dumplings on top.

## SOUSED HERRINGS WITH MUSTARD SOUR CREAM
SERVES 10 AS AN HORS D'OEUVRE
10 herring fillets
3 pickled dill cucumbers
1 tbsp hot German mustard
1 medium-sized onion, cut into rings
1 tbsp capers

FOR THE COURT BOUILLON
2 cups water
⅔ cup cider vinegar
1 bayleaf
6 peppercorns
2 cloves
4 allspice berries
4 juniper berries, crushed
1 tsp salt
FOR THE DECORATION
finely sliced raw onion rings
flat-leaved parsley sprigs
FOR THE MUSTARD SOUR CREAM
⅔ cup carton dairy sour cream
2 tbsp wholegrain mustard
salt and black pepper

1. Preheat the oven, setting the temperature control to 325°.
2. Wash the herring fillets and check for bones. Cut the pickles into quarters.
3. Lay the fillets skin-side down and spread with a little mustard. Scatter over the onion, capers and place a piece of pickle at the narrow end of each fillet.
4. Roll the fillets up and secure with a wooden toothpick. Pack the rolls tightly in an ovenproof dish and add the ingredients for the court bouillon.

5. Cover the dish and bake for 30 minutes. Allow the fish to cool in the liquid.
6. Lift the herrings out and drain well. Arrange on a serving dish and decorate with a few whole peppercorns from the court bouillon, raw onion rings and whole parsley leaves.
7. Mix the sour cream with the mustard and season with salt and ground black pepper. Serve in a separate dish.

## HOT PLATTER OF SMOKED MEATS AND SAUSAGES
SERVES 10
2lb assorted smoked sausages
    (frankfurters, bierwurst, etc.)
1lb blood sausage (black pudding)
1lb smoked ham
1lb smoked loin of pork

*Below* A generous helping of smoked meats and cooked sausages (here, frankfurters bratwurst, bierwurst and black pudding), boiled potatoes with caraway and cabbage stewed with apples, served with German mustards and lager.

TO SERVE
*a selection of mustards*

1. Place the smoked sausages and the black pudding in a large pan of water that is just off the boil. Not-too-hot water will prevent the skins from splitting.
2. Cut the ham and smoked loin of pork into thick strips. Put them in a steamer or colander on top of the simmering sausages. Cover them tightly with a lid or foil and leave them over the heat for a further 20 minutes.
3. Pile all the sausages and meats onto a hot serving platter and hand mustard separately.

## BOILED POTATOES WITH CARAWAY
SERVES 10
*4lb new or small potatoes*
*¼ cup butter*
*1 tbsp caraway seeds*
*salt and ground black pepper*

1. If the potatoes are new, leave the skins on and just scrub them. Peel old potatoes.
2. Cook the potatoes in boiling salted water until tender. Drain.
3. Melt the butter in a small pan over low heat and add the caraway seeds and cook for one minute.
4. Toss the potatoes in the butter and caraway seeds.

## RED CABBAGE WITH APPLES
SERVES 10
*1 medium-sized red cabbage*
*¼ cup dripping or bacon fat*
*1 large onion, sliced*
*2 cooking apples, peeled and sliced*
*2 dessert apples, peeled and sliced*
*1 tbsp brown sugar*
*1 tbsp vinegar*
*⅔ cup red wine*
*4 cloves*
*1 bay leaf*
*salt and ground black pepper*

1. Shred the cabbage and discard the hard stalks. Rinse well.
2. Melt the dripping in a large heavy-based pan, and fry the onion until soft.
3. Add the drained cabbage, apples, sugar, vinegar, wine, cloves and bay leaf, season with salt and ground black pepper.
4. Cover the pan tightly and cook the cabbage over a very low heat, stirring occasionally until the cabbage mixture is soft and greatly reduced in bulk, about 2 hours. Check the seasoning.

## CHERRY STRUDEL
SERVES 10
FOR THE STRUDEL PASTRY
*2 ½ cups all-purpose flour*
*pinch of salt*
*1 egg*
*⅔ cup water*
*1 tsp oil*
FOR THE CHERRY FILLING
*1 cup sugar*
*⅔ cup water*
*stick of cinnamon*
*2 ½lb cherries, stoned*
*½ cup melted butter*
*4 tbsp browned breadcrumbs*
*½ cup ground almonds*
TO SERVE
*confectioners' sugar*
*whipping or heavy cream*

1. Sift the flour and salt into a bowl. Mix the egg with the water and oil and stir into the flour to form a soft dough.
2. The pastry now has to be beaten: lift the whole mixture up in one hand and with a flick of the wrist throw it on to a lightly floured board. Continue until it no longer sticks to your fingers and the whole mixture is smooth and very elastic. Cover and leave in a warm place for 15 minutes.

*Above* A light flowery Moselle or hock (riesling from the Rhine) could be drunk as an aperitif or with the cherry strudel. Good strudel can be made with very finely rolled bought puff pastry instead of strudel pastry.

3. Gently heat the sugar, water and cinnamon in a pan until the sugar is dissolved. Add the cherries, cover and simmer gently until the fruit is soft. Drain and remove the cinnamon.
4. The pastry is now ready for rolling and pulling: flour a tablecloth and roll the pastry out as thinly as possible. Flour your hands well and gently stretch and pull the pastry until it is evenly paper thin.
5. Preheat the oven, setting the temperature control to 400° and grease a baking sheet.
6. Trim off the thick edges of the pastry and brush it with half the melted butter. Sprinkle with the crumbs and ground almonds. Spread the cherries on top.
7. Using the tablecloth to help, roll up the strudel and turn it on to the greased baking sheet. Gently curl each end of the strudel round to form a horse-shoe. Brush with the remaining butter.
8. Bake for 20 to 30 minutes. Take out and dust with confectioners' sugar.

# APHRODISIAC DINNER
*for two*

**Ginseng**
*This is the most legendary of aphrodisiacs. The Chinese called it the root of heaven. It is used as a tonic and to increase sexual vitality. Ginseng can be bought as a root or in powder form and taken as tea or in tablets or capsules.*

ALMOST EVERY FOOD KNOWN TO MAN SEEMS TO HAVE contained magical properties for someone at some time. So planning an Aphrodisiac Dinner is not hard. For a first course you might have bird's nest soup – the Chinese swear by it, though its constituent parts of sea swallow spit, fish spawn and seaweed do not promise well. Casanova and Brillat Savarin (the great French philosopher-gastronome) both thought oysters did the trick, and indeed any seafood is supposed to be pretty stirring stuff, mainly because Aphrodite, Goddess of Love, was born in the sea and was the unlikely offspring of the sea foam and a scallop shell. Less exotic but just as good might be a mussel soup, or shrimp and melon pieces, marinaded together in vinaigrette dressing with ginger (ginger is supposed to further lovers' desires too).

Virility (if not submissive compliance) has always been associated with "good red meat", preferably high and gamey. Spanish wives used to beg the butcher for a cut off the "bravest bull" after a bullfight – to guarantee their husbands' powers. If the cook can contrive beef with a good garlicky sauce, then success must surely be certain – garlic, according to the great herbalist Culpeper "sends up strong fancies to the head". Even celery and carrots "serve well in love matters".

Tomatoes are of course "apples of love". Go easy on the green salad though – Aphrodite is said to have thrown herself on to a bed of lettuce to calm her desires. And there is nothing so cooling as cucumber.

Peaches, grapes, passionfruit, lychees, strawberries and cherries are all lovers' fruits. You might serve them with coeurs à la crème (p. 52) or in a syrup with a dash of champagne.

As this dinner is unashamedly aimed at seduction, the cook-seducer had better plan things well. It's no good getting hot and bothered over the omelets while the intended cools on the couch. So fix things so that the minimum of cooking is last-minute. The food should happen effortlessly and as if by magic, with as little fuss and as much élan as the Emperor Concerto swelling out of the record player.

The table should be laid, the champagne in the bucket, the flowers on the table, the music on the turntable before the door bell rings. The food should be waiting its entrance out of sight.

Because seduction, not cooking, is the whole point of the proceedings, we have planned a wildly expensive and intensely

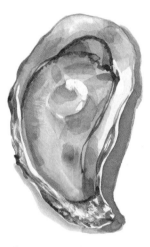

Cold-water oysters from the east coast or tiny Olympia oysters from the west are the gourmet's choice, even if the chances of a hidden pearl are remote. Keep them in a bucket at the bottom of the refrigerator for not more than 24 hours. Make sure they are lying rounded side down – if they open up a little they won't lose their juices.

**Stuffed Eggs**
*If you can't rise to oysters (or if you are someone who dislikes them), then stuffed eggs can be made quite luxurious. For curried eggs mix the hard-boiled yolk with a little curry paste and cream. Top plain stuffed eggs with strips of smoked salmon or a little red or black caviar. Mix chopped shrimp with the egg yolk; spoon into the white and decorate with a whole shelled shrimp.*

*Left* Oysters are said to be great aphrodisiacs. Hot oysters in champagne followed by figs with more champagne might, with any luck, lead to oyster-silk sheets before the evening is over.

*Right* Luxury open sandwiches of beef and asparagus or smoked salmon and shrimp (on the left). On the right, Beluga caviar on ice surrounded by traditional garnishes of hard-boiled egg, chopped parsley and chopped shallots with triangles of rye toast.

glamorous version of the open sandwich for the main course. Sandwiches may not normally equate with glamor but this one does. It is a veritable cliché of rich wooing – smoked salmon, caviar, and rare beef. The first course is exotic and rich without being much trouble to make. The dessert, if the participants have not left for the bedroom before they get to it, is wicked and wonderfully delicious – a chocolate truffle par excellence.

## WINE
Champagne of course – only the best and most expensive vintages naturally – followed by the best red wine that money can buy. Finally a half bottle of Château d'Yquem or other excellent dessert wine to follow the chocolate. Don't drink it *with* it. That would be too much of a good thing. Have it with the grapes.

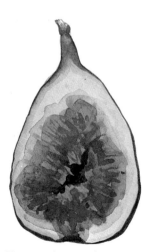

Figs somehow combine freshness with decadence. Buy them on the ripe side, squashy and tender.

Serving Wine
*Most white wines and the lighter reds and rosés are at their best at lower temperatures. Served between 40° and 48°. Chilling wine in an ice bucket will be more efficient if the bucket is filled with ice cubes and cold water rather than ice cubes alone.*

### THE MENU
*Oysters in Champagne*

*Brown Bread with Smoked Salmon and Shrimp in Lime Mayonnaise*
*Rye Toast with Caviar*
*Rare Roast Beef on Sesame Bread*

*Chocolate Truffle Pots*

*Grapes, Pomegranates or Figs*

## GETTING AHEAD
*Days in advance*
○ Arrange the rendezvous.
○ Buy champagne, wine and liqueurs.
○ Make fish stock and freeze.
○ Make cheese sablés pastry and freeze.

Cheese Sablés
*Make cheese pastry (use half the quantity given for Cheshire Cat cookies p. 214), roll it out to ⅛in thick. Stamp out small rounds with a plain pastry cutter. Chill for thirty minutes, dust with paprika and bake at 400° for 8-10 minutes.*

*Left* Chocolate truffle dessert decorated with chocolate rose leaves. The mixture is as rich as it is boozey so serve modest helpings lest sleep overtake the object of your affections.

### The day before

○ Make a list from the recipes and buy all the shopping, except for the oysters which should be ordered specially.

○ Make the sauce for the oysters in champagne.

○ Make the chocolate truffles and paint the chocolate leaves. Chill.

○ Defrost sablés pastry and bake. Store in an airtight container.

### The day of the dinner

○ Set the table and arrange candlelight, flowers, elegant wine glasses and champagne bucket.

○ Set the tray for coffee. Arrange a bowl of grapes, pomegranates or figs and put them on the coffee tray. Leave space to stand the chocolate truffle so that there is no need to leave the table once the dessert stage is reached.

○ Chill the champagne and any wine.

○ Chop the chervil or parsley for the oysters in champagne.

○ Organize the music.

### An hour before the dinner

○ Put the sauce for the oysters in a pan ready to reheat. Open the oysters (if not opened already) and have them and their juices ready to add at the last minute.

○ Make the coffee cream for the truffle, pipe it and decorate with leaves and set on the coffee tray.

○ Make the open sandwiches and cover firmly with plastic wrap, keep in a cool place.

○ Arrange the caviar and decoration, cover and keep cool. Slice the rye bread and have it ready with butter to toast at the last minute.

### After the victim has arrived

○ Heat the champagne sauce and add the oysters just before serving.

○ Toast and butter the rye bread.

○ Turn on the music and slide into action.

**Oysters**
*The best time for buying these is in the autumn when they are not spawning. Most are eaten raw. Serve them on the half shell on a bed or crushed ice with wedges of lemon and Tabasco. Pacific oysters are tough and usually cooked.*

**Caviar**
*This is the salted roes of the sturgeon. Beluga caviar has the largest grains and is the most sought after. Sevruga is smaller-grained. Salmon caviar is red and is good served with smoked salmon and a wedge of lime. All caviar should be kept cool and eaten within two days of opening.*

**Rye Bread**
*This is made with rye flour mixed with varying proportions of wheat flour. Light rye bread has caraway seeds added. Both light and dark rye bread have a slightly sour flavor and are best used thinly sliced for sandwiches.*

# APHRODISIAC DINNER RECIPES

## OYSTERS IN CHAMPAGNE
*1 tbsp butter*
*1 shallot, finely chopped*
*2 scallions, finely chopped*
*1 tsp all-purpose flour*
*⅔ cup strong fish stock*
*⅔ cup champagne*
*12 oysters and their juices*
*salt and ground white pepper*
*chopped chervil or parsley*
TO SERVE
*cheese sablés (see margin note, p. 116)*

1. Melt the butter in a heavy-based pan and gently fry the shallot and scallions until soft but not at all colored.
2. Add the flour and continue to cook for a further minute. Slowly pour on the stock and champagne, stirring continuously until the liquid is boiling. Simmer for 15 minutes.
3. Add the oysters and juice, season with salt and white pepper and simmer for 5 more minutes.
4. Sprinkle in the chervil and serve immediately with cheese sablés.

NOTE:
To open the oysters, wrap a dish cloth around your left hand and in it place an oyster with the deeper shell downwards (to catch the juices). Push a wide bladed, short rigid knife hard into the hinge and twist to open. Or better still, have the fish shop to do it for you – a scratched hand could interfere with romance and spoil the whole evening.

## BROWN BREAD WITH SMOKED SALMON AND SHRIMP IN LIME MAYONNAISE
*2 slices wholewheat bread*
*butter for spreading*
*4 × 1oz slices smoked salmon*
*salt and ground black pepper*
*2 tsp thick mayonnaise*
*1 lime*
*1oz shelled shrimp*
FOR DECORATION
*cayenne pepper*
*watercress*

1. Thickly butter the bread. Fold each slice of smoked salmon in half and place two on each slice of bread.
2. Grate a little of the lime rind, and add it to the mayonnaise with a squeeze of juice and salt and pepper, if necessary. Cut two thin slices from the lime and set aside.
3. Stir the shrimp into the mayonnaise and place a spoonful on top of the salmon to one end of each slice of bread.

4. Make a small cut in the slices of lime, twist into an S shape and place near the spoonful of shrimp mayonnaise.
5. Sprinkle cayenne pepper over the shrimp mixture and decorate with a small bunch of watercress.

## RYE TOAST WITH CAVIAR
*1 hard-boiled egg*
*small jar Beluga or Sevruga caviar*
*1 shallot, finely chopped*
*chopped parsley*
*thin slices rye bread*
*butter for spreading*

1. Separate the egg yolk from the white, sieve the yolk and chop the white finely, using a stainless steel knife.
2. Put the caviar jar on to a plate and decorate the plate with a cluster of chopped shallot, egg yolk, egg white and chopped parsley.
3. Serve with hot buttered rye toast.

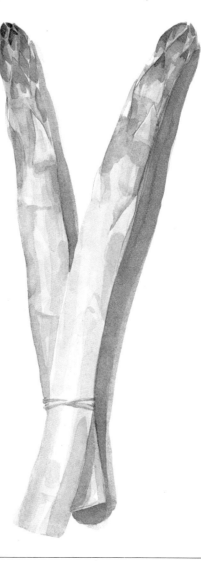

## RARE ROAST BEEF ON SESAME BREAD
*4 small round slices sesame bread*
*butter for spreading*
*1 tbsp horseradish cream*
*12 thin slices rare rolled rib roast*
FOR DECORATION
*watercress*
*4 spears cooked asparagus*

1. Butter each slice of bread and spread with horseradish cream.
2. Fold the slices of beef in half and place three on each slice of bread with the fold uppermost to give height.
3. Decorate with a small bunch of watercress and spears of asparagus.

NOTE:
Buttering the bread thickly will prevent the sandwich from becoming soggy if made in advance. Make sure that all the sandwiches are covered (loosely but with no air-gaps) in plastic wrap to prevent drying out.

## CHOCOLATE TRUFFLE POTS
*6 Amaretti-type cookies*
*2 tsp brandy*
*3oz bittersweet chocolate*
*3 tbsp heavy cream*
FOR DECORATION
*1oz bittersweet chocolate*
*2 leathery rose leaves or pliable holly leaves*
*2 tbsp heavy cream, whipped*
*½ tsp instant coffee powder*

1. Put the cookies into the bottom of two small china pots or elegant shaped glasses. Sprinkle one teaspoon of brandy into each.
2. Melt the chocolate in a basin set over a pan of simmering water. Allow to become cool but not set.
3. Whip the cream, fold in the cooled but still liquid chocolate and spoon on top of the ratafia cookies. Chill for several hours until set.
4. Meanwhile make the decoration: melt the chocolate over a pan of simmering water. Wash and dry the rose or holly leaves. With a small paintbrush paint the *underside* of the rose or holly leaves with melted chocolate and leave, chocolate side up, to set. Fold the instant coffee powder into the whipped cream and place in a pastry bag fitted with a ½in star nozzle.
5. When the chocolate truffle has set, pipe a whirl of coffee cream on top of each one. Peel the rose or holly leaves off the chocolate and decorate each whirl of cream with a chocolate leaf.

*for twelve*

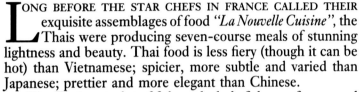

**Saté**
*Serve tiny saté sticks as an additional snack (see recipe in Barbecue in the Backyard, p. 175). Cut the meat into ½in cubes before marinading. Thread on to toothpicks and broil. Serve on a round plate with peanut sauce in the center.*

LONG BEFORE THE STAR CHEFS IN FRANCE CALLED THEIR exquisite assemblages of food *"La Nouvelle Cuisine"*, the Thais were producing seven-course meals of stunning lightness and beauty. Thai food is less fiery (though it can be hot) than Vietnamese; spicier, more subtle and varied than Japanese; prettier and more elegant than Chinese.

The Thais eat a lot of fish, and whole fish are often served in beautiful fish-shaped china dishes. The whole baked sea bass in our Al Fresco Lunch is a Thai recipe, and would make a good alternative to the gaeng ped nua on a buffet table.

If the food can be wittily made to look like something else – if a carrot looks like a fern leaf, a radish like a lotus blossom, and a sandwich like a tiny fish or a pagoda, so much the better.

Flowers, particularly orchids and jasmine (which grow like weeds in Thailand) are a national addiction. Floral garlands hang on everything – bedside lamps, the prow of a boat, the rear-view mirror of a truck, the handlebars of a bike and, most certainly, around the necks of honored guests.

Cooking a Thai dinner is not difficult if the ingredients are available, which they are in the major American and European centers. But Westerners will not behave with the gentle and civilized manners of the Thais. They won't bring their hands together in front of the face (eyes level with fingertips and head bowed) in greeting and farewell. They won't sit neatly, soles of the feet on the ground or tucked away lotus-fashion – to point the feet at anyone is deeply insulting. There won't be, as there are in high-born Thai households, servants shuffling round the table on bended knee, carefully keeping their heads below the level of the guests' and bowing out smiling and backwards. But never mind. If the food is genuinely Siamese, a few Thai-like flower bowls are arranged, and perhaps some Thai pottery or ornaments assembled, an unusual and undoubtedly delicious party can be had.

**A Thai Menu**
*A classic Thai menu centers around a large bowl of plain boiled or steamed rice. This is surrounded by dishes of soup and dishes of steamed or fried food, a curry, salad and dipping sauces. Dessert would be fresh fruit and a sticky sweetmeat.*

*Below* (From the left) fresh lychees, ripe rambutans and kumquats.

Lemon Grass
*This is one of the ingredients which gives Thai food its aromatic quality. Occasionally it can be found fresh, in ethnic supermarkets. If not, use it dried or substitute fresh lemon balm leaves.*

Our menu is long and complicated – with a selection of snacks to start with, then soup, then a Thai curry and rice, a salad and finally fruit. The snacks could be omitted from the buffet or could be served on their own at a Thai-flavored drinks party. They are very typical and pretty, however, and easier to make than they appear.

THE MENU

*Fried Crab Cakes*

*Pork in a Green Net*

*Quail-Egg Flowers*

*Thai Mushroom Soup*

*Gaeng Ped Nua*

*Steamed Rice*

*Shrimp and Papaya Salad*

*Thai Fruit Tray*

*Peanut Flower Cookies*

NOTE:

Some of the ingredients for an authentic Thai flavor such as nam pla (Thai fish sauce) can only be had from specialist Thai shops, or sometimes from Chinese supermarkets. For this reason, we have given both the English and Thai names for little-known foodstuffs.

GETTING AHEAD
*Weeks or days before the buffet*
○ Telephone the guests to invite them or send invitations made of cards and pressed flowers.
○ Make a shopping list from the recipes, buy the dry goods and the Thai ingredients.
○ Organize some delicate pottery to serve the meal on.
○ Find some bowls to arrange flowers in.

*Two days before the buffet*
○ Shop for the fresh ingredients.
○ Make the Thai mushroom soup, but do not add the scallions. Cool, cover tightly and then chill.
○ Make the spicy red beef to stage 2. Cool, cover and chill.
○ Make the peanut flower cookies and store in an airtight container.

*The day before the buffet*
○ Pick or buy some fresh flowers and fill the dining room with exotic flower arrangements. Make several flower bowls for the table and for decorating coffee and drinks trays. Keep back 12 flowers to make napkin rings with.
○ Make and steam the crab cakes, cover and leave overnight.
○ Make and shape the pork sausages, but do not cook them. Cover and chill. Prepare the cucumber strings.
○ Boil the quails' eggs for 3 minutes. Shell and store in a bowl of cold water overnight.
○ Make the dressing for the shrimp and papaya salad.

*Right* A Thai fruit-basket arranged on woven fresh banana leaves and served with coarse salt. The reddish-brown hairy fruits (here half-peeled) are rambutans, the unpeeled ones are lychees. Sliced papaya (the pink strips) and mango. The mini-oranges are kumquats which are eaten raw and whole.

Scallion Flowers
*These can be made for dipping into sauces. Use small scallions and trim them to 2in long. Cut the green part into fine shreds, leaving the white part of the scallion whole. Soak in iced water for at least two hours. The green will curl like petals.*

Quail-egg flowers made with pickled cucumber ends and quail eggs make amusing cocktail snacks.

Fine ribbons of cucumber give spicy cocktail sausages a new look.

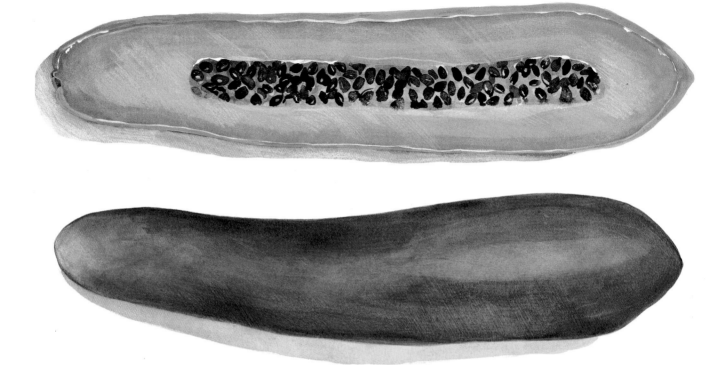

*Above* Thai papayas (malagos) are occasionally available from specialist food shops. Green when underripe, the flesh gradually becomes pink and the seeds black. Serve as melon with sugar or salt.

**Custard Apples**
*These have soft, light green segmented rind. When the fruit is ripe the segments break away, exposing the creamy custard-like pulp. It is native to Asian countries and is also known as the sugar apple.*

### On the day

○ Set the table, making it look as pretty as possible with flowers and delicate-colored table linen.
○ Bind the napkins with flowers and colored ribbons.
○ Arrange a drinks tray and coffee tray with a small bouquet of flowers on each.
○ Set the peanut flower cookies on a small plate to serve with coffee.
○ Make the cucumber flower cups and soak them.
○ Turn the quails' eggs in the soy mixture and leave to cool.
○ Shred the scallions for the soup.
○ Slice the red peppers for the spicy red beef.
○ Fry the pork sausages and wrap in the cucumber nets.
○ Prepare the ingredients for the shrimp and papaya salad.

### An hour before the guests arrive

○ Arrange the shrimp and papaya salad but do not dress. Cover and chill.
○ Prepare the Thai fruit tray, cover and chill.
○ Put the quails' eggs in the cucumber flowers and arrange on a serving plate with the pork in green nets, decorate with flowers.
○ Put the mushroom soup and spicy red beef in pans ready to heat up.
○ Put plates into the oven to keep warm.
○ Rinse the rice in cold water.

### After the guests arrive

○ Fry the crab cakes and serve them immediately with the other snacks.
○ Heat the soup and add the scallions just before serving.
○ Heat the spicy red beef and add the remaining ingredients.
○ Cook the rice.
○ Dress the salad.

**Peanut Cookies**
*Chill the peanut cookies for 30 minutes before baking to make sure that they retain their shape.*

**Steaming**
*This is one of the simplest and fastest methods of cooking food. A whole meal can be cooked in a multi-tiered steamer. Steamed foods retain their color, texture, flavor and almost all the nutrients.*

# THAI BUFFET RECIPES

## FRIED CRAB CAKES
MAKES 12
*3 eggs*
*oil or butter*
*6 tbsp chopped fresh coriander (cilantro)*
*    leaves*
*1 tsp freshly ground black pepper*
*2 cloves garlic, crushed*
*8oz frozen white crabmeat*
*¼ cup creamed coconut*
*2 tbsp nam pla (Thai fish sauce)*
*juice of half a lime*

1. Separate the eggs. Oil or butter 12 small ramekins or foil cases.
2. In a food processor beat to a paste all the ingredients except one egg yolk and the egg whites.
3. Beat the egg whites to a stiff snow that will hold its shape.
4. Fold the whites into the crab mixture, and fill the containers.
5. Use the remaining egg yolk (beaten with a little salt) gently to brush the top of the little soufflés.
6. Steam for 15 minutes or bake sitting in half-an-inch of hot water in a roasting pan at 300° for 25 minutes. Cool, then turn out of the molds.
7. Just before serving fry the crab cakes in hot oil to brown them.

## PORK IN A GREEN NET
MAKES ABOUT 12
FOR THE NETS
*the skin of a cucumber*
FOR THE PORK BALLS
*8oz extremely finely ground pork or*
*    sausage meat*
*2 tbsp nam pla (Thai fish sauce)*
*2 tsp sugar*
*3 tbsp fresh coriander (cilantro) leaves,*
*    chopped*
*1 small clove garlic, crushed*
*2 red fresh chilies, seeded and chopped*
*salt and pepper*
*2 tbsp frying oil*

1. Mix the pork ball ingredients together, adjusting the amount of chili used to taste. (Fry a little mixture if you are reluctant to taste it raw.) Shape into about 12 small sausages.
2. Fry the pork sausages in a little oil in a wok or frying-pan, rolling them about to brown them well. When firm and cooked, drain and allow to cool.
3. To make the green nets: simply peel the cucumber in long strips and cut the strips into the finest strings. Plunge the strings of peel quickly into boiling water for one minute, then rinse, drain and cool them.

4. When the sausages are cold use the cucumber strings to bind them by winding the cucumber round and round the sausages or in a criss-cross pattern. Oil the sausages to make the cucumber stick to them. Stick a toothpick into one end of each sausage.

## QUAIL-EGG FLOWERS
MAKES 12 FLOWERS
*6 small, fat, pickling cucumbers*
*3 tbsp wine vinegar*
*3 tbsp sugar*
*3 tbsp water*
*1 tbsp salt*
*oil for frying*
*1 clove garlic, crushed*
*½ tsp black peppercorns, coarsely crushed*
*pinch ground coriander*
*4 tbsp soy sauce*
*1 tbsp brown sugar*
*12 hard-boiled quails' eggs*

1. Cut a 1in piece from each end of each cucumber. It is the ends that are used, so reserve the middle sections for use in a later dish.
2. With a melon baller, scoop most of the flesh out of the cucumber ends to make thick small cups. With a sharp knife cut the rims of the cups deeply, zig-zag fashion, to form flower cups with petals.
3. Mix the wine vinegar, sugar, water and half the salt together and soak the cucumber flowers in this for half an hour.

*Above* Quail-egg flowers and pork in a green net decorated with an orchid. Top left, radish roses and fresh lime.

4. Heat a tablespoon of oil in a wok or frying-pan and when hot add the remaining salt, garlic, pepper, coriander, soy sauce and brown sugar.
5. Shell the eggs carefully and turn in the hot soy mixture until evenly brown. Allow to cool in the sauce, turning occasionally.
6. When cold put a quail egg into each cucumber flower (well drained) and spear a wooden toothpick through both, like a stalk, to hold them together.

## THAI MUSHROOM SOUP
SERVES 12 SMALL PORTIONS
*10 large dried Chinese mushrooms*
*5 cloves garlic, peeled*
*2 tbsp coriander (cilantro) leaves, chopped*
*1 tsp black peppercorns*
*2 tbsp soya oil*
*10 cups good chicken stock*
*2 tbsp nam pla (Thai fish sauce)*
*3 skinless, boneless chicken breasts, cut into*
*    even small shreds*
*1 bunch very fine scallions, washed*

1. Soak the mushrooms in hot water. Leave for one hour or until pliable.
2. In a coffee grinder or mortar, pound the garlic, coriander (cilantro) leaves and peppercorns.

*Left* Fried crab cakes (surprisingly easy to make and quite delicious) here are decorated with radish roses and coriander leaves.

3. Heat the soya oil and in it fry the coriander and garlic paste, stirring over the heat for a minute or two.

4. Remove the stems from the mushrooms, cut the rest into pieces. Add the chicken stock, nam pla and mushrooms to the hot paste.

5. Bring to the boil, then turn down the heat and simmer very gently until the mushrooms are tender – perhaps 20 minutes.

6. Add the chicken shreds and poach gently until they are cooked (about 2 more minutes).

7. Using a very sharp knife, shred the white ends of the scallions with a little of the green, lengthwise.

8. Add the scallion shreds to the soup one minute before serving – just long enough to allow the onions to soften slightly without spoiling their bright color at all.

## GAENG PED NUA
### (spicy red beef)
SERVES 12 SMALLISH PORTIONS
*2 tbsp Thai red curry paste*
*3lb braising steak cut in strips*
*3 tbsp oil for frying*
*1 stalk lemon grass, cut into short pieces*
*few makrut (citrus) leaves*
*5 cups coconut milk made from blending*
*    together 1½ blocks creamed coconut and*
*    4 cups water (or use canned coconut milk)*
*2 tbsp nam pla (Thai fish sauce)*
*½ tsp sugar*
*2 red peppers, seeded and cut in strips*
*bunch fresh horabha (basil)*

*Above* Thai mushroom soup with scallions and coriander is delicious and would make a pleasantly unusual starter to a more conventional dinner too.

*Below* Gang ped nua (spicy red beef) served with rice.

1. Fry the curry paste in the oil in a large wok or pan for a minute or so, then add the strips of beef and fry while turning, to coat the meat well in the paste. Cover with water and add the lemon grass, and broken-up makrut leaves.

2. Simmer until the meat is tender (about one hour), then add the coconut milk and reduce until the sauce is thick and oily.

3. Add the fish sauce, sugar and red peppers and simmer until the peppers are just cooked.

4. Finally add the horabha leaves.

5. Serve the gaeng ped nua with steamed or boiled rice.

NOTE:
If the sauce curdles (which it frequently does with no ill effects) it can be "brought back" by beating vigorously.

## SHRIMP AND PAPAYA SALAD
SERVES 12
*1 small head Chinese cabbage*
*2 small papayas*
*3 ripe firm tomatoes*
*small bunch thin scallions*
*1lb cooked, shelled shrimp*
*4 tsp salted peanuts*
FOR THE DRESSING
*3 fresh small green chilies*
*4 limes*
*3 tsp nam pla (Thai fish sauce)*
*1 tsp sugar*

1. Wash, dry and finely shred the Chinese cabbage.

2. Peel, seed and thinly slice the papayas.

3. Dip the tomatoes into boiling water for 10 seconds, peel them and cut into slivers.

4. Wash the scallions and shred them lengthwise.

5. Split the chilies and remove the seeds. Cut the flesh very finely.

6. Grate the rind of one of the limes very finely and squeeze the juice of all of them.

7. Mix the lime rind, juice, nam pla, sugar and shredded chilies together.

8. Choose a large, shallow bowl and in it arrange all the salad ingredients as prettily as possible.

9. Sprinkle the salad evenly with the dressing.

## THAI FRUIT TRAY
Buy as many exotic fresh fruits as possible. Typical Thai fruits would be rambutan, lychee, papaya, mango, carambola (star-fruit), prickly pear,

loquat, custard apple, mangosteen, pummelo, jackfruit. Persimmons are not Siamese but no matter – probably no one will know, and they certainly look wonderful.

Peel or prepare each fruit and arrange on a large tray, preferably covered with a banana leaf, in a formal pattern. Do not pile the fruit up in the Western fashion. There should only be one layer. Decorate with fresh flowers or leaves.

Put a pile of small plates or saucers and paper napkins next to the fruits and perhaps a large communal fingerbowl full of slices of fresh lime and floating rose petals.

Provide a dish of coarse sea salt too. Fruit is often served with salt in Thailand.

#### RAMBUTAN
Leave some of the rambutans whole and cut through the hard shell of the others so that you can remove half of it, leaving the fruit lying in the other half-shell.

#### LYCHEE
Leave the lychees whole, and preferably in bunches for the guests to tackle themselves.

#### PAPAYA
Skin and slice the papayas and provide wooden toothpicks for the guests to help themselves.

#### MANGO
As for papaya.

#### PRICKLY PEAR
Wearing rubber gloves, rub the prickly pears in a newspaper or cloth to remove all the prickly spines. Peel and slice across into rounds. Leave one or two whole for decoration.

#### LOQUAT
Leave the loquats whole and in bunches if possible.

#### CUSTARD APPLE
Split a few custard apples in half and provide spoons to eat them with. The flesh is creamy.

#### MANGOSTEEN
These are very difficult to deal with. Carefully cut each mangosteen as if you would slice it in half but only cut through the thick purple shell and not into the

*Right* Peanut flower cookies and whole raw kumquats with, above, pink rose petals in a finger bowl. A drop of rose flower water will perfume the water too.

fruit. Lift one side of the shell off, leaving the whole fruit lying in the other half-shell. The flesh should be pure white, not stained with brown or purple (which indicates bruising).

#### PUMMELO
Peel and extract the juicy segments, and arrange them attractively.

#### CARAMBOLA (STAR-FRUIT)
Slice one fruit across into star-shaped discs, and leave one or two whole.

#### PERSIMMONS
Cut the fruit into neat quarters, and then again into eighths, as one would a tomato.

#### JACKFRUIT
Jackfruit are enormous, and very sticky to deal with. Wear rubber gloves and remove the skin and the spongy, pulpy, tasteless flesh. What is eaten is the flesh around each brown seed. Remove the seeds with the surrounding layered flesh, pile them in a corner of the tray, each one speared with a toothpick for easy management. (The seeds are not eaten raw but can be roasted or baked like potatoes.)

*Above* Shrimp and papaya salad makes a light, unusual and exceptionally pretty dish, perfect for a hot day.

## PEANUT FLOWER COOKIES
MAKES ABOUT 80 COOKIES
⅔ cup butter
1 cup sugar
1 large egg, beaten
⅔ cup smooth peanut butter
½ tsp vanilla
1¾ cups all-purpose flour
1 tsp baking powder
½ tsp salt

1. Cream the butter and sugar together until smooth, light and soft.
2. Beat in first the egg, then the peanut butter and vanilla.
3. Sift the flour with the baking powder and salt and stir into the mixture.
4. Roll all but one large tablespoon of the mixture into marble-sized balls with the fingers and put, well apart, on three ungreased baking sheets.
5. With a sharp small knife cut each ball across, as if to cut it in half, but without cutting more than halfway through the ball. Repeat the cut at right angles so that the ball now has four segments.
6. Gently ease the four "petals" open. Make a tiny ball from the reserved mixture and put into the middle of the "flower", like a bud.
7. Bake for 12 minutes or until the cookies are pale brown.
8. While hot, gently ease off the baking sheet and lift, with a metal spatula, on to a cooling rack.
9. Store in an airtight container.

# ONE PLATE DINNER *for Sixty*

*Left* A single plate of good imaginative food, perhaps the spicy babotie or pasta with clams and squid in garlicky sauce, can mean the difference between a run-of-the-mill drinking party and something rather special.

**Emergency Supplies**
*It is a good idea to have emergency supplies in store in case disaster strikes. Keep plenty of dried pasta, cans of good condensed soup and cheese. Boil the pasta and make a sauce by diluting the condensed soup with milk, or milk and cream; mixing it with plenty of grated cheese, and warming over a low heat. Stir into the cooked pasta and season well with salt and ground black pepper. Add fried garlic, mushrooms or crisp bacon if you have them.*

SOMETIMES THERE'S NO ROOM, OR NO MONEY, TO FEED A lot of people lavishly, but sometimes Wine-and-Cheese just won't do. A single plate of good food can mean the difference between a run-of-the-mill drinking party, and something rather special. It needn't cost more either. People tend to drink rather less if they are not hungry, and booze costs more than lasagne.

A single dish of something warming and old-fashioned, like meatballs and rice, hot and creamy chicken and ham pie, a plateful of pasta, or maybe a vegetarian curry with all the trimmings, served when the party is well under way, will give the proceedings a welcome fillip. It's a chance for trapped guests to escape their interlocutors, for the eager to get closer to the object of their desire (be that man, woman, the groaning table or just the bar), and for the host or hostess to show off. It is, even for the inexperienced cook, quite easy to get one good dish wonderfully right, so that there will be a satisfying degree of "Oo-ing" and "Ah-ing".

The dish should be one that can be prepared well in advance, and should need no more than a plate and a fork per person. Disposable plates, if they are good quality (stiff and deep) will just do, but best of all are those large old-fashioned hotel soup bowls with a broad rim. These will contain any sauce without spilling. The bowl means they'll hold a goodly portion that should satisfy the hungriest guest, and the rim allows the diner to grip the thing firmly without getting his thumb in the gravy.

Green salad, cut up small enough to be easily handled with a fork, goes well with most hot food. Though recipe books seldom recommend it, there are few things as delicious as salad turned in chicken sauce or meat ball gravy. Rice is good too, or mashed potatoes. The main thing is to ensure that everything can be gotten on one plate and eaten with ease standing up.

A word of warning: if making a hot dish, like cassoulet or chicken fricassé, do it in smallish quantities (our recipes are for 10) rather than in one large pot. It is easy to burn or overcook large quantities and, worse, they cool so slowly they can easily go bad. Discovering that the whole lot is fermenting just as the guests arrive is not funny and, of course, it is potentially extremely dangerous as well. See page 10 for "Catering in Quantity".

For a chunky salad, try to get all the pieces roughly the same size, either in uniform chunks or matching sticks or even slices. Cucumber peel, provided it is not bitter, adds color and texture to the salad.

**Wine Boxes**
*Good quality wine can be bought from many supermarkets or liquor stores in large quantities, packaged in thick plastic containers inside a cardboard box. As the wine is purchased in a larger quantity it is inexpensive and, being lighter than glass bottles, is easy to carry. The wine is served from a small tap pulled out of the bottom of the box for easy help-yourself-service. As the wine is drawn off, the plastic container collapses without allowing air to enter and spoil the remaining wine.*

## WINE

Of course this party could start with the usual mixed bar, with whisky, gin and all the mixes, but it is important to offer wine once the guests are eating. Or wine could be served throughout the party. A choice of red or white would be best but certainly much more red than white will be drunk with the babotie and with the bacon roll. Both would be good with a rich soft zinfandel or a cabernet sauvignon. Or you might like to serve a burgundy with the babotie. The pasta dishes would be good with a chilled Italian soave or similar dry white wine although many people would prefer red wine regardless of the conventions – so offer both.

**Pasta and Sauces**
*As a rough guide, rich or meaty sauces go best with chunky short pasta; tomato sauces with long thin pasta or small short shapes; olive oil and garlic sauces with long, thin pasta shapes and sauces which are based on cream, butter or béchamel go well with small, delicate pasta shapes.*

| MENU 1 | MENU 2 | MENU 3 |
|---|---|---|
| *Babotie* | *Mixed Pasta with Seafood Sauce* | *Giant Cheese and Bacon Roll with Tomato Sauce* |
| | *or* | *or* |
| | *Mixed Pasta with Chicken and Mushroom Sauce* | *Mustard Sauce* |

## GETTING AHEAD

*Months in advance*
- Invite the guests.
- Choose the menu.
- Check plates, knives and forks. Collect large soup bowls or buy paper plates.
- Check glasses.
- Buy the alcohol.
- Make a shopping list from the recipes, remembering to include ingredients for green salad, potatoes or rice that you may be serving with the main dish.
- Buy the dry ingredients.

*Weeks before the party*
- Cheese and bacon roll: make the pastry and freeze it in one pound packs.

*Two days before the party*
- Babotie; do all the shopping. Roast the lamb.
- Pasta: do all the shopping with the exception of the seafood if you are making the seafood sauce. Order fresh fish to collect on the day. If making the chicken sauce, poach the chickens. Grate the Parmesan cheese.
- Cheese and bacon roll: do all the shopping. Make the tomato or mustard sauce. Take the pastry out of the freezer and put into refrigerator. Dice the bacon.

*The day before the party*
- Babotie: mince the lamb, make the babotie and the custard but do not put the two together.
- If serving rice, cook and butter it.
- Pasta: make the chicken sauce or prepare the tomato sauce base for the seafood.
- Cheese and bacon roll: make the cheese and bacon roll but leave the pastry raw. Cover with plastic wrap and chill.
- If serving salad, buy the ingredients.

**Invitation Cards**
*To let the guests know that this is an informal supper party use paper plates as invitation cards, perhaps writing "Come for Supper" in bold colored ink and giving the time and date. Use the smallest, flattest plates available, writing the address and sticking the stamp on one side, the invitation on the other.*

Some possibilities for the mixed pasta: *conchiglie* (shells), *farfalle* (butterflies), and *eliche* (propellers).

**Babotie**
*This is the South Africans' answer to shepherd's pie. The cooked, ground lamb is spiced with curry and sweetened with chutney and fruit. The heavy mashed potato top is replaced with a light egg custard, delicately flavored with lemon leaves.*

Get clams opened (shucked) by the fish shop, or buy them ready-shucked and frozen or canned.

*Right* Paper napkins and good-sized plates are essential for a one-plate dinner. Hotel soup bowls with a broad brim are ideal.

○ Count out and polish glasses, plates and forks.
○ Chill the wine and make plenty of ice cubes.
○ Make flower arrangements or table decorations.
○ Put out paper napkins.

*On the morning of the party*
○ Pasta: collect the seafood. Finish the seafood sauce, cool quickly and then chill.
○ Set the table and organize the bar.
○ Dish the mustard sauce and chill.
○ If serving salad, prepare leaves and dressing.

*An hour before the guests arrive*
○ Babotie: pour the custard on half the baboties and cook.
○ Put the rice in the oven or warmer to heat. A shallow roasting pan is best.
○ Pasta: heat the sauce.
○ Cheese and bacon roll: brush the rolls with egg and bake in relays if necessary.
○ Salad: toss most of it in dressing. Reserve some undressed.
○ Put Parmesan or mustard sauce on the table.

*30 minutes before the guests arrive.*
○ Baboties: keep the cooked baboties warm and cook the rest.
○ Pasta: keep the sauce warm in an ovenproof dish.

*15 minutes before the guests arrive*
○ Cheese and bacon roll: warm the cooked rolls. Heat the tomato sauce.

*After the guests arrive*
○ Cook the pasta.

Preparing the Table
*When serving the meal, arrange a stack of plates and wrap a knife and fork for each guest in a paper napkin. There is no need to spend hours on table decorations. Large chunky candles and an earthenware jar full of flowers and greenery from the garden will set the scene prettily and informally.*

Alternative Pastry Filling
*Use 2lbs sausage meat, 1 medium onion, finely chopped, 3 tbsp finely chopped parsley, mixed well together and seasoned with salt and black pepper. Spread half down the center of the pastry rectangle and top with 5 hard-boiled and floured eggs. Cover with the remaining sausage meat.*

Shellfish
*This is usually sold live, frozen or cooked as it quickly deteriorates once dead. Keep cooked shellfish refrigerated and eat within three days. Store live shellfish in an open container covered with a damp cloth in the bottom of the refrigerator.*

# ONE PLATE DINNER RECIPES

Even an inexperienced cook will find it quite easy to get one good dish really right. Here is a selection from the three alternative menus. From left to right: freshly grated Parmesan, chicken and mushroom sauce, mustard sauce for the roll, seafood sauce, babotie, giant cheese and bacon roll and tagliatelle.

QUANTITY NOTE:
Remember to adjust the quantities if catering for a large number. If serving the babotie, pasta or the roll without a first course, dessert or cheese, make 6 dishes of the pasta or babotie for 60 people or make 10 giant cheese and bacon rolls. If you are serving rice with the babotie, allow 2 tbs dry rice per person. For pasta, allow 3-4oz per head. If you are serving salad, judge the quantity by the handful. (Allow one small clutch of leaves per person. You should have 4 large bowls of dressed leaves and 1 prepared undressed bowl by in reserve.) See Catering in Quantity, p. 10.

## BABOTIE
SERVES 10
*3 slices white bread*
*4 cups milk*
*2½lb cooked, ground lamb*
*2 medium-sized onions, chopped*
*2 apples, chopped*
*⅓ cup butter*
*2 heaped tbsp curry powder*
*2 tbsp chutney*
*½ cup chopped almonds*
*¼ cup raisins*
*3 tbsp vinegar or lemon juice*
*salt and black pepper*
FOR THE TOP
*3 eggs*
*salt and black pepper*
*lemon leaves or bay leaves*

1. Soak the bread in the milk, squeeze dry and place in a mixing bowl, with the minced lamb.
2. Preheat the oven, setting the temperature control to 350°. Grease an ovenproof dish.
3. Fry the onion and apple slowly in the butter. Add the curry powder and cook for a further minute.

4. Mix the apple and onion with the lamb and bread, add the chutney, almonds, raisins and vinegar or lemon juice. Season with salt and black pepper.
5. Pile into the greased dish and place in the warm oven for about 10 minutes to form a slight crust on top.
6. Meanwhile, mix the eggs with the milk in which the bread has been soaked. Season with salt and pepper.
7. Pour this over the meat, place the lemon or bay leaves on top and continue to bake until the custard has set and browned (about 30 minutes).

## MIXED PASTA WITH SEAFOOD SAUCE OR CHICKEN AND MUSHROOM SAUCE
SERVES 10
THE PASTA
*3lb fresh mixed green and white pasta*
*2 tbsp olive oil*
*salt and black pepper*
*½ cup melted butter*
*2 tbsp chopped parsley*

1. You will need to cook the pasta in two pans that hold not less than 6 quarts of water each (preserving pans would be ideal). Half-fill the pans with water and add oil and salt.

2. Bring to the boil and add the pasta, boil rapidly, uncovered, for about 10 minutes (but check the manufacturer's instructions – pastas vary) when it should be just tender. Drain and rinse with boiling water. Toss in melted butter and season with black pepper.

3. Pile the pasta into hot serving bowls. Pour the sauce on top. Sprinkle with the chopped parsley. Serve immediately with Parmesan cheese.

FOR THE SEAFOOD SAUCE
*2 tbsp olive oil*
*2 large onions, finely chopped*
*3 cloves garlic, crushed*
*2lb canned tomatoes*
*1¼ cups red wine*
*⅔ cup water*
*2 tbsp tomato paste*
*1 tsp coriander seeds, crushed*
*1 tsp basil*
*salt and black pepper*
*3lb fresh round clams or 2lb canned or*
*    bottled*
*⅔ cup oil for frying*
*1lb squid*
*2lb cooked shrimp*
TO SERVE
*freshly grated Parmesan cheese*

1. Heat the olive oil and fry the onion and garlic until transparent.

2. Add the canned tomatoes, red wine, water, tomato paste, coriander and basil. Season with salt and pepper. Bring to the boil and simmer for 30 minutes or until the sauce has reduced by about a third and is rich in flavor.

3. Meanwhile prepare the seafood. Clean the clams and fry them in a little oil until the shells open. Discard any that do not open. Add the juices to the sauce. Remove clams from their shells. Clean the squid and cut into thin slivers.

4. Once the sauce has reduced, add the squid and simmer gently for 5-10 minutes until tender. Add the clams and shrimp and heat through.

FOR THE CHICKEN SAUCE
*3lb cooked chicken meat*
*12oz button mushrooms*
*¼ cup butter*
*2½ cups milk*
*bay leaf, parsley stalk, peppercorns, slice of*
*    onion, blade or large pinch of mace*
*⅓ cup butter*
*¾ cup flour*
*2½ cups chicken stock*
*1¼ cups heavy cream*
*salt, black pepper and nutmeg*
*1 tbsp fresh or 1 tsp dried oregano*

1. Cut the cooked chicken into bite-sized chunks. Cut the mushrooms into quarters and fry them in the butter.

2. Place the milk and flavorings together in a pan. Bring to simmering point, then turn down the heat and leave for 10 minutes to infuse. Strain.

3. Melt the butter in a heavy-based pan, add the flour and cook for one minute. Gradually add the infused milk and chicken stock, stirring constantly until the sauce is smooth and simmering.

4. Add the chicken and mushrooms and any juices that the mushrooms were cooked in and season with salt and black pepper. Simmer for 5-10 minutes.

5. Remove from the heat. Stir in the cream. Add the nutmeg and oregano.

## GIANT CHEESE AND BACON ROLL
SERVES 8
FOR THE PASTRY
*4 cups all-purpose flour*
*1 cup butter*
*2 eggs, beaten*
*⅔ cup dairy sour cream*
*½ cup grated Parmesan cheese*
*salt and black pepper*
*pinch dry English mustard*
*pinch cayenne pepper*
FOR THE FILLING
*1lb bacon*
*1 medium-sized onion*
*1 medium-sized potato*
*2 tsp mixed fresh sage, rosemary and parsley,*
*    chopped finely*
*black pepper*
*beaten egg*

1. Sift the flour into a mixing bowl and rub in the butter.

2. Beat the eggs and mix them with the sour cream.

3. Stir the cheese, salt, black pepper, mustard and cayenne into the flour. Pour in the eggs and cream. Using a knife and then fingertips draw the mixture together to form a soft but firm dough. Chill for 30 minutes.

4. Remove any rind from the bacon and cut into tiny ½in cubes. Peel the onion and potato and dice a little smaller than the bacon. Mix together in a bowl and season with fresh herbs and black pepper.

5. Preheat the oven, setting the temperature control to 375°.

6. Roll out the chilled pastry to an oblong 12in × 14in. Spoon the bacon filling in a strip down the center.

7. Fold the sides of the pastry over the filling to form a large sausage roll. Brush the edges with egg and seal them well together. Turn the roll on to a baking sheet so that the join is underneath.

8. Brush with egg. Use the pastry trimmings to decorate the roll and brush again with egg.

9. Bake for 45 minutes until the roll is golden brown. Serve hot with mustard or tomato sauce or cold with mustard sauce only.

## TOMATO SAUCE
SERVES 8
*1 tbsp oil*
*1 small onion, chopped*
*1 clove garlic, crushed*
*1 stick celery, chopped*
*1lb canned tomatoes*
*1 bay leaf*
*1 fresh parsley stalk*
*salt*
*black pepper*
*2 tsps vinegar*
*1 tsp sugar*
*dash of Tabasco*
*pinch of basil*

1. Heat the oil in a heavy-based sauce-pan, add the onion, garlic and celery and fry gently until soft and transparent.

2. Add all the remaining ingredients, bring to the boil and simmer for 40 minutes.

3. Liquidize or sieve the sauce. Return to a clean pan. Bring back to the boil and check the seasoning.

## MUSTARD SAUCE
SERVES 8
*⅔ cup thick mayonnaise (p. 93)*
*1 tbsp milk*
*⅔ cup heavy cream, whipped lightly*
*2 tbsp wholegrain mustard*
*salt and pepper*

1. Put the mayonnaise into a mixing bowl and thin with milk to the same consistency as the whipped cream.

2. Fold in the cream and mustard. Season with salt and pepper.

# VIP DINNER

*for Four*

*Left* Good plain ingredients can make unusual and elegant dinners. The top half of the picture shows the ingredients for our winter dinner (pheasant, red wine, root vegetables, cassis). In the foreground, the food for our light summer menu of avocado, turbot and fruit.

EVERYONE, HOWEVER SOPHISTICATED, SUFFERS AT LEAST a pang of anxiety when faced with entertaining someone "important", the boss being the archetypal example. Usually the dinner guests who give us the most qualms, and put us most on our mettle, are people we do not know well or who are amazingly good hosts or cooks themselves, or – which shouldn't matter but it does – are famous or VIPs. We all know perfectly well that the Head of the Federal Reserve Board, or the President of the United States, is only human, and probably loves simple home cooking, but it does not stop us fretting about getting everything right.

So the trick is to plan things well, and allow oneself time to get everything really right, with as much done well in advance as possible. A last-minute scramble for ice cubes, last-minute boiling and draining of vegetables, a flustered dash to lay the table, make for anxious hosts and uneasy guests. If time is allowed for a leisurely bath, and a bit of personal preening in front of the mirror, or even for a nip of Dutch courage, dread will give way to pleasurable anticipation.

The two menus suggested, one for summer and one for winter, combine sophisticated and pretty presentation with what is really very simple cooking. Nothing requires too much last-minute attention – and if the countdown is followed to the letter, there is plenty of time for relaxed chatting with your guest over a drink before dinner is served.

Cautionary Note
*It is best to plan dishes that have been tried before and are known to be successful. If an interesting new recipe inspires you, experiment first.*

---

### THE SUMMER MENU
*Avocado with Tomato Water Ice*

*Turbot Wrapped in Spinach with Saffron Sauce*
*Steamed New Potatoes with Lima Beans*

*Raspberries and Seedless Grapes*

### THE WINTER MENU
*Hot Smoked Fish and Spinach Mold*

*Pheasant and Chestnut Pie*
*Purée of Root Vegetables*
*Brussels Sprouts*

*Grape and Cassis Brûlée*

---

Buying Pheasant
*Hen pheasants are smaller and juicier than cock pheasants. Feel the width of the breast to see if it is plump and check that the legs are smooth and the feet supple.*

Turbot
*This is a large flat fish and can weigh up to 45lb. It has firm, delicately flavored flesh and is usually sold as fillets or steaks, though trimmings can be bought for kebabs. Because of its excellent flavor, turbot is best simply poached, steamed or broiled.*

## WINE

A small dinner for VIPs is the ideal time to splash out on something special. Ask a good wine shop's advice and tell them what food you are serving. For the winter menu they might suggest a chablis for the first course, followed by a good red burgundy, and for the summer menu a light, refreshing Loire or colombard with the avocado, followed by a rich, rather special white pinot chardomay. Good dessert wines can sometimes be bought surprisingly cheaply in half-bottles and a half-bottle of sauternes would give each person one small glass – the perfect way to end a meal.

## GETTING AHEAD

SUMMER MENU ○ WINTER MENU ● SUMMER AND WINTER MENU ◑

*A month in advance*
- ◑ Arrange a date for your guests to come.
- ◑ Choose the menu and make a shopping list.
- ◑ Choose some special wine to complement the menu and check on your stock of pre-dinner drinks, brandy and port.

*Two days before the dinner*
- ○ Do all the shopping, except the turbot and fruit.
- ○ Make the tomato water ice.
- ◑ Give the house a good going-over.
- ◑ Check and iron tablecloth and napkins.
- ◑ Clean the silver and best glasses.
- ● Do all the shopping, except the sprouts and cream.
- ● Cook the smoked haddock.
- ● Marinate the pheasant.

*The day before the dinner*
- ◑ Arrange some flowers.
- ◑ Put fresh candles in holders.
- ◑ Put hand towels in the bathroom.
- ● Make the filling for the pheasant and chestnut pie.

**Dessert Wines**
*For an excellent dessert wine look for abboccato from Orvieto in Italy, a "Spanish sauternes" or a sweet white graves. Excellent sauternes start from the mid price range. For extra special occasions the fine German wines cannot be matched. Look for the words "Beerenauslese" or "Trockenbeerenauslese" on the label. Champagne or sparkling white wine are good to serve with a light or fruit dessert.*

**Avocados**
*When the fruit is ripe it should give a little when squeezed gently between the palms of the hands. Bullet-hard avocados can be ripened wrapped in paper and left in a warm dark place. The flesh turns brown when exposed to air so prepare the pears at the last minute and brush the surface with lemon juice.*

**Asparagus**
*This is a delicious alternative starter to a summer dinner. To cook asparagus, bind it in bundles and stand it upright in a pan of boiling salted water. Use an inverted saucepan as a lid so that the stalks boil while the tips steam.*

**Button Onions**
*These are easier to peel if first soaked in boiling water for 2 minutes. Cook them with the root still attached to keep them from falling apart during cooking. Snip the root off just before serving.*

**Ice Creams and Sorbets**
*Large crystals of ice form when ice creams and sorbets are frozen. Beating the mixture during freezing breaks the crystals down. The more an ice cream or sorbet is beaten, the smoother the texture will be.*

*Left* Carefully laid tables, whether as stylish as this or not, can make an instant visual impact. Take care to line up the bottom ends of the cutlery carefully and space everything accurately.

**Pheasant and Chestnut**
*The filling for the pheasant and chestnut pie can also be made into a delicious casserole. Add an extra 1¼ cups stock and at the end of cooking leave the pheasant on the bone and thicken the liquid with a little butter-and-flour paste.*

- Make the purée of root vegetables.
- Sprinkle the grapes with cassis. Cover with whipped cream.

*The day of the dinner*
○ Buy the turbot, raspberries, seedless grapes and cream.
○ Scrub the new potatoes.
○ Pod the lima beans, cook them and remove the outer skins.
○ Cook the spinach leaves, prepare the turbot parcels and refrigerate. Make the fish stock.
◑ Set the table, prepare the bar for pre-dinner drinks, set a tray for coffee and liqueurs.
◑ Put out all serving dishes and eating plates.
○ Put raspberries and seedless grapes together in a clear glass bowl. Whip the cream.
- Buy the sprouts and prepare (but do not cook) them.
- Prepare mixture for the smoked fish and fill the ramekins.
- Sprinkle the brûlées with sugar and broil them.
- Cover the pheasant pie with pastry, decorate, brush with egg, and refrigerate.

*Half an hour before the guests arrive*
○ Steam the new potatoes, dish up and keep warm.
○ Put a steamer ready to cook the fish.
○ Make the saffron sauce, and keep warm.
- Put a roasting pan ready for the smoked fish. Boil some water.
- Heat the vegetable purée, dish up and keep warm.
- Cook the pheasant and chestnut pie.

*After the guests arrive*
○ Halve the avocados and fill with tomato sorbet.
○ Cook the fish.
○ Reheat the lima beans in butter and add to the potatoes.
- Cook the fish molds.
- Cook the Brussels sprouts.

**Bath and Change**
*Our schedule allows a breathing space two hours before your guests are due for you to have a bath and a cup of tea (or something stronger?). Afterwards dress for dinner but be sure to put on an apron.*

*Right* Black triangle: winter menu course of pheasant and chestnut pie with purée of root vegetables and Brussels sprouts served with good red burgundy. White triangle: light summer main course of turbot wrapped in spinach with saffron sauce served with new potatoes and lima beans.

**Cheat Crème Brûlée**
*Make the caramel top by melting soft brown sugar in a heavy-based pan until it turns a dark golden brown. Pour a thin layer over the top of the chilled cream.*

Seedless green grapes happily are in season when raspberries are at their cheapest. Mixed together and served with cream they make an unbeatable dessert. The deep-flavored black grapes are perfect for the rich winter brûlée.

**Cassis**
*This is the French word for blackcurrant and it is also used for the name of a blackcurrant liqueur. Crème de cassis (used in our brûlée) is the finest variety of this.*

# THE SUMMER VIP DINNER RECIPES

## AVOCADO WITH TOMATO WATER ICE

**SERVES 4**

*2 ripe avocados*
**FOR THE TOMATO WATER ICE**
*2 cups tomato juice*
*2 tsp tomato paste*
*salt and freshly ground*
*    black pepper*
*1 tsp sugar*
*1 bay leaf*
*2 parsley stalks*
*6 leaves fresh basil*
*6 peppercorns*
*1 slice of onion*
*1 stick of celery*
*squeeze of lemon juice*
**TO SERVE**
*juice of half a lemon*
*sprigs of fresh basil*

1. Put all the tomato water ice ingredients together in a pan. Slowly bring to the boil and simmer for 15 minutes. Strain the mixture.
2. Allow to cool, check the seasoning.

3. Pour the mixture into a metal tray and place in the freezer. Beat with a fork every 30 minutes until the water ice has completely frozen.
4. To serve the avocados: cut each one in half and remove the stone. Brush the cut edges with lemon juice.
5. Pile the tomato water ice into each avocado. Stand on individual plates and decorate each one with a sprig of basil. Serve immediately with brown bread and butter or brown rolls.

NOTE:
For a more elegant, but more troublesome presentation, skin the avocado halves, lay them, rounded side up on the plates, cut them into slices, brush with lemon juice and serve the scooped water ice next to the row of slices.

## TURBOT WRAPPED IN SPINACH WITH SAFFRON SAUCE

**SERVES 4**

*4 × 6oz boneless turbot steaks*
*12oz fresh spinach*
*salt*
*ground white pepper*
**FOR THE STOCK**
*8oz fish bones, heads and skins*
*1¼ cups water*
*2 slices onion*
*1 leek*
*1 bay leaf*
*2 parsley stalks*
*4 peppercorns*
**FOR THE SAUCE**
*4 strands saffron*
*2 tsp cornstarch*
*⅓ cup butter*
*lemon juice*
*salt*
*ground white pepper*

1. Wash the spinach and remove the tough stalks, keeping the leaves as whole as possible.
2. Drop into boiling salted water for one minute, drain and rinse well with cold water. Lay the leaves flat on a clean dish cloth.
3. Put all the stock ingredients together in a pan, simmer for 20 minutes and strain.
4. Season the turbot and wrap each steak in the spinach leaves.
5. To make the sauce: add the saffron to the fish stock and bring slowly to the boil.
6. Mix the cornstarch with a little cold water, add some of the hot liquid to it, then add this to the hot stock and stir until boiling.

7. Gradually beat in the butter to make a shiny yellow sauce. Strain to remove the saffron strands. Season with lemon juice, salt and pepper. Keep warm by standing in a pan of hot water.
8. Steam the fish over boiling water for about 10 minutes. A Chinese-style steaming basket is ideal for this. The fish is done when it feels firm to the touch.
9. Make a lake of saffron sauce on four warm dinner plates. Carefully lay a fish parcel on each plate and serve immediately.
NOTE:
This recipe may also be made with fresh salmon or halibut.

## STEAMED NEW POTATOES WITH LIMA BEANS

**SERVES 4**

*1lb tiny new potatoes*
*1½lb shelled lima beans*
*sprig of mint*
*melted butter*
*salt*
*black pepper*
*chopped mint or chives*

1. Scrape or just scrub the potatoes. Sprinkle with salt.
2. Place in a steamer or sieve, with the sprig of mint, over a pan of boiling water. Cover tightly and cook for 30 minutes until the potatoes are tender. Drain and keep warm.
3. Boil the lima beans in salted water for 5-10 minutes.
4. Cool under running water, then remove the grey skin from each bean.
5. Toss the beans in melted butter over moderate heat until hot, then mix with the potatoes, season with salt and black pepper and sprinkle with the chopped herbs.

## RASPBERRIES AND SEEDLESS GRAPES

**SERVES 4**

*1lb fresh raspberries*
*½lb seedless grapes*
**TO SERVE**
*ice cream or whipped cream*
*sugar*

1. Avoid washing the raspberries if you can. Tip them out gently into a shallow serving dish.
2. Pull the grapes from their stalks. Wash and dry them, and sprinkle over the raspberries.
3. Serve with the cream and sugar handed separately.

# THE WINTER VIP DINNER RECIPES

## SMOKED FISH AND SPINACH MOLD
SERVES 4
*4oz smoked haddock*
*⅔ cup milk*
*onion, bay leaf and peppercorns*
*4oz spinach*
*1 tsp cornstarch*
*⅔ cup light cream*
*2 eggs*
*2 scallions, finely chopped*
*black pepper*
FOR DECORATION
*2 large tomatoes*
*1 tbsp butter*
*1 tsp fresh dill or a pinch of dill weed*
*salt*
*black pepper*

1. Preheat the oven, setting the temperature control to 350°. Put the smoked haddock into an ovenproof dish with the milk and flavorings, cover and poach in the oven for about 25 minutes.
2. Skin and flake the fish. Strain the milk and reserve.
3. Finely chop the spinach and put in a bowl, with the fish.
4. Thicken the reserved milk with the cornstarch. Cool a little and mix with the light cream and beaten eggs.
5. Pour the custard on to the fish and spinach and mix very thoroughly. Add the chopped scallions and season with black pepper. For a really smooth texture liquidize briefly in a blender.
6. Butter four ramekin dishes. Divide the haddock and spinach mixture between them. Stand the dishes in a roasting pan full of hot water. Bake in the oven for 15-20 minutes, until just set.
7. Skin and seed the tomatoes. Cut the flesh into tiny cubes. Melt the butter in a pan, add the tomato flesh and fry quickly for 30 minutes. Add the dill and season.
8. Turn the molds out on to individual plates. Serve with a spoonful of tomato.

## PHEASANT AND CHESTNUT PIE
SERVES 4
*2 small hen pheasants or Cornish game hens*
FOR THE MARINADE
*1 onion, sliced*
*1 carrot, sliced*
*1 stick celery, sliced*
*6 juniper berries*
*2 whole allspice berries, slightly crushed*
*1 bay leaf*
*6 peppercorns*
*red wine*
*juice of ½ an orange*

FOR THE PIE FILLING
*oil and butter for frying*
*2 slices bacon, diced*
*6oz pearl onions, peeled*
*4oz button mushrooms*
*1¼ cups chicken stock*
*2 tbsp butter*
*3 tbsp flour*
*2 tsp redcurrant jelly*
*salt*
*black pepper*
*4oz cooked whole chestnuts*
FOR THE TOP
*8oz puff or rough puff pastry, defrosted if frozen*
*beaten egg*

1. Two days before the dinner, cut the birds into four neat pieces. Put all the marinade ingredients together in a bowl. Add the birds, mix well, cover, and leave refrigerated overnight.
2. The following day, preheat the oven, setting the temperature control to 350°. Lift the birds out of the marinade and pat dry. Strain marinade and reserve.
3. Heat the oil and butter in a heavy-based frying-pan and in it brown the pheasant or hen pieces quickly on both sides. Transfer them to a casserole.
4. In the same pan brown the bacon and onions and add them to the casserole. Brown the mushrooms and put aside.
5. Pour a little chicken stock into the pan, stir well, scraping off any sediment, and pour into the casserole.
6. Melt the butter in the pan, add the flour and cook for one minute. Pour on the remaining stock and the marinade, stir until boiling and smooth. Pour over the pheasant or game hens.
7. Stir in the redcurrant jelly and season with salt and black pepper. Simmer in the oven for about 40 minutes until the flesh is tender. Cool.
8. Before the sauce is stone-cold, remove the joints and strip off the flesh.
9. Skim the fat from the sauce, then replace the meat and add the mushrooms and chestnuts. Check the seasoning and pour into a deep ovenproof dish.
10. Turn the oven temperature control up to 400°.
11. Roll the pastry to the thickness of a penny. Cut a long strip a little wider than the lip of the pie dish, brush the lip with water and press on the strip of pastry.
12. Brush the pastry strip with water, lay the remaining sheet of pastry over the pie and press down firmly. Cut away the excess pastry. Decorate with pastry leaves.

13. Brush the pastry with beaten egg and bake in the oven for 30 minutes until the pastry is golden brown.

## PURÉE OF ROOT VEGETABLES
SERVES 4
*8oz celeriac (celery "root")*
*8oz rutabaga*
*4oz carrot*
*1 medium-sized parsnip*
*1¼ cups milk*
*2 medium potatoes, cooked and mashed*
*salt and black pepper*
*¼ cup butter*
*chopped parsley*

1. Wash, peel and thinly slice the celeriac, rutabaga, carrot and parsnip. Place in a thick-bottomed saucepan and add the milk, salt and pepper. Simmer slowly until the vegetables are tender.
2. Purée in a food processor or push through a sieve.
3. Return to a clean pan, melt the butter, add the purée and the mashed potato. Beat well over the heat, adding a little more milk if the purée is very thick.
4. When piping hot, season well with salt and black pepper. Sprinkle with chopped parsley just before serving.

## BRUSSELS SPROUTS
SERVES 4
*1½lb small firm Brussels sprouts*
*melted butter*
*salt and black pepper*

Wash and trim the sprouts. Boil in salted water for 5-8 minutes until just tender. Drain well, toss in melted butter and season with salt and black pepper.

## GRAPE AND CASSIS BRÛLÉE
SERVES 4
*4oz black grapes*
*4 tsp crème de cassis*
*1¼ cups heavy cream*
*a few drops of vanilla*
*¼ cup light soft brown sugar*

1. Peel and halve the grapes, remove the pips. Put in the bottom of four ramekin dishes. Sprinkle one teaspoon of cassis over each.
2. Whip the heavy cream and fold in the drops of vanilla. Spoon on top of the grapes and spread absolutely flat. Cover and refrigerate overnight.
3. The following day: heat the broiler until it is red hot. Sift the sugar over the top of each ramekin. Put them under the broiler for a few minutes until the sugar is bubbling all over. Allow the brûlée to become cool and hard before serving.

# FUND RAISER'S PARTY

## for Two Hundred

Left *Left* Bright decorations and multi-colored balloons can make even a hired hall with folding chairs and trestle tables look festive. Among the aftermath of the lottery, tangerines in a thick, shiny caramel sauce.

THE REAL TRICK – AND IT IS NO MEAN FEAT – TO RAISING funds is to make the separation of the donor from his money not only painless but pleasurable. Brave words. But how to do it?

The first principle must be to give value for money so that ticket-buyers can justly feel that they are getting a good deal, and are not paying over the odds for the privilege of being charitable. Almost any of the parties in this book could be used to raise funds. The Harvest Supper could be a public affair with admission tickets costing something and every glass of cider or helping from the buffet costing a bit more. The Hogbake could be transformed into a community fair with side shows and stalls, fortune-tellers, beetle races and skittles to boost the takings.

The success of any charity event depends, more than on anything else, on good organization. Outdoor events need fine weather too, but that factor is in the lap of the gods. Good organization is more surely attainable. Weeks of committee meetings and action plans may be necessary. The first meeting of the organizers must form that committee and allocate responsibilities to the members along the lines described for the Creole street party, p. 185.

Our Fund Raiser's party is a dance and dinner. The Berlin theme (p. 109) would be an excellent one, as would Harlequin (p. 83). The party does *need* a theme. A decorated hall or house lifts the spirits as one enters it. The guests, sensing the effort and time that have gone into the decorations, the food and general organization, respond with a subconscious resolve to enjoy themselves, or with the unvoiced recognition that this is obviously going to be a party to remember.

Assuming the party is to be a fairly grand affair raising money for a well-known cause, then the first thing to ensure is a patron of fame, and preferably of fortune too. Famous faces, whether pop singers or media celebrities, are the surest guarantee of support. If the invitation can say "In the presence of HRH Stanislavsky of Ruritania", or better still "HRH Stanislavsky requests the pleasure of the company of Mr and Mrs Jones in Ruritania Palace" – wonderful. If he'll lend the palace for free, more wonderful. Of course the party might be in the local school gym, but the principle still applies. Once Prince Stanislavsky is involved, persuasion is a lot easier. The

**Don't Scrimp!**
*It is wise to invest money to make money. If services are not donated, pay for them willingly in order to ensure guests receive value for money.*

**A Touch of Glamor**
*Help the fund-raising by adding a touch of glamor to inexpensive ingredients. For example, add lobster to chicken mayonnaise; decorate egg mayonnaise with asparagus or mock caviar, mix crab with a Waldorf salad or smoked salmon with a pasta salad.*

**Advertising Space**
*If you're producing any kind of printed program for the occasion, it's a good idea to try and sell advertising space to local firms or services who may like to support your cause in this way.*

supermarket might be talked into donating the hams, the liquor store might provide the wines at cost price, the pop group and/or bands might play for a small cut of the ticket sales rather than for astronomical fees, and so on.

Our party assumes a guest list of 200, sitting at tables, each seating 10. With any luck each committee member (and there will need to be at least 10) will undertake to fill a table by selling tickets to friends. That will leave half the tables still to be filled by local advertising (many local newspapers have cheap rates for charities), and word of mouth. One committee member must be given the unenviable task of ticket-sales and seating arrangements – juggling the foursomes and twosomes and singles to make up tables, and possibly persuading the contractor to make last-minute changes with table sizes to accommodate parties of 6 or 8 instead of 10. (See p. 13 for room measurements, table and chair sizes, etc.)

A slightly outrageous atmosphere on such a night is no bad thing. The best fund raisers' parties spend money to make money and if hired "kissogram" girls from an entertainment agency can be kissed for a fee, gorillas on roller skates can be danced with for a donation, if the raffle is so organized that the participants write their names on folding money, and scantily-clad girls – or fellows – strut round the tables collecting the loot in bra or bikini, then the general atmosphere will be merry and, with any luck, merriness will lead to generosity if not to reckless spending.

On the same risqué tack, belly dancers can collect an astonishing amount of money by wriggling their navels at diners. No one can refuse to tuck a dollar or two into a G-string or bikini top when surrounded by encouraging friends. But it's important not to overdo the demands. If the guests feel forcibly fleeced rather than laughingly persuaded, they might not come next year – and the chances are that the fund raiser will need their support again.

Black gas balloons, with the table host's name on them, can be tethered to the middle of each table to make finding one's place easier.

After dinner an auction might be held. It needs to be short, or boredom will strike. The items auctioned should be amusing and worth having. A pair of Elton John's irridescent socks or lunatic specs will fetch more than his old fountain pen. Bidding for a life-size cardboard cut-out of Ronald Reagan will be hotter than for a framed picture of him.

One word of warning: it is vital not to embarrass the diners with amateurish speeches, bad auctioneering or lackluster music. Even if professional bands, belly dancers, auctioneers or comics cannot be persuaded to forego their fees, it is generally better to pay them and charge more than to keep the ticket price down and have the guests squirming in their seats while Lucy's cousin does her dreadfully bad impersonations, and then crossly refusing to put their hands on their check books.

## WINE

At charity affairs people expect to be charged for their wine separately. But, unless efficient and honest barmen and waiters can be got for nothing, loss of cash is common. The cost of proper staff can equal the profit on the drink but amateur sellers frequently get the change wrong, lose the float,

A Magic Touch
*A roving magician or fortune-teller visiting tables after dinner will be an amusing way of passing the time until the dancing or auctioneering begins.*

Planning the Evening
*Space the money-making activities throughout the evening. Lotteries and competitions could be held before dinner; a raffle during the dessert course; the auction should follow dinner and more raffles could be held during the rest of the evening.*

Staff Wages
*It is not wise to handle large amounts of cash at a function. Count out staff wages and seal them in individual envelopes beforehand.*

The Workers
*Barmen, musicians and waitresses make a big contribution to the success of the evening. It is important to look after them well, giving them a proper break and a good meal.*

fail to charge for bottles and end up with a deficit. So unless selling is likely to be watertight, it might be better to include wine in the ticket price for dinner, and allow about ¾ bottle per head. The choice had better be limited to all-purpose red or white, but of sufficiently good quality not to cause wry faces. It is false economy to produce undrinkable wine. The guests may not drink much of it, but they may not come again either.

Insurance
*Check with a broker in case you need public liability or any other insurance. It is a good idea to display disclaimer notices in cloakrooms and parking areas.*

---

**THE MENU**

*Chicken and Lobster Mayonnaise*

*Nutty, Spicy Rice Salad*

*Marinated Mushroom, Tomato and Pepper Salad*

*Chestnut Roulade*

*Caramel Tangerines*

---

## GETTING AHEAD

*One year before the party*
○ Form the committee and delegate the jobs (see Creole Party, p. 185 and Harlequin Masked Ball, pp. 86-7).
○ Set a date and book a venue or arrange for a marquee/tent company to inspect the site.
○ Choose a theme and discuss the best devices for parting guests from their cash. Remember to hire cash registers to collect takings in.
○ Design invitations (include donation slips or pleas for lottery prizes, items to be auctioned, etc).
○ Discuss famous names to be approached to add luster to the proceedings.
○ Ensure that all committee members will beg or borrow for their requirements before they offer to pay for them.
○ Decide the best form of advertising.

*Six to three months ahead*
○ The committee should meet to discuss progress. By now the venue should be firmly booked and firm arrangements made for provision of food, hire equipment, serving staff, drinks, bar-tenders, music, bands, lotteries, auctions, singing telegram companies, etc.
○ Find helpers to serve food and drink, or hire professionals.
○ Send invitations.
○ Place advertisements.
○ *The committee in charge of food:* Agree who is going to cook what and make lists of ingredients required.

Book Ahead
*In America the summer is the season for many parties and charity functions. Plan ahead as caterers, tent and equipment-hire companies can become booked as far as a year in advance.*

Tent Floor
*It is worth spending money on a proper floor for a tent as rush matting on grass can become cold and damp during the evening and is easily tripped over.*

*Above* Don't worry about peeling off every scrap of pith. Once soaked in a thick caramel syrup, the pith is unnoticeable on the glistening tangerines.

*One month before the party*
○ Hold another meeting to ensure that absolutely everything is properly organized and arranged.
○ Appoint a competent supervisor to oversee the servers on the evening.
○ Check on the number of acceptances or tickets sold and roughly calculate the number of guests that will be attending.
○ Pass this information on to those in charge of supplying food, drink and hire equipment.
○ If necessary arrange for a security guard to be on duty the night before the party to protect the tent and its contents.

*One week before the party*
○ Organizer to check on number of guests attending and give firm numbers to food, drink and hire equipment committees.

*Three days before the party*
○ *Food committee:* Take delivery or shop for all the ingredients except the lobster meat.

*Two days before the party*
○ If using a tent it should be put up today.
○ Check arrangements with the security guard.
○ *Food committee:* Cook the chicken, make the mayonnaise, make the chestnut roulades, enough for one per table, but do not fill them. Make the caramel sauce. Keep everything well refrigerated.

*One day before the party*
○ *Food committee:* Collect the cooked lobster and cut up the flesh.
○ Strip the meat from the chicken carcasses.
○ Prepare the marinated mushroom and pepper, cut up the tomato but keep separately. Cover and chill.
○ Boil the rice.
○ Place fresh damp dish cloths over the roulades (to prevent them from cracking).
○ Peel the tangerines and leave soaking in the sauce overnight.
○ Decorate the venue, except for flower arrangements.
○ Bring the tableplan up to date with the guest list.
○ If numbers have increased make sure that the food committee know.

Caramel tangerines
*These make a refreshing dessert served with a large brandysnap filled with whipped cream.*

Chicken and Lobster Mayonnaise
*To add flavor to the chicken and lobster mayonnaise, mix the lobster meat and thinned mayonnaise together the day before.*

**Placemats**
*If the party is a casual affair, placemats can be cut out of thick colored paper and will be less expensive than table linen. Write the place names on them in bold letters so they can double as name cards.*

○ Set up tables and chairs for the appropriate number of guests and label them clearly for waitresses setting the tables.
○ If anything of value is left overnight, make sure that the tent is protected by security or the venue safely locked.

### The morning of the party
○ Two servers should arrive to set up the tables and put cloths on the buffet. Coffee cups and saucers should be placed ready on tables.
○ Arrange flowers.
○ Bands or discos to arrive to set up speakers, amplifiers, etc.
○ Set up lotteries, raffles and auctions.
○ Set up the bars. There should be at least two for 200 guests.

### The afternoon of the party
○ *Food committee:* Dish up the chicken and lobster mayonnaise, add the decoration except for the lumpfish roe.
○ Add the tomatoes to the marinated mushroom and pepper.
○ Finish the rice salad and dish up.
○ Fill and roll up the roulades and put on serving plates.
○ Dish up the caramel tangerines allowing one bowl per table.
○ Deliver all the food to the venue.
○ Divide the food equally between the two buffet service points.
○ Arrange a dish of chicken and lobster mayonnaise, and one of each type of salad together at various points on each service station. Place a pile of plates near each selection of food so that there is plenty of access for the guests.
○ See the plan for buffet-and-waiter service on p. 93 (Harvest Supper).
○ Instruct the staff to clear empty plates from the tables when the guests have finished their main course. They can then serve one roulade and one bowl of tangerines to each table. Once dessert is finished the plates can be cleared and a pot of coffee with cream and sugar delivered to each table.

### Half an hour before
○ Bands or discos, lotteries, raffles and bars should all be manned and ready to go.
○ Make sure you are dressed well in advance and arrive at the function early. You may need to escort famous guests.
○ Have someone on the door to collect tickets or invitations and ward off gate-crashers.
○ *Food committee:* Add the lumpfish roe to the chicken and lobster mayonnaise. Turn the salads with a fork to make them look fresh and shiny. Slice the roulades and dust with confectioners' sugar just before serving.

### After the party
○ Make sure any takings, checks, alcohol, valuable items not sold, etc. are safely stored for the night.
○ Make sure the bar stocks are checked and takings correct.
○ Leave the venue tidy.

### Next day
○ Bank the takings and calculate the profit.
○ Inform all voluntary helpers of the party's success (both financial and pleasurable) and thank them for their efforts.
○ Make sure the contractors have collected everything from the venue and left it neat and clean.

**Tableplan**
*Remember to draw up a large master tableplan to be displayed so that guests will be able to locate their seats easily.*

**Boiled Rice**
*Boil rice in a large pan of salted water at a fast boil to prevent the grains from sticking together. White rice will take 10-15 minutes to cook and brown rice up to 45 minutes. When cooking rice in large quantities, rinse it first in hot water and then in cold. Spread it thinly in a colander and make holes to allow the steam to escape.*

**Peppers and Mushrooms**
*Peppers are found in considerable varieties and can be mild, sweet, hot or fiery. Generally speaking, the smaller the pepper, the hotter it will be. The most commonly used are green bell peppers for salads and casseroles. Button mushrooms are best for salads as they retain their white color. Large flat mushrooms have more flavor and can be used for soups and sauces.*

**Lines**
*A long line for food can spoil the evening. Give careful thought to the position of the buffet tables and serving arrangements. There must be a clear "IN" and "OUT" of the service area and as much access to the food as possible.*

**The Takings**
*The bank will expect the cash takings to be counted and sorted into the appropriate amounts. Check with the bank what these are and collect money bags from them beforehand.*

# FUND RAISER'S PARTY RECIPES

QUANTITY NOTE:

Adjust the quantities downwards if catering for a large number of guests. If part of a buffet for 200 people, you will need to make only 15 times the recipes for the chicken and lobster mayonnaise, the spicy nut salad and the marinated tomato and pepper salad and the chestnut roulade. For the caramel tangerines, 10 times the recipe should be sufficient for 200 if part of a buffet. See Catering in Quantity, p. 10.

## CHICKEN AND LOBSTER MAYONNAISE
SERVES 10
*2 medium-sized roasting chickens*
*1 bay leaf*
*6 peppercorns*
*1 sprig parsley*
*1 carrot*
*1 slice onion*
*1 stick celery*
*12oz lobster meat (1½lb–2lb) cooked lobster*
  *in the shell*
*2 cups mayonnaise*
*⅔ cup milk or light cream*
*salt*
*ground black pepper*
*lemon juice*
*Tabasco*
FOR DECORATION
*a few lettuce leaves*
*lobster shells, if available*
*red lumpfish roe (bought in jars)*
*wedges of lemon*

1. Rinse the chickens and put them in a large pan with the flavorings and cover with water. Simmer gently for 1¼ to 1½ hours until the thighs are tender and the drumsticks will wobble loosely. Remove from the pan and set aside to cool.
2. Strip the chicken meat from the carcasses, keeping the pieces as whole as possible. Cut the chicken into bite-sized chunks.
3. Cut the lobster meat into pieces about the same size as the chicken.
4. Mix the mayonnaise with enough of the milk or cream to thin it to a coating consistency.
5. Reserve a quarter of the mayonnaise. Mix the chicken and lobster meat with the rest and season well with salt, ground black pepper, lemon juice and Tabasco.
6. To serve: finely shred the lettuce leaves and arrange around the edge of a large serving platter. Pile the chicken and lobster mixture in the center of the dish. Use the remaining mayonnaise to coat the top of the meat.
7. Decorate with the lobster shells and a few teaspoons of red lumpfish roe in front of each one. Arrange the lemon wedges neatly around the outside of ring of the shredded lettuce.

## NUTTY SPICY RICE SALAD
SERVES 10
*2 tbsp oil*
*1 medium onion, finely chopped*
*1 tsp garam masala or mild curry powder*
*½ tsp turmeric*
*pinch cayenne pepper*
*½lb cooked rice*
*1 tart eating apple*
*⅔ cup assorted dried apricots, bananas and*
  *golden raisins, coarsely chopped*
*1 cup assorted nuts, coarsely chopped*
*1 tbsp chopped fresh herbs*
FOR THE DRESSING
*⅔ cup walnut oil and salad oil mixed*
  *half and half*
*1 tbsp wine vinegar*
*1 tbsp lemon juice*
*salt*
*ground black pepper*

1. Heat the oil, add the onion and fry gently until soft. Stir in the garam masala, turmeric and cayenne pepper and continue to fry the mixture for one minute.
2. Place the cooked rice in a mixing bowl and fork the onion and spice mixture into it.

3. Core and slice the apple and add to the rice with the dried fruit, chopped nuts and herbs. Mix them all together thoroughly.
4. Mix all the dressing ingredients together and use to moisten the salad. Season well with salt and ground black pepper.

## MARINATED MUSHROOM, TOMATO AND PEPPER SALAD
SERVES 10
*1lb button mushrooms*
*10 tomatoes*
*1 large green pepper*
FOR THE DRESSING
*2 tbsp olive oil*
*2 shallots, finely chopped*
*1 clove garlic, crushed*
*1 tsp coriander seeds and fennel seeds,*
  *crushed*
*2 tbsp white wine*
*juice of ½ lemon*
*1¼ cups water*
*salt*
*ground black pepper*
FOR DECORATION
*chopped coriander (cilantro) leaves*

1. Wipe the mushrooms, skin the tomatoes and cut into eighths, remove the core and seeds from the green pepper and cut into slices.
2. Heat the olive oil in a heavy-based pan and in it briskly fry the mushrooms and pepper for 2 minutes. Remove from the pan and set aside.

*Right* On the left nutty spicy rice salad and marinated mushrooms, tomato and pepper, with chicken and lobster mayonnaise top right.

3. Add the shallots and garlic to the pan and fry gently until softened. Add all the remaining ingredients, bring to the boil and simmer until the liquid has reduced by half.
4. Return the mushrooms and peppers to the pan and set aside to cool.
5. Stir the prepared tomatoes into the salad and leave to stand for an hour.
6. Turn the salad into a serving dish and sprinkle with coriander (cilantro).

## CHESTNUT ROULADE
SERVES 10
*5 eggs*
*¾ cup sugar*
*grated rind of 2 oranges*
*12oz unsweetened canned chestnut purée*
*1¼ cups heavy cream*
*4 tbsp orange liqueur*
*a little confectioners' sugar*

1. Preheat the oven, setting the temperature control to 350°. Line a large roasting pan or jelly roll pan with greased wax paper or foil.

2. Separate the egg yolks and whites.
3. Add the sugar to the yolks and beat until pale and mousse-like.
4. Fold in the chestnut purée.
5. Beat the egg whites until they form soft peaks. Add a spoonful to the chestnut mixture and mix thoroughly. Gently fold in the remaining whites.
6. Pour the mixture into the prepared tin and bake in the preheated oven for 12 to 15 minutes or until the roulade feels a little firm, and dry on top, when pressed with the finger tips.
7. Remove the roulade from the oven and cover immediately with a damp dish cloth. Leave to cool, preferably overnight.
8. Whip the heavy cream and fold in the orange liqueur. Turn the roulade out on to a clean dish cloth or sheet of wax paper and remove the backing paper. Spread the cream evenly over the cake and roll up like a Swiss roll.
9. Trim the edges and put the roulade on to a serving dish. Dust with confectioners' sugar.

## CARAMEL TANGERINES
SERVES 10
*20 tangerines or satsumas*
*1 cup granulated sugar*
*2½ cups water*

1. Peel the tangerines and remove as much pith as possible (do not worry about all the pith as it will not show when soaked in the caramel sauce).
2. Put the sugar into a heavy-based pan with a little water to moisten it. Stand the pan over a low heat until the sugar has completely dissolved.
3. Once the sugar has dissolved boil until the liquid turns dark golden brown. Pour in the remaining water – take great care at this stage as it will hiss and splutter furiously. Re-boil, stirring continuously until any lumps of sugar have dissolved, then boil to a syrupy consistency. Cool.
4. Put the tangerines in a glass bowl and pour over the caramel sauce.
5. Leave the tangerines to stand in the sauce for at least one hour in the refrigerator before serving.

# PUNK PARTY
## *for Forty*

*Left* Lurid colors, zany glasses, zips and safety-pins and the uninhibited use of a spray gun could turn the cellar or garage into Punks' Paradise.

THE WORD "PUNK", IN SHAKESPEAREAN TIMES, MEANT prostitute and in the eighteenth century it meant trash or worthless rubbish, or something moldy or rotten. Today it means anything from a carefully contrived Mohican hair-do and black make-up, to torn jeans and a safety-pin through the nostril. So a Punk Party might be a young or not-so-young person's fancy dress – assuming that for the majority of guests punk gear is not everyday wear.

A make-up kit with plenty of purple, black, white and grey in it would seem essential. Trousers with carefully engineered tears and holes would help. Safety pins, paper clips, pieces of foil, or indeed any *objet trouvé* that appeals could somehow be worked into hair, or attached to ear-rings or jacket. The whole point, of course, is to run to excess, so on no account invite anyone too stuffy to join in.

As to the food: well, punk culture does not run to gastronomic heights. Most punks, like young people the world over, eat fast-food and drink cola. But, if the party is intended as a merry send-up of disaffected youth, that is no reason to eat their bland burgers and greasy fries.

Our Punk Supper is delicious, simple and vulgarly colorful – the multi-colored boiled eggs may not get eaten (the most adventurous of us tend to balk at weird-colored food) but they don't cost much and can provide a laugh or a shudder. The face-cake is another joke, but a delicious-tasting one. And the rest of the menu should satisfy everyone.

**Marbled Eggs**
*Follow the directions for Tea Eggs (see Easter Treasure Hunt and Lunch, p.101), but boil the eggs in water with food coloring. Add plenty of color to ensure that the eggs take on a good lurid shade.*

*Right* Repeat the safety-pin or zip motif on the invitation card. Or add a single earring or a tuft of orange nylon hair.

A squashed cola can makes a decidedly "alternative" flower vase for a single bloom.

## Invitation Cards
*Buy metallic colored card to make invitations. Cut it into odd shapes and write and draw the message in graffiti-style writing. Punch a hole in the corner of the card and clip a safety-pin through it.*

THE MENU

*Pizza*

*Ham and Pea Cream Quiche*

*Devilled Sausage Cartwheels*

*Marbled Eggs*

*Red, Green and Yellow Pepper Salad*

*Baby Beets in Sour Cream*

*Green Potato Salad*

*Face Cake*

## Music
*Don't forget the music. The Sex Pistols, The Clash, The Damned, The Vibrators and The Exploited are all musts. Turn it up loud – that's how Johnny Rotten, Sid Vicious, Richard Hell et al. would like it . . .*

## GETTING AHEAD
*A month before the party*
- ○ Send invitations (many punk cards can be bought, or make outrageous collages on postcards with cut-outs from magazines).
- ○ Collect make-up, jewelry, spray-on hair dyes and glitter and clothes to wear. Have a few extra for guests who forget they are meant to be punks and arrive looking too conservative.
- ○ Buy some vividly colored crêpe paper or posters to transform the room where you will be holding the party.
- ○ Buy party poppers, spray streamer or any other items available from joke shops.
- ○ Order the extra-long sausages and freeze them.
- ○ Buy garish paper napkins, candles and table decoration.
- ○ Make the quiche pastry and the sponge base and freeze.

### Rainbow Drops
*These can be used to decorate the face cake. Arrange them as dangly ear-rings, hair slides, make-up or simply place them in between the piped, whipped cream as a border for the cake.*

### Cocktail Sausages
*Large sausages can be made into two cocktail-size ones by gently twisting them in the center and then cutting them in half.*

*Two days before the party*
- ○ Do all the shopping.
- ○ Make the marbled eggs.
- ○ Make the pea purée for the quiche.
- ○ Make the devilled sauce.
- ○ Check cutlery, plates and service equipment.
- ○ Defrost the quiche pastry.

### Jumbo Sausages
*These are now available to caterers and in a few supermarkets. If they cannot be bought, advise the butcher in plenty of time so he can fill sausage meat into large sausage skins without twisting them into separate links.*

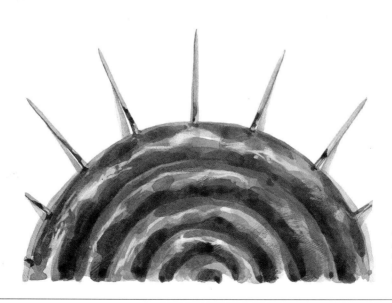

**Right** Hold a coil of sausage together for cooking with a ring of spiky sticks.

### Safety Note
*If you're including razor blades as part of your decor, make sure they are well out of reach or that the blades are protected.*

Potato Skins
*Many of the nutrients occur just beneath the potato skin and for this reason, it is best to serve young potatoes with their skins on. If the potatoes are too old and unattractive-looking to be served with their skins, peel them very thinly, or scrub them and boil them in their skins and peel them while they are still hot.*

*The day before the party*
○ Make the quiches and prepare (but do not bake) pizzas and chill them
○ Roll up the sausages.
○ Cook the potatoes and remove the skin.
○ Take the cake base out of the freezer.
○ Decorate the room or rooms for the party.

*The morning of the party*
○ Set up a buffet table and put out plates, cutlery and napkins.
○ Decorate the room and put out party jokes.
○ Leave make-up, hair sprays and odd scarves, pieces of jewelry in the bathroom for guests to help themselves to, with a sign, graffiti-style, in lipstick on the mirror inviting them to do so.
○ Set up the bar. Chill the wine.

Pasta
*Pasta is made from extra-hard wheat flour, mixed with water or egg and water. It is sold in some six hundred shapes and may be flavored with spinach, tomato or even chocolate when it is served as a dessert with butter, sugar and cream. Fresh pasta freezes well or will keep refrigerated for two or three days wrapped in a damp cloth.*

*Right* Curious, but easily achievable and delicious, Mohican face cake and marbled eggs with pasta dyed with food coloring. For a milder version of the pasta use bought, flavored pastas (tomato, spinach, wholewheat or plain white).

Pizzas
*The flat and deep-dish pizzas overflowing with rich tomato sauce and many toppings that we serve today bear little resemblance to pizza as it was originally made: a flattish yeast-leavened bread dough with a thin coating of spaghetti sauce scraped over the top.*

*Two or three hours before the guests arrive*
○ Finish the green potato salad.
○ Make the pepper salad.
○ Prepare the beets and sour cream but do not combine.
○ Finish the face cake.
○ Peel the boiled eggs and serve in a bowl.
○ Bake the pizzas from frozen.

*Half an hour before the guests arrive*
○ Brush the sausages with devilled sauce and cook them.
○ Heat the pizza.
○ Toss the beets in sour cream.

Pineapple
*Buy pineapples with a deep yellow skin and a strong fragrant smell. To serve fresh pineapple in its shell, slice off top and bottom. Cut around the inside of the skin from both ends, gradually working towards the middle to release the flesh so it can be pushed out in one piece. Cut it into neat slices and remove the woody core. Put the fruit back in the shell, sprinkle with kirsch and then replace the top.*

# PUNK PARTY RECIPES

QUANTITY NOTE:
For 40 guests make 3 times the recipes for pizza, quiche and salads and 2 times the sausage cartwheels. See Catering in Quantity, p. 10.

## PIZZA
SERVES 10
*2oz fresh yeast*
*2 cups lukewarm milk and ⅔ cup water mixed together*
*4 cups all-purpose flour*
*2 tsp salt*
*4 tbsp olive oil*
FOR THE FILLING
*1 medium onion, finely chopped*
*2 cloves garlic, crushed*
*2 tbsp olive oil*
*2lb canned tomatoes*
*salt*
*black pepper*
*1 tbsp chopped fresh basil or oregano or 1 tsp dried*
*4oz mushrooms, sliced*
*1 green pepper, sliced*
*4oz salami, thinly sliced*
*1⅓ cups (8oz) shelled cooked shrimp*
*1lb canned artichoke hearts, drained and sliced*
*4 tbsp olive oil*
*6oz Mozzarella cheese*
*20 small black olives*

1. Mix the yeast to a paste with a little of the warm liquid and the sugar.
2. Sift the flour and salt into a warmed mixing bowl. Make a well in the center and pour in the liquid. Mix to a firm, soft dough. Knead it for about 10 minutes.
3. Put the dough into a clean, oiled bowl and leave to rise in a warm place until it has doubled in bulk.
4. Punch the dough down and roll into two huge rounds a good 12in in diameter. Place them on a baking sheet.
5. To make the filling: gently fry the onion and garlic in the oil until soft and transparent. Add the canned tomatoes, bring to the boil and simmer until thick. Season with salt and black pepper. Add the herbs.
6. Preheat the oven, setting the temperature control to 400°. Spread the tomato mixture over the base of each pizza. With the back of a knife mark five segments on each one. Arrange the mushrooms, green pepper, salami, shrimp and artichoke hearts each in a section. Sprinkle liberally with olive oil. Add the Mozzarella cheese cut into thin slices, and then scatter the olives over the top of the pizzas.

7. Allow the pizzas to stand for 10 minutes, then bake in the hot oven for 20 to 30 minutes. The filling should be hot and bubbling and the crust crisp and golden.

## HAM AND PEA CREAM QUICHE
SERVES 10
FOR THE SHORTCRUST PASTRY
*2 cups all-purpose flour*
*pinch of salt*
*¼ cup butter*
*¼ cup lard*
*3 tbsp cold water*
FOR THE PEA CREAM
*8oz frozen peas*
*2 tbsp butter*
*2 tbsp heavy cream*
*salt and black pepper*
*nutmeg*
FOR THE FILLING
*1 medium onion, finely chopped*
*1 tbsp butter*
*4oz cooked ham*
*2 cups whole milk*
*3 eggs*
*salt and black pepper*
*3 tbsp grated Parmesan cheese*

1. Preheat the oven, setting the temperature control to 400°.
2. Sift the flour and salt into a mixing bowl. Rub in the butter and lard, add the water and mix to a firm dough.
3. Roll the pastry to a circle large enough to line a 12in flan ring or tart pan. Chill in the refrigerator for 30 minutes.
4. Line the pastry case with wax paper and fill with rice or baking beans. Bake the pastry case for about 30 minutes, removing the paper and beans halfway through cooking.
5. Cook the peas in boiling, salted water for 5 minutes, drain well and push through a sieve or purée in a blender. Beat in the butter and cream, salt, pepper and nutmeg.
6. Prepare the filling: lightly fry the chopped onion in the butter. Spoon into the cooked pastry case. Cut the ham into thin strips and scatter on top of the onion.
7. Turn the oven temperature control down to 375°.
8. Mix together the milk and eggs, season with salt and black pepper. Pour into the flan ring and bake in the oven for 20 minutes until the filling is slightly set, but still a little runny.
9. Put the pea purée into a pastry bag fitted with a ½in plain nozzle. Remove

the quiche from the oven and carefully pipe the pea purée in a spiral beginning at the center of the quiche and moving to the outside edge.
10. Sprinkle the Parmesan cheese over the top.
11. Return the quiche to the oven and continue to cook for a further 20 minutes until it is lightly golden and just firm.
12. Serve hot or cold.

## DEVILLED SAUSAGE CARTWHEELS
SERVES 10
*2lb beef sausage meat in one or two continuous thin sausages (see note p. 148)*
FOR THE SAUCE
*2 tbsp tomato ketchup*
*1 tsp clear honey*
*1 tsp vinegar*
*2 tbsp chutney*
*1 tsp dry English mustard*
*2 tsp Worcestershire sauce*
*3 drops Tabasco sauce*
*salt*
*coarsely ground black pepper*

1. To make the sauce: mix all the sauce ingredients together.
2. Preheat the oven, setting the temperature control to 375°.
3. Roll the sausages up like coiled snakes and secure with toothpicks.
4. Put each one on to a large flat ovenproof dish or tray. Prick all over with a fine needle.
5. Brush all over with the devilled sauce.
6. Bake for 25 minutes brushing the sauce over them occasionally until they are firm and brown.
7. Serve hot.

## RED, GREEN AND YELLOW PEPPER SALAD
SERVES 10
*1 large green pepper*
*1 large red pepper*
*1 large yellow pepper*
*1 small onion, finely sliced*
FOR THE DRESSING
*4 tbsp olive oil*
*1 tbsp wine vinegar*
*pinch of mustard*
*squeeze of lemon juice*
*salt*
*black pepper*

1. Remove the core, pips and any tough membrane from the peppers, keeping them whole.

2. Slice the peppers into rings. Arrange them in overlapping circles on a shallow serving dish. Scatter the onion over the top.

3. Put all the dressing ingredients together in a screw-top jar and shake well. Pour over the salad.

## BABY BEETS IN SOUR CREAM
SERVES 10
*3lb fresh or mildly pickled baby beets, cooked*
*1 cup dairy sour cream*
*a few tbsp milk*
*salt*
*black pepper*
*finely chopped parsley or chives*

1. Peel the fresh beets or drain the pickled. Place in a mixing bowl.
2. Mix the sour cream with a little milk to a thick coating consistency. Season with salt and pepper.
3. Just before serving pour the sour cream over the beets and mix a little, so that the sour cream and beet juices are marbled bright pink and white. Tip into a clean glass bowl and sprinkle with chopped parsley or chives.

## GREEN POTATO SALAD
SERVES 10
*3lbs potatoes*
FOR THE GREEN MAYONNAISE
*3oz frozen spinach, cooked and well drained*
*1¼ cups mayonnaise (p. 93)*
*milk*
*⅓ cup finely chopped walnuts*
*salt*
*black pepper*

1. Wash the potatoes and boil in salted water until just tender. Drain and cool, then remove the skins.
2. Purée the spinach in a blender or processor, or push through a sieve to obtain a smooth purée.

*Above* Everyday ingredients (fresh dates, cherries, the top of a pineapple, a chocolate bar, orange segments and two green grapes) make the features of our punk face cake.

3. Mix the spinach purée with the mayonnaise and, if necessary, thin to a coating consistency by adding a little milk. Add the chopped walnuts and season with salt and black pepper.
4. Cut the potatoes into bite-sized pieces. Mix with the green mayonnaise and tip into a clean serving dish.

## FACE CAKE
SERVES 20
*2 cups soft "tub" margarine*
*2 cups sugar*
*grated rind and juice of 2 lemons*
*8 eggs*
*4 cups self-raising flour*
FOR THE FILLING
*5 cups heavy or whipping cream*
*⅔ cup kirsch*
*1 small pineapple*
*8oz strawberries*
*2 bananas*
FOR DECORATION
*the top of the pineapple*
*2 fresh dates*
*2 green grapes*
*2 cherries*
*2 large orange segments*
*1 thick chocolate bar*
*pink coloring*
*toothpicks*

1. Line a 12in round deep layer pan with a double layer of greased wax paper. Preheat the oven, setting the temperature control to 350°.
2. Cream the margarine, sugar and lemon rind together until pale, light and fluffy.
3. Gradually beat in the eggs.
4. Sift the flour twice and fold into the mixture with just enough of the lemon juice to form a soft dropping consistency.
5. Turn the mixture into the prepared pan and bake for one hour. Test the cake by pressing the top lightly with the fingertips. If the cake feels firm it is cooked: if not, turn the oven temperature control down to 300° and continue to cook for another half an hour. Cool the cake on a wire rack and remove the wax paper.
6. To finish the cake: lightly whip the cream and add the kirsch. Remove the skin from the pineapple and cut the flesh first into slices and then into chunks. Save the top leaves for the decoration. Hull and slice the strawberries and slice the bananas.
7. Mix a third of the whipped cream with the fruit. Split the cake into three layers, fill with the fruit and cream and sandwich back together again.
8. Reserve 2 tablespoons of the cream and color it pink. Use the remaining cream to completely cover the whole of the top and sides of the cake with a smooth layer.
9. Cut the pineapple top in half lengthways and clean by wiping with oiled paper. Place it in the top center of the cake to look like a Mohican hair-do.
10. Use the rest of the decoration ingredients (and your imagination too) to create a punk face. (See the illustration on p. 149.)

# VICTORIAN WEDDING

*for Eighty*

*Left* Fresh flowers,
controlled pretty colors and
pristine linen sets off the
romantic wedding cake and
gives a look of yesteryear.
Left back, veal and ham pie;
right back, mustard and
honey-glazed ham.
Foreground, from the left,
smoked salmon and shrimp
rolls with stuffed anchovy
eggs, potted kipper and beet
and scallion salad.

I**T IS OBVIOUSLY NOT A GOOD IDEA TO CATER FOR YOUR** own wedding unless you are the calmest of brides (or grooms) and the most efficient of cooks. But the bride's mother, or brother, or aunt could well take it on, and save the bride's father a fortune. Catering for a wedding is no more difficult than coping with any other party, and many of the cocktail, tea or buffet menus in this book would make excellent wedding fare, with the addition of the wedding cake and, if the party is to be a day-time one, tea or coffee.

Getting the proceedings hiccup-free is a matter of planning with meticulous, even pedantic, care; of making lists and checking them religiously. We have provided a schedule for our groaning Victorian sideboard, which, if not suitable for the wedding you plan, may at least serve as a model when making your own plans. See also the lists in Catering in Quantity, pp. 10-13.

We have assumed that the wedding is to be a morning one, with the reception guests arriving just before lunch. But the length of the wedding service or ceremony and the distance between the church or registry office and the reception will obviously make a difference, so make careful calculations of your own. It is vital that catering matters are well under control so the family can stand, if they wish to, in a formal receiving line to welcome the guests.

Our party has a romantic Victorian theme, and is a spring-time affair, with the predominant color themes primrose yellow and white. We have assumed that waitresses or students can be hired for the day and can be persuaded to arrive in full-length black skirts and white blouses. They could wear black bows, neckties or bow-ties at the throat, and mob caps on the back of their heads. Mob-caps are easy enough to make, or fabric shower caps with the plastic lining removed look very good. Or flat cooks' hats or waitresses' lace head-bands can be cheaply bought from catering suppliers. Nothing has to be at all authentic as long as the general old-fashioned look is achieved. Floral printed long cotton skirts, Edwardian-looking waistcoats, even straw boaters, if worn by all the waiting staff, will give unusual charm to the party.

Buffet tables can be given a romantic look by the addition of small bouquets pinned to the ruched and draped table-cloths. Thin filmy modern materials, like cheap curtain lining,

Marking the Route
*The church or reception may be
difficult to find. As well as
enclosing a map with the
invitations, mark the route
with balloons.*

Flowers
*Bouquets of flowers look pretty
and old-fashioned with a
white paper doily fastened to
the back, giving the
arrangement a frilly white
edge. Order extra flowers to
decorate the plates of food and
matching flowers for the
wedding cake.*

Florists' primulas
(polyanthus) last better than
wild primroses when picked
but try to get soft, pale
colors.

**Tablecloths**
*Gold or pink damask tablecloths can be hired and look attractive with white lace shawls or cloths set over the top.*

drape beautifully and can be used for the front and sides of a buffet. Or lace tablecloths or even lace shawls set diagonally over plain white sheets or hired tablecloths will disguise their "caterer's" look.

Flowers should as far as possible reflect the theme – tight Victorian bouquets tied with trailing ribbons and lace will look far better than the usual florist's triangular arrangements. The bridesmaids and bride could carry similar nosegays or bunches of primroses, and garlands of flowers and leaves look enchanting set squarely or slightly back on the head. If using a professional florist, find pictures in old books or magazines of exactly the shape of bouquet or headdress you want. No florist will come up with the right thing if all she has to go on is a verbal description, and being presented with the wrong thing on the day of the wedding, when it is too late to do anything about it, is very disappointing.

If coping with the flowers yourself, do them the day before and keep them overnight in a cool room, or even outside, but under cover, overnight. Small bouquets, bouttonieres and hair bands should be made as late as possible the night before, the flower stems wrapped in wet cotton wool, oasis or other florist's material, and wrapped in foil to prevent drips. These should be put in a plastic box or lightly covered with plastic wrap and kept cool, even refrigerated if the extra cream, milk and food is not already making impossible demands on the refrigerator space.

Which brings up the next matter – refrigeration. You simply cannot have enough, especially if the house is centrally heated or the weather is at all warm. So make arrangements to borrow a neighbor's refrigerator, and ask the fish merchant to get you large polystyrene cool boxes. They are used to keep wet fish fresh and are generally thrown away after use. They will need a scrub to remove the fishy smell. Buy or borrow as many cold packs as possible. These are bags, or sometimes bottles, filled with a liquid which once solidly frozen retains its chilling properties for many hours. A few of these put in the polystyrene boxes (or in insulated picnic boxes) with the food or flowers will keep them cold and fresh very effectively. For best results put the cold packs *on top* of the food (but not on top of flowers of course) – cold air *sinks*, remember. It will not be possible to cool all the milk needed, the wine or champagne, or orange juice for the children, in the refrigerator, however capacious. So order ice and hire ice-baths or borrow plastic babies' baths, or any other suitable containers. The bath would be ideal but it is seldom near the point where you wish to set up the bar and running up and down stairs can be a nuisance. Figure on 50lbs of ice for chilling drinks for 100 people. The thing to remember is that wine cools quickest in *water* containing plenty of ice rather than lying on top of ice cubes. The icy water more effectively surrounds and cools the whole bottle. The trick is to put the bottles in the bath first. Pour on the ice and add the water (it is hard to get the bottles through the ice if they are added last). But one word of warning: if the wine has been bought from a liquor store on a "sale-or-return" basis, the labels must be intact on any bottles returned to him. Most liquor stores will supply wine and champagne on this basis, happily agreeing to over-supply you in the hope that you will keep more of the wine than you intended to. They will sometimes lend glasses free of charge too.

A silver coin stuck into the first champagne cork popped is a traditional lucky memento.

**Food Temperatures**
*Remember that polystyrene is an insulator so it will keep food warm as well as cool. It is vitally important to cool the food quickly and thoroughly before storing in insulated containers.*

**Strawberry Tarts**
*Strawberry tarts are a good addition to a summer wedding – but fiddly to make so only attempt them for a small wedding party. Bake rich shortcrust pastry shells; mix Petit-Suisse or cream cheese with a little sugar and place a spoonful in the base of each pastry case. Arrange strawberries on top and carefully coat them with hot redcurrant jelly.*

**Wine Labels**
*Bottles of white wine or champagne steeped in icy water are likely to lose their labels. Take care not to have too many bottles chilling as the reception draws to its close as bottles without labels cannot be returned to the supplier.*

Pretty China
*Pretty china plates and serving dishes can easily be found in second-hand shops and on junk stalls in markets. Also look for Victorian jelly molds with tiers and fluted edges.*

To give the food a Victorian look, beg or borrow a few ham stands, cake stands or epergnes – anything that will raise some of the food above the rest. Even pretty plates on upturned bowls, as long as they are steady, will do. Make pyramids of fruit and leaves on sideboards or mantelpieces. If you have or can borrow some jelly molds, use them for jellies or molds such as our blackberry jelly, or to give shape to potted meats or pâtés. Tiered cake stands, even modern ones, look quaintly Victorian, and big old-fashioned platters and serving dishes will lend much elegance and charm.

## THE INVITATION
Wedding invitations should go out a good six weeks before the event to far-away relatives and friends to give them time to make arrangements. Victorian wedding invitations were very like ours, but were sometimes more sentimental, with engraved orange-blossom or entwined initials on them.

## WINE
Champagne is the obvious, if expensive choice. German Sekt or French or Californian sparkling wines make good alternatives. But look for the words "Méthode Champenoise" on the label. They denote classic champagne-like making of the wine, rather than the injection of carbon dioxide – the method used in making soda water – to get bubbles. Do not make the common mistake of starting with a glass of good champagne then following with inferior bubbly. Better start as you mean to go on. Or offer the best wine for the toast to the couple at the end of the proceedings. Grading up is a pleasanter experience for the drinker than grading down.

Wine
*Instead of serving champagne throughout the reception, it makes a refreshing change to offer a selection of wines. A light red wine, a medium German wine and a dry French one would be a good choice. White wine could be made into kir or wine-coolers (mixed with soda water).*

---

**THE MENU**

*Potted Kipper*

*Chicken and Veal Pie*
*Cumberland Sauce*

*Mustard and Honey-Glazed Ham*
*Stuffed Anchovy Eggs*
*Smoked Salmon and Shrimp Rolls*
*Beets with Scallions*
*Simple Tossed Salad*

*Blackberry Gelatin with Port*
*Coffee and Orange Mini-Meringues*

*Victorian Wedding Cake*

---

Selecting the Menu
*When choosing the menu remember the guests making a long journey. There is nothing worse than arriving at a reception having missed lunch only to be offered a few canapés. Plan a substantial meal or lay on something simple but filling beforehand – say French bread, Brie and celery.*

## GETTING AHEAD
*One year to six months before the wedding*
○ Choose a date and confirm this with the church or Registry Office.
○ Draft a list of guests to establish the approximate number.
○ Find a venue for the reception. Arrange for access the afternoon before the wedding.
○ Make the wedding cake and "feed" with brandy.

To open champagne, hold the bottle almost horizontally, grip the cork firmly in one hand and twist the bottom of the bottle with the other. To stop it bubbling over, dip a wet finger into the top or keep the bottles as near lying down as possible. And remember flying corks are dangerous.

**Wedding Invitations**
*A printer will be able to produce many elaborate and curly typefaces to choose from and it is possible to have paper napkins, or the boxes designed for sending small slices of cake to absent friends (available from stationers, and large department stores) overprinted in the same way.*

*Six to two months before the wedding*
○ Order the invitations (make maps and directions of how to reach the ceremony and reception).
○ Find some helpers so that once the buffet is arranged you can become a guest and the helpers will take care of everything. For eighty guests you will need at least four. Check they have long black skirts and mob caps or straw hats and vests.
○ Arrange for some of the helpers to assist with the food preparation.
○ Decide on the things you need in the way of tables, chairs, cutlery, plates, glassware, linen, coffee and tea urns, etc. See check lists in Catering in Quantity, p. 10.
○ Arrange to borrow or hire them.

*Two months before the wedding*
○ Send the invitations.
○ Make an arrangement for the supply of drinks. Order ice.
○ Choose the flowers: either order them from a florist or find a friend to deal with them, but do not attempt to produce food and flowers alone. Remember you will need flowers to decorate the plates of food and cake, and perhaps for button-holes and corsages.
○ Find Victorian-looking serving dishes and a few ornaments to decorate the buffet.
○ Arrange to borrow extra refrigerator and freezer space.
○ Collect cool boxes and polystyrene containers.

*One month before the wedding*
○ Marzipan the wedding cake.
○ Make the potted kipper to stage 5 and freeze.
○ Draw up shopping lists for the meat, fish, fruit, vegetables, dairy and dry goods.
○ Place orders for everything except the dry goods so that all you have to do when you need them is to pick them up or have them delivered.
○ Arrange for the drinks, etc. to be delivered directly to the reception place on the morning of the wedding. Make sure someone is there to take delivery and check the order; nothing goes astray more easily than alcohol.
○ Buy as many of the dry goods as possible.

*Three weeks before the wedding*
○ Coat the wedding cake with icing.

*Two weeks before the wedding*
○ Make the meringues and store in an airtight container.
○ Coat the cake with a second layer of icing.
○ Make ham frill.

*One week before the wedding*
○ Arrange to collect the hams and soak them.
○ Make the Cumberland sauce, mayonnaise and salad dressing (don't add fresh herbs).
○ Make the blackberry purée for the gelatin.
○ Do a final count of guests and adjust food orders.

*Three days before the wedding*
○ Collect the meat.
○ Make the chicken and veal pies and the jellied stock.
○ Cook the ham and glaze with mustard and honey.
○ Pipe shells around the cake and add lace and ribbons.

**Wedding Cake**
*Our fruit wedding cake can be made up to a year in advance. Leave the wax paper from lining the pan attached to the cakes to keep them moist, and store wrapped in foil or in a cake pan in a cool place. The cakes can be enriched by pricking small holes in the top of each one, pouring over a little brandy or rum and allowing it to soak in.*

**A Sponge Wedding Cake**
*You might like to make a sponge wedding cake instead of a traditional fruit one. It could be lemon or chocolate flavored and filled with fruit and cream mixed with any liqueur. Bake 3 different-sized tiers; pile them on top of each other (smallest on the top) and cover the outside with fresh whipped cream or molded fondant icing (p. 171). Decorate the tiers with chocolate hearts, whole strawberries and fresh flowers.*

**Staff**
*As a rough guide you will need 1 member of staff per 20 guests for a buffet and 1 per 40 to serve canapés and champagne.*

**Butter**
*Potted meats and fish keep better if made with butter rather than cream or cream cheese. If sealed with clarified butter, smoked fish pâtés will keep, refrigerated, up to 3 days and potted meats and pâtés up to 10 days. To clarify butter, heat gently until just foaming, then strain through a doubled piece of fine muslin.*

**Smithfield Ham**
*This is the best known of American "country-style" hams. It is cured by a lengthy and elaborate process. The ham is coated with salt, sodium nitrate and sugar, refrigerated for 5 days; salted and refrigerated again; smoked for 10 days and finally aged for 6-12 months.*

*Above right* Blackberry gelatin with port, and orange and coffee meringues.

### Two days before the wedding
○ Fill pies with jellied stock.
○ Boil the eggs.
○ Defrost the potted kipper.
○ Make the blackberry gelatin with port.

### The day before the wedding
○ Take delivery of the hire equipment. Get the tables set up.
○ Collect the fruit and vegetables, dairy and fish order.
○ Add the clarified butter and decorate the potted kipper.
○ Cut the anchovy eggs in half, mix up the filling but keep both separate and covered with plastic wrap overnight.
○ Fill the salmon rolls with shrimp and cream cheese.
○ Chop the scallions.
○ Peel and slice the beets.
○ Wash the lettuce and shake dry. Wash the cherry tomatoes, cut up the cucumbers.
○ Chop mint and chives for decoration and dressings. Refrigerate overnight covered with plastic wrap.
○ Make the orange cream and the cinnamon cream.
○ Deliver all non-perishables to the place of the reception.

### The morning of the wedding
○ Delegate two of your helpers to go to the venue to set places at the tables, put the plates on the buffet and arrange the room.
○ They must check that the glasses and drinks have been delivered as ordered.
○ The two helpers should set up the bar and immediately put the champagne on ice.

### Meanwhile at home, you plus three helpers
○ Fill the anchovy eggs.
○ Dish up the pies, glazed ham, eggs and salmon rolls.
○ Finish the beet and lettuce salads.
○ Turn out the gelatin.
○ Fill the coffee meringues.
○ Check you have all creams and accompanying sauces.
○ Deliver all to the reception place.
○ Arrange the buffet with two or three service points and decorate the food with flowers.
○ Add flowers and trailing ribbons to wedding cake.

**Raised Pie**
*When molding the pastry for a raised pie make sure that there are no cracks or the jelly will seep out. If cracks appear after cooking, seal them with a little butter. The jelly will moisten the pie and hold the meat and pastry together.*

Stuffed anchovy eggs form part of the main buffet but they could also make a delicious first course.

Smoked salmon should be a transluscent pale orange. Opaque pink salmon has been frozen too long.

# VICTORIAN WEDDING RECIPES

QUANTITY NOTE:
Adjust the quantities if catering for large numbers. For 80 people make 3 times the recipes for potted kipper and Cumberland sauce; 8 times the stuffed eggs and the salmon and shrimp rolls; 4 times the chicken and veal pie and the beet salad. One 15lb ham should be sufficient. See Catering in Quantity, p. 10.

## POTTED KIPPER
SERVES 10
*1lb kippered herring*
*¾ cup softened butter*
*¼ cup cream cheese*
*black pepper*
*lemon juice*
FOR DECORATION
*¼ cup clarified butter*
*a few bay leaves*
*juniper berries*

1. Lay the kippers in a roasting pan. Cover with boiling water and leave to stand for 10 minutes. Drain.
2. Remove the skin and any bones from the fillets.
3. Cream the butter with the cream cheese until very soft.
4. Mince the fillets, and beat into the butter and cream cheese mixture. (Alternatively place the butter, cream cheese and kipper fillets in a food processor and blend until smooth.)
5. Season to taste with black pepper and lemon juice.
6. Pile into earthenware dishes and flatten the top. Pour the clarified butter on top. While the butter is still runny, decorate with bay leaves and juniper berries. Chill.

## CHICKEN AND VEAL PIE
SERVES 10
FOR THE PASTRY
*4 cups all-purpose flour*
*1 tsp salt*
*2 eggs and 1 yolk, beaten*
*¾ cup water*
*¼ cup butter*
*⅓ cup shortening or lard*
*½ cup all-purpose flour*
FOR THE FARCE
*¾ cup ground or finely chopped chicken*
*¾ cup ground or finely chopped veal*
*1½ cups sausage meat or fatty ground pork*
*½ small onion, minced*
*ground allspice*
*ground nutmeg*
*salt*
*coarsely ground black pepper*

FOR THE FILLING
*8oz chicken breasts*
*8oz veal, cut in thin stripes*
*chopped parsley*
*flour for dusting*
TO FINISH
*1 beaten egg*
*2½ cups jellied stock*

1. Make the pastry: sift the flour and salt together into a bowl. Add the eggs and cover with the flour.
2. Put the water, butter and lard together in a saucepan and bring slowly to the boil.
3. Once the liquid has boiled, pour it immediately on to the flour and stir vigorously with a knife. Knead the pastry until the egg streaks have gone and the pastry is smooth.
4. Wrap the pastry in a piece of plastic wrap and leave at room temperature for 30 minutes.
5. Meanwhile make the farce by mixing all the ingredients for it together.
6. Preheat the oven, setting the temperature control to 375°.
7. Roll the pastry to a round approximately 12in in diameter and cut a wedge from a quarter of it. Reserve this for the lid, keeping it wrapped in plastic wrap and at room temperature.
8. Use the rest of the pastry to line a 9½in (3qt) springform pan. Mold the pastry well into the corners and press the joins together.
9. Spread half of the farce in the bottom of the pastry case. Sprinkle with chopped parsley.
10. Dust the chicken breasts and veal slices well with flour and lay them on top. Add more parsley. Cover with the remaining farce.
11. Roll the pastry for the lid to a circle an inch larger than the pie. Brush the edge of the pie with beaten egg. Press the lid on to the pie, sealing the edges well and crimping them by pinching between the thumb and forefinger.
12. Brush the top with egg. Make a small hole in the center of the pastry with a small round pastry cutter. Use the trimmings to make pastry leaves and elaborately decorate the top. Brush again with egg.
13. Bake for 1 hour, then turn the oven temperature control down to 200° and bake for two more hours or until firm when pierced with a skewer.
14. Remove the outer ring of the pan and then cool the pie overnight but do not chill.

15. The following day, warm the stock until it is liquid then cool again until syrupy. Using a funnel in the hole of the pastry lid, fill up the pie with jelly. Keep adding stock until you are sure the pie is completely full. Refrigerate before serving. Hand Cumberland sauce separately.

## CUMBERLAND SAUCE
SERVES 10
*2 oranges*
*1 lemon*
*½ cup (8oz) redcurrant jelly*
*1 shallot, chopped*
*⅔ cup port or red wine*
*½ tsp mild pale Dijon mustard*
*pinch of cayenne pepper*
*pinch of ground ginger*

1. Remove the zest of one orange and the lemon finely, using a potato peeler. Remove only the outer skin, but no pith. Cut the rind into needle-fine shreds.
2. Squeeze all the fruit juice and strain into a pan, add the remaining ingredients with the shreds. Simmer for 10 minutes. Leave to cool.

## MUSTARD AND HONEY-GLAZED HAM
SERVES 40
*1 whole country ham weighing approximately 15lb*
*1 large onion*
*2 carrots*
*2 bay leaves*
*a handful of fresh parsley*
*peppercorns*
*4 tbsp clear honey*
*2 tsp prepared English mustard*
*a handful of cloves*
FOR DECORATION
*a white paper ham frill*

1. Soak the ham in cold water for 3-4 days.
2. Place it in a large pan of fresh water and add the onion, carrots, bay leaf, parsley and peppercorns.
3. Bring the water slowly to the boil. Cover the pan and turn the heat down so that the water is barely simmering. Cook for three hours or until the flesh is tender when pierced, and has shrunk away from the bone.
4. Allow the ham to cool slightly in the stock before lifting out and carefully pulling off the skin without removing any of the fat. With a small sharp knife score the fat to make a diamond pattern.
5. Preheat the oven, setting the temperature control to 425°.

6. In a small saucepan warm the honey. Mix with the mustard to form a smooth paste. Spread evenly over the fat. Stick a clove in the center of each diamond.

7. Bake the ham in the hot oven for 10 to 20 minutes until golden brown and slightly caramelized. Watch carefully as the glaze burns very easily.

8. Allow to cool. Tidy the meat around the edge of the bone. Place the frill on the bone and serve on a ham stand.

## STUFFED ANCHOVY EGGS

*To go with the Salmon and Shrimp Rolls*

MAKES 10 STUFFED EGGS

5 hard-boiled eggs
1 tbsp mayonnaise
anchovy essence
salt, black pepper and Tabasco
FOR DECORATION
anchovy fillets
a little milk
watercress
lemon slices

1. Cut the eggs in half lengthways.

2. Remove and sieve the yolks, or purée them in a food processor. Mix with the mayonnaise to make a soft but not sloppy paste.

3. Season well with the anchovy essence, salt, pepper and Tabasco.

4. Place the mixture in a pastry bag fitted with a ½in fluted nozzle and pipe a small whirl into the hollows of the egg whites.

5. Soak the anchovy fillets in a little milk for an hour to remove some of the saltiness. Drain, then cut the fillets into long slivers and use them to make a cross or lattice pattern on top of each egg.

6. Arrange the eggs on a serving dish in alternate rows with the smoked salmon rolls. Decorate with wedges of lemon and watercress.

## SMOKED SALMON ROLLS AND SHRIMP ROLLS

*To go with the Anchovy Eggs*

MAKES 10 ROLLS

8oz sliced smoked salmon
8oz cream cheese
1⅓ cups (8oz) shelled cooked shrimp
2 tbsp milk
a little grated rind and juice of lemon
2 tsp finely chopped fresh dill
salt and black pepper
FOR DECORATION
lemon
watercress

1. Trim the salmon into strips approximately 3in × 6in. Save the trimmings.

2. Soften the cream cheese. Purée the smoked salmon trimmings with a little milk and mix with the cream cheese. Add the grated lemon rind and juice, dill and enough of the milk to make a soft but not sloppy mixture.

3. Fold in the shrimp and season to taste with salt and black pepper.

4. Place a spoonful of the mixture at the top of each salmon strip and roll up.

5. Arrange the rolls on a serving dish in alternate rows with the eggs. Decorate with slices of lemon and watercress.

## BEETS WITH SCALLIONS

SERVES 10

1lb cooked beets
8 scallions
FOR THE DRESSING
3 tbsp salad oil
1 tbsp wine vinegar
pinch dry English mustard
pinch brown sugar
salt
black pepper

1. Peel the beets and cut into ¼in slices. Arrange in overlapping layers in shallow serving dishes.

2. Clean the scallions and chop finely. Sprinkle over the beets.

3. Place all the dressing ingredients in a screw-top jar and shake well, season to taste with salt and black pepper. Pour over the salad.

## SIMPLE TOSSED SALAD

SERVES 10

1 small romaine lettuce
1lb cherry tomatoes
½ cucumber
FOR THE DRESSING
4 tsp salad oil
1 tbsp wine vinegar
squeeze of lemon juice
1 tsp finely chopped chives
1 tsp finely chopped mint

1. Wash the lettuce and shake dry. Discard outside leaves and break the largish leaves into small pieces. Leave the best and smallest ones whole.

2. Leave the cherry tomatoes whole. Cut the cucumber half neatly into small sticks approximately 2in long and ¼in wide.

3. To serve the salad: place all the dressing ingredients together in a screw-top jar and shake well. Arrange the lettuce around the edge of a large, round, shallow serving platter. Toss the tomato and cucumber in the dressing and pile into the center of the dish.

## BLACKBERRY GELATIN WITH PORT

SERVES 10

2lb blackberries
1 cup sugar
⅔ cup ruby port
4 tbsp unflavored gelatin
TO SERVE
2½ cups whipping cream
2 tsp ground cinnamon

1. Put the berries and sugar into a saucepan and cover with water. Boil until soft (about 5 minutes). Liquidize in a blender and push through a sieve.

2. Put ⅔ cup water in a saucepan and sprinkle the gelatin evenly over it. Allow to soak for 10 minutes. Heat very gently until the gelatin is clear and liquid, but do not boil. Pour into the blackberry mixture and stir.

3. Add the port and enough water to make up to 8 cups. Mix well.

4. Pour into two wet jelly or other decorative molds and refrigerate until set.

5. To serve the jellies, dip the molds briefly into hot water – just enough to loosen them without melting the jelly. Put the serving dish over the mold and invert so that the jelly falls on the plate.

6. Whip the cream lightly. Sift the cinnamon into the cream and gently fold in.

## COFFEE AND ORANGE MINI-MERINGUES

MAKES 20 MERINGUES

3 egg whites
½ cup soft brown sugar
1 tsp instant coffee powder
FOR THE FILLING
2 cups heavy cream
1 tbsp Grand Marnier
grated rind of 1 orange

1. Preheat the oven, setting the temperature control to 225°.

2. Place wax paper on four baking sheets and brush with oil.

3. Beat egg whites until stiff but not dry.

4. Add 1 tbsp of sugar and beat again until stiff and very shiny.

5. Fold in remaining sugar and the instant coffee powder.

6. Put the meringue into a pastry bag fitted with ½in plain nozzle. Pipe the meringue into small whirls.

7. Bake in the oven for about two hours until the meringues are dry and will lift easily off the paper. Leave to cool.

8. Whip the cream, fold in the Grand Marnier and orange rind. Sandwich the meringues together in pairs.

QUANTITY NOTE:

This recipe is sufficient to fill a 8in cake tin. For our Victorian Wedding cake make three times this quantity to fill a 6in pan, a 8in pan and a 12in pan. Make the mixture in two or three batches, smaller quantities are easier to deal with. The large cake will take about 3½ to 4 hours to cook, the middle-sized cake will take about 2½ to 3 hours and the small one about 2 hours.

## VICTORIAN WEDDING CAKE

BASIC FRUIT CAKE
¾ cup butter
¾ cup soft dark brown sugar
rind and juice of 1 lemon
4 eggs
2 cups all-purpose flour
½ tsp ground allspice
½ tsp nutmeg
½ tsp cinnamon
½ tsp mace
1 tbsp black molasses
1⅓ cups currants
3 cups golden raisins
2½ cups raisins
2oz candied peel
8oz candied cherries
1 cup flaked almonds
⅔ cups dry cider or brandy
1 grated apple

1. Line the base and sides of a 8in deep layer pan with a double layer of greased wax paper.
2. Preheat the oven, setting the temperature control to 350°.
3. Cream together the butter, sugar and lemon rind until they are light and pale in color. Gradually beat in the eggs one by one.
4. Sift together the flour and spices and fold into the mixture. Stir in the remaining ingredients.
5. Spoon the mixture into the prepared pan. Tie a few layers of brown paper or newspaper around the outside of the pan to stop the edges from burning.
6. Bake in the preheated oven for one hour then turn the oven temperature control down to 300° for the remaining cooking time. (Test after a further 2½ hours.)
7. The cake is cooked when a skewer will emerge dry having been pushed into the middle of the cake. If the top is in danger of over-browning cover it with doubled wax, or ordinary brown paper.
8. Leave the cakes to cool before wrapping them and storing in an airtight container until you are ready to ice them.

FOR THE MARZIPAN
Make three times the recipe for our 3-tier cake
1 cup sugar
2 cups confectioners' sugar
4 cups ground almonds
2 egg yolks
2 whole eggs
2 tsp lemon juice
⅛ tsp vanilla
APRICOT GLAZE
¾ cup apricot jam
⅔ cup water

1. To make the marzipan: sift the two sugars together into a bowl and stir in the ground almonds.
2. Beat the egg yolks and the whole eggs together and add to the dry ingredients with the lemon juice and vanilla. Mix them lightly with a wooden spoon.
3. Dust the work surface with confectioners' sugar and knead the marzipan until smooth. Take care not to overwork the mixture as if you do, you will draw the oils out of the almonds, giving a greasy paste.
4. Divide the marzipan into half and then divide one of the halves again into ⅔ and ⅓. Repeat the following process to marzipan each cake. Take one third of a piece of the marzipan and roll it into a circle a little larger than the top of the cake.
5. Measure the circumference of the cake with a piece of string and roll the remaining marzipan to a strip as long as the piece of string and just a little wider than the height of the cake.
6. Heat the apricot jam with the water. Bring to the boil and brush over the sides of the cake. Turn the cake on its side and roll on to the strip of marzipan, sticking on the marzipan as you go.
7. Turn the cake the right way up and brush the top with more hot jam. Make sure that the circle of marzipan for the top of the cake is dusted with plenty of confectioners' sugar to prevent it sticking to the work surface. Place the cake upside down on top of the circle.
8. Use a palette knife to work the joins together and make sure that the marzipan is smoothed down the sides to meet the table top. (This will give a perfect square edge.)
9. Turn the cake the right way up and brush off any excess confectioners' sugar with a clean dry pastry brush.
10. Cover the cakes with wax paper and leave them to dry for at least forty-eight hours before icing them.

FOR THE ROYAL ICING
Make twice the recipe for our 3-tier cake
6 cups confectioners' sugar
2 egg whites
2 tsp glycerine
squeeze of lemon juice
16in cake board

1. Sift the confectioners' sugar into a bowl. Beat the egg whites until frothy.
2. Gradually beat enough of the sugar into the whites until the mixture is smooth and will stand up in peaks like meringue. Add the glycerine and lemon juice and continue to beat the icing to a light spreading consistency.
3. Place the large cake on the cake board then stand the middle and small cakes on top, making sure that they are placed symmetrically.
4. Spread the icing smoothly over the three cakes. Do not worry if the finish is not perfect, most of it will be covered with ribbons and decorations. However, if you feel unhappy with the first coat of icing, allow it to dry for two or three days, shave off the rough edges with a sharp knife, thin down the remaining icing with a little egg white (or make fresh icing) and apply a second coat to the cake. Allow to dry for one week.

TO FINISH THE CAKE
2yds ½in wide daisy lace
wide white ribbon
narrow pastel-colored ribbon
1 roll white gift-wrap ribbon
extra flowers for the sides
bouquet of little flowers for the top of the cake
(in a low bowl)

1. Make up a half quantity recipe of royal icing (see above).
2. Use a medium-size star nozzle to pipe a row of shell shapes around the bottom of each cake.
3. Attach the daisy lace to the top edge of each cake, making it secure with royal icing or large-headed pins. (Remember to warn whoever cuts the cake to remove the pins.) Stick the narrow and wide ribbons around the side of each cake, either on top of each other or below each other.
4. Arrange the extra fresh flowers around the tiers of cake, using royal icing to stick them on if necessary.
5. Cut the gift-wrap ribbon into assorted lengths and "curl" it by pulling a knife or scissor-blade over the surface. Attach the ribbons to the top of the cake, allowing them to trail down the sides. Stand the bouquet of flowers on top.

# MIDDLE EASTERN MEZZEH

*for twenty*

Pitta bread, broken or cut into sticks, crisp lettuce leaves and carrot batons make fresh and delicious scoops for savory dips.

THIS PARTY IS AN UNASHAMED MISH-MASH OF MIDDLE Eastern styles. It includes the Egyptian falafel, an Armenian version of the Lebanese tabouleh, a Syrian hummus, salads from Israel and dips from everywhere. The essential thing about a Mezzeh (Meze in Greece and Maza in Israel) table is its variety – dozens of small plates or saucers containing every kind of appetizer. A modest pavement café may offer a couple of dozen dishes with your drinks – Feta cheese, tomato salad, two or three types of olives, fish in oil, tahina, hummus, miniature kebabs, avocado salads, walnut and cheese mixtures – anything and everything providing it is colorful, tasty and can be eaten with the fingers or scooped up with bread or a lettuce leaf.

Mezzeh in the Middle East are served as snacks, or as a prelude to a meal, or instead of one. Our mezzeh table is the whole point of the party. Of course a table such as this could be provided as the buffet for any kind of stand-up party, but it seems a pity to relegate so much effort and such variety and beauty to a side-show. So ask your guests to a Middle Eastern Mezzeh party, at lunch time, preferably in the blazing heat. It may not be possible to conjure up the glare of whitewashed café walls, or the cool interior of a Bedouin's tent, or the palm-shaded inner courtyard of a potentate's palace, with deep blue tiles, orange trees and splashing fountains. But think along those lines.

Use as many different-patterned or shaped saucers or small plates as you can lay your hands on. Variety is all. Although serving three dozen dishes on matching saucers may appeal to the organized designer, it also makes the offerings look mass-produced and as if provided by caterer or hotel.

Do not be tempted to have too much of anything. The whole point is that the choice is large, but the dishes are small. The mezzeh is traditionally a great repository for left-overs, and very good it can be too. A little of yesterday's chopped liver, spiked with a bit of fresh onion, a left-over red mullet mashed in good olive oil, a couple of meatballs sliced, a little pickle, a fresh salad made of no more than one large tomato and a green pepper. And so on.

How much to prepare? The easiest way to calculate this is to allow two dishes per person. Of course there can be some repeats – for 20 people forty little saucers each containing a

*Mezzeh Dishes*
*Greek, Turkish, Syrian, Israeli, Egyptian, Arabian and Persian dishes are suitable for a mezzeh party. The Spanish version of a mezzeh is called tapas and some of the dishes served in this could also be included here – for instance, Spanish omelet, shrimp or potatoes in strong garlic-flavored mayonnaise, steamed clams or mussels, marinated raw fish or fried quails' eggs.*

*An Unusual Cocktail*
*Cut the top third off a watermelon. Scoop out the flesh and seeds and put them in a colander and catch the juice in a bowl. Fill the melon with the fruit juice, vodka and a little sugar. Wedge it in a bed of cracked ice (or better still, for a beach party, bury it in the sand). Pierce holes in the lid of the melon and issue guests with straws to take a passing swig!*

different and delicious food, would be amazing and wonderful, but perhaps not practicable. Two of everything would do nicely, and would be less of a performance to prepare. But remember that many of the dishes need not be elaborate home cooking. Middle Eastern delicatessens will provide many excellent ready-prepared dishes in small quantities, and simple things like olives, nuts, Feta cheese, fresh dates, canned ratatouille, canned tahina, chopped fresh cucumber with mint and lemon, can fill the gaps. Try to vary texture as well as taste and color – perhaps crispy-fried rings of squid, or fresh crudités to contrast with the soft pastes like taramasalata and hummus.

Provide plates for the guests on which they can put their selection, and forks if the mixtures can neither be scooped up with a carrot stick or small crisp lettuce leaf, nor eaten cleanly with the fingers. Put a stack of paper napkins on the table too, and make sure there are enough crackers, pitta bread, breadsticks and crudités for dipping.

## DRINKS

The peoples of the Middle East are not great drinkers. Good Muslims would not drink any alcohol at all of course and even the Christians seem to drink more water and strong sweet coffee ("Greek" or "Turkish" according to whose side you are on) than wine. But Westerners, dependent on a bit of artificial stimulation to break down the barriers of reserve, might be offered the Greek ouzo, well chilled, or retsina, the famous resinated wine that is loved or loathed by tourists. For the less adventurous provide a sunny red wine from California or a well chilled white wine.

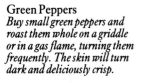

Turkish Delight and strong, black coffee make the perfect end to your mezzeh.

**Feta Cheese**
*This is a crumbly, white Greek cheese made from goats' or ewes' milk and ripened in brine. It can be eaten alone, used in cooking or crumbled into a salad with tomato, black olives, and raw onion and tossed with olive oil and oregano.*

**Ouzo**
*This is a fiery, colorless spirit flavored with aniseed. It belongs to the same family as arrack, anis and pernod. Serve a small amount in a liqueur glass with ice, or in a tumbler topped up with water.*

### THE MENU

Sardines
Avocado Salad
Green, Red and Yellow Peppers
Labna Cheese
Tzatziki
Hummus
Taramasalata
Eggplant Dip
Black and Green Olives
Fresh Dates
Ceviche
Armenian Bulgar
Fried Squid
Ful Medames
Tomato and Zucchini Salad
Falafel
Kofta Kebabs
Tuna Fish and Butterbeans
Anchovy Salad
Mushroom Salad
Feta Cheese

**Green Peppers**
*Buy small green peppers and roast them whole on a griddle or in a gas flame, turning them frequently. The skin will turn dark and deliciously crisp.*

*Right* A bit of sun, a whitewashed wall, and a table outside provide the perfect setting for sitting over ouzo (or retsina) and Greek mezzeh. Here pitta bread for dipping in taramasalata, black olives and Feta cheese and, behind, pepper salad.

Prepare two lots of each dish (or four of half of them) for 40 people.

*Above* Outer circle (large plates only), from the top: kofta kebabs, black olives with Feta cheese, taramasalata with pitta bread sticks, mushroom salad, Armenian bulgar. Inner circle, top right: fried squid, falafel, tomato and zucchini salad, fresh dates, anchovy salad. In the center, raw vegetable sticks for eating with the various savory mixtures in small dishes (from the top right: sardine dip, hummus, avocado salad, labna cheese and tzatziki).

## GETTING AHEAD
*A few weeks in advance*

○ Invite the guests by invitation or by telephone.
○ Decide how simple or lavish the party is to be. It could be a laden table in the house or garden. If hiring large palms in tubs, order them now.
○ Collect numerous small dishes, saucers and bowls for serving the mezzeh in.
○ Buy small cocktail-size paper napkins.
○ Make a shopping list from the recipes (remember to include crackers, breads and vegetables to make the crudités for serving with the mezzeh).

Pitta Bread Sandwiches
*Pitta bread makes good sandwiches with a difference. Split them in half and fill them with a selection of mezzeh.*

**Vine Leaves**
*These can be bought vacuum-packed in brine or ready-stuffed in cans. Stuffing for vine leaves can be made from spiced ground lamb or cooked rice flavored with onion and mint.*

○ Buy the dry goods.
○ Decide on drinks to be served and buy them.

*Two days before the party*
○ Do the remaining shopping, including exotic fruit and flowers for display.

*The day before the party*
○ Make plenty of ice for drinks.
○ Arrange the buffet and area where the party is to be held.
○ Make an exotic arrangement of fruit or flowers to decorate the buffet.
○ Drain the yogurt for the labna cheese; make the hummus, eggplant dip and the taramasalata.
○ Slice and marinate the fish for the ceviche.
○ Peel the tomatoes, chop mint, coriander leaves and parsley for the Armenian bulgar. Cover and chill.
○ Clean and slice the squid.
○ Boil the eggs for the ful medames and the anchovy salad.
○ Peel the tomatoes for the tomato and zucchini salad and the anchovy salad.
○ Mix the ingredients for the kebabs; put on sticks and chill.
○ Cut the Feta cheese into cubes, dish up and cover.

*The morning of the party*
○ Mash and dish up the sardines.
○ Slice the pepper salad and cover with vinaigrette dressing.
○ Shape the labna cheese into balls and cover with olive oil and seasoning.
○ Soak cucumber for tzatziki, drain and dry. Make dressing.
○ Dish up the olives and the dates.
○ Add chili to the ceviche and dish up.
○ Soak the wheat for the bulgar, prepare vegetables and mix them all together.
○ Prepare lemon wedges for the squid.
○ Mix the ful medames with seasonings, dish up and add onion.
○ Cook zucchinis, cool, mix with tomatoes and season.
○ Make and shape the falafel.
○ Make and dish up the tuna and beans.
○ Soak anchovies, chop and mix with tomato.
○ Fry mushrooms for the mushroom salad and mix with the dressing. Dish up and cover.

*The morning of the party*
○ Put forks and napkins on the buffet bar.
○ Set up the bar and drinks.
○ Prepare the vegetables and arrange crackers and bread to serve with the mezzeh.

*Just before the guests arrive*
○ Mix the tzatziki.
○ Decorate the hummus with coriander leaves.
○ Decorate the taramasalata with lemon or black olives.
○ Mix the Armenian bulgar with a fork before serving.
○ Dish up the eggplant dip.
○ Dust squid with flour and fry.
○ Dust falafel with flour and deep fry.
○ Decorate ful medames and the anchovy salad with egg.
○ Grill the kofta kebabs.
○ Make and dish up the avocado salad.
○ Put out everything on the mezzeh table.

**Yogurt**
*This is used throughout the Middle East in soups, as a marinade, in stews and in salad dressings. It can be eaten plain or with fresh dates and honey. Low-fat yogurt can be made to taste like rich Middle Eastern yogurts by the addition of cream.*

**Crudités**
*It is easier to scoop dip with crudités cut into short sticks, no longer than 2in. Put them in a bowl of iced water to crispen before serving.*

**Olives**
*Black olives are simply fully-ripened green olives. The riper the olive, the higher the oil content. Store olives in the refrigerator and, if keeping them for a long time, freshen them up before serving by rolling them in olive oil and a few crushed coriander seeds or chopped coriander (cilantro) leaves.*

**Cleaning Squid**
*Pull the head and tentacles from the body. Cut off the tentacles and discard the head and entrails. Wash the body, rub off the skin and remove the clear cartilage. Cut the body into rings and the tentacles into small pieces.*

**Bulgar Wheat**
*This is cracked wheat (whole wheat grains cracked between rollers) that has been parboiled. It can be boiled and served like rice, baked in a pilaf or soaked and served as a salad.*

# MIDDLE EASTERN MEZZEH RECIPES

NOTE:
In addition to the mezzeh recipes, you should serve small crisp crackers (such as Ritz crackers), crisp bread sticks, fingers of pitta bread, and crudités (such as crisp small romaine lettuce leaves, chicory leaves, carrot sticks, celery sticks, cucumber sticks, raw turnip sticks, raw asparagus with the tough skin peeled off the stalks) for dipping. The quantities in each of the recipes given below would serve 4 people as a starter.

## SARDINES
Allow about 8oz of canned sardines in oil, mash the sardines well, removing any bones and season with salt, pepper and lemon juice.

## AVOCADO SALAD
Use 2 ripe avocados. Remove the stone and outside skin. Chop the flesh and mix with oil, lemon, chopped walnuts and season with salt and freshly ground black pepper.

## GREEN, RED AND YELLOW PEPPERS
Use one small pepper of each color. With a sharp knife cut around the stalks and lift them out with the seeds attached. Slice the peppers into very fine rings, taking care to discard any seeds left inside as you go. Arrange in small dishes and serve in vinaigrette dressing.

## LABNA CHEESE
*3 cups full fat yogurt*
*2 tsp sesame seeds*
*2 tsp chopped thyme*
*1 tsp paprika*
*4 tbsp olive oil*

1. Line a sieve with muslin and stand it over a bowl. Pour the yogurt into the muslin, cover and leave it to drain through overnight.
2. The following day: shape the drained yogurt into small balls and put into serving dishes. Pound together the sesame seeds, thyme, paprika and oil. Pour over the cheese balls.

## TZATZIKI
*1 cucumber, peeled and finely diced*
*2 cloves garlic, crushed*
*2 heaped tbsp finely chopped mint*
*1¼ cups plain yogurt*
*1 tbsp lemon juice*
*3 tbsp whipping cream (optional)*
*salt and ground black pepper*
*extra chopped mint*

1. Put the cucumber into a sieve and sprinkle with salt. Leave for 1 hour.
2. Meanwhile mix all the remaining ingredients together and season to taste.
3. Rinse the cucumber in cold water and dry well. Mix with the yogurt dressing.
4. Serve with a little extra chopped mint sprinkled on top.

## HUMMUS
*1lb canned chick peas, drained*
*6 tbsp cold water*
*2 cloves garlic, crushed*
*⅔ cup tahini*
*juice of 1 lemon*
*1½ tsp salt*
*ground black pepper*
*pinch cumin*
*pinch chili powder*
*chopped coriander (cilantro) leaves*

1. Mash the chick peas and water in a food processor or blender, or push them through a sieve.
2. Gradually beat in the garlic, tahini and lemon juice to taste. The mixture should spread easily. Add a little more water if it is very thick.
3. Season with salt and ground pepper, cumin and chili powder. Decorate with chopped coriander leaves.

## TARAMASALATA
*1 slice crustless white bread*
*1 clove garlic, crushed*
*8oz smoked cod's roe, skinned*
*⅔ cup vegetable oil*
*⅔ cup olive oil*
*lemon juice*
*freshly ground black pepper*

1. Soak the bread in cold water and squeeze it dry. Put it into a bowl with the crushed garlic and cod's roe. With a wooden spoon or electric beater gradually beat the oils in drop by drop, mixing all the time. Season with lemon juice and black pepper.

NOTE:
This can also be made in a food processor or blender.

## EGGPLANT DIP
*1 large eggplant*
*vegetable oil*
*1 slice crustless white bread*
*1 clove garlic, crushed*
*1 shallot, finely chopped*
*1 tbsp parsley, finely chopped*
*1 tsp fresh marjoram, chopped*
*salt*
*ground black pepper*
*4 tbsp olive oil*
*lemon juice*

1. Preheat the oven, setting the temperature to 375°. Brush the outside of the eggplant with oil and bake in the oven for 40 minutes to 1 hour until soft. Set aside and leave it to cool.
2. Cut the eggplant in half and scoop the flesh into the bowl of a blender or food processor.
3. Soak the bread in cold water and squeeze dry, add to the eggplant flesh with the crushed garlic, shallot, herbs and salt and pepper. Blend the mixture until smooth.
4. Gradually add the oil, beating all the time.
5. Season to taste with salt, black pepper and lemon juice.

## BLACK AND GREEN OLIVES
Buy 6oz each of the large, loose kind from a delicatessen.

## FRESH DATES
Buy 12oz from a specialty grocer or fruit and vegetable shop.

## CEVICHE
This is a Mexican, not Middle Eastern dish, but very suitable nonetheless.

*1lb any white fish (monkfish, halibut, turbot, red snapper or sea bass)*
*juice of 2 limes*
*1 small onion, sliced finely into rings*
*2 tbsp olive oil*
*1 red chili*
TO SERVE
*extra wedges of lime*

1. Cut the fish into wafer-thin slices and then into ¼in strips. Place in a dish and cover with the lime juice, onion and olive oil. Cover the dish and chill overnight.
2. The next day, split the chili in half and carefully remove all the seeds. Chop the chili finely.
3. Add to the fish and marinate for a further 15 minutes before serving. Serve with extra wedges of lime.

## ARMENIAN BULGAR
*½ cup fine bulgar (cracked wheat)*
*4 tomatoes, peeled, seeded and finely chopped*
*½ cucumber, finely chopped*
*1 green pepper, seeded and finely chopped*
*½ medium-sized onion, finely chopped*
*4 tbsp chopped coriander (cilantro) leaves or*
    *chopped parsley*
*1 tbsp finely chopped mint*
*juice of 2 lemons*
*4 tbsp olive oil*
*salt*
*freshly ground black pepper*

1. Soak the bulgar in cold water for about 1 hour.
2. Drain well, wrap in a clean dish cloth and squeeze out all the excess moisture.
3. Spread the wheat on a tray to dry.
4. Put the prepared vegetables into a mixing bowl with the soaked wheat. Stir in the parsley, mint, lemon juice and olive oil.
5. Season well with salt and freshly ground black pepper.

## FRIED SQUID
*1 whole medium-sized squid*
*½ cup all-purpose flour*
*salt*
*black pepper*
*oil for deep frying*
*wedges of lemon*

1. To prepare the squid, cut the tentacles into bite-sized pieces and slice the body into neat rings.
2. Just before serving toss the pieces of squid in flour seasoned with salt and pepper and fry in deep fat until crisp.
3. Serve hot, sprinkled with a little salt and decorated with lemon wedges.

NOTE:
For instructions on cleaning squid, see the margin note on p.165.

## FUL MEDAMES
*1lb canned Egyptian brown beans*
    *(ful medames)*
*4 tbsp olive oil*
*1 tbsp lemon juice*
*salt*
*black pepper*
FOR DECORATION
*1 small onion, sliced into fine rings*
*2 hard-boiled eggs*

1. Drain the beans and rinse well. Mix in a bowl with the olive oil and lemon juice, season with salt and black pepper.
2. Turn the beans into a small serving dish and decorate with rings of onion and wedges of hard-boiled egg.

## TOMATO AND ZUCCHINI SALAD
*2 beefsteak tomatoes*
*8 zucchini*
*olive oil*
*butter*
*lemon juice*
*salt and black pepper*

1. Cut the tomatoes into quarters and then cut each quarter into slices.
2. Wash the zucchini and cut diagonally into ¼in-thick slices. Heat one tablespoon of oil in a frying-pan, add one tablespoon of butter and when foaming quickly fry the zucchini over a high heat. Drain and leave to cool.
3. Mix the tomatoes and zucchini together and moisten with more olive oil and lemon juice. Season with salt and black pepper.

## FALAFEL
*1lb canned chick peas*
*1 egg lightly beaten*
*½ tsp turmeric*
*2 tbsp chopped coriander (cilantro) leaves*
*¼ tsp ground cumin*
*¼ tsp cayenne pepper*
*1 clove garlic, crushed*
*1 tbsp tahini*
*3 tbsp bulgar, soaked and dried*
*salt*
*ground black pepper*
*½ cup all-purpose flour*
*oil for deep frying*

1. Put the chick peas into a food processor or blender with the egg, turmeric, coriander leaves, cumin, cayenne pepper, garlic, tahini and soaked cracked wheat. Blend until smooth and season with salt and black pepper. (In the absence of a machine, finely chop or sieve the chick peas and beat in all the other ingredients.)
2. Using your hands, shape the mixture into 1in balls and flatten them slightly. Dust with flour and deep fry until the balls are lightly browned.
3. Drain well on paper towels and serve hot.

## KOFTA KEBABS
*1lb boneless lamb*
*1 tsp coriander seeds, ground*
*1 tsp cumin seeds, ground*
*1 tbsp chopped mint*
*1 tbsp chopped parsley*
*salt and ground black pepper*
*wooden saté sticks (small kebab sticks)*

1. Chop the lamb or mince it in a food processor. Add all the seasonings and mix very well.
2. Take small pieces of the mixture and roll it into sausages. Thread the sausages on to the saté sticks. Broil or cook over a barbecue for 10 minutes.

## TUNA FISH AND BUTTERBEANS
*1lb canned tuna fish in oil*
*1lb canned butterbeans*

Break the fish into chunks. Drain the butterbeans and mix with the tuna. Decorate with slices of raw onion.

## ANCHOVY SALAD
*2oz canned anchovy fillets*
*a little milk*
*2 beefsteak tomatoes, peeled*
*3 hard-boiled eggs, peeled*
*vinaigrette dressing*

1. Drain the oil from the anchovies and soak in milk for 1 hour. Pat dry and chop coarsely.
2. Seed the tomatoes and coarsely chop the flesh. Cut the hard-boiled egg into wedges.
3. Toss all the ingredients together in vinaigrette dressing.

## MUSHROOM SALAD
*4 cups button mushrooms*
*oil for frying*
*2 tsp coriander seeds, crushed*
*⅔ cup natural yogurt*
*2 tbsp light cream*
*2 tbsp chopped coriander (cilantro) leaves*
*salt and ground black pepper*
*lemon juice*

1. Heat the oil in a heavy-based frying-pan and briskly fry the mushrooms with the coriander seeds. Drain on paper towels and leave to cool.
2. Mix the fried mushrooms together with the yogurt, cream and coriander leaves. Season with salt, pepper and lemon juice. Serve warm or cold.

## FETA CHEESE
Buy 8oz Feta cheese. Cut into ¼in cubes and mix with black olives.

# TRAMPS PARTY
*for Fourteen*

Costume children's parties are generally wonderful fun for the children and a real headache for parents. If young Tom wants to turn up at his friend's birthday party dressed as a cornflake packet, as David Bowie or as the Archangel Gabriel, it is usually Mom who has to put cardboard and glue together, and it is Mom who receives the complaints that wings dig into shoulder blades, that the crown is not made of genuine jewels and that the standard of design and execution is not a patch on Geraldine's mother's.

A Tramps Party has none of these problems. The children will like nothing better than vandalizing Daddy's old pyjamas or ancient coat, blackening their faces with burnt cork and opening up too-small sneakers so that their toes can protrude. The joy of it is that the parent's contribution stops at providing the old clothes and sanctioning their destruction. And the children have almost as much fun filthying themselves up as they do at the party. For sheer pleasure there is nothing like forbidden fruit – getting dirty, not having to wash hands and comb hair, eating with the fingers, and best of all, eating on the move instead of demurely at table. There are also the pleasures of eating food in the wrong order (like jam tarts before fish and chips) and wolfing it down like a dog.

A Tramps Party is ideal for busy working parents with little time for organization and cooking. Everything can come from the supermarket or the local fast-food joint. Cupcakes, candy, potato chips and snacks in their packages can simply be hidden in large plastic trashcans among some contrived "trash" – old newspapers, empty cartons, etc. The children can scavenge in one can for newspaper-wrapped parcels of fried chicken, polystyrene boxes containing hamburgers or spare ribs. The second can could contain anything and everything children clamor for when out shopping – candy bars, potato chips or animal crackers. If adding (for health and conscience sake) some fresh fruit, choose fruit that needs peeling. Strawberries or grapes off the floor might be carrying authenticity too far. But bananas and oranges might spill out of the trashcans without worrying the hygienist.

A Tramps Party is not really suitable for very young children. Three- and four-year-olds get grubby all the time anyway, so dirt is hardly a treat. They are still at the age of "party dresses" and "best trousers". But after six or seven,

Entertainment
*A professional entertainer might be persuaded to dress as a Gentleman of the Road or as an old-fashioned clown, complete with strings of sausages and bags of candies. Older children enormously enjoy old movies like Buster Keaton, Charlie Chaplin or Laurel and Hardy.*

Edible Games
*A lot of fun can be had from edible games. Large iced cookies can be cut before baking into jigsaw puzzles. Small rounds of chocolate and plain shortbread make good draught counters to be eaten when out of the game. Giant-sized X's and O's made out of currant-bun dough can be played on a large marked board or cloth on the floor.*

*Left* Clean "trash" provides decor that the children will enjoy fixing to walls and scattering about. Painted orange crates make suitable tables or stools. In the center trashcan cake, complete with filling of candies and a sugar mouse on the lid.

when children are expected to behave in a civilized manner, behaving in a normally totally unacceptable way is good fun. Disco-aged children like it too, and will spend hours making their tramps gear somehow fashionable as well as tattered.

Most children cling to the traditions to some degree, and few would be happy to forego the birthday cake and candles altogether. A broken cake from the trashcan would not sufficiently honor the attainment of nine whole years for John or the longed-for status of a "teenager" for Isabel. So make a proper birthday cake. But to continue the tramp theme it might be fun to make the cake in the shape of a trashcan. Bake three cakes in the narrowest and tallest cake pans and stack them one on top of the other. Ice them with fondant icing, colored a dirty grey (achieved by lightly coloring white icing with black color). If black color proves hard to find, a red or green trashcan will do too, or mixing red and green will produce a dirty brown.

The final recommendation of this sort of party is the minimum of washing up for the grown-ups. Everything having been wrapped in paper, eaten with the fingers, or drunk in disposables, it is a simple matter of emptying the "pretend" trashcans into the real ones. There'll be a bit of sweeping up however. Cake crumbs and broken cookies will litter the floor if the party has been held indoors. If it took place in the backyard perhaps the dog and the birds will help you to clear up, even if your children won't.

## GETTING AHEAD

*A month or so before the party*
- Use suitable scraps of paper to invite the children and be sure to explain the type of party and dress.
- Get the children to collect suitable cartons and papers for "clean trash" to serve the food in.
- Decide on a menu and make a shopping list.
- If supplying fried chicken and chips or hamburgers and fries give the local fast-food franchise warning.
- Buy plenty of cans of soft drink.
- Make the birthday cakes and freeze them.
- Find some old clothes for your children to make costumes out of (and a few extra for inappropriately clad guests to dress up in).
- Sort out music and games if you need them.

*The day before the party*
- Buy all the shopping (and remember to include lots of trash bags).
- Defrost the cakes.

*The morning of the party*
- Confirm your order with the fast-food franchise.
- Finish the birthday cake.
- Start arranging sacks of "clean trash" with fruit, chocolate bars, cupcakes, etc.
- Clear plenty of space.
- Organize music and games.
- Check your children's costumes.

*Just before or after the children arrive*
- Arrange to collect the hot food from the fast-food franchise and distribute in trash sacks. (You may want to arrange for a friend to do this for you so as not to leave the party unsupervised.)

**Homemade Food**
*This can be prepared by the children. Hollowed-out French rolls filled with tuna and egg mayonnaise make interesting sandwiches. Or try chocolate-coated rice crispie or cornflake cookies or frozen banana lollies made from banana halves on toothpicks, wrapped in foil and frozen, then dipped in melted chocolate and refrozen. Eat them while still cold and firm.*

**Sugar Mice**
*These are usually only sold in the shops at Christmas time, but they are simple to make with molded icing. Knead the icing until smooth and make a pear shape. Make snips at the pointed end with scissors for whiskers. Color a little icing pink and shape into a long thin tail and two small pink ears. Pipe on two white and chocolate eyes.*

**Drinks**
*Coke or fizzy pop could be served from a wheelbarrow, bin or battered cardboard carton. No glasses of course. However, for still orange soda or milk, cardboard boxes or old yogurt pots would not spoil the theme. And excellent pure fruit juices can be bought in one-portion sizes with straws attached.*

Candies, if they are likely to end up on the floor, should be individually wrapped or in tubes or packets.

# TRAMPS PARTY RECIPES

## TRASHCAN CAKE

**FOR THE CAKE**
*1½ cups soft margarine*
*1½ cups sugar*
*6 eggs*
*2¼ cups self-raising flour*
*¾ cup cocoa powder*
*4 tsp baking powder*

**FOR THE BUTTER FROSTING**
*½ cup unsalted butter*
*2 cups confectioners' sugar, sifted*
*2 tsp cocoa powder, dissolved in 1 tbsp*
*    boiling water*

**FOR THE MOLDED ICING**
*8 cups confectioners' sugar, sifted*
*2 egg whites*
*2 tbsp light corn syrup*
*a few drops of water*
*a little cornstarch*
*gravy coloring*

**TO FINISH THE CAKE**
*apricot jam*
*1 package liquorice candies, lollipops and*
*    other candies*
*sugar mouse, plastic spiders and insects*
*1 candle approximately 4in long*
*4oz royal or glacé icing (see p. 160)*
*food coloring*
*9in round cake board*

1. Preheat the oven, setting the temperature to 375°. Grease three 6in diameter ring molds (see Note I). Grease a 7in layer cake pan and line the base with greased wax paper.
2. Put all the ingredients for the cakes together in a large mixing bowl. Beat with an electric mixer for 5 minutes until the mixture is smooth and fluffy (see Note II).
3. Divide the mixture between the prepared cake pans and bake for 30 to 40 minutes, until the cakes are golden brown and feel firm when pressed on top with the fingertips. Cool on a wire rack.
4. To make the butter frosting: beat the butter until soft and fluffy. Gradually beat in the confectioners' sugar and cocoa until the mixture is light and smooth.
5. To make the molded icing: put the confectioners' sugar into a mixing bowl, add the egg whites and syrup. Mix with a wooden spoon and then with your hand until the mixture forms a ball, adding a few drops of water if the mixture is hard and crumbly. Sprinkle the work top with cornstarch and knead the icing until smooth and pliable. Use the cornstarch sparingly as too much will spoil the flavor of the icing.
6. Save a golf-ball-sized piece of icing, cut a quarter off the remaining icing and color it dark brown with the gravy coloring. Color the rest pale brown (or use food color to get a suitably sludgy shade). Keep the icing well sealed in a plastic bag.
7. To assemble the cake: sandwich the three ring cakes together with the butter icing. Roll the large piece of molded icing into a strip as deep as the cakes and long enough to wrap all the way round them. Lay the piece out flat and make indentations using the edge of a ruler or knife, to look like the ridges on the side of a trashcan. Brush the sides of the cakes with hot, melted, apricot jam and wrap the icing round the outside of the cake. Make a neat join, and stand the cake on the cake board.
8. Take the dark brown molded icing and save a small piece to make handles for the trashcan lid and for the sides of the can. Roll the remaining icing into a circle large enough to cover the top and sides of the Victoria sandwich. Brush the Victoria sandwich with hot apricot jam and lay the molded icing on top.
9. Fill the center of the cake with candies and lollipops, piling them up to one side. Rest the lid on top at an angle and, if necessary, secure it with a toothpick. Attach the handles to the top of the lid and to the sides of the can. Arrange the sugar mouse, spiders and insects on top or crawling round the bottom and sides of the trashcan.
10. Wedge the candle firmly into the candies poking out at the top of the

Change the hamburger stand's paper wrapping for colored newspaper comics – more fun for the children and color printing smudges less than genuine newsprint.

trashcan, making sure that it will be safe to light. Roll the extra piece of white molded icing to look like a scrap of paper; while still pliable hang it out of the trashcan and write happy birthday on it in colored royal or glacé icing. Attach it with more icing under the lid.

**NOTE I**
In the absence of three ring molds, the cakes can be made one by one in a single pan. But do not mix all the cakes at once – divide the quantities by 3 and mix them one at a time. There may be some mixture over each time (the whole recipe is enough for the layer cake pan) but it cannot be helped. Use the extra for cup cakes and freeze them. Finally make the layer cake pan, again using one-third of the recipe.

**NOTE II**
In the absence of an electric mixer it would be advisable to make the cakes one by one. Beating the mixture for all the cakes at once by hand would be impossibly tiring.

# BARBECUE IN THE BACKYARD

*for Ten*

*Left* A home-built barbecue
made with loose bricks is
stable and good-looking.
Use an old-fashioned metal
scraper-mat for the grill and
make sure there are air
spaces in the bottom of the
barbecue to allow a draft.
Homemade herb-flavored
hamburgers are a far cry
from frozen ones. On the
side, chicken and lamb saté.

THE HOGBAKE ON PAGE 59 IS A SUGGESTION FOR the ambitious party-giver who is not daunted by the thought of a whole pig over the coals and the Clambake (p. 79) is the best beach picnic in the world.

But for most of us a barbecue is a backyard or a terrace affair for a dozen close friends or for the family and the children's friends. On still warm evenings when it is too hot to eat indoors and too fine to want to, sitting outside is wonderfully peaceful and pleasant. The smell of sizzling burgers or spicy saté from the fire, the clink of ice cubes in long tall glasses and the satisfyingly distant sound of children playing seem to sum up what is best in family holidays.

But to get the thing right, a good, tried and trusty barbecue is essential. Making a fire like a boy scout is out. It takes too long. The smoke gets in your eyes and food comes off it charred on the outside and raw in the middle. There are dozens of well-designed cheap barbecues on the market which are easy to light, economic in charcoal (which can often cost as much as the meat) and safe to operate. The more expensive ones can turn into smoking ovens, can stand up to being left in the rain, or can operate on gas or perhaps even have "extras" like rotisseries or kebab holders.

But for our party all you need is a small barbecue (preferably with a wind-shield so you can stop the smoke blowing your way), about 10lbs charcoal briquets, a firelighter to enable you to start the fire without fuss, and a grill tray to support the burgers and saté.

Safety Note
*Children are always keen to help with barbecues but great care should be taken to prevent accidents. Never leave the barbecue unattended by an adult; avoid heating sauces in pans with long handles that stick out and can be knocked over.*

*Below* For perfectly cooked burgers, have them at room temperature rather than chilled before you begin. Do not turn them over till the first side is well browned and droplets of juice show on the uncooked top side. They are done when they no longer have the squashy feel of raw meat when pressed with a thumb.

Lighting
*Camping gas lights hung in trees provide an easy way of lighting the garden. Many types of torch-like candle are now on the market to stand in the earth. They usually have insect-repelling properties. Place them where they won't be knocked over and do not move them while they are alight – the liquid wax is dangerously hot.*

If the party is a more serious matter than two families getting together for supper, check through the list in Catering in Quantity on p. 12. Otherwise just make sure you have some method of keeping flying insects at bay, and that there is enough light to see what you are doing after the sun goes down, and a table by the barbecue for the cook's gear. A water-spray of the kind used for spraying plants and laundry is useful for dousing unwanted flames.

Our menu might seem a lot for a mere ten people, but it is surprising how much more meat people will eat at a barbecue. The smell of the cooking keeps bringing them back for another burger or spare rib. So be generous with the catering and allow one of everything for everybody.

Mini-Kebabs
*Make hot mini-kebabs of bacon and scallop, or spicy sausage and red pepper, threaded on to toothpicks and grilled.*

---

THE MENU

*Hamburgers*

*Spare Ribs*

*Lamb and Chicken Saté*

*Hot Bread with Savory Butters*

*Pasta Salad*

*Chocolate and Apricot Cheesecake*

---

## GETTING AHEAD

*A month to two weeks before the party*
○ Send invitations, or just telephone your guests.
○ Make a contingency plan in case it should pour with rain.
○ Check the barbecue and buy a bag of charcoal; if you like the food to have a specially smoky taste buy some hickory wood chips too.
○ Arrange for outside lighting, etc. if the party is to be held at night. Also insect repellent.
○ Stock up with paper napkins and plates. Buy the drinks: wine, beer and soft drinks, cocktails would be suitable (see Thirties Cocktail, p. 197), also ice cream floats.

*Two days before the party*
○ Make a shopping list from the recipes and buy all the food.
○ Trim the lamb and chicken for the saté and cut into cubes, and marinate them.

*The day before the party*
○ Marinate the spare ribs.
○ Shape the hamburgers; keep well chilled.
○ Cook the pasta.
○ Make the savory butters (see margin note).
○ Make the cheesecake.

*The morning of the party*
○ Set up the barbecue.
○ Arrange tables and chairs.
○ Arrange a drinks tray and a coffee tray.
○ Organize candles, lighting.
○ Arrange the music.
○ Buy the French bread.

Fire Precautions
*Keep a bucket of water handy and a domestic fire-extinguisher if you have one. And NEVER use petrol or kerosene to start the fire.*

Bread and Savory Butters
*Serve hot French bread with anchovy, or garlic and scallion butter. For each loaf use ⅓ cup softened butter pounded together with either two anchovy fillets and a drop of anchovy essence, or 2 finely chopped scallions and a crushed clove of garlic. Season well with lemon juice, salt and ground black pepper. Slice the bread diagonally, spread with one of the butters, wrap in foil and warm just before serving.*

An ordinary candle set upright in a glass jam jar gives an attractive gentle glow and won't be blown out by the wind. A line of them along a path or wall top looks good.

**Hamburgers**
*Use best quality ground beef to make hamburgers. Tough meat will result in a tough burger. The addition of a little cereal or breadcrumbs will moisten and add flavor to the burger as it will absorb some of the fat which would otherwise run out when heated.*

*Two or three hours before the guests arrive*
○ Put out mustards, mayonnaise, relishes, salt and pepper, plates, napkins, etc.
○ Prepare sliced onion, tomato and lettuce.
○ Make the peanut sauce. Leave in a heavy pan to heat over the barbecue.
○ Thread the lamb and chicken on to kebab sticks; put the remaining marinade into a small bowl so that the barbecue chef can pour it over at the last minute.
○ Arrange all the meat on trays ready to be sent outside.
○ Finish the pasta salad.
○ Decorate the cheesecake.
○ Fill the French bread with the savory butters and wrap in foil.

*An hour before the guests are due to arrive*
○ Check your fire safety precautions.
○ Light the barbecue and allow the coals to burn down.
○ As soon as the coals are low enough, start cooking the spare ribs.
○ Arrange all the food on the buffet table.

*After the guests arrive*
○ Heat the bread.
○ Cook the hamburgers and saté (the saté will probably be cooked first so guests can come back for hamburgers and spare ribs as they are ready).

**Warming Area**
*If possible, arrange a warming area on the barbecue. This is easily done if you are building your own barbecue. A low wall of bricks behind the fire will retain the heat and keep cooked food warm for about half an hour.*

**Saté**
*This is a South-East Asian dish of tiny meat or fish kebabs. The meat is marinated in oil, soy sauce and subtle spices, and served with a peanut and coconut sauce. The fish is coated with a thick marinade of coconut milk, nuts, garlic and lemon grass which is baked on to the food during cooking.*

*Below right* To the side of the barbecue, clockwise from top left: spare ribs in a rich and sticky sauce, multi-colored pasta salad, anchovy butter, scallion and garlic butter, peanut sauce and a hamburger in a sesame bun. On the barbecue chicken and lamb saté and hamburgers sizzle over glowing charcoal.

# BARBECUE IN THE BACKYARD RECIPES

## HAMBURGERS

SERVES 10

*3lb lean ground beef*
*salt and ground black pepper*
*2 tbsp parsley, finely chopped*
*2 tbsp marjoram, finely chopped*
*10 sesame hamburger buns*
*2 onions, thinly sliced*
*4 sliced tomatoes*
*handful washed lettuce leaves*
*mustard, mayonnaise, ketchup, assorted*
*    bought relishes*

1. Put the ground beef on the worktop and flatten it. Sprinkle evenly with the salt, black pepper and fresh herbs. Knead the meat until all the seasonings are mixed. (If using a machine take care not to overbeat the meat. Overworking leads to rubbery-textured meat when cooked.) Divide into ten equal portions and make into round flat shapes.
2. Cook the hamburgers on the barbecue until they are dark brown and charred on the outside and still pink in the middle (about 3-4 minutes per side).
3. Serve the burgers with toasted or warmed buttered buns and let everyone help themselves to salad and relishes.

## SPARE RIBS

SERVES 10

*5lb pork spare ribs*
FOR THE MARINADE
*4 tbsp clear honey*
*4 tbsp soy sauce*
*⅔ cup orange juice*
*1¼ cups tomato ketchup*
*2 garlic cloves, crushed*
*1 tsp dried basil*
*salt and pepper*

1. Mix all the marinade ingredients together. Put the spare ribs into a shallow container, pour the marinade over, cover and refrigerate overnight.
2. To barbecue the ribs, have the barbecue rack well above the fire or make sure that the heat is not too fierce. The ribs need to cook for 20-30 minutes to be tender. Should the flame be too high the outside will be burnt before the inside can cook. Keep basting the ribs with marinade while they are cooking.

NOTE:
If not using a barbecue, set the oven temperature control to 375°. Put the spare ribs, with the marinade, into a roasting pan and bake for one hour. Or heat and bake the ribs in the oven for 45 minutes, finishing them on the barbecue to give them a char-grilled flavor.

## LAMB AND CHICKEN SATÉ

SERVES 10

*1½lb boneless lean lamb*
*One 4½lb roasting chicken*
FOR THE MARINADE
*1 small onion, sliced*
*2 cups peanut oil*
*2 tsp coriander seeds, crushed*
*1 tsp fennel seeds, crushed*
*2 cardamom pods, crushed*
*2 allspice berries, crushed*
*1 tsp garam masala*
*1 tsp chopped lemon grass*
*1 lemon*
*salt*
PEANUT SAUCE
*(See recipe in Al Fresco Lunch, p. 209)*

1. Cut the lamb and chicken flesh into small cubes (discarding the bones and skin).
2. Mix all the marinade ingredients together except the lemon. Squeeze the juice from the lemon, then finely slice the lemon skin and add both to the marinade.
3. Mix the cubes of meat with the marinade, cover and leave overnight.
4. The following day, drain the cubes of meat from the marinade. Thread alternate pieces of chicken and lamb on to skewers or wooden saté sticks.
5. Barbecue or broil the kebabs for 12 minutes, turning halfway through cooking and basting constantly with the marinade.
6. When the meat is cooked, scatter the raw marinated onion over the kebabs and serve them hot with the onion and warm peanut sauce.

## PASTA SALAD

SERVES 10

*12oz shell pasta, white or assorted colors*
*salt*
*olive oil*
*4oz black olives, halved and stoned*
*1 shallot, finely chopped*
FOR THE DRESSING
*⅔ cup mayonnaise*
*grated rind and juice of one lemon*
*½ cup whole milk*
*salt*
*black pepper*
*parsley, finely chopped*

1. Cook the pasta for 5 minutes if fresh (12 minutes if dried), in a pan of boiling salted water with a spoonful of olive oil. Drain, rinse in hot water, and drain again. Turn occasionally to ensure all the water runs out of the pasta shapes.

2. Mix the mayonnaise with the lemon juice and rind and add only enough of the milk to give a thin cream. Season well with salt and black pepper.
3. Mix the pasta with the black olives, finely chopped shallot and dressing. Turn into a clean salad bowl and decorate with parsley scattered over the top.

## CHOCOLATE AND APRICOT CHEESECAKE

SERVES 10

FOR THE CRUST
*1 package of chocolate wafer cookies*
*¼ cup melted butter*
FOR THE FILLING
*1lb canned apricot halves*
*2 tbsp unflavored gelatin*
*1½ cups cream cheese*
*⅔ cup heavy cream*
*⅓ cup sugar*
*½ tsp vanilla extract*
FOR DECORATION
*⅔ cup whipping cream*
*4 apricot halves, reserved from the filling*

1. Put the cookies into a plastic bag and crush them with a rolling pin.
2. Mix the cookies with the melted butter and press into the base of a 12in loose-bottomed tart pan or spring-form pan.
3. Drain the apricots. Reserve 4 tablespoons of syrup and 4 pieces.
4. Put three tablespoons of the syrup into a small pan, sprinkle over the gelatin and leave to soak. Purée the rest of the apricots using 1 tablespoon of the fruit syrup to moisten.
5. Soften the cream cheese and beat in the cream, sugar and vanilla extract. Add the apricot purée.
6. Dissolve the gelatin over a gentle heat. When it is clear and warm pour it into the cream cheese mixture, stirring well. Pour the mixture on top of the cookie base and refrigerate.
7. Cut the remaining apricots halves into slices. Pipe shells or rosettes of cream around the edge of the cheesecake and place a slice of apricot in between each one.

NOTE:
Gelatin should always be of a similar temperature to the mixture to which it is being added. If it is too hot it will set as soon as it touches the colder mixture and will form "ropes" of gelatin. This is not only unpleasant to eat but the mixture will not set as the gelatin is not evenly distributed.

# COLOR DINNERS
## for Six

**Color Cocktails**
*Mix cocktails to match the color of the party. Wine can be flavored with food coloring which will not affect flavor, or with a drop of brightly-colored liqueur.*

SOMETIMES A VERY SPECIAL AND UNUSUAL DINNER PARTY can be had by the simple expedient of color co-ordinating the food. It sounds crazy, but, providing the desire for the right color has not meant the inclusion of un-suitable food, the result can be amusing, visually stunning, and delicious to eat. Our color dinners are designed for 6 people but of course the theme could be carried through on a larger scale. The Golden Wedding on p. 217 is a good example.

If the decor can be made to match (say deep purple table-cloths or black silk sheets used as tablecloths, dark purple paper napkins, black candles, black china), so much the better. Flowers are surprisingly easy to get right. Dark dahlias, almost black chrysanthemums, dark violets, dark Nicotiana, near-black petunias are available in the autumn, while pale yellow narcissus, primroses, daffodils, jonquils and yellow tulips bloom in the spring. But a bit of cheating is in order anyway. Wonderful crêpe paper flowers of exactly the right shade can be mixed in with the real thing and artificial fabric flowers are now comparatively cheap and most beautifully made.

A word of warning. An all-white dinner can look anemic and dull unless the deliberate whiteness is well emphasized by white cloths, white flowers, white napkins, white china. A meal of Stilton soup, chicken with rice and ice cream could just look like an unhappy accident if the color theme is not made blindingly obvious. It is often best to play safe and opt for Pink-and-White or Green-and-White or Yellow-and-White. Other single color schemes, even if set against a non-matching background, like a white cloth or a polished table, jump out at the diner determinedly and obviously – it's hard not to notice if all the food is purple for example.

Written invitations for small dinners are rare but it might be nice to send ones of the right color and possibly requesting some co-operation from the guests. The men invited to an all-pink dinner might turn up in pink shirts, the women with pink earrings, flowers, beads or dresses. At least if they know they are attending a "Primrose Lunch" all the work and effort in producing primrose decor and pale lemon-colored food will get noticed and admired.

We have only space to give the main or more unusual recipes in this chapter, and ideas for others. If making up your own "color" menus, beware of ending up with an unbalanced

**Fish Terrines**
*Layered fish terrines can be adapted for many different color parties. White or pink fish can be used layered with spinach, herbs, spicy breadcrumbs or whole slices of blanched vegetables.*

If color co-ordinating the decor, choose a section from the spectrum and stick to it. Try to confine yourself to 2 or 3 shades at most and not more than 1 contasting color.

Interior designers' color swatches might provide inspiration. Or you could build your color scheme round a favorite bedspread or fabric and use them as a tablecloth.

meal. For example, it is easy to rely on too much cream and egg for a pale dinner: a cream-laden soup, a cream-laden main course, rice or mashed potatoes and an eggy, creamy pudding.

## THE ALMOST BLACK DINNER

The first course consists quite simply of a few slices of black pudding (blood sausage or "*boudin noir*"), accompanied by raw peeled beets, cut in matchsticks and marinated in a mustardy vinaigrette with a pinch of cumin. Get a good spicy sausage and cut it fairly thickly.

The secret of good red cabbage is very slow, prolonged cooking. Ours was cooked for 3 hours in a low oven and contains (besides one red cabbage, sliced) 2 cut-up apples, 2 tablespoons golden raisins, 3 tablespoons vinegar, 1 tablespoon sugar, a pinch of ground allspice, and salt and pepper, but no added water.

The recipe for blackberry gelatin is given in the Victorian Wedding, p. 159. Or a black fruit salad made with autumn fruits such as black figs, blackcurrants, blackberries, blueberries, damsons and black plums looks wonderful in a glass bowl. Black grapes, halved and seeded, may be added to this too if they were not used in the pigeon dish.

> **THE MENU**
>
> *Black Pudding with Raw Beet Salad*
>
> *Pigeon Breasts with Black Grapes*
>
> *Red Cabbage (p. 113)*
>
> *Blackberry Gelatin (p. 159)*
> *or*
> *Black Fruit Salad*

## THE PINK AND GREEN DINNER

This dinner is spectacularly summery and pretty. Salmon and strawberries is the quintessential luxury menu for the rich and privileged in June and our menu is a slightly cheaper relative of that theme. Good trout from a fish farm where they feed keratin in the diet are as pink and pretty as salmon if not quite so *recherché*. Green asparagus are plentiful and not prohibitively expensive in midsummer, and would fit the demands of color – especially if served with a pink (tomato-flavored) mayonnaise. Equally, avocados sliced and fanned out on white plates with a strawberry dressing (see St Valentine's Day Dinner, p. 30) would fit the bill.

Salads are easy. If it's green and pretty it will look right and be appropriately summery. Chopped fresh herbs will improve it too, and the dressing should be light and lemony.

For dessert, a green fruit salad made of kiwi fruit, green grapes, melon, green-skinned apple and greengage plums would be a possible alternative to the strawberry mousse and ice cream.

The dinner-table decor is easy to achieve. Pink flowers abound in the summer, as do white ones. Green flowers (Hellebores, Nicotiana, Euphorbias) are beautiful if you can get them. Or an unusual and pretty table decoration can be had

Dark autumn fruits such as blackcurrants, dark plums, blackberries or blueberries make an unusually full-flavored fruit salad.

**Black Grapes**
*It is only the skin on black grapes that gives them their color; once removed they will look little different from white grapes.*

**Pigeon**
*Pigeons or squab (specially reared young pigeons) have most of their meat on the breast. The remainder of the carcass is best used for stock. Old birds can be very tough so check that the feet and breast bone are supple to make sure of getting a young one.*

**Black Pudding**
*This is traditionally associated with the north of England. Although a member of the sausage family, it is called a pudding because it contains cereal as well as meat. The color comes from pigs' blood, hence its other name "blood sausage".*

*Right* A black, shiny table, black china and black tulips provide the perfect sophisticated setting for an almost black (actually deep red or purple) dinner. Here the first course is simplicity itself: spicy blood sausage, raw beet salad and red lettuce.

Pink and green fruit are easy
to obtain. Try a pink and
green fruit salad made with
water melon, crisp green
apples and ripe greengage
plums.

*Right:* The Primrose
Dinner main course (below
left): chicken in yogurt curry
sauce, saffron rice with
almonds and julienne of
rutabegas and carrots with
straw-colored white
burgundy. Center: The
Pink and Green Dinner first
course, the tomato aspic
ring with cucumber salad
and a rosé de provence
wine. On the right The
Almost Black Dinner main
course: pigeon breasts,
black grapes and red
cabbage with burgundy.

by putting a whole open lettuce in a shallow bowl of water and
tucking tiny pink flowers between its leaves.

Candles can be had in any color or variation of color.
Candy-striped pink and green ones are particularly pretty.
Candy-striped or spotty pink or green fabric can be bought for
an instant tablecloth, and any amount of pretty and chic paper
table napkins can be bought. Also, printed wallpapers can
make very effective table coverings.

All in all the Pink and Green is probably one of the easiest
and most satisfying themes to achieve.

THE MENU

*Tomato Aspic Ring with Cucumber Salad*

*Cold Pink Trout with Watercress Sauce*

*Shrimp in Green Mayonnaise*
*Pink Potatoes with Herbs (p. 182)*

*Strawberry Mousse (p. 182)*
*with Pistachio Ice Cream*

## THE PRIMROSE DINNER
Make the chicken mildly curried and thicken the cooking
liquid slightly with cornstarch for the sauce. Mix the cooked
rice with saffron shreds, fried onions and fried almonds. The
gelatin is made with yellow-colored fruit juice, boiled and
sweetened and set with 1 tbsp gelatin to 2½ cups liquid.

Cucumber and Strawberry
*These could be included as a
salad in a pink and green
dinner. Neatly slice a cucumber
and arrange the slices
overlapping in a circle on a flat
serving dish. Hull and quarter
the strawberries and toss in
mint-flavored vinaigrette. Pile
in the center of the cucumber
ring.*

**Pumpkin**
*This is a member of the squash family. The puréed flesh can be used for soups, pies and bread. Wedges of pumpkin can be baked with butter and sugar as a vegetable. Use the hollowed-out shell to make a pretty soup tureen.*

Good yellow alternatives to our menu might be a yellow tomato and Swiss cheese salad (the tomatoes in slices, the cheese in strips), followed by a creamy smoked haddock flan, and the meal rounded off with peeled nectarines or peaches simply sliced and served with a splash of brandy.

Yellow flowers are easy, but it is important to stay away from the orange-reds. Stick to pale primrose, whites, buffs and clear yellows. If primroses are available, tiny individual bouquets at each guest's place might be nicer, and take less room than a central flower arrangement.

A good shop will provide pretty patterned paper tablecloths or, failing that, giftwrap or wallpaper might provide the right color range for your menu.

An alternative menu for a yellow dinner could start with a salad made from yellow tomatoes and Swiss cheese and finish with ripe peaches or nectarines.

> **THE MENU**
>
> *Pumpkin Blossom Soup*
>
> *Chicken in Yogurt Curry Sauce*
>
> *Saffron Rice with Almonds*
>
> *Julienne of Rutabegas and Carrots*
>
> *Gelatin and Fruit*

**Saffron**
*This is the world's most expensive spice. It is made from the dried stamen of the saffron crocus and each flower has only three stamen which must be gathered by hand. It is available in strands or powder.*

## GETTING AHEAD
*A few weeks before the party*
- ○ Telephone or send invitations to your friends.
- ○ Choose a color scheme then collect appropriate table linen, glasses, plants, flowers, and any other decorations.
- ○ Select a menu and make a shopping list.
- ○ Buy the dry goods.
- ○ Buy the wine, drinks and mixers.
- ○ See "Getting Ahead for Food".

*The day before the party*
- ○ Do all the shopping.
- ○ See "Getting Ahead for Food".

*The morning of the party*
- ○ Decorate the room.
- ○ Set the table, arrange the flowers.
- ○ Prepare a tray for coffee with appropriate colored cups, tray cloth or even sugar. (Sugar can be speckled with a few drops of coloring.)
- ○ See "Getting Ahead for Food".

*When the guests arrive*
- ○ See "Getting Ahead for Food".

## GETTING AHEAD FOR FOOD
**THE ALMOST BLACK DINNER**

**Gelatin Molds**
*If a gelatin or mold proves difficult to turn out, dip the mold briefly in hot water to melt the gelatin a little and loosen it. Turn the gelatin on to a wet plate so that it can easily be moved if not centrally placed.*

*The day before*
- ○ Make the dressing for the beet salad.
- ○ Marinate the pigeon breasts.
- ○ Make the stock.
- ○ Cook the red cabbage.
- ○ Make the syrup for the fruit salad.
- ○ Prepare gelatin and chill.

**Marinades**
*A marinade is a mixture of oil, wine, vinegar, spices and flavorings. It is used to tenderize, add flavor and to moisten the food. Marinating meat or fish can be kept in the refrigerator for up to five days.*

**Fruit Salad**
*Instead of making a sugar syrup to moisten fruit salads, simply pour fruit juice and white wine over the prepared fruit. Sprinkle over sugar to taste.*

*The morning of the party*
○ Cut beets into strips.
○ Slice black pudding.
○ Cook pigeon, seed grapes, chop walnuts and make the croûtes.
○ Prepare fruit salad.

*When the guests arrive*
○ Toss beets in dressing, arrange on plates with black pudding and decorate with radicchio.
○ Heat pigeon and decorate and reheat the red cabbage.
○ Turn out the gelatin.

THE PINK AND GREEN DINNER
*Days or weeks before*
○ Make plain mayonnaise for the trout and shrimp.
○ Make and freeze the pistachio ice cream.

**Pink Potatoes**
*Peel the potatoes and cut them into walnut-sized pieces. Boil them in salted water for 10 minutes. Drain and cool. Fry the pieces in butter and paprika. Drain on paper towels and sprinkle heavily with chopped fresh herbs.*

*The day before*
○ Make and chill the tomato aspic ring.
○ Cook the trout. (See p. 87 for poaching fish.)
○ Add watercress to the mayonnaise for the shrimp.
○ Peel and boil the potatoes.
○ Make and chill the strawberry mousse.

*The morning of the party*
○ Prepare the dressing for the cucumber salad. Slice the cucumber skin.
○ Skin the trout and decorate with lemon wedges and watercress. Hand sauce separately.
○ Chop the herbs for the potatoes.
○ Decorate the mousse.

*When the guests arrive*
○ Seed and slice cucumber flesh, turn out ring, toss salad and put in ring. Decorate.
○ Dress the shrimp with the green mayonnaise.
○ Reheat the potatoes by tossing them in melted butter and sprinkle heavily with paprika and herbs.
○ Transfer ice cream to the refrigerator 40 minutes before serving.

**Thawing**
*Almost all food is best thawed before cooking. Ideally this should be done as slowly as possible to help retain the texture and moisture. If thawing has to be done rapidly, seal the food in a plastic bag and submerge in cold water.*

THE PRIMROSE DINNER
*Days or weeks before*
○ Make the pumpkin blossom soup; freeze without the cream.

*The day before*
○ Defrost the soup.
○ Make the chicken curry.
○ Peel and shred the rutabegas and carrots.
○ Make the fruit gelatin.

*The morning of the party*
○ Beat or reprocess the soup to restore texture and add cream.
○ Prepare ingredients for the rice.
○ Turn out the gelatin and slice the fruit.

**Peppers and Tomatoes**
*Sweet yellow peppers are ripened green peppers. The sweetness is gained in the ripening process. Yellow tomatoes are a different variety from red ones, although they will taste the same.*

*When the guests arrive*
○ Heat the soup and serve with saffron rolls.
○ Reheat the chicken.
○ Cook the rice and add the almonds at the last minute.
○ Drain the julienne of rutabegas and carrots and pat dry. Fry in butter.

**Strawberry Mousse**
*Beat 5 egg yolks with ⅔ cup sugar and stir in ⅔ cup puréed strawberries. Dissolve 1 tbsp gelatin in 3 tbsp water and stir into the strawberry mixture. Fold in ⅔ cup whipped cream and three whisked egg whites. Pour into a soufflé dish, chill until set and decorate with whole strawberries.*

Take care to cut or slice vegetables evenly. Beet matchsticks, cucumber slices or a carrot julienne all look incomparably better if they are neatly executed.

# COLOR DINNERS RECIPES

## PIGEON BREASTS WITH BLACK GRAPES
SERVES 6

*9 plump young pigeons*
*oil and butter for frying*
*1 medium-sized onion, finely diced*
*1½ cups pigeon or chicken stock*
*1 tbsp butter*
*1½ tbsp flour*
*1 tbsp blackcurrant jelly*
*grated nutmeg*
*salt and freshly ground black pepper*
*few drops gravy coloring*
*3 tbsp pickled walnuts, chopped*
*4oz black grapes, halved and seeded*
FOR THE MARINADE
*1 onion, sliced*
*1 carrot, sliced*
*1 stick celery, sliced*
*1 clove garlic, crushed*
*1 slice lemon*
*6 juniper berries, 6 peppercorns and*
*    2 allspice berries, crushed*
*1½ cups red wine*
*2 tbsp wine vinegar*
FOR THE STOCK
*pigeon carcasses*
*1 onion*
*1 carrot*
*1 stick celery or 1 leek*
*bay leaf*
*parsley stalks*
*thyme*
*peppercorns*
*water*
FOR DECORATION
*3 slices white bread*
*oil for frying*
*salt*
*finely chopped parsley*

1. The day before: remove the breasts from the pigeons with a small, very sharp knife, by running the knife along the length of the breast bone and carefully scraping downwards against the rib cage.
2. Mix all the marinade ingredients together and add the pigeon breasts. Cover and chill overnight.
3. Put the pigeon carcasses into a large pan with the other stock ingredients and enough water to cover them. Bring to the boil, remove any scum that rises to the top and simmer for at least two hours until the stock is well reduced and full in flavor.
4. The following day: preheat the oven, setting the temperature control to 350°. Remove the pigeon breasts from the marinade and pat dry. Strain the marinade and reserve.

5. Heat the oil and butter in a heavy frying-pan and in it quickly brown the pigeon breasts on each side. Lift the breasts out and transfer them to a casserole.
6. In the same pan fry the onion until dark golden brown and add to the casserole.
7. Pour a little of the stock into the pan. Stir well, scraping any sediment from the bottom of the pan, and pour it into the casserole.
8. Melt the butter in the pan, add the flour and cook for one minute, pour on the remaining stock and reserved marinade, stir until smooth and boiling. Add the blackcurrant jelly and nutmeg and season to taste with salt and black pepper. Pour over the pigeon.
9. Cover the casserole and cook in the preheated oven for two hours until the pigeon breasts are tender and the sauce is reduced and shiny. If necessary add a little gravy coloring to give a dark sauce. Stir in the chopped walnuts and cook for a further 10 minutes.
10. Meanwhile make the decoration: cut 2 heart-shaped pieces from each slice of bread. Heat the oil in a frying-pan. Fry the pieces of bread on each side until crisp and brown. Drain and sprinkle with salt. While still warm dip the corner of each heart in chopped parsley.
11. Warm the grapes briefly in the oven or microwave. Arrange the pigeon breasts on a heated serving dish and spoon the sauce over. Put the heart-shaped croûtes around the edge of the dish and the grapes, skin side up, on top.

## TOMATO ASPIC RING WITH CUCUMBER SALAD
SERVES 6

*1lb canned Italian tomatoes*
*1 clove garlic, peeled and crushed*
*5 leaves basil or 1 tsp dried basil*
*juice of half a lemon*
*1 tsp sugar*
*1¼ cups dairy sour cream*
*2 tbsp water*
*1 tbsp aspic or unflavored gelatin*
FOR THE CUCUMBER SALAD
*1 cucumber*
*2 tbsp mayonnaise (see recipe p. 93)*
*1 tbsp heavy or whipping cream*
*squeeze of lemon*
*salt and ground black pepper*

1. Put the tomatoes, garlic, basil, lemon juice and sugar together in a blender and blend until smooth. Strain to remove the tomato seeds.

2. Beat in the sour cream.
3. Put the water into a small pan and sprinkle over the aspic or gelatin. Leave to soak for 10 minutes. Heat gently until runny and clear, add to the tomato mixture and mix well.
4. Season to taste with salt and black pepper, pour into an oiled ring mold and chill until set.
5. To make the cucumber salad: peel the cucumber and reserve the skin. Cut the cucumber in half lengthwise and scrape out the seeds with a teaspoon. Cut the flesh into thin slices.
6. Drop the cucumber skin into a pan of boiling water for one minute then plunge it immediately into cold water. Pat dry on paper towel and cut into the thinnest strips possible.
7. Mix the mayonnaise with the cream, lemon, salt and pepper. Add the sliced cucumber just before serving.
8. To serve the mold: turn it out on to a wet plate. Push it gently to get it dead-center. Mop up any water. Arrange the strips of cucumber skin around the ring like the spokes of a wheel. Pile the cucumber salad into the center of the ring.

## PUMPKIN BLOSSOM SOUP
SERVES 6

*12oz pumpkin blossoms (or 3 cups cubed*
*    pumpkin flesh if flowers are unavailable)*
*¼ cup butter*
*1 large onion, finely chopped*
*4 cups chicken stock*
*salt*
*ground white pepper*
*2 egg yolks*
*⅔ cup heavy or whipping cream*

1. Discard the stems from the blossoms and chop the flowers coarsely. (Or peel, seed and chop the flesh.)
2. Melt the butter in a large pan and gently fry the onion until soft and transparent. Add the blossoms and fry them gently for a further 3 to 4 minutes. If using pumpkin flesh, peel it and slice it and then cook for 10 minutes, slowly.
3. Pour in the stock, season with salt and white pepper. Cover and simmer until the flowers (or pumpkin cubes) are tender.
4. Purée the soup in a blender or a food processor.
5. Mix the egg yolks with the cream, then whisk in 1 cup of the hot soup. Return this to the rest of the soup and cook without boiling, until it has slightly thickened. Serve the soup immediately.

# CREOLE PARTY

*for Thirty or Three Hundred*

*Left* Paper cups, plastic cutlery, crêpe paper flags and funny hats add merriment (and mess!) to a street party. Disposable containers (cola cans, bowls, etc.) can easily be discarded along with the spent streamers and party whistles but willing cleaners-up are essential. In the center, jambalaya with spicy rice, pork and shrimp.

To STAGE A MARDI GRAS BALL ON THE SCALE THAT THE exclusive clubs for the white aristocracy of New Orleans once did would take the resources of an Onassis. Costumes for the revellers cost thousands of pounds, and each club's organized street procession, complete with floats, black torch-bearers *et al.*, vied with its rivals for splendour, expense and baroque extravagance. Most of the stratified, but all traditional and snobbish clubs still hold costume balls on *Mardi Gras* (the Tuesday before Lent) and each club chooses a king and queen (more by social standing than by charm or looks), and attendant dukes and duchesses. Invitations are almost impossible to get, so outsiders (non club-members) must content themselves with the street parties and parades that take place for five days during which the main Canal Street is closed to all traffic other than carnival floats and revellers. Recently the black and Creole parades have stolen the limelight, with their good-humored merriment, outrageous costumes (many of which have taken all year to make), steel bands and exuberant dancing.

Our *Mardi Gras* party is frankly a hotchpotch of Creole, Caribbean, and anyone else's carnival. In any event in Northern America and Northern Europe, *Mardi Gras* is no time for revelling in the streets. It is just too cold. But high summer brings people out on the tarmac and the English Notting Hill carnival, which takes place in August, with its merry mixture of West Indians and Africans exotically attired, sweeping through West London while the British bobby looks benignly on, has now become the biggest street festival in the world.

Of course it is not possible to take over the main street of your home town just because you want to hold a street party, but the key to a Carnival is showing off – dressing up, parading, music, singing and dancing *in public* – not in the privacy of your own home. So a street party might be an excellent town festivity, or a community affair for one street, or one block with each household contributing food and drink, and sharing the expenses of music, hired equipment, etc. It should go on, if not for days at a stretch, at least for many hours, culminating with open-air dancing to very loud, live Caribbean music. Entirely impracticable for most of us? Well, yes, but at least we could have an open-air party where the guests come exotically masked, eat Creole food and dance the night away.

**New Orleans**
*The restaurants of New Orleans have made the city a gastronomic center of the United States. Creole dishes are hot, spicy and skilfully blended so that no one seasoning overpowers the dish. The cuisine is a mélange of French, Spanish and Indian styles, modified by black cooks.*

**Filé Powder**
*Filé powder is one of the aromatics that give Creole food its distinct flavor. It is made of powdered sassafrass leaves and should be added to dishes at the last minute and never boiled.*

**Music**
*New Orleans has a lively musical life. Country and Western musicians long to perform at the Grand Old Opry and many important jazz musicians have come from the city. New Orleans is famous for its funeral processions accompanied by a band playing sad music to the cemetry and joyful music back home.*

**Cajuns**
*Cajuns are descendants of the French Acadians displaced from Newfoundland. While Acadian dishes have remained very French, they have lent a French influence to Creole cooking.*

Café Brulot
*This is a New Orleans concotion of strong expresso coffee flavored with cloves, cinnamon, orange and lemon peel and flamed with brandy.*

## PLANNING A STREET PARTY

A community party takes a few committee meetings to get off the ground. It also requires some very painstaking organization, great tact, steely determination, gentle patience and the forbearance of a saint to get it right. The first meeting should discuss: time; date; place; what the party is to consist of; where the money is to come from; and who is to be invited.

The willing organizers must then form themselves into subcommittees or co-opt their friends so that the work does not fall on to the unfortunate fellow who had the bright idea in the first place. One group should be responsible for the food, which means getting it cooked, begging or borrowing trestle tables, plates, cutlery, etc. One group should worry about drinks, which includes soft drinks for the children, ice, glasses, trays, etc. Someone else should cope with the authorities – if it is to take place in a town square, for example, the police should be told; if open braziers or torches are planned the fire department must be consulted. First aid needs to be considered, perhaps with the advice of the local ambulance people. If drinks are to be sold instead of given away, the organizers will need a liquor licence to do so – they may need to co-opt a local bartender to be the licensee. If there is to be a parade, the traffic authorities and the police need to be asked for their permission and co-operation. Someone needs to obtain the services of a steel band, and hire anything unusual (tented awnings in case of rain? braziers for warmth and glamor? electric twinkling lights to string along the street? floats for the parade?).

The second meeting, and subsequent ones, should check on everyone's progress so that, if someone is proving too feeble to get things done, he can be ruthlessly replaced in good time by someone better. Community parties, even more than most, depend on good planning and the committee will be heartily blamed if the party is not a success. If it's a triumph the organizers can glow with well-founded pride.

Safety
*When planning a party of this size, safety is of the utmost importance. Advice should be taken on first aid, fire precautions and from the police in the early stages of planning.*

Jambalaya
*If making this in quantities to be reheated later, fry the meats, peppers and spices as described. Allow to cool. Cook the rice separately in the chicken stock with tomatoes. Keep separate until reheating, then combine meats, rice and shrimp. Reheat, stirring over moderate heat, or in a shallow open dish in the oven. Add parsley at the last minute.*

Bread Pudding
*New Orleans bread pudding is a simple, though calorific, dessert. Make a sauce by melting butter and sugar together. Mix with bourbon and simmer for 2 minutes. Pour over chunks of French bread and serve straightaway.*

THE MENU

*Jambalaya*

*Crawfish Pie*

*Southern-Baked Chicken*

*Tomato and Okra Salad*

*Baked Bananas with Pecan Nuts*

*Shoofly Pie*

*French Vanilla Ice Cream*

## GETTING AHEAD
*One year before the party*

○ Gather together the committee to organize the party. See "Planning a Street Party" above for subjects to be discussed. Before proceeding further contact the local police to ensure they will be agreeable to blocking off the street from traffic and check with them for any other legal requirements (liquor licence, fire precautions, first aid, etc).

Delicious pecans are widely sold in supermarkets but walnuts would make a good substitute if pecans are unobtainable.

Live Shellfish
*If buying live crawfish, use them promptly as they will soon spoil.*

○ Form subcommittees to organize food, drinks, dealing with local authorities, parade, music and facilities, etc. (see "Planning a Street Party").
○ Arrange a second meeting to check on progress.

*At the second meeting*
○ Choose the menu.
○ Decide on drinks to be offered, apply for a licence if required.
○ Agree on facilities needed (such as temporary toilets) and make necessary arrangements.
○ Check on progress with local authorities and that all their requirements can be met.
○ Agree on music. Bands or discos should be booked immediately.
○ Agree on invitations and arrange to have them printed in plenty of time.

*During the next few months*
○ Hold the occasional meeting to ensure that all is going well and constantly urge along the committees by telephone.
○ Put up posters and send invitations.
○ *Food committee:* Leader to delegate the making of one dish to each member. The leader should check that adequate cooking and storage facilities and equipment will be available. Use disposable plates or cutlery or ask guests to bring their own. Arrange to hire anything necessary.

Crawfish
*Also called spiny or rock lobster, crawfish have large tails filled with sweet tender meat like proper lobsters but have no claws. Crayfish, freshwater shellfish that look like miniature lobsters, are traditionally used for "crawfish pie" in Louisiana where crayfish are confusingly known as crawfish. We use proper crawfish in our recipe as their larger size makes less work.*

　　Discuss in detail with each committee member the ordering, preparation, storage and collection of the food and how it will be served at the party. Buffet service is probably the easiest although it may be possible to dish up the food in batches of 10 or 20 to be delivered to tables of seated party guests. Find helpers to deal with the food on the day.
○ *Drinks Committee:* Make a list of drinks required, and order them. Include extras like straws and lemons. Buy plastic glasses, arrange for hired glasses with the music and facilities committee. Check that plenty of bottle openers will be available. Order bags of ice. Organize bartenders.
○ Parade committee: Check that all is going well with the local authorities. Arrange floats and in addition make sure there will be plenty of costumes and paraders to walk alongside. Check with the music and facilities committee that the bands will be included in the parade. You may have to arrange for their costumes.
○ *Music and facilities committee:* Check arrangements for bands or discos. Hire an amplifier and speakers; borrow records and tapes. Arrange for the hire of awning, toilets and also for the hire of any equipment needed by the other committees.

*One month before the party*
○ *Food committee:* Shopping lists should be made from the recipes. Dry goods bought. Ice cream frozen, pastry for the shoofly and crawfish pies frozen.

*One week–two days before the party*
○ *Drinks committee* should have purchased all the stocks, be in possession of the glasses, bar equipment and liquor licence and have helpers organized.
○ *Parade committee:* Check that all parties making a float are still doing so and that they will be able to put them together on the morning of the party.

"Bayou"
*The New Orleans area is surrounded by inland waterways called "bayou". They provide a plentiful supply of crawfish, much used in Creole dishes.*

Plastic straws are pleasanter to drink from than paper ones and the wide pretty ones, in bright rastafarian colors, with bendable ends make drinking a Coke from the can pleasant even for conservative adults.

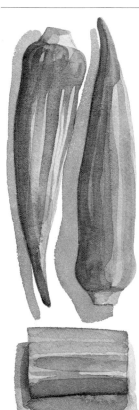

Fresh okra is delicious if cooked with care and goes well with tomatoes. Avoid the canned variety which lacks flavor.

Shoofly Pie
*This originated from the deep South where it is said that flies attracted by the sweet sticky filling had to be shooed away.*

*Two days before the party*
○ *Music and facilities committee:* Tents, toilets and any other equipment should all be delivered and erected.
○ *Food committee:* Complete all shopping with the exception of the shellfish for the jambalaya and crawfish pie. Defrost the pastries and bake the pie cases.

*The day before the party*
○ *Food committee:* Prepare the onions and peppers for the jambalaya, cut up the pork loin and spicy sausage.
   Buy the shrimp and crawfish and refrigerate. Make the filling for the crawfish pie.
   Egg and flour the chicken breasts, cover tightly and leave overnight.
   Skin the tomatoes, cook the okra and make the salad dressing.
   Prepare the fruit juice and rind for the baked bananas, put together in a bowl and cover.
   Chop the pecans.
   Make the shoofly pies.
○ *Drinks committee:* Set up the bar (but do not put out glasses or drinks).
○ *Parade committee:* Check that all participants are ready with their costumes and props for the floats and that they all know the right time to congregate.
○ *Music and facilities committee:* Check with bands to make sure they will arrive on time. Inform them about changing facilities and make sure some refreshments will be reserved for them.

*The day of the party*
○ *Food committee:* Finish jambalaya (see margin note for cooking in quantity and reheating, p. 186).
   Put the crawfish filling into the pie, sprinkle with Parmesan cheese and broil, serve warm or cold.
   Bake the chicken at the last minute and immediately take to the party so that it will be just warm for serving.
   Toss the tomato and okra salad.
   If there are heating facilities at the party take the bananas in skins. Simmer the butter, sugar and fruit juice until syrupy and take along with the pecans. Cook the bananas on site. If there are no facilities, cook the bananas at home and take piping hot.
   Serve the shoofly pie cold. Take the French vanilla ice cream out of the freezer 40 minutes before serving. If necessary keep it cold in an insulated box with freezer bags.
○ *Drinks committee:* Set out all the drinks and glasses at the bar area ready for service. Take delivery of ice. Do not leave the bar unguarded.
○ *Parade committee:* Make sure that the floats arrive first thing in the morning and that the participants are there to dress them. Check that the local police have cordoned off the street. Check fire and first aid safety precautions. Assemble bands, floats and others for the start of the parade.
○ *Music and facilities committee:* See that all equipment is there and working well and that helpers are on hand to repair anything that should break. Make sure that the bands have arrived and know where to play after the parade. If using recorded music make sure that it is playing and that someone is in charge of keeping the music going.

Gumbo
*The most famous of Creole soups, this makes a hearty dish. It is made with meat and shellfish and seasoned with filé. The shellfish is served complete with shell which makes eating a messy business. Provide large linen napkins and finger bowls.*

Okra
*This is a young seed pod. Sauté the okra before adding to soups and stews to improve the mucilaginous texture.*

*Right* Bright paper cloths, paper plates and colored streamers create a carnival background for the delicious food: on the left Southern-baked chicken with lemon and lime slices. Center, shoofly pie with a crusty spiced sugar top and on the right tomato and okra salad.

# CREOLE PARTY RECIPES

QUANTITY NOTE:
Adjust the quantities for large numbers. For 30 people, make twice the recipes for jambalaya, crawfish pie, baked bananas and shoofly pie; 1½ times the Southern-baked chicken and 3 times the tomato and okra salad. See Catering in Quantity, p. 10.

## JAMBALAYA
SERVES 10
*2lb pork loin*
*oil for frying*
*1 large onion, finely chopped*
*2 cloves garlic, crushed*
*1 tsp turmeric*
*2 tsp ground ginger*
*1 tsp paprika*
*2 green peppers, seeded and sliced*
*1 cup rice*
*1lb canned tomatoes*
*2 cups chicken stock*
*salt and pepper*
*squeeze of lemon juice*
*8oz hot spicy sausage (e.g. chorizo) cut into chunks*
*1lb (2¾ cups) shrimp, cooked and shelled*
FOR DECORATION
*½ cup shrimp in shells*
*chopped parsley*

1. Trim the pork and cut it into slices ½in × 2in. Heat the oil in a heavy-based pan and quickly brown the meat on all sides. Lift out the pieces and put them to one side.

2. Put the onion in the pan and fry gently until soft and transparent. Add the garlic, turmeric, ginger and paprika and continue to fry for one minute. Now add the green pepper, and fry a further minute.
3. Stir the rice into the vegetable mixture, add the tomatoes, chicken stock, and browned meat. Bring to the boil, season with salt, pepper and lemon juice, cover and simmer for 10 minutes.
4. Stir in the spicy sausage and shrimp, simmer for 10 more minutes until the stock has all been absorbed.
5. Pile the jambalaya on to a heated serving dish. Scatter the shrimp in shells over the top. Allow them to warm through in the oven.
6. Sprinkle with chopped parsley before serving.

## CRAWFISH PIE
SERVES 10
*pastry for two 8in pie shells*
FOR THE FILLING
*1½lb raw crawfish tails*
*1¼ cups milk*
*1 small onion, sliced*
*1 carrot, sliced*
*1 stick celery, sliced*
*1 bay leaf*
*¼ cup butter*
*1 small onion, finely chopped*
*4½ tbsp all-purpose flour*
*1 tsp dry mustard*

*good pinch cayenne pepper*
*3 tbsp dry sherry*
*Worcestershire sauce*
*salt and ground black pepper*
*⅔ cup heavy cream*
*¼ cup grated Parmesan cheese*
*paprika*
*extra butter*

1. Roll the pastry out thinly and line two 8in tart pans. Chill the pastry cases for 30 minutes.
2. Preheat the oven, setting the temperature control to 400°. Prick the base of the pastry with a fork and line with foil or wax paper and baking beans. Bake for 30 minutes, removing the lining halfway through cooking to allow the pastry to brown.
3. To make the filling: remove the flesh from the crawfish shells. Crush the shells and put them together in a pan with the milk, onion, carrot, celery and bay leaf. Bring slowly to the boil, simmer for 10 minutes, strain.
4. Poach the crawfish in the strained milk for 3 to 4 minutes, taking care that the milk does not boil. Strain. Reserve the milk and cut the crawfish flesh into chunks.
5. Melt the butter in a saucepan, and gently fry the chopped onion. Add the flour, mustard and cayenne pepper and fry for one minute. Gradually add the reserved milk, stirring constantly to make a smooth sauce.

6. Stir in the dry sherry, Worcestershire sauce and season with salt and black pepper, bring to the boil and simmer for two minutes. Add the cream and crawfish flesh.

7. Pour into the cooked tart case. Sprinkle the Parmesan cheese and paprika over the top and dot with a little butter. Brown under the broiler. Serve warm or cold.

## SOUTHERN-BAKED CHICKEN
SERVES 10
*10 chicken breasts, with skin attached*
*3 cups self-raising flour*
*2 tsp baking powder*
*2 tsp ground cumin*
*¼ tsp cayenne pepper*
*2 tbsp chopped parsley*
*grated rind of one large lemon*
*salt*
*black pepper*
*2 eggs*
*⅔ pt milk*
*1 cup dripping, lard or shortening*

1. Cut the chicken breasts in half.
2. Mix the flour, baking powder, cumin, cayenne pepper, parsley and lemon rind together in a shallow container. Season well with salt and black pepper.
3. Beat the eggs and milk with a large pinch of salt. Pour into a shallow dish.
4. Dip the chicken pieces first into the egg and milk and then into the seasoned flour. When each piece has been coated once repeat the whole process until all the flour is used. Lay the chicken on a baking sheet, cover and refrigerate for one hour. By then the egg and milk will have soaked into the flour to make a batter-like coating.
5. Preheat the oven, setting the temperature control to 400°. Put the fat into a roasting pan and melt in the heated oven until sizzling hot.
6. Lay the chicken in the hot fat and cook for 15 minutes. Turn the pieces over and cook for a further 15 minutes or until the chicken is tender all the way through.
7. Drain the chicken on paper towels. Serve hot or cold.

## TOMATO AND OKRA SALAD
SERVES 10
*1 lb fresh okra*
*10 tomatoes, skinned*
*½ small onion, finely chopped*
FOR THE DRESSING
*⅔ cup vegetable oil*
*2 tbsp chili or wine vinegar*
*½ tsp tomato paste*
*pinch dry mustard*
*pinch brown sugar*
*dash of Tabasco*
*salt and ground black pepper*
*1 tbsp chopped parsley*

1. Wash and dry the okra. Trim the top and bottom of the pods, and cut into 1in lengths. Boil in salted water for 5 minutes or until tender. Drain and rinse well in cold water.
2. Cut the tomatoes into eighths and put in a bowl with the okra and the chopped onion.
3. Place all the dressing ingredients, except the parsley, in a screw-top jar and shake well.
4. Toss the vegetables in the dressing and leave to marinate for one hour.
5. Before serving, turn the salad into a bowl and sprinkle with chopped parsley.

## BAKED BANANAS WITH PECAN NUTS
SERVES 10
*10 bananas*
*juice of one lemon*
*⅔ cup butter*
*grated rind and juice of 2 oranges*
*½ cup sugar*
*1 cup pecans, chopped*
TO SERVE
*cream or ice cream*

1. Preheat the oven, setting the temperature control to 375°.
2. Peel the bananas and split them in half lengthways. Brush them with lemon juice to prevent them turning brown.
3. Melt the butter in a pan, add the orange juice and rind, sugar and any remaining lemon juice. Simmer till syrupy and pour over the bananas.
4. Bake the bananas for 10 to 15 minutes, basting once or twice, until they are just tender.
5. Scatter the pecans on top of the bananas and serve immediately with cream or ice cream.

## SHOOFLY PIE
SERVES 10
*8 oz flan pastry (see Tarte Maison, p. 19)*
FOR THE FILLING
*½ cup dried apricots*
*⅔ cup raisins*
*½ cup stoned whole dates, chopped*
*½ cup dried figs, chopped*
*⅓ cup soft brown sugar*
*½ tsp baking soda*
*⅔ cup dark rum*
FOR THE TOPPING
*2 cups all-purpose flour*
*1 tsp cinnamon*
*1 tsp grated nutmeg*
*½ tsp ground ginger*
*½ cup butter*
*⅓ cup soft brown sugar*
TO SERVE
*whipped cream, ice cream or sour cream*

1. Soak the dried fruit, brown sugar together with the baking soda in the rum overnight.
2. Roll out the pastry thinly and use to line a 12in tart pan. Prick the base of the pastry with a fork and chill for 30 minutes.
3. Preheat the oven, setting the temperature control to 400°. Line the pastry case with foil or wax paper and baking beans. Bake for 30 minutes, removing the foil or wax paper lining half way through cooking to allow the pastry to brown. Leave to cool.
4. Turn the oven temperature control up to 425°. Sift the flour and spices together into a large mixing bowl. Rub in the butter.
5. Spoon the soaked fruit into the tart case. Spread the topping over the fruit and sprinkle the sugar on top.
6. Bake in the heated oven for 15 minutes. Lower the oven temperature to 375° and cook the pie for a further 20 minutes.
7. Serve warm or cold.

## FRENCH VANILLA ICE CREAM
SERVES 10
*8 egg yolks*
*¾ cup sugar*
*3¾ cup whipping or heavy cream*
*1 vanilla pod or 2 tsp vanilla extract*

1. Beat the egg yolks and sugar until light and frothy.
2. Put the cream and vanilla pod (but not the extract) into a pan and heat until steaming.
3. Remove the vanilla pod from the cream and pour the cream on to the egg yolk mixture, beating all the time.
4. Place the bowl over a pan of simmering water and stir until the mixture has become thick and creamy and will coat the back of a wooden spoon. If using vanilla extract, add it now.
5. Allow the custard to cool completely, pour into a clean container and freeze, beating every 30 minutes until the ice cream is completely frozen.
6. Place in the refrigerator for 30 minutes before serving.

# THIRTIES COCKTAIL *for Fifty*

The traditional olive for dry martinis is the firm green (unripe) variety. Cherries bottled in maraschino are generally used for sweeter drinks.

Bar Equipment
*You will need the following equipment: shaker, small strainer, measure, mixing glass, long-handled spoon, teaspoon, dish cloth, fruit juice squeezer, crushed ice, electric blender with several goblets, corkscrew, bottle opener, hot water for cleaning the utensils.*

COCKTAILS, IF NOT COCKTAIL PARTIES, ARE VERY MUCH back in fashion, having suffered an eclipse for about forty years. Today fashionable youth flings back slings and knocks back blockbusters in thirties-style bars all over America and Europe. Most of the famous cocktails of the twenties and thirties, the Manhattans, Daquiris and Brandy Alexanders, are back in favor but the best-selling concoctions today are far more popular than they were when dreamed up by New York, Paris or London barmen fifty years ago. Some are strictly 1980s rather than 1930s, but never mind – the main thing is that they should taste great and look spectacular. And the very names Harvey Wall-banger, Tequila Sunrise or Singapore Sling suggest a good time – this is not run-of-the-mill drinking – it's a deliberate celebration.

To stage a really spectacular twenties or thirties cocktail party, a professional cocktail barman is a must. Which means that the party will have to be held on his night-off from bar or hotel, and the first thing to do before inviting anyone, is to book him. A proper barman is not essential of course, but the practised speed with which a really good cocktail-maker works is a pleasure to watch, and the sheer theatricality of his performance is one of the factors that fills a bar with fashionable patrons. Also, he'll produce better drinks much quicker and with less mess than an amateur. His expertise will also mean that a wide variety of cocktails can be offered. If the host is to stir martinis, shake whisky sours, and pack ice into juleps, he could end up having a horribly flustered time and the guests could end up cross and thirsty.

So if the host or hostess is to play barman, the choice of drinks should be very limited – perhaps one cocktail based on bourbon, one on gin and one on rum – with not more than five in total. The basic juices and flavorings can be mixed in smallish quantities in advance leaving only the alcohol and the ice to be added. A silver cocktail shaker is a theatrical and atmospheric prop, but most cocktails can be more efficiently and speedily made in an electric blender. The blender also eliminates the need for ready-crushed ice. For most drinks it can be crushed in the goblet with the whizzing drink. Beg or borrow as many blenders as you need to avoid having to rinse the goblet between drinks, and make sure you have sufficient electrical outlets to operate them.

Cut plenty of orange and lemon slices to go with the cocktails and keep them refrigerated until needed.

Ready-Mixed Cocktails
*If the budget does not run to a professional barman, the host can minimize the work by buying some ready-mixed cocktails.*

**Cocktail Decorations**
*Before the party prepare a supply of slices of fruit and twists of rind. Cherries, olives, toothpicks, straws, swizzle sticks and paper parasols all make good decorations.*

Set up the bar to resemble a professional one as closely as possible – with counter in front and shelves and work surface (perhaps an emptied bookcase or kitchen dresser) behind. If it is possible to organize matters so that the bar-counter is at customer-elbow height with (behind and slightly below it) a work-top on which rinsing bowl, cloth, cut-up fruit, etc. are concealed, so much the better. Try to lay things out in an organized manner with drink bottles behind, chilled mixes on ice (they could be lying in a baby-bath or wash-tub) to one side on the floor, glasses on the work surface, herbs in a jug or counter-top – everything within reach.

A thirties look can be given to the room by the replacement of pictures with thirties posters, by the addition of potted palms and art-deco objects or lights. Marvellously-shaped cocktail glasses can be fairly cheaply bought and thirties-style saucer-shaped champagne glasses can be hired.

## MUSIC

A full El Morocco orchestra with a reincarnation of Harry James on the trumpet is probably out of the question, but records like Ray Noble's *Little White Lies*, Cole Porter's *Begin The Beguine* and the recordings of the Tommy and Jimmy Dorsey, Glen Miller and Benny Goodman orchestras playing favorites such as *In The Mood, Deep Purple* and *String Of Pearls* would supply the right period sound.

## THE INVITATION

The invitations should specify that the party is a nostalgia trip to the thirties or twenties (or both) so that guests can come appropriately dressed, the women in drippy, straight, low-waisted dresses, costume beads and even perhaps forehead bandeaux or saucy feathered hats; the men in almost anything remotely twenties or thirties – blazers, straw hats, stripes, dinner jackets, white tie, pleated trousers or Bertie Wooster tweeds. It doesn't matter if the gear is not authentic – it's the thought that counts.

## THE FOOD

The drinks are obviously more important than the food for this party and we have given the recipes for the most popular fizzes and slings, punches and "shorts". A teetotaller's tipple is a good idea too – a non-alcoholic but sophisticated-looking and interesting-tasting drink that the non-drinker can nurse without being constantly asked "Don't you want something stronger?" (See margin note, p. 194.)

But *some* food should be provided. If the party is genuinely a drinks-time only one, then nuts and potato chips plus a few plates of our rather formal hotel canapés would suit the hour and the atmosphere, as would little hot pastry bouchées filled with mushroom or shrimp mixtures, or a basket of boiled quails', gulls' and plovers' eggs (left in their shells for the guests to peel) with a bowl of sea-salt for dipping them in. Or even an upturned half-melon stuck à la porcupine with sticks containing cheese-and-grape-bites and melon cubes with smoked ham. But if there is any danger of guests staying on and making a night of it, then something more substantial should be provided after a couple of hours of drinking – the dishes suggested in the One Plate Dinner (pp. 130-1) would do or the Creole jambalaya (p. 189) might be appropriately sobering.

Really fresh bought chips and peanuts (buy them vacuum-packed) are adequate nibbles if supper is to be served later. But more substantial snacks are better for an extended drinks party.

*Right* High-tech bar stools, thirties lights and shiny chrome set the scene for a sophisticated period cocktail party. From the left: tequila, Russian vodka, Galliano liqueur and crème de menthe form the basis for many strange and wonderful cocktails.

**Glasses**
*You will need the following glasses: 4 fl oz V-shaped cocktail glasses; Old Fashioned glasses (short tumblers); highball glasses (tall tumblers holding approximately 8 fl oz); champagne glasses – either tulips or saucers (saucers are more "thirties").*

**Hot Cocktail Food**
*Serve hot cocktail food decorated with watercress and skewered with a toothpick. Arrange paper napkins on the serving dish for guests to help themselves to.*

**Salmon Pie**
*Flat salmon pie served with a simple green salad makes a perfect meal after the party. Make any type of rich savory pastry. Roll one-third into a base and lay on a baking sheet. Cover with a layer each of cream cheese, smoked or fresh salmon, and chopped, cooked spinach. Sprinkle with a little white wine and lemon juice and season with salt and black pepper. Cover with the rest of the pastry. Bake at 400° until golden brown.*

THE MENU

*Toothpicks:*
*Cubes of Cheddar with Cocktail Onions*
*Melon Pieces wrapped in Parma Ham*
*Pieces of Brie wrapped in Salami*
*Peeled Shrimp with Seedless Grapes*

*Quails', Plovers' and Gulls' Eggs with Seasoned Salt*

*Aspic Toasts with Salami, Kipper, Ham and Lobster**

*Steak Tartare on Toast**

*Devils on Horseback**

*Angels on Horseback**

**Recipes included*

Small pieces of two contrastingly flavored foods make interesting cocktail bites. On top, pieces of Cheddar with cocktail onions. Above melon in Parma ham. Choose firm, fairly dry melon and cut long strips of ham to wrap right round, lest they fall apart.

Take care not to push the toothpicks right through the food – it makes the mouthful awkward to eat. On top, Brie wrapped in salami. Choose slightly under-ripe Brie and keep cool. Dark Italian salami, thinly sliced, is a good buy. Above, peeled shrimp with a seedless grape.

## GETTING AHEAD

*A month or so before the party*
- If hiring a barman, book him as soon as possible. Check with him if there are any special ingredients or equipment you should provide.
- Send the invitations. Use a period card or picture postcards with a thirties look.
- Decide where the bar will be and how you will organize it.
- Buy, borrow or rent any items you need for the bar, or equipment for making the cocktails. (See margin note on Bar Equipment, p. 191.)
- Arrange to rent glasses either from a wine and liquor merchant or hire-firm.
- Make a list of drinks from the recipes and buy them, preferably on a "sale or return" basis. Consult Catering in Quantity, p. 10 when calculating quantities.

*Two weeks before the party*
- Buy small paper napkins to hand out with the food.
- Collect posters and thirties *objets* to decorate the room. Large palms and aspidistras can be hired.
- Buy or borrow suitable tapes or records.
- Make a shopping list from the recipes.
- Buy the dry goods.
- Buy an assortment of nuts, savory biscuits, cocktail onions, gherkins, olives, etc.
- Decide whether or not to provide more substantial food for "stayers on" and make preparation for this. (See our recipe for salmon pie on p. 192.)
- Order the quails', plovers' and gulls' eggs, oysters and lobster meat from a good delicatessen.

*Two days before the party*
- Make plenty of ice, crack it or crush it (see margin note) and store it in the freezer in plastic bags.
- Do all the shopping except for the quails', plovers' and gulls' eggs, oysters, lobster and the steak.
- Start decorating the room with posters, plants and suitable thirties *objets*.
- Take delivery of the drinks and glasses and check them carefully.

Sweet Martini
*For a sweeter martini, substitute sweet vermouth for dry. Or add a dash of orange bitters to a dry martini and serve it with a cherry instead of an olive or twist of lemon peel.*

Teetotaller's Tipple
*Make 1¼ cups strong black tea and in it dissolve 2 tbsp brown sugar. Mix with 1¼ cups water, 2 tbsp lime juice cordial and slices of orange, lemon and cucumber. Chill well. Just before serving add a small bottle of tonic water, plenty of ice cubes and decorate with mint leaves.*

Ice
*"Cracked" ice is roughly chopped ice. "Crushed" ice is chopped to the texture of coffee sugar crystals. Both can be achieved in a food processor and returned to the freezer until needed.*

## Quails' Eggs
*These are speckled brown and about one-third of the size of a chicken's egg. They make a delicious "salad tiède" when medium-boiled and served with chicken or duck liver lightly fried in butter.*

*Below* The tiny quails' eggs look beautiful on a plain dish or arranged in a "nest" of radicchio. As they are commercially farmed, they are available most of the year. Gulls' eggs and plovers' eggs only in late spring.

### The day before the party
○ Make the devils on horseback, undercooking slightly.
○ Make the dried bread croûtes for steak tartare.
○ Make kipper or ham topping for aspic toasts.
○ Set out the bar. If a barman is coming he will set out all the drinks, glasses and everything he needs. However, if you are doing the bar with the help of friends it may be a good idea to set out bottles and polish the glasses now.
○ Make the salmon pie (or an alternative) for stayers on.
○ If you have space, put the cocktail glasses in the refrigerator to chill.

### The morning of the party
○ Finish setting up the bar, except for the ice and the chilled drinks.
○ Shop for oysters, quails', plovers' and gulls' eggs, lobster meat and steak.
○ Cook the eggs in boiling water (quails' eggs for 3 minutes, plovers' for 5 and gulls' for 7).
○ Cut up cubes of cheese, ham, melon, etc. for toothpicks and cover with plastic wrap.
○ Put eggs, unpeeled, in a basket with a bowl of seasoned salt and a dish for the debris beside the basket.
○ Make lobster topping.
○ Make steak tartare.
○ Make angels on horseback, undercooking slightly, and keep chilled.
○ Finish aspic toasts and chill (but do not cut them yet).
○ Put out paper napkins.
○ Put out bowls of nuts, potato chips and pickles, etc.

### A few hours before the guests arrive
○ Put the angels and devils on horseback into a roasting pan ready to be heated.
○ Thread the prepared food on to toothpicks and spike into a pineapple, melon or cabbage.
 ○ Cut the aspic toasts into fingers and arrange them carefully on a serving dish.
  ○ Put the steak tartare on to dried bread and decorate with the hard-boiled egg.
   ○ Have serving dishes and extra toothpicks ready to serve hot food and watercress to decorate.
    ○ Cover all cold food lightly with plastic wrap.
    ○ Cut up fruit and squeeze fresh juices for the bar.

### Just before the guests arrive
○ Uncover cold food.
 ○ Put ice on the bar and lightly break up cracked or crushed ice if this has been stored in the freezer.
  ○ If you do not have a professional barman, frost the rims of the cocktail glasses (wet the rims with egg white and dip them into sugar or salt).
   ○ Put on the music.

### After the guests arrive
○ Heat angels and devils on horseback.

From top to bottom: quails', plovers' and gulls' eggs look beautiful left in their shells. Provide celery salt, sea salt, cayenne pepper and perhaps mayonnaise, and leave the guests to peel the eggs themselves. Don't forget a debris dish.

## Hard-Boiled Eggs
*It is the pocket of air trapped inside the membrane at the fat end of an egg which expands and causes the egg to crack when boiled. To avoid this, pierce a hole in that end of the egg with a darning needle or egg pricker.*

# THIRTIES COCKTAIL RECIPES

## ASPIC TOASTS
**MAKES ABOUT 50 OF EACH VARIETY**

For each type of filling you will need ten slices of toast (each slice will cut into five or six fingers) and approximately ¾ cup aspic or unflavored gelatin. Commercial gelatin can be used as only the thinnest layer should coat each slice. A little sherry can be added to the gelatin to improve the flavor.

To coat the toasts with gelatin: place them on a wire rack, put the liquid gelatin into a metal jug and cool until it is starting to set and looks syrupy. Then spoon a little gelatin over to completely cover the filling. If the gelatin is too set or lumpy remelt it by standing the jug in warm water. If it is too liquid, cool it by standing in iced water. The trick is to use it when it is *just* liquid, smooth and syrupy – neither too runny nor too set.

## FILLINGS
**SALAMI**
*20 wafer-thin slices of salami*
*8oz (1 cup) cream cheese*
*a little milk or cream*
*grated horseradish*
*sprigs of chervil to decorate*

Soften the cream cheese with a little milk or cream. Add grated horseradish to taste. Spread a thick layer over each slice of toast and carefully lay the salami on top. Decorate with flat leaves of chervil dipped in the liquid gelatin to secure them to the salami; chill. Coat with gelatin and chill again to set. Cut each slice of toast into fingers.

**POTTED KIPPER**
(see p. 158 but halve the quantities)
*black olives to decorate*

Spread the potted kipper evenly over each slice of toast. Decorate with halved black olives and coat with a thin layer of gelatin. Cut into small fingers.

**HAM**
*8oz (1⅓ cups) smoked ham, finely chopped*
*½ cup softened butter*
*1 tbsp chopped parsley*
*1 tsp seed mustard*
*ground black pepper*
*cucumber skin cut into diamond shapes*

Beat the ham and butter together until smooth. Add the chopped parsley and mustard, season with black pepper. Spread evenly over the toast. Decorate with cucumber, coat with aspic, allow to set and cut into fingers.

*Right* Above, aspic toasts: crisp toast topped with savory mixtures and a fine sheen of aspic. Here lobster topped with red mock caviar and potted ham decorated with a diamond of cucumber skin. Below them, devils on horseback (prunes stuffed with chutney and wrapped in crisp bacon).

**LOBSTER**
*⅓ cups cooked lobster meat, chopped*
*2 tbsp mayonnaise*
*2 tbsp whipped cream*
*salt, pepper, Tabasco*
*lemon juice*
*1 tbsp gelatin*
*aspic jelly*
*lobster coral or red caviar*

Mix the lobster meat with the mayonnaise and whipped cream, season with salt, pepper, Tabasco and a squeeze of lemon juice. Put a spoonful of water into a small pan and sprinkle the gelatin over, leave to soak for 10 minutes, then warm over a gentle heat until clear and runny. Add to the lobster and mix well.

Spread the lobster mixture over the toast and coat with aspic. Leave until the lobster and the aspic have set. Cut the slices into fingers and decorate each one with a little lobster coral or red caviar.

## STEAK TARTARE ON TOAST
**MAKES ABOUT 50**
**FOR THE STEAK TARTARE**
*14 slices white bread*
*8oz fillet or rump steak*
*2 tbsp oil*
*2 raw egg yolks*
*½ small onion, finely chopped*
*2 tsp parsley, finely chopped*
*salt and freshly ground black pepper*
*Worcestershire sauce*
*2 hard-boiled hens' eggs or 10 quails' eggs*

1. With a small round cutter cut four rounds out of each slice of bread. Bake in a cool oven until crisp and dry. Cool.
2. Trim the steak and chop or mince it two or three times until it is very smooth. Mix in all the ingredients except the hard-boiled eggs and season with salt, pepper and Worcestershire sauce.
3. Put a spoonful of steak tartare on top of each round of baked bread and decorate with sieved hard-boiled egg yolk, and chopped egg white or slices of hard-boiled quails' eggs.

## DEVILS ON HORSEBACK
**MAKES ABOUT 50**
*25 slices fairly fat bacon*
*50 cooked prunes*
*1 jar chutney*
*wooden toothpicks*

Stretch the streaky bacon with the back of a knife and cut each slice in half. Remove the stones from the prunes. Fill the center of each prune with a little chutney. Roll the prunes in the bacon pieces and lay them side by side in a roasting pan. Set the oven temperature to 425°. Bake the devils on horseback for 10 minutes until they are browned. Pierce each roll with a toothpick and serve when slightly cooled.

## ANGELS ON HORSEBACK
**MAKES ABOUT 50**
*25 slices fairly fat bacon*
*50 oysters, fresh or frozen*
*wooden toothpicks*

Stretch the bacon slices with the back of a knife and cut each slice in half. Roll the oysters in the bacon slices and lay them side by side in a roasting pan. Set the oven temperature control to 425°. Bake the angels on horseback for 10 minutes until they are browned. Pierce each roll with a toothpick and serve when slightly cooled. (If using fresh oysters, ask the fish shop to open them for you but be sure to use the oysters on the same day. If you have to open the oysters yourself, see the Note on how to do it in Aphrodisiac Dinner, p. 118.)

## MARTINI

½ gin and
⅛-½ dry vermouth
1 dash Angostura bitters (optional)
olive or a twist of lemon peel
cracked ice

Put some cracked ice into a cocktail glass. Add the gin, vermouth and bitters if wished. Stir gently and drop in the olive or lemon peel.

## GIN FIZZ

4 cubes cracked ice
1 measure gin
2 tbsp lemon juice
1 tsp sugar
½ egg white
1 tsp crème de menthe
soda water
FOR DECORATION
a little egg white, sugar and a slice of lemon

Put the ice into a cocktail shaker. Add the gin, lemon juice, sugar, egg white and crème de menthe. Dip the rim of a tall tumbler into the extra egg white and then in sugar. Shake the cocktail, strain into the glass, top up with soda and decorate with the slice of lemon.

## SINGAPORE SLING

2 cubes cracked ice
1 measure gin
½ measure cherry brandy
¼ measure Cointreau
1 tbsp lemon juice
soda water
FOR DECORATION
slice of lemon, cherry, slice of pineapple and a paper parasol

Put the cracked ice into a tall tumbler. Add the gin, cherry brandy, Cointreau and lemon juice. Top up with soda water and stir. Drop the lemon and cherry into the sling. Stick the parasol into the pineapple slice, and hook over the edge of the glass. Drink with straws.

## MANHATTAN (SWEET)

cracked ice
½ rye bourbon
½ sweet vermouth
dash Angostura bitters
FOR DECORATION
twist of lemon peel and a cherry

Put some cracked ice into an Old Fashioned glass. Mix the bourbon, vermouth and bitters in a shaker, pour over the ice and stir once. Add the lemon peel and cherry on a toothpick.

NOTE:
(A dry Manhattan may be made with dry vermouth and decorated with an olive.)

## OLD FASHIONED

1 sugar lump
dash Angostura bitters
2 dashes soda water
2 ice cubes
1 measure bourbon
FOR DECORATION
half slice orange

Put the sugar lump into an Old Fashioned glass, shake the dash of bitters on to the sugar cube and add the soda. Stir until the sugar has dissolved. Add the ice and coat with the dissolved sugar. Add the bourbon, stir, then float the slice of orange on top.

## SIDECAR

1 measure brandy
½ measure Cointreau
½ measure lemon juice
2 cubes cracked ice
FOR DECORATION
a twist of lemon

Put the brandy, Cointreau, lemon juice and cracked ice into a cocktail shaker and mix. Strain into a cocktail glass and decorate with the lemon.

## HARVEY WALL-BANGER

3 cubes cracked ice
2 measures orange juice
1 measure vodka
2 tsp Galliano
FOR DECORATION
toothpick with cucumber, orange peel, pineapple and cherry

Put the cracked ice into a tall tumbler, pour on the orange juice and vodka. Add the Galliano and stir well. Decorate with the toothpick and fruit.

## BLACK RUSSIAN

2-3 cubes cracked ice
2 measures vodka
1 measure Kahlua

Put the cracked ice cubes into an Old Fashioned glass. Pour over the vodka and Kahlua and stir.

## BRANDY ALEXANDER

1 measure brandy
1 measure crème de cacao
1 measure cream
2 cubes cracked ice
grated nutmeg

Put the brandy, crème de cacao, cream and ice into a cocktail shaker and mix well. Pour into a cocktail glass and sprinkle grated nutmeg on top.

## TEQUILA SUNRISE

3 cubes crushed ice
3 cubes ice
1 measure tequila
2 measure orange juice
2 tsp grenadine

Put the crushed ice, orange juice and tequila into a cocktail shaker and mix well. Put the cubes of ice into a tall tumbler and pour over the tequila mixture. Just before serving slowly add the grenadine, allow to settle and stir once.

## DAIQUIRI

1 cube crushed ice
2 measures white rum
1 measure lemon or lime juice
1 tsp sugar

Put the crushed ice, white rum, fruit juice and sugar into a cocktail shaker and mix until the sugar has dissolved. Pour into a cocktail glass and serve with short straws.

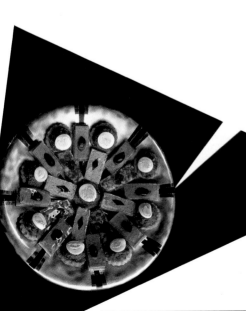

*Left* Outer circle, steak tartare with a slice of quail's egg on toast; kipper pâté with a slice of black olive and a fine coat of aspic. Inner ring, salami decorated with chervil sprigs and potted ham with cucumber skin.

# WATERLILY DINNER *for Eight*

*Left* A single, simple theme (here making everything waterlily-shaped) can give style and wit to a party. In the middle, a paint-sprayed artichoke serves as a waterlily set in a bowl amidst floating candles. Above it, butter pieces arranged in a flower shape and below it a simple salad given a waterlily look. For each guest a first course of artichoke served with aïoli in a flower-carved lemon skin and a flower-bud bread roll.

THIS DINNER, PLANNED FOR EIGHT, IS AN ELABORATE, but fairly easily achieved, concept. It combines true elegance, a dash of wit, and a good measure of fun. But you cannot do it half-heartedly. For the theme to work, it must be carried through from start to finish. If you only bother with the waterlily effect for, say, some of the food, forgetting the napkins and the flowers, the result could look affected and pretentious. After all, cutting melons *à la zig-zag* is not new – third-rate hotels specialize in such tricks. But if everything reflects the waterlily theme – floating candles among the lily-pads in a great shallow bowl, pale yellow or white napkins folded like waterlilies, perhaps a tablecloth made of pale blue lining fabric (or better still water-taffeta), handpainted with lily-pads, even the butter curled into waterlily petals – the effect will be witty and pretty.

But what if you can't get waterlilies? Well, the effect is the thing, and large white chrysanthemums floating sparsely in the bowl will do. Or you can cheat – use artichokes, sprayed yellow, pink or white. (The ones in our photograph are artichokes with their petals trimmed to sharper points, and sprayed white. Expensive. But they last for weeks before drying out and

## Zig-Zag Cuts
*To be effective zig-zag cuts must be very neatly carried out. Use a really sharp knife to score a fine line marking the top and bottom of the points of the zig-zags and then use them as guidelines when making the cuts.*

Fresh chrysanthemums are exotic blooms more easily available than waterlilies. Buy the large mop-head or frilly oriental type.

dying.) Or you could contrive a rose dinner instead, with tomato skins peeled to make roses, radishes cut into roses, the spikes of the watermelon rounded to rose-petal shape, and the yellow and white color scheme swapped for rose-pink. You could go further, with a rose-hip sorbet served with crystallized rose-petals and rose-petals in the salad.

If the theme is chrysanthemums you can even eat the petals in soup or salad. The Chinese serve a clear chicken soup with a handful of chrysanthemum petals thrown in at the table – their color intensifies for a few seconds, and the effect is very pretty.

Our menu sticks to the waterlily theme, however, but we have included a few rose and chrysanthemum tricks and recipes too.

## THE INVITATION
The chances are that you could find postcards of a waterlily or a rose, or you could draw or trace pictures of them on to writing paper. Or if you plan your dinner well ahead you might be able to press roses or chrysanthemums (waterlilies are too waxy) in a

### Waterlily Radishes
*Take small radishes, remove the roots, but leave the leaves (if fresh) intact, or at least leave a short length of stalk. Cut almost through each radish from root tip to stalk to divide it almost in half. Then cut across again at right angles to the first cut, so that the radish is now in not-quite-severed quarters. Then twice more to produce eighths. Soak the radishes in iced water, which will make the "waterlily petals" open up.*

### Rose Radishes
*Take small round radishes, and trim off the roots, while leaving at least some green stalk or leaves. With a very sharp small knife shave four petals from the skin of each radish round the tip, taking care not to cut too deeply, nor to sever the petals completely. Then shave another ring of petals round the middle of the radish, perhaps five this time, then a final ring of petals near the base. Drop the cut radishes into iced water to open up.*

WATERLILY INVITATION

*Left* Contrive a colored collage or pop-up waterlily invitation with thin artists' card or shiny gummed paper.

flower press or between sheets of blotting paper under a pile of books and include them in a folded invitation? Or, if the budget will bear it, get a florist to deliver your invitation with a single rose in a box. Such obvious care will alert your guests to a very special evening. You might not like to go as far as suggesting they turn up dressed as water-nymphs, but the women (and the men?) might be encouraged to wear flowers at their bosom, or in hair or buttonhole.

## WINE
The menu is sophisticated enough to require wine slightly out of the ordinary – perhaps a rich white pinot chardomay for the first course, followed by a pinot noir or good petite sirah with the steak. A really silky sticky dessert wine would be a treat.

### Crystallized Rose Petals
*Shake the petals off the roses making sure they are absolutely dry. Brush with egg white and then dust both sides with sugar. Leave to dry overnight on wax paper in a warm room.*

### Butter Roses
*Chill a block of butter. Scrape off a curled central bud, then large flat petals. Attach the petals to the central piece and freeze on a foil-covered saucer.*

**Cooking Steaks**
*The secret of cooking a juicy steak is to seal both sides over a really fierce heat, then to lower the heat to cook it according to your liking. The softer (squashier) the meat feels when pressed, the rarer it is.*

**Yeast**
*Store baker's yeast in a loosely tied plastic bag in the refrigerator where it will keep for up to a month. Dried yeast can be kept for up 6 months in an airtight container.*

THE MENU

*Grapefruit and Crab Lily Cocktail*
*or*
*Artichokes with Aïoli*

*Tournedos Lilies on Spinach Lake*
*Tomato Lily with Pea Purée*
*Waterlily Endive Salad*

*Waterlily Melon with Mint*
*or*
*Rose-hip Sorbet*

## GETTING AHEAD

*Weeks in advance*
○ Get the invitations (pressed flowers, hand-drawings, pretty postcards) made and sent.
○ Get the tablecloth made, the flowers ordered or at least planned.
○ Buy floating candles (available from large stationers or gift shops) and odorless oil to float them on, such as peanut or vegetable oil.
○ Plan what you are to drink, and stock up.

*Days in advance*
○ Make the sorbet if opting for this rather than the watermelon.
○ Make the aïoli for the artichokes.
○ Make the chervil butter for the tournedos.
○ Fold the napkins.
○ Make the mayonnaise for the crab cocktail.
○ Make the bread rolls and freeze them.

**Artichokes**
*It is important to remove all of the fibrous choke which is very inedible. Small artichokes are the tenderest. The heart is the best part so the fewer outside leaves the better.*

*The day before*
○ Chill white wine.
○ Make the crab cocktail mixture, cut the grapefruit skins and keep in a plastic bag in the refrigerator.
○ Boil the artichokes.

*Below* To make flower-bud rolls, shape the dough into balls. Once risen, cut the dough deeply into petals, brush carefully with beaten egg and bake.

Chrysanthemums
*These make an excellent alternative to waterlilies. White chrysanthemum heads floating in a glass bowl filled with water, lit from above, make an attractive centerpiece.*

*Below* At each place, grapefruit and crab cocktail in a flower-fashioned grapefruit skin; tornedo lilies on a spinach lake with tomato buds filled with creamed peas. In the center, rose-hip sorbet arranged with crystallized rose petals and rose leaves, and a watermelon and mint fruit salad in a watermelon skin. On the small plate, a decoration of tomato skins thinly pared in strips and rolled up into buds.

○ Make the pea purée.
○ Make the salad dressing.
○ Make the croûtes for the tournedos lilies.

*On the morning of the dinner*
○ Prepare the room, lay the table, set up drinks, wine, etc. Do the flowers.
○ Trim the artichokes and cut out the fibrous chokes.
○ Thaw the bread rolls.
○ Cut the tomatoes and fill with the pea purée, brush with butter ready for baking.
○ Prepare the salad, arrange in a bowl, and cover with plastic wrap.
○ Make the fruit salad (or dish up the sorbet, without leaves, and return to the freezer).
○ Set up coffee tray.
○ Fry the steaks, but do not bake them. Cool and then refrigerate.
○ Make the spinach sauce.

*Before the guests arrive*
○ Dish up the crab cocktail or the artichokes. Keep cool.
○ Dress the salad.
○ Put the croûtes in a low oven to heat.
○ Warm the spinach sauce.

*Just before supper*
○ Put the stuffed tomatoes in the oven to bake at 400°. Put the crab cocktail or artichokes on the table.
○ Just before sitting down to the first course, put the steaks in the oven under the tomatoes. They will take about 10 minutes to cook to medium rare.

*During supper*
○ Assemble the steaks on individual plates.
○ Add the leaves to the sorbet.

Chrysanthemum Soup
*Into clear chicken soup, or fairly pale beef consommé, scatter fresh chrysanthemum petals – either into the soup tureen in the middle of the table or into each guest's bowl. But do it at the table. The intense color effect is fleeting. (The petals have very little taste, and are quite harmless.)*

Tomato Rose
*The hotel chef's favorite trick. Inedible, or almost, but gives spectacular emphasis to a flower theme. Take a very red firm tomato and peel the skin off it, as you would an apple, starting at the rounded end and working towards the stalk end. Then roll the skin up quite tightly to resemble a rose-bud.*

# WATERLILY DINNER RECIPES

## GRAPEFRUIT AND CRAB LILY-COCKTAIL
SERVES 8
*4 grapefruit*
*1 ¼ cups homemade mayonnaise*
*4 tbsp heavy or whipping cream*
*1lb white king crabmeat (frozen or canned)*
FOR THE CURRY SAUCE
*1 small onion, chopped*
*2 tsp oil*
*2 tsp curry powder*
*½ tsp tomato paste*
*3 tbsp water*
*1 small bay leaf*
*⅓ cup red wine*
*salt and pepper*
*2 tsp apricot jam*
*1 slice lemon*
FOR DECORATION
*paprika*
*young mint leaves*

1. Using a sharp vegetable knife, cut each grapefruit in half with deep zig-zag cuts around the center.
2. With a grapefruit knife cut round each segment of grapefruit to lift it into a bowl, leaving the membrane and pith behind. Remove pips. Collect any excess juice. Pull the membranes from the grapefruit skins.
3. To make the curry sauce: heat the oil in a frying-pan and gently cook the chopped onion until soft and transparent; add the curry powder and continue to cook gently for about one minute.
4. Add the tomato paste, water, bay leaf, wine, salt, pepper, jam, lemon slice and simmer for 8 minutes. Push the mixture through a sieve.
5. Use enough of the sauce to flavor the mayonnaise to the desired strength. Thin it to a just-runny consistency with water if necessary.
6. Half whip the cream and stir into the flavored mayonnaise.
7. Defrost the frozen crab meat slowly, and season with grapefruit juice, salt and pepper.
8. Drain the crab meat well and place in a mixing bowl with grapefruit chunks. Mix with enough of the sauce to coat the crab meat, keeping a little sauce back for decoration.
9. Spoon the mixture into the grapefruit cases. Coat the top of each cocktail with a little of the reserved sauce. Sprinkle with paprika.
10. Tuck mint leaves into the sides of each cocktail to emphasize the waterlily effect.

## ARTICHOKES WITH AÏOLI
SERVES 8
*8 medium-sized artichokes*
*1 slice lemon*
*1 tsp oil*
AÏOLI
*3 cloves garlic*
*2 egg yolks, at room temperature*
*pinch of salt*
*1 tsp Dijon mustard*
*⅔ cup olive oil, at room temperature*
*⅔ cup peanut oil, at room temperature*
*squeeze lemon juice*
*2 tbsp wine vinegar*
*freshly ground black pepper*

1. Cut away the stalks of the artichokes and any of the very tough leaves. Trim the base so that the artichoke will stand upright.
2. Plunge the artichokes into a pan of boiling salted water. Add the slice of lemon and teaspoon of oil. Cook for about 45 minutes or until a leaf can be easily pulled away from the whole. Drain well. Turn upside down on a rack and leave the artichokes to cool.
3. To make the aïoli: crush the garlic and place in a bowl with the egg yolks, salt and mustard. Beat well with a wooden spoon.
4. Mix the oils together and add them drip by drip, beating all the time. The mixture should be very thick by the time half the oil is added. Add the lemon juice.
5. Resume pouring the oil rather more confidently, but alternating the dribbles of oil with small quantities of vinegar. Add the pepper to taste. Place in 8 individual serving dishes, or in 8 "lily"-shaped lemon skins cut *à la zig-zag* with the flesh and pith scooped out.
6. To serve the artichokes: pull out the center leaves and with a teaspoon carefully scrape out the fibrous "choke", making sure that every particle is removed. Place the artichokes on individual serving plates each accompanied by a small dish of aïoli.

## TOURNEDOS LILIES ON SPINACH LAKE
SERVES 8
*½ cup butter*
*squeeze lemon juice*
*2 tbsp chervil, finely chopped (use parsley or chives if chervil is not available)*
*salt and black pepper*
*14 slices white bread*
*oil for frying*
*8 × 5oz fillet steaks, neatly trimmed*
*⅔ cup madeira*
*1 ¼ cups beef stock or bouillon*
*12oz spinach, cooked and chopped or puréed or 4oz frozen spinach, cooked and finely chopped*
*⅔ cup heavy cream*

1. Cream the butter, stir in the lemon juice and chervil. Season to taste. Place in a pastry bag fitted with a fluted nozzle and pipe eight rosettes on to a sheet of wax paper. Leave the rosettes in the refrigerator to harden.
2. Cut 40 petal-shaped slices of bread for the croûtes. Heat the oil in a heavy frying-pan and fry the bread on both sides until crisp and brown. Keep warm on a serving platter.
3. Heat a teaspoon of oil until it is beginning to smoke. Brown the steaks on both sides by fast frying. If doing this well in advance, lift out now and set aside while still raw in the middle. If cooking at the last minute, lower the heat to cook the steaks to your liking (4-5 minutes a side for well done, 3 minutes a side for medium and 2 minutes a side for rare). Lift them out when ready and keep warm.
4. While the pan is still hot, pour in the madeira, stirring and scraping the sediment off the bottom of the pan. Add the beef stock or bouillon, bring to the boil and reduce by half.
5. Stir in the spinach and continue to stir until boiling. Add the cream and season with salt and pepper.
6. Liquidize the sauce until smooth.
7. If the steaks were pre-browned, finish cooking them now, either for 5-10 minutes in the oven with the temperature set at 400° or in a frying-pan.
8. The steaks are served individually. Coat the base of each plate with spinach sauce. Arrange five croûtes to look like a flower on top of the sauce to one side of each plate. Place a fillet steak in the center of each flower. Take the chervil butter and place in the center of each steak with the hot tomato waterlily beside it.

## TOMATO LILY WITH PEA PURÉE
SERVES 8
*8 large tomatoes*
*melted butter*
FOR THE PEA PURÉE
*1 small onion*
*2 tbsp butter*
*4 tbsp strong chicken stock*
*8oz frozen peas*
*salt*
*pepper*
*4oz boiled potatoes*

1. Using a sharp-pointed vegetable knife and making zig-zag cuts, slice a quarter off each tomato at the rounded end. Scoop out the flesh and seeds. Place the tomato shells on a greased baking sheet.
2. Chop the onion finely and put it with the butter, stock, peas and salt and pepper into a saucepan. Cover the saucepan and simmer the ingredients together until the peas are tender.
3. Preheat the oven, setting the temperature control to 375°.
4. Push the boiled potatoes through a wire sieve. Do not use a food processor – it makes the potatoes glue-y.
5. Liquidize the peas with any remaining stock or push through a sieve. Turn into a bowl.
6. Gradually beat the potatoes into the peas. Taste for seasoning.
7. Place the purée in a pastry bag fitted with a fluted nozzle. Pipe rosettes of the mixture into the tomato shells. Brush with melted butter. Bake until the tomatoes are just soft and the purée is hot all through (about 10 minutes).

NOTE:
The purée must not be too watery or it will collapse when baked in the oven. Moisten with butter rather than extra stock or milk.

## WATERLILY ENDIVE SALAD
SERVES 8
*2 heads Belgian endive*
*2 lamb's lettuces*
*1 curly endive (chicory)*
*1 bunch watercress*
*1 tbsp chopped chives*
FOR THE DRESSING
*3 tbsp vegetable oil*
*1 tbsp olive oil*
*1 tbsp wine vinegar*
*1 tbsp French mustard*
*1 small clove garlic, crushed*
*salt and pepper*

1. Wash and dry all the salad leaves, discarding any tough stalks and keeping each type of leaf separate.
2. Put the dressing ingredients together in a screw-top jar and shake well.
3. To serve the salad: arrange the Belgian endive leaves around the edge of a large salad bowl. The tips should be pointing upwards like a large lily. Arrange the lamb's lettuce in the same way inside the chicory.
4. Toss the curly endive, watercress and chives together in a bowl with the dressing and pile into the center of the lettuce and endive lily. (The endive and watercress can be replaced by any kind of salad leaves. See the various suggestions made for leaf salad in Al Fresco Lunch, p. 210.)

## WATERLILY MELON WITH MINT
SERVES 8
*1 medium-size round watermelon*
*1lb strawberries*
*⅔ cup orange juice*
*2 tbsp Grand Marnier*
*1 tsp chopped mint*
FOR DECORATION
*a few whole mint leaves*

1. Using a sharp knife and making long, thin zig-zag cuts, slice a third off the top (rounded end) of the watermelon.
2. Carefully scoop out the flesh of the melon, keeping it in as large pieces as possible. Cut a thin slice off the bottom of the melon skin to prevent wobbling or rolling on the plate.

3. Cut the melon flesh into 1in chunks. Discard all the black pips. Hull the strawberries. Cut any very large strawberries in half.
4. Soak the melon and strawberries in the orange juice and Grand Marnier for about 2 hours.
5. Mix the chopped mint with the fruit and carefully pile the mixture into the melon shell, scattering the mint leaves on top.

NOTE:
Long watermelons cut across *à la zig-zag* will make 2 melon 'lilies'. A similar salad can be made in golden orange colors and in individual portions. Use halved charentais or canteloupe melons. Discard the seeds. Scoop out the flesh and cut into chunks. Mix the melon chunks with slices of mango or halved apricots and soak in the orange juice or liqueur. Add chopped mint and pile the fruit salad into the melon shells.

## ROSE-HIP SORBET
SERVES 8
*Measurement by volume (any large cup will do) is the easiest and quickest way to get the quantities right for a sorbet.*

*2 cups rose-hips*
*water to cover*
*4 cups sugar*
*juice of a lemon*
FOR DECORATION
*Flower-shaped orange skins or rose leaves*

1. Simmer the rose-hips in the water until really squashy and tender. (If they are very ripe this will only take 10 minutes; if they are rock-hard it may take two hours, and the water will need constant topping-up.)
2. When they are done, push them and the liquid through a sieve.
3. Measure the juice obtained and either make it up to two cups with more water, or boil it down to two cups. Then put it back on the heat with the sugar and the lemon juice and heat slowly, stirring, until the sugar is dissolved. Cool, then freeze, beating when almost frozen to ensure a smooth creamy sorbet.
4. Serve in flower-shaped orange skins or in a glass bowl decorated with shiny leaves.

NOTE:
The leaves will have to come from an evergreen or "florist's" rose – the ones with the hips will be bare, or distinctly autumnal by now.

# ELEGANT AL FRESCO LUNCH

*for Fourteen*

*Blazing sun can be very tiring. The ideal protection is the dappled shade of a vine-covered arbor. Failing that, tables can often be hired with accommodation for the umbrellas in the middle. Or umbrellas can be free-standing and placed next to the tables.*

THE GREAT THING TO REMEMBER WHEN PLANNING AN *al fresco* lunch of inordinate elegance is that the chances are it may not be *al fresco* at all, but consumed indoors while wind lashes the windows and rain buckets down. So try to have a contingency plan up your sleeve. Where will you set up the drinks if inside? Where will everyone sit? The trick is to have everything intended for the outside checked and clean and ready (plates counted, silver polished, etc.) but not laid out until you are *sure* the heavens will not open.

If the weather is doubtful but not doomed, it is better to settle for *inside*. Then if, as happens in some areas, if not in California, the skies suddenly clear at ten-minutes-to-lunch-time, the guests can be dragooned into helping with the exodus. No one minds a last-minute removal to the terrace, but a defeated scamper for cover would certainly have a dampening effect on the party.

Jugs of flowers on outdoor dining tables are wonderfully romantic and, should it rain, will make the inside seem sunnier. Best of all are wild flowers (they look casual and pretty in jam jars – you can pretend the children just gathered them from the fields that morning) but greenery and simple daisies will do. What won't do is a formal, stately florist's arrangement.

Tablecloths outside always give an old-world elegance to a party. White or colored sheets will do, and look particularly Victorian and charming if covered with smaller lace tablecloths – or even with a lacy shawl. But beware of bright white table-cloths in blazing sun. They can be very dazzling and tiring to the eyes.

Our party is for 14 people. If they can be accommodated at one huge table, or two long tables pushed end to end, so much the better. If not, two or three tables – it doesn't matter if they are different shapes and sizes so long as the seating plan is careful. A seating plan, with place names (tucked into or under the glasses to stop them blowing away in the wind), is a good idea for an elegant lunch. The slight feeling of a treasure hunt while the guests search for their names and the agreeable (one trusts) surprise of discovering who their neighbours are to be, heightens the general mood of pleasant expectancy.

Of course all the usual organization that applies to sit-down parties applies equally to this one. But, *because* it is outside, a few extra problems might show their ugly heads.

Wind
*Tablecloths can be secured with special caterer's metal clips (which can be hired with tables, chairs and linen) or with large bulldog clips from an office supply, fixed strategically with thumbtacks under the table (at the corners is best because the folds will hide all) or even, at a pinch, with heavy pebbles to weigh them down.*

Cold
*Tell everyone you are eating al fresco so that if they come beautifully dressed as for an elegant garden party (as one hopes they will), they will also bring a sweater or wrap.*

Tuck place names into or under the wine glasses so that the breeze cannot carry them off.

**Chicken Salad**
*This can also be served as a main course. Our recipe will be enough for 8 people. Arrange the salad on a large serving dish with the meat, melon and mango in neat rows on a bed of noodles. Serve the sauce separately.*

**New Potatoes**
*Buy new potatoes in small quantities as they quickly lose their flavor. They will retain their flavor and their nutritional value best if scraped or scrubbed rather than peeled, and then steamed over a pan of vigorously boiling water.*

## THE MENU

We have planned this menu so that it can be served up in seven-portion dishes, which can be set on the table, one dish at each end. A whole huge sea bass for 14 might be more impressive but it would be difficult to buy and would take agonizingly long to serve.

The menu looks curious – a cold chicken dish followed by a hot sea bass. But the chicken dish is not much more than a light and pretty salad starter. The sea bass will happily stay hot in the oven while the guests eat the first course and, because they are all *à table* when the hot fish are brought out, they are in the right position to gasp and clap. Also it can be served promptly.

Strictly speaking, clean, hot dinner plates should arrive with the fish but they really are not necessary. The remains of the light peanut dressing from the chicken won't spoil the coriander-flavored sea bass and, though the fish will obviously cool faster on cold plates, it does not matter much. It is delicious hot, warm or cold.

Hot new potatoes would be good with the fish but, for ease of serving, we have suggested only an unusual leafy salad. The redcurrant snow, which is light and voluminous, is spectacular served in huge cocktail glasses, sundae glasses or brandy balloons. It can, of course, be served from a large bowl on to plates, but it does not look as pretty on a flat plate or in a pudding bowl.

**Melon**
*To test a melon for ripeness, press it gently with the thumb at the opposite end to the stalk. If it gives a little, the melon is ripe. Ogen, charentais and cantaloupe melons have a strong, fragrant smell when ripe.*

**Tuiles Cups**
*Tuiles can be made into "cups" by molding them round an oiled orange or lemon. Fill them with redcurrant snow or any flavored ice cream or mousse.*

### THE MENU

*Chicken Salad with Noodles, Melon and Mango*
*Peanut Dressing*

*Baked Sea Bass with Coriander*
*Leaf Salad*

*Three Seasoned Soft Cheeses*

*Redcurrant Snow with Mint*

*Almond Tuiles*

## THE INVITATION

Of course a phone call would do, but it might be wittier to send an impressionist painter's postcard – perhaps Manet's *Déjeuner sur l'Herbe* or a Pissarro park scene or one of Monet's hatted women in a poppy-spotted field. Or get a child to draw an outdoor feast and photostat it. It will probably feature fish fingers, sausages and ice-cream cones but no matter. It will cause a smile. Or you might play it safe and be very specific.

Flowers sandwiched between blotting paper and pressed under a pile of books make amusing and charming decorations for the invitation cards.

*Right* Crisp white linen, casually but carefully arranged flowers, and attention to detail, give this outdoor lunch elegance and sophistication. On the dinner plates chicken salad with noodles, melon and mango and a peanut dressing. In the center, a fresh leaf salad and to the right a whole sea bass baked with scallions and coriander leaves.

## GETTING AHEAD

*Months in advance*
- Send invitations.
- Plan table seating for outside, and make contingency plan for inside.
- Collect jugs or jars to hold flowers.
- Sort out tablecloths, lace coverings, and napkins and iron them.
- Find out where to hire clips to secure tablecloths, or buy thumbtacks or bulldog clips.
- Make place names.
- Borrow or hire sun-umbrellas if needed.
- Make a shopping list for drinks and food.

*Two days before the party*
- Order the sea bass.
- Do all the shopping.
- Keep the fresh pasta refrigerated and covered by a damp dish cloth.
- Poach the chicken and reduce the stock. Keep refrigerated.

*The day before the party*
- Cook the noodles, turn in oil, cover and refrigerate.
- Make the peanut dressing and liquidize.
- Cut the chicken into chunks. Refrigerate.
- Collect the sea bass. Marinate it and leave ready to bake next morning.
- Make the soft cheeses. Refrigerate.
- Make the salad dressing.
- Prepare the redcurrants. Refrigerate.
- Make the almond tuiles and store in an airtight container.
- Collect wild flowers for the table, arrange them and put them somewhere cool.

*The evening before the party*
- Set out plates and serving dishes.
- Collect all the cutlery, napkins, tablecloths, salt, peppers, etc. on a tray ready to set up inside or out.
- Lay the tray for coffee.
- Set up glasses, drinks, ice, sliced lemon, etc.
- Chill the wine.

*The morning of the party*
- Dish up the peanut dressing in sauce boats.
- Prepare melon and mangoes and mix with the chicken.
- Arrange the soft cheeses on a board with vine leaves and cheese mats.
- Wash the salad leaves and leave to drain.
- Make the redcurrant snow but do not decorate.
- Arrange the almond tuiles on a serving plate.
- Decide if the weather is stable or not and set the table inside or outside accordingly.

*Half an hour before the guests arrive*
- Preheat the oven.
- Dish up the chicken noodle salad and keep covered.

*Once the guests have arrived*
- Put the sea bass in the oven.
- Toss the salad.
- Put the first course on the table.
- Decorate the redcurrant snow.

*One of the glories of the late summer is fresh redcurrants, shiny, tart and tight with juice.*

*Right* Lunch prolonged into the sunshine. Top left: two of the seasoned soft cheeses (walnut cheese and soft blue cheese with herbs); in the center: goats' cheese in oil. Top right: redcurrant snow with mint. Bottom left: almond tuiles.

## CHICKEN SALAD WITH NOODLES, MELON AND MANGO AND PEANUT DRESSING

SERVES 14 AS A STARTER

*2 medium-sized roasting chickens*
*2½qts chicken stock (or water with 1 bay*
*    leaf, 6 peppercorns, 2 sprigs of parsley,*
*    1 slice of lemon, sprig of fresh thyme,*
*    1 carrot, 1 onion and 1 stick of celery)*
*1lb fresh tagliatelle or 8oz dried tagliatelle*
*4 tbsp peanut oil*
*1 large honeydew, canteloupe or galia melon*
*2 ripe mangoes*
*1 bunch scallions*

FOR THE PEANUT DRESSING

*1 tbsp peanut oil*
*1 medium onion, finely diced*
*2 cloves garlic, crushed*
*1oz fresh ginger, peeled and grated*
*¾ cup crunchy peanut butter*
*1¼ cups chicken stock*
*¼ cup coconut cream, dissolved in*
*    1¼ cups water*
*juice of 1 lime*
*salt*
*freshly ground black pepper*

1. Rinse the chickens and place in a saucepan of simmering stock or of water with flavorings.
2. Cover the pan and cook the chickens gently for 1¼-1½ hours, until the thighs are tender. Remove the chickens from the saucepan and set aside to cool, reserving the stock.
3. Strain the stock, reserve 1¼ cups for the sauce and put the rest into a large clean pan.
4. Strip the chicken meat from the carcasses, keeping the pieces as whole as possible. Cut the meat into bite-sized chunks.
5. Cook the tagliatelle in the boiling chicken stock for 3 minutes until just tender. (Dried pasta will take 10 minutes or so.) Drain and rinse with cold water. Drain well again, then toss in the peanut oil and season with salt and pepper.
6. Peel the melon and mangoes. Cut them into chunks the same size as the chicken.
7. Clean the scallions and cut them into fine needleshreds. Place in iced water to make them curl.
8. To make the peanut sauce: heat the oil in a heavy frying-pan. Gently fry the onion, garlic and ginger until soft. Add the crunchy peanut butter, chicken stock and diluted coconut cream and stir over heat until smooth.
9. Liquidize the sauce and season with salt, black pepper and lime juice. Cool the sauce but do not refrigerate it.
10. Serve the salad on individual plates: drain the scallions well. Mix with the tagliatelle. Place a portion of this over the base of each plate.
11. Toss the chicken with the mango and melon and when it is well mixed pile on top of the pasta.
12. Serve the peanut sauce in a sauceboat, handed separately.

NOTE:

This dish can be arranged in the same way but on one large serving platter if preferred. (See the margin note Chicken Salad on p. 206.)

## BAKED SEA BASS WITH CORIANDER

SERVES 14

*Two 4lb fresh whole sea bass*

FOR THE MARINADE

*1 tsp sugar*
*1 tsp salt*
*1 tsp coarse ground black pepper*
*⅔ cup sesame oil*
*squeeze of lemon juice*
*1 bunch scallions, chopped*

FOR THE SAUCE

*dry vermouth*
*sunflower oil*
*2 tbsp soy sauce*
*2 tbsp sesame oil*

FOR DECORATION

*4 tbsp fresh coriander (cilantro) leaves*

1. Clean the sea bass and pat dry. Lay the fish in 2 ovenproof dishes. Mix all the marinade ingredients together. Pour over the fish, cover tightly and chill for three hours.
2. Preheat the oven, setting the temperature control to 350°. Remove the fish from the refrigerator and bake for 35-40 minutes, or until a skewer slides easily through the flesh.
3. Lay the fish on 2 serving dishes and keep warm in a low oven. Put all the ingredients for the sauce together in a pan and bring to the boil.
4. Scatter the chopped coriander leaves over the fish and pour on the sauce.

## LEAF SALAD

2LB LEAVES SERVES 14

Toss a mixture of curly endive, young spinach, sorrel, arugula, dandelion and lamb's lettuce leaves in a dressing made of 4 parts vegetable oil (half of it olive) to one part wine vinegar, with a squeeze of lemon, salt and pepper and a little Dijon mustard to flavor.

## THREE SEASONED SOFT CHEESES

(These three recipes, together, will be sufficient for 14)

Serve the cheeses on a straw cheese mat and decorate them with fresh vine leaves and grapes.

### WALNUT CHEESE

*1½ cups cream cheese*
*⅓ cup finely grated mature Cheddar*
*¼ cup freshly grated Parmesan*
*1 tsp Dijon mustard*
*salt, black pepper*
*a pinch of cayenne*
*⅔ cup finely chopped walnuts or pecans*

1. Soften the cream cheese, then beat in the two hard cheeses. Season to taste with the mustard, salt, pepper and cayenne.
2. Chill for two hours until firm.
3. Shape the cheese into small balls and roll each one in the chopped walnuts.
4. Chill before serving.

### GOATS' CHEESE IN OIL

*3 rolls chèvre cheese (about 5oz each)*
*1¼ cups olive oil*
*peppercorns (black, green and pink if available), coarsely crushed*
*2 cloves garlic, crushed*
*1 shallot, finely chopped*

FOR DECORATION

*2 tsp chopped coriander (cilantro) leaves*

1. Slice the chèvre into pieces 1in thick. Place them in a dish a little deeper than the slices.
2. Mix together the remaining ingredients and pour over the cheese. Cover and refrigerate overnight.
3. To serve, drain the cheeses from the oil. Place the oil in a sauce-boat and hand a small amount separately. Or leave the cheeses in a glass or earthenware jar. Or dish up in the oil and provide a fork for the guests to extract them with. Add the chopped coriander just before serving.

### SOFT BLUE CHEESE WITH HERBS

*1½ cups cottage cheese (small curd)*
*1 cup grated blue cheese*
*⅓ cup heavy cream, whipped*
*salt and black pepper*
*4 tbsp mixed chopped parsley, chervil and chives*

1. Blend together the cottage cheese and blue cheese. Fold in the whipped cream.
2. Season with salt and pepper and one tablespoon of the chopped herbs.
3. Shape the cheese into several little cakes. Turn each cake in the remaining chopped herbs.

## REDCURRANT SNOW WITH MINT

SERVES 14

*2lb ripe redcurrants*
*2½ cups heavy cream*
*1¼ cups natural (plain) yogurt*
*¾ cup sugar*
*6 egg whites*
*2 tbsp chopped mint*

FOR DECORATION

*14 sprigs of mint*

1. Pull the redcurrants off their stalks. Wash and drain the fruit well.
2. Whip the cream until stiff. Stir in the yogurt and sugar.
3. Beat the egg whites, until they form soft peaks, and fold into the yogurt and cream.
4. Reserve a few of the currants for decoration. Gently stir in the remaining fruit and the mint.
5. Serve the redcurrant snow in tall goblets. Scatter a few redcurrants over the top of each one and decorate with a sprig of mint.

## ALMOND TUILES

MAKES ABOUT 30

*⅓ cup blanched (peeled) almonds*
*1 cup sugar*
*4 egg whites*
*1 cup all-purpose flour*
*1 tsp vanilla extract*
*½ cup melted butter*

1. Preheat the oven, setting the temperature control to 350°. Lightly grease three baking sheets and a rolling pin.
2. Cut the almonds into fine shreds.
3. Beat the sugar into the egg whites with a fork. The egg white should be frothy but by no means snowy.
4. Sift in the flour and add the vanilla extract and almonds.
5. Cool the butter (it should be melted but not hot) and stir into the mixture.
6. Place the mixture in teaspoonfuls at least 5in apart on the baking sheets and flatten well.
7. Bake in the oven until a good brown at the edges and pale beige colored in the middle (about 6 minutes). Remove from the oven and cool for a few seconds.
8. Lift the cookies off carefully with a palette knife. Lay them, while still warm and pliable, over the rolling pin to form into a slightly curved shape.
9. As soon as the tuiles are stone-cold, put them all into an airtight container or into a sealed plastic bag to keep them crisp overnight.

# — THE MAD HATTER'S TEA PARTY —

*for Fourteen*

The costumes of the Mad Hatter and the Dormouse are ideal for dressing up.

CHILDREN BETWEEN FIVE AND TEN (AND OFTEN OLDER) love to dress up, and a children's costume tea party is an inexpensive birthday treat.

Choosing the winner in the best costume is agony for the judge – should he be influenced by imagination, effort, or Lucinda's quivering bottom lip? The answer is probably that the Birthday Boy or Birthday Girl had better win it, with the actual best effort coming second and everyone else getting mini-prizes.

The principal characters, for readers who have forgotten their childhood classics, are the White Rabbit who wears white kid gloves, a waistcoat, and carries a fob watch and fan; the caterpillar who smokes a hookah and sits on the magic mushroom; the Duchess who has a huge medieval headdress and a baby that turns into a piglet; the Cheshire Cat who wears nothing but his grin; the King and Queen of Hearts, their son the Knave and their gardeners, courtiers, soldiers, all "nothing but a pack of cards", and the Mock Turtle who weeps all the time. Then there is Old Father William whose hair "has become very white" and who has "grown most uncommonly fat". He spends his time standing on his head, doing backward somersaults and balancing eels on his nose; and there's the Lobster, the Snail and the Tortoise. If *Through the Looking Glass* characters are acceptable too (and why not?), then the choice includes Tweedledum and Tweedledee, the Walrus and the Carpenter, Humpty Dumpty, the Jabberwock, the Red and White Queen and the Lion and the Unicorn.

## THE INVITATION

It might be wise to list characters on the invitations, which should go to the birthday child's friends a good three weeks before the day to allow a little time for costume design. If a copy of Alice's adventures with the original Tenniel drawings can be had (most libraries have one) the original Mad Tea Party picture could be traced or photostatted for the invitation.

Though Alice in Wonderland provides wonderful scope for dressing up, it must be admitted there is little in the way of food. The so-called Mad Hatter's tea party (actually it was the March Hare's) was no kind of party at all. The Hatter, and the Dormouse (who was asleep most of the time) were the only guests; Alice was a gate-crasher and no one had anything more

An Alice costume is easily achievable with a little-girl dress and a wide hairband, though the March Hare may be more appealing to small children.

## The Program
*There is a time-honored program for children's parties which goes like this: 3.00-3.30 children arrive and are left to their own devices until shyness evaporates. 3.30-4.15 party games. 4.15 everyone to the restroom. 4.30-5.00 food, ending with birthday cake. 5.00-5.30 children left to rollick. 5.30 children collected and given going-home presents.*

exciting to eat than bread and butter, and not all of them got that. Everyone was very rude to everyone else, especially to Alice, and the Dormouse ended up in the teapot. So our menu is a far cry from Alice's meagre fare. A few bought sugar mice might be a good idea as most of the menu is the sort of simple savory food most young children seem to prefer.

The cake might be a plain rectangular chocolate sponge (not too rich) covered in white frosting and decorated to represent a playing card – 9 of Hearts for a nine-year-old, etc.

## Party Games
*These should be energetic to start with (musical chairs, potato spoon races and musical statues); then quieter towards food time to calm the children down (pass the parcel and dead lions – in which the children lie spread-eagled while the grown-ups threaten to tickle them; if they move they're out).*

---

THE MENU

*Card Sandwiches*

*Cheshire Cat Cheese Crackers*

*Caterpillar Cake Bread*

*Queen of Hearts Tarts*

*"Pack of Cards" Birthday Cake*

*"Drink Me" Potion*

---

## Prizes
*Party Packs containing paper hats, masks, games and small toys can be bought to hand out as the children arrive. Have plenty of tiny prizes or candies to dish out to game winners and balloons or party whistles for going-home presents.*

## GETTING AHEAD
*One month or two before the party*
○ Make or buy invitation cards, paper cloths and plates.
○ Think of suitable games to play and buy some small prizes.
○ Make the birthday cake base and freeze.

*A week before the party*
○ Make a shopping list from the recipes and buy all the dry goods. Supply tea and food for grown-ups and additional soft drinks.
○ Check replies to the invitations and estimate numbers.
○ Find bottles with airtight tops for the "Drink Me" potion.

*The day before the party*
○ Make the pastry for the Cheshire Cat cheese crackers.
○ Make the caterpillar cake bread.
○ Make the pastry for the tarts, roll it out and line the tart cases, cut scraps into heart shapes and chill overnight.
○ Buy fresh ingredients and defrost the birthday cake.
○ Make the "Drink Me" potion base.
○ Hide any prizes if the games require it. Wrap "pass the parcel" parcels and the "going-home" presents.

*The morning of the party*
○ Clear as much space as possible in the rooms to be used for the party, making sure any breakable items are stored safely.
○ Set up the table with cloth, napkins, paper plates, cups and candies.
○ Decorate the caterpillar cake bread and the birthday cake.
○ Cut out and bake the crackers; fill and bake the tarts.
○ Add fruit juice to the "Drink Me" potion and pour into bottles.

*Two hours before the children arrive*
○ Decorate the Cheshire Cat cheese crackers.
○ Make the card sandwiches and cover with a damp cloth.
○ Arrange all the food on the table.

*Left* Children and artistic parents could join in the creation of a Wonderland (if not strictly Alice's) of toadstools and cut-out trees. The giant teapot could be filled with candies though children generally enjoy savory food more than their parents imagine. Here Cheshire Cat cheese crackers and peanut butter and egg sandwiches.

Our "Drink Me" Potion is based on fresh oranges and lemons but any popular drink can be poured into suitable bottles and labelled.

# THE MAD HATTER'S TEA PARTY RECIPES

## CARD SANDWICHES
SERVES 14
*16 slices white bread*
*16 large slices brown bread*
*butter for spreading*
FOR THE FILLINGS
*salt and pepper*
*peanut butter*
*4 hard-boiled eggs*
*mayonnaise*
*honey*
*raspberry jam*
FOR DECORATION
*chopped watercress*

1. Butter the bread and lay it out on the work top.
2. Mash the boiled eggs and mix with a little salt, pepper and mayonnaise.
3. Using the brown bread make four rounds of peanut butter sandwiches and four rounds of egg.
4. Do the same with the white bread, filling it half with honey and half with raspberry jam.
5. Stamp out the bread with diamond, heart, club and spade-shaped cutters (they can be bought about 2in long), cutting two shapes from each round of sandwiches.
6. Arrange them on a plate decorated with chopped watercress.

## CHESHIRE CAT CHEESE CRACKERS
MAKES ABOUT 15-20
*2 cups all-purpose flour*
*⅔ cup butter*
*1 cup Cheddar cheese, finely grated*
*salt and black pepper*
*beaten egg*
FOR THE TOP
*¼ cup cream cheese*
*1 tsp tomato ketchup*
FOR DECORATION
*watercress*

1. Preheat the oven, setting the temperature control to 375°.
2. Sift the flour into a mixing bowl. Rub in the butter and add the grated cheese and salt and pepper.
3. Bind the mixture with enough beaten egg to form a stiff dough. Chill.
4. Make a thick cardboard template of the round face of a cat with ears on top. Roll the cheese pastry out to ⅛in thick. Using the template as a guide, cut out as many cat faces as possible.
5. Place the faces on a baking sheet and bake for 8 to 10 minutes until crisp and brown. Cool on a wire rack.

6. Fit a small pastry bag with a writing nozzle. Mix the cream cheese and ketchup together. Pipe an outline for the ears, slanting eyes, whiskers and a huge grinning mouth on the top of the crackers.
7. Serve the Cheshire Cat crackers on a bed of watercress so that the faces appear to be staring out of bushes.

## CATERPILLAR CAKE BREAD
*1oz fresh yeast*
*¼ cup sugar*
*1¼ cups lukewarm milk*
*4 cups all-purpose flour*
*1 tsp salt*
*1 tsp ground allspice*
*¼ cup butter*
*⅓ cup currants*
*⅓ cup golden raisins*
*grated rind of ½ lemon*
*2 eggs*
*milk for glazing*
FOR DECORATION
*2 glacé cherries*
*2 sticks of angelica 2in long*
*cake candles if to serve as birthday cake*
FOR THE ICING
*1 cup confectioners' sugar*
*squeeze of lemon*
*boiling water to mix*

1. Cream the yeast with the sugar and a little milk.
2. Sift the flour with the salt and allspice into a warmed mixing bowl. Rub in the butter and add the dried fruit and lemon rind.
3. Make a well in the center and pour in the yeast mixture, beaten eggs and enough milk to mix to a soft dough. Beat the mixture with your hand until it will leave the sides of the bowl.
4. Knead the dough for 10 minutes. Place in a clean bowl and cover with oiled plastic wrap. Leave to rise until it has doubled in bulk, about one hour.
5. Preheat the oven, setting the temperature control to 400°. Grease a flat baking sheet.
6. Knead the dough again for 5 minutes and divide into 8 to 10 pieces of varying size.
7. Shape each piece into a ball, then flatten the balls a little. Arrange the dough to look like a slightly curving caterpillar, with the flat sides of the balls pressed together and the rounded part facing upwards. Put a few small pieces at one end to form the caterpillar's head, fatter ones in the middle for its body and trailing off to small ones at the tail.

8. Leave to rise for 15 minutes. The dough should now be stuck together. Brush the caterpillar with milk, and push two glacé cherries into the head to make its eyes.
9. Bake for 30 to 40 minutes until firm and brown. Cool on a wire rack.
10. Mix the confectioners' sugar with the lemon juice and a little boiling water to a "just runny" consistency. Pipe the icing over the top of the caterpillar.
11. Stick the pieces of angelica on top of the head for the antennae, and the appropriate number of candles into the body, if wanted.

## QUEEN OF HEARTS TARTS
MAKES 14
FOR THE PASTRY
*2 cups all-purpose flour*
*pinch of salt*
*½ cup butter*
*1 egg yolk*
*very cold water*
FOR THE FILLING
*2 tbsp strawberry jam*
*2 tbsp greengage or other plum jam*
*2 tbsp lemon curd*
*pastry trimmings*

1. Sift the flour with the salt and rub in the butter.
2. Mix the egg yolk with a little cold water and add it to the mixture. Mix to a firm dough adding a little extra water if necessary.
3. Roll out the pastry thinly and stamp out rounds with a fluted pastry cutter. Use to line 14 tartlet pans. Chill for 30 minutes.
4. Preheat the oven, setting the temperature control to 375°.
5. Fill each one with jam or lemon curd, dividing the colors evenly. Cut small pastry hearts from the trimmings and place one in the center of each tart.
6. Bake until the filling is bubbling and the pastry hearts cooked (about 15 minutes). Cool before serving.

## "PACK OF CARDS" BIRTHDAY CAKE
FOR A SIX-YEAR-OLD
*2oz bittersweet chocolate*
*2 cups all-purpose flour*
*½ tsp baking powder*
*¼ tsp salt*
*4 large eggs, separated*
*1½ cups sugar*
*1¼ cups milk*
*½ cup unsalted butter, melted but cool*
*vanilla extract*

*Right* Uncomplicated food amusingly presented is popular with children. From the right, clockwise: Queen of Hearts tarts, Cheshire Cat cheese crackers, card sandwiches, caterpillar cake bread and "Pack of Cards" birthday cake.

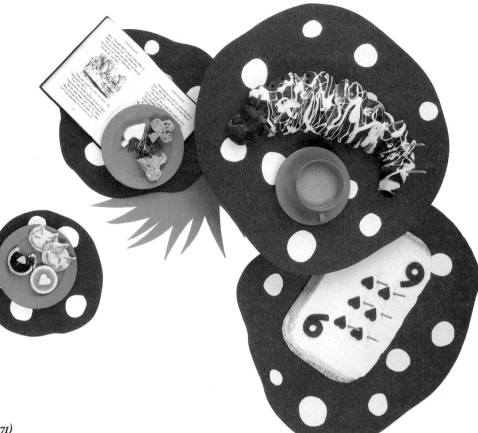

FOR THE FROSTING
*1 cup confectioners' sugar, sifted*
*¾ cup unsalted butter*
*4 tbsp condensed milk*
FOR DECORATION
*4oz marzipan or molded icing (see p. 171)*
*red food coloring*
*candles*
*candleholders*

1. Preheat the oven, setting the temperature control to 325°. Line the base and sides of a rectangular pan 10in×8in with greased wax paper and dust with flour.
2. Melt the chocolate over a pan of simmering water. Cool until still melted but not hot.
3. Sift the flour, baking powder and salt together.
4. Beat the egg yolks with half the sugar until pale, mousse-like and thick.
5. Beat the egg whites until stiff and gradually beat in the remaining sugar, a spoonful at a time.
6. Alternately fold the milk, sifted flour and melted butter into the egg yolk mixture, one-third at a time. Gently fold in the beaten egg whites, taking care not to overmix.
7. Divide the cake mixture in half. Add the cooled chocolate to one half and a few drops of vanilla extract to the other half.
8. Put assorted spoonfuls of chocolate and vanilla mixture into the cake pan. Bake the cake in the preheated oven for 40 minutes or until the top feels firm when pressed with the fingertips. Turn out of the pan and cool on a wire rack.
9. To make the frosting: beat the confectioners' sugar and butter together until light and fluffy, then gradually beat in the condensed milk.
10. Remove the paper from the cake, split it in half and fill with one-third of the icing. Sandwich the cake together and spread the remaining frosting over the top and sides of the cake. Smooth the top of the cake and using a fork or the serrated edge of a knife or comb, make horizontal ridges round the cake to look like the side of a pack of cards.
11. Color the marzipan or molded icing as deep a red as possible. With a small heart-shaped cutter cut out six hearts and two number sixes. Arrange them on the top of the cake to look like the six of hearts. Place a candle to the left hand side of each heart.

NOTE:
Of course the Pack of Cards birthday cake could be made for a child of any age up to ten by simply adjusting the card number.

### "DRINK ME POTION"
*6 oranges*
*4 lemons*
*¾ cup sugar*
*5 cups water*

1. Thinly pare the rind from the oranges and lemons and put the peeled rind together in a pan with the sugar and water.
2. Place the pan over a low heat, allow the sugar to dissolve, then bring to the boil and simmer gently for 15 minutes.
3. Strain the liquid into a bowl and allow to cool.
4. Squeeze the juice from the oranges and lemons and add them to the "Potion".
5. Chill and serve in airtight bottles with "Drink Me" tags round the necks.

NOTE:
Older children may prefer the "Drink Me" potion to be a cider cup instead of a fruit juice mixture. Use equal quantities of cider, lemonade and undiluted orange soda. Mix them all together in a large container and serve with plenty of ice cubes.

# GOLDEN WEDDING PARTY

*for twenty*

**Vark**
*Celebrate with a touch of luxury. In India festive dishes are sometimes decorated with wafer-thin pieces of silver or gold tissue called Vark. Small pieces gently laid on top of the carrot and coriander soup or on the honey and orange sauce will take on a golden hue. It is sold in specialty Asian food stores.*

NO ONE ACHIEVES TWO GOLDEN WEDDINGS IN A LIFE-time and most of us do not see one. So the excuse for celebration is even greater than for a wedding. A wedding is a kind of prayer for the future; a golden wedding is a thanksgiving for the past fifty years.

The obvious theme – gold – is happily also one of the easiest to manage successfully. As with nearly every largish party, it pays to go right over the top. Do not be afraid of vulgarity. Just get going with glitter in one hand and spray-on gold paint in the other.

Because it is likely that some of the guests (and almost certainly the Golden Wedding couple) will be in their seventies or more, a sit-down meal will be less exhausting and more suitable than a stand-up affair, and twenty close friends and relatives will probably give more pleasure than a hundred acquaintances.

This menu assumes twenty guests at four round tables, each seating five. Family parties almost always contain more women than men, which makes the conventional seating plan of boy-girl-boy-girl impossible. So make a virtue of necessity: five is a good number for conversation, a round table is cosy and pretty and if there are four of them in the room they will lend the atmosphere of a small elegant restaurant.

The food will require either professional help in the kitchen or willing friends to do last-minute dishing up, etc. But almost the whole meal is cooked in advance.

When it comes to decor, the possibilities are endless. Gold-colored (really a sort of buff-yellow) tablecloths and napkins can be hired, gold-colored paper napkins are easily available, gold-foil doilies can be used under food, glasses, coffee cups, side plates – anywhere and everywhere to give a formal lacy effect.

Flowers come in all shades of yellow and orange, and will look wonderful. Truly gold leaves can be had with a can of gold-spray paint. (Do the spraying outside or in a well-ventilated room, and lay the leaves – which must be dry or the paint won't stick – on newspaper. If spraying leaf arrangements once they are in place, take care to protect the walls and floor, or table top, immediately behind the leaves.) Gold-foil flowers, hanging doves, mobiles and decorations are easy to make (get a book on paper decor out of the library). Gold artificial flowers

*Left A celebratory golden glow is surprisingly easy to create. Use shades of yellow, bronze and gold for everything. Here the low leafy "gilt" table decorations are simply fresh ivy sprayed with gold paint. The roses on the napkins are similarly gilded and gold candelabra, chairs and "old-gold" linen can be hired. On the main-course plates honey-glazed chicken breasts with layered butternut squash. For a first course, smoked haddock pâté.*

Tiny bouquets of yellow flowers or leaves make pretty individual (one for each guest) table decorations.

**Floral Decorations**
*"A host of golden daffodils" is only possible in early spring but roses, polyanthus, lilies and the daisy-like chrysanthemums in shades varying from buff to clear yellow or pale orange mixed with gold-sprayed leaves look charming.*

are available at fancy food shops or shops where cake decorations are normally bought.

White china with a gold band is the usual caterer's hireware and sometimes amber-stemmed hock glasses can be hired. If they cannot, stick a band round each glass with gold foil sticky tape. Yellow balloons or even gold-foil balloons are pretty and childishly indicate a party. Gold – or at least yellow – streamers can be trailed among the gold-sprayed ivy leaves on the tables, or thrown by exuberant guests while drinking a glass of champagne with the dessert.

## THE INVITATION

This should, of course, be gold too, either hand-made or grandly printed. Gold-inked felt-tip pens are widely available and wonderful invitation cards can be made by sticking gold sequins all over picture postcards – perhaps of a celebratory feast, a bunch of flowers or a luscious still life. Or a sepia-tinted photograph of the celebrating couple's wedding fifty years ago could be set in a double gold paper frame.

INVITATION

## ENTERTAINMENT

After dinner 50-year-old home-movies will make family and friends both laugh and cry.

---

**THE MENU**

*Carrot and Coriander Soup*

*Smoked Haddock Pâté*

*Chicken Breasts with Honey and Orange
Layered Butternut Squash*

*Peaches in Champagne*

---

## GETTING AHEAD

*Far in advance*

○ Order gold invitations or arrange for copies of wedding photographs to be printed for invitations.

○ Order four 3ft 6in diameter tables and 20 gilt chairs to be delivered 48 hours before the party.

○ Check cutlery, china, glassware and tablelinen and hire them if necessary.

○ When the invitations are ready, make up the guest list and send them off.

**Removing Chicken Breasts**
*Lay the bird breast-side up and remove the legs. Cut through the breast flesh to one side of the bone and loosen by carefully scraping downwards against the rib cage. Snip through the flesh where it is attached to the wing.*

**Cooking Fish**
*Fish contains very little fat and therefore dries and toughens easily. Use the most gentle cooking methods and start testing the fish halfway through the recommended cooking time. A fish is cooked the moment the flesh will flake.*

○ Arrange for help (perhaps someone to dish up the food and wash up).
○ Make and freeze the basic sponge cake for anniversary cake.

*One month before the party*
○ Buy gold candles and balloons, paper napkins and doilies.
○ Make gold doves and flowers or any other paper decorations.
○ Spray dried leaves and flowers with gold paint.
○ Order flower arrangements from the florist or just the flowers to arrange yourself.
○ Buy dry goods, champagne and wine, spirits and mixers.
○ Make the carrot and coriander soup without adding the cream, and freeze it.

*Two days before the party*
○ Spray fresh leaves with gold paint.
○ Clear the rooms being used for the party.
○ Do all the shopping.
○ When the hired equipment is delivered make sure the contractors assemble the tables where you want them and arrange the chairs.
○ Check all the equipment to see that everything ordered is there, note any items damaged.
○ Sort out serving dishes.
○ Cook and flake the smoked haddock.
○ Take the soup out of the freezer and refrigerate.

*The day before the party*
○ Finish making the smoked haddock pâté, shape and chill on a flat tray.
○ Set the tables and trays for coffee.
○ Make the flower arrangements, decorate the room.
○ Organize the bar, chill wine and champagne.
○ Defrost sponge cake for anniversary cake.

*The morning of the party*
○ Prepare the butternut squash ready to go in the oven.
○ Grate the rind and squeeze the juice from the oranges, squeeze the lemon juice.
○ Measure the chicken stock and add 2 tablespoons honey, the vinegar and soy sauce.
○ Make the peaches in champagne and chill.
○ Chop coriander leaves for the soup, wipe and trim endive and radicchio leaves for the smoked haddock pâté, slice oranges for the chicken.
○ Make caramel top for anniversary cake.

**Radicchio**
*This is a type of chicory introduced from Italy. It looks like a small lettuce with ruby-red leaves but has a bitter taste. Make a pretty salad by mixing radicchio with green lettuce leaves.*

*Below* Smoked haddock pâté can be shaped with 2 spoons to form golden eggs. The center leaves of frilly endive are pale and crisp. Or radicchio leaves would provide an attractive color contrast.

*Above left* A simple cake given star treatment with elaborate gold ribbons and baubles (bought from the gift-wrap counter), and a garland of piped coffee cream around the edge. Use a gold felt-tip for writing the place names and gold doilies under the champagne glasses. On the left, the best of golden drinks – champagne.

Anniversary Cake
*To make the anniversary cake: make double the quantity cake recipe for coffee and walnut layer cake (see Celebration Tea, p. 72) and bake it in three 12in layers. Keep the best-looking layer for the top and spread the remaining two with thick layers of apricots and cream. Put 1 cup sugar into a heavy-based pan and melt over a low heat to a golden caramel. Put the top layer of cake on a wire rack standing over an oiled baking sheet. Oil the longest knife you have. Pour the caramel evenly over the cake and quickly mark it into portions with the knife before the caramel sets hard. Put the layers on top of each other with the caramel on top. Decorate with a gold collar around the edge and gold baubles and ribbons on top.*

*One hour before the guests arrive*
○ Put the squash in the oven.
○ Glaze the chicken breasts, brown them, pour on the sauce and cook in the oven.
○ Put the soup ready to heat in a large pan. Measure the cream and leave to one side.
○ Dish up the smoked haddock pâté, cover and leave.
○ Whip cream to serve with peaches.
○ Fill cake with apricots and cream, wrap gold collar around edge of cake and decorate the top with gold baubles and ribbons.

*15 minutes before the guests arrive*
○ Put the soup on gentle heat.
○ Strain the sauce for the chicken, thicken with cornstarch, add the butter, arrange on the serving dish, cover and keep warm.
○ Put the dinner plates in to warm.

*After the guests arrive*
○ Add cream and coriander leaves to the soup.
○ Decorate the chicken.
○ Light the candles.
○ Make toast to serve with the smoked haddock pâté.
○ Turn out butternut squash.
○ Add the extra ⅔ cup champagne to the peaches just before serving them.

Adding Butter to Sauces
*Butter is beaten into a sauce to thicken and enrich it and to add a shine. Beat the butter in teaspoon by teaspoon – too much at once could cause curdling.*

# GOLDEN WEDDING PARTY RECIPES

QUANTITY NOTE:
For 20 people make twice the recipes given below.

## CARROT AND CORIANDER SOUP
SERVES 10
*2lb carrots*
*2 medium-sized potatoes*
*1 large onion*
*¼ cup butter*
*½ tsp ground ginger*
*½ tsp ground mace*
*6 cups chicken stock*
*2 tsp crushed coriander seeds*
*salt and black pepper*
*⅔ cup milk*
*⅔ cup light cream*
FOR DECORATION
*finely chopped coriander (cilantro) leaves*

1. Peel and slice the carrots, potatoes and onion.
2. Melt the butter in a heavy-based saucepan, add the vegetables and fry gently until they are soft but not at all colored. Add the ginger and mace and cook for one minute.
3. Pour on the chicken stock. Add the coriander and season with salt and black pepper. Simmer for 30 to 40 minutes until all the vegetables are soft.
4. Purée the soup in a blender or food processor. Check the seasoning.
5. Reheat until just boiling, add the cream and serve immediately, sprinkled with chopped coriander leaves.

## SMOKED HADDOCK PÂTÉ
SERVES 10
*1lb smoked haddock*
*⅔ cup milk*
*1 bay leaf*
*2 slices white bread, with the crusts removed*
*½ tsp turmeric*
*pinch of mixed spice*
*pinch of white pepper*
*1 cup unsalted butter*
FOR DECORATION
*lettuce and radicchio (red endive) leaves*

1. Poach the haddock in the milk with the bay leaf for about 20 minutes.
2. Strain the milk and put it together with the bread into a blender or food processor and blend to a paste.
3. Turn the paste into a small pan and stir over a low heat until it becomes thick and sticky. Add the turmeric, spice and pepper and cook for a further minute.
4. Remove the skin and any bones from the fish. Mince, or blend in a food processor. Gradually beat in the bread

paste and the butter. Check the seasoning and chill for one hour.
5. Wash and shake dry the lettuce and radicchio leaves. Tear into small pieces.
6. Using two small spoons dipped in water, mold the mixture into egg shapes. Serve two to each person on an individual plate decorated with lettuce and radicchio.

## CHICKEN BREASTS WITH HONEY AND ORANGE
SERVES 10
*10 chicken breasts*
*3 tbsp runny honey*
*2 tbsp oil*
*4 tbsp butter*
*juice and rind of 2 oranges*
*1¼ cups chicken stock*
*2 tbsp lemon juice*
*2 tbsp dry cider or vinegar*
*2 cloves*
*2 tbsp soy sauce*
*1 tsp cornstarch*
*a little extra butter*
FOR DECORATION
*1 orange, halved and sliced*
*1 bunch of watercress*

1. Warm one tablespoon of the honey with a dessertspoon of water. Brush this glaze over the chicken breasts. Preheat the oven to 375°.
2. In a heavy-based frying-pan, heat the oil and butter, add the chicken breasts a few at a time and brown on all sides. Transfer to an ovenproof dish.
3. Make the orange juice and chicken stock up to 2½ cups with either stock or water. Pour into the frying-pan and scrape any sediment from the bottom of the pan. Add the remaining honey, orange rind, lemon juice, cider or vinegar, cloves and soy sauce. Bring to the boil and pour over the chicken. Cover and bake in the oven for 30 to 40 minutes or until the chicken breasts are tender and still moist.
4. Turn the oven to very low. Remove the breasts and keep warm in the oven.
5. Pour the sauce into a pan. Skim any fat from the top of the sauce, then boil rapidly until it has reduced by about a third and is of a syrupy consistency. Mix the cornstarch to a smooth paste with 2 teaspoons water. Pour on a little of the hot sauce and return to the pan. Stir until the sauce is boiling and gradually beat in the rest of the butter a little at a time. Check the seasoning.
6. Pour a lake of the sauce over the base of a heated serving dish. Arrange the

chicken breasts neatly on top. Decorate with slices of orange and a small bunch of watercress. Hand any extra sauce separately.

## LAYERED BUTTERNUT SQUASH
SERVES 10
*2 small young butternut squash or 2lb pumpkin*
*1 onion*
*5 yellow tomatoes, peeled*
*6 tbsp melted butter*
*salt and black pepper*
*1 tbsp chopped fresh tarragon*

1. Use a little of the butter to grease an ovenproof dish. Set the oven temperature control to 375°.
2. Peel and slice the squash or pumpkin, and the onion.
3. Dip the tomatoes into boiling water for 10 seconds, then peel and slice them.
4. Arrange a neat row of overlapping butternut slices in the bottom of the dish, then put all the vegetables into the dish, alternating the layers and adding melted butter, salt and black pepper, and a little tarragon between each layer.
5. Bake for 1½ hours or until very tender and beginning to brown on top. Pour off excess liquid and turn out on to a serving plate. Or serve in its dish if preferred.

## PEACHES IN CHAMPAGNE
SERVES 10
*10 large, ripe peaches*
*1¼ cups water*
*1¼ cups champagne*
*1¼ cups sugar*
*juice of 1 orange*
*2 tbsp Southern Comfort (or any other golden-colored liqueur or spirit)*
*⅔ cup extra champagne*
TO SERVE
*whipped cream*

1. Dip the peaches into boiling water for 10 seconds and remove the skins. Place the peeled peaches in a glass serving bowl.
2. Place the water, champagne and sugar together in a pan. Slowly dissolve the sugar, then bring to the boil and boil rapidly to form a sticky syrup.
3. Add the orange juice and Southern Comfort or other liqueur. Pour the syrup over the peaches and chill.
4. Add the extra champagne just before serving to give the syrup some 'fizz'. Serve with whipped cream handed separately.